WILLIAM HENRY HOLMES
AND THE REDISCOVERY OF
THE AMERICAN WEST

WILLIAM HENRY HOLMES
AND THE REDISCOVERY OF
THE AMERICAN WEST

Kevin J. Fernlund

University of New Mexico Press

Albuquerque

Library of Congress Cataloging-in-Publication Data

Fernlund, Kevin J.
    William Henry Holmes and the rediscovery of the American West /
Kevin J. Fernlund.—1st ed.
        p. cm.
Includes bibliographical references and index.
    ISBN 0-8263-2127-5 (alk. paper)
        1. Holmes, William Henry, 1846–1933. 2. Anthropologists—West (U.S.)
—Biography. 3. Archaeologists—West (U.S.)—Biography. 4. Archaeologi-
cal surveying—West (U.S.)—History. 5. Archaeological geology—West
(U.S)—History. 6. Indians of North America—West (U.S.)—Antiquities.
7. Indians of North America—West (U.S.)—Social life and customs.
I. Title.
    E76.92—dc21
99-050896

For my Mother,
Shirley Ann Fernlund

Contents

Contents

Illustrations

Acknowledgments

For financial support, I am grateful to the Dorothy Woodward Memorial Fellowship of the University of New Mexico's History Department. This assistance made possible my travel to and research at the Smithsonian Institution, the National Archives, and the Library of Congress. The "Douglas and Shirley Fernlund Foundation" rendered to me on a number of critical occasions aid to buy a meal or pay a bill. There is no way I can adequately express my appreciation for the support of my parents. I have incurred many other debts in the course of writing my dissertation and turning it into a book. Among my many creditors are Richard W. Etulain at the University of New Mexico's Center for the American West and Durwood Ball at UNM Press for their support, encouragement, and patience; I also owe thanks to the late Wallace Stegner and to William H. Goetzmann for their advice and insights; to Mrs. Laughlin A. Campbell for kindly allowing me access to the William Henry Holmes materials that remain with the family; to María E. Montoya and her family for kindly allowing me to stay in their lovely home in Arvada, Colorado, while I was doing research in Denver; to Ferenc Szasz, Paul Hutton, Jonathan Porter, William Sturtevant, Lois Fink, Pamela Henson, William Truettner, Judy Johnson, Marta Zulauf, Ira Plotkin, María E. Montoya, Liping Zhu, Jo Ann Chavez, William Broughton, Daniel Churchill, Lori Lahlum, Tobias Kreidle, Paul Christensen, Mark Stoll, and Christopher Huggard for their time, help, criticism, conversation, and friendship; to Carol Edwards of the Field Records Library of the United States Geological Survey and to Susan Glenn and James Glenn of the Smithsonian Institution Archives and the National Anthropological Archives, respectively, for their very generous help; to Beverly Whitman, Mary A. Davis, and Rosemary Lewis Engle of the Yellowstone Research Library; to Paul Fees of the Buffalo Bill Historical Center; to Kristine Haglund of the Library and Archives of the Denver

Museum of Natural History; and to Becky Shepard of the Harrison County Genealogical Society for their assistance. I would like to acknowledge Erik Moore for his photographs of the Holmes sketches and government illustrations located in the Field Records Library of the USGS and Jacqueline V. Nolan for her map of Holmes's West. I am particularly grateful for Clifford M. Nelson's critical reading of the entire manuscript. And finally I would especially, and above all, like to thank my wife Sharon Corn Fernlund for her help and understanding. Still, for all of this wonderful help, I alone, of course, am responsible for everything that follows.

Introduction

AFTER FINISHING HIGH SCHOOL in the late 1970s, I left my home in
Tucson and went to school at Northern Arizona University in Flagstaff.
Having grown up in the Sonoran Desert, I was attracted to the prospect of
winters with snow, the San Francisco Peaks, which watch over everything like
omnipresent gods, the Grand Canyon, the Painted Desert, Oak Creek, and
the hundreds of other natural wonders that make up the southwestern Colorado Plateau. I soon fell into a pleasant routine of studying for my classes
during the week and escaping on the weekends to hike and explore this open
country with its inexhaustible scenic marvels. And along with the rest of my
friends, I started reading the literature the area inspired, such as the works by
Edward Abbey. In fact, the ability to quote Abbey became de rigueur in conversations around the campfire.

I majored in European history, my special interest being the British Raj in
India. Not surprisingly, in retrospect, I gradually developed an interest in the
history of a much closer conquered province—the Four Corners. This area,
which director John Ford made famous in his John Wayne westerns and
which has appeared in countless television commercials and magazine adver-
tisements, includes northern Arizona, northern New Mexico, southern Utah,
and southern Colorado. It was Wallace Stegner's books, however, namely
Mormon Country and *Beyond the Hundredth Meridian*—more than any others—that excited my historical imagination and taught me to look at this region's cultural stratigraphy, which in its own way stands as exposed today in
the lives of its peoples as the colorful bands of rock strata that are visible at
every turn.

I became especially intrigued by Stegner's discussions of the artist and explorer of the American West, William Henry Holmes (1846–1933), who was
arguably the first to draw the Grand Canyon and get it right. I was intrigued
by this fellow who brilliantly produced panoramic views of the West in "in-

destructible lines," to use Stephen Pyne's words. The result was a still-unrivaled opus of scientific illustration, scattered over ten years of government publications. Somehow Holmes managed to draw western landscapes in scientific as well as aesthetic terms that are as fresh and vital today as they were a hundred years ago. It takes a certain genius to be able to do that, and Holmes possessed it in full.

To my surprise, there was no biography of this gifted individual. Surely Holmes deserved further study, I thought, maybe even a doctoral dissertation. I was not certain so I wrote to Wallace Stegner seeking his advice on the matter. In a typed note, which now adorns a wall in my office next to a large framed print of Thomas Moran's *The Chasm of the Colorado,* he indicated that he thought Holmes was certainly a subject worthy of a dissertation. That letter meant a great deal to me and Stegner's endorsement of the idea of undertaking a biography of Holmes gave me the confidence to take the next step, to apply for admission into the history program at the University of New Mexico, which was known for its emphasis in western and southwestern America.

I then learned that none other than William H. Goetzmann, the author of the Pulitzer Prize-winning *Exploration and Empire: The Explorer and the Scientist in the Winning of the American West* (1966) and leading authority on western exploration, was planning to write a biography of Holmes, whom he called "perhaps the greatest artist-topographer and man of many talents that the West ever produced."[1] Well, so much for my study. But before I started to explore other topics, I wrote to Goetzmann who kindly shared with me his decision some time earlier to pursue writing projects other than the Holmes biography.

By now I had come to realize that Holmes was much more than a great topographical artist who had rendered scenes of the West from the Grand Canyon of the Yellowstone to the Grand Canyon of the Colorado. He was also very active in the transformation of the sciences in the last years of the nineteenth century from patrician concerns to professional disciplines, making significant contributions along the way in geology, archaeology, anthropology, and museum exhibition. Holmes's tireless efforts in destroying the claims for the existence of a paleolithic man in North America ran parallel to Cyrus Thomas's work in repudiating the fanciful speculations about the origins of the mound builders. In so doing, however, Holmes set the standards of evidence that were eventually used to establish the now universally accepted fact that nomadic people arrived in the Americas during, rather than after, the ice ages. The dispute today, which is as lively as it was in Holmes's time, is again over the antiquity of the first arrivals and it is as polarizing as the other great question in American archaeology: the size of the Native American population at the time of contact. The work of Holmes represented another victory of the expert over the Sunday-afternoon amateur, and was part of a general movement that would have far-reaching consequences for America's democratic and scientific culture. In addition to all of these things, Holmes served science and art in other important ways as well. For years, he worked as an administrator at the Smithsonian Institution, serving in a number of capacities including chief of the Bureau of American Ethnology and director of the Smithsonian's National Gallery of Art. In short, the more I read about Holmes the more it became evident to me that here was an individual whose life was not only significant to the cultural history of the Four Corners but would help fill in the picture of America's intellectual growth in those pivotal years between 1870 and 1920 when the United States modernized and became a world power. This was indeed a story well worth telling.

To make sense of Holmes's long and rich career, I found Goetzmann's discussion of exploration particularly helpful. The author of *Exploration and Empire* makes the point that the exploration of the American West had a profound influence on the East's intellectual growth and development, in much the same way that the exploration of the Americas endlessly ramified the cultural life of Europe. The relationship between new lands and the older centers of power, then, is the key to understanding what Goetzmann called a "process and activity," in order to distinguish exploration from some great game of "Pin the Tail on the Donkey." In this sense, the term *discovery* is something of a misnomer, suggesting as it does a random act or single dramatic event. Explorers are given a "purpose or mission," Goetzmann wrote, which they then try to carry out. A famous case in point is Thomas Jefferson's instructions to Lewis and Clark stating what they should look for as they journeyed into the unknown West. To quote Goetzmann further on this important subject, exploration's

> purposes, goals, and evaluation of new data are to a great extent set by the previous experiences, the values, the kinds and categories of existing knowledge, and the current objectives of the civilized centers from which the explorer sets out on his quest.

In short, exploration is an activity "'programmed' by some older center of culture," and discovery, that is, the collection of new information, is anticipated as a matter of course.[2]

Stegner, on the other hand, takes the more romantic and traditional view. In referring to John Wesley Powell's second voyage down the Colorado River, Stegner stated flatly: "The second passage down the river was not an exploration, but a survey; what rendered it scientifically important rendered it dramatically second-hand. Exploration like seduction puts a premium upon the virgin."[3] In this sense, there was little in the American West that Holmes "discovered"; but as we shall see, there was much that he *rediscovered.* And while the story of rediscovery may not be as dramatic as that of the first encounter with a new land or people, it is one that is perhaps more meaningful to those of us who wish to rediscover the American West for ourselves.

With Goetzmann's guidelines in mind, I myself as an armchair explorer of an explorer had some idea as to what to look for as I proceeded to write my dissertation on Holmes's life. Indeed, it seemed to me that it would be hard to find an individual whose career better illustrates Goetzmann's view of exploration than that of William Henry Holmes. Whether Holmes served with the Hayden Survey, the Smithsonian Institution, or the Field Museum, he was carrying out a part of a broad cultural agenda. What is more, Holmes was active at both ends of the process of exploration: he took part not only in implementing the "program," he also, in Jeffersonian fashion, helped design it. This less dramatic but more powerful position was evident in his roles as scientific authority, museum curator, and administrator.

In researching Holmes's professional career, I found abundant materials, including a multivolume, bound scrapbook that Holmes assembled, called "Random Records of a Lifetime, 1846–1931." Holmes was apparently preparing to write an autobiography. Frederick S. Dellenbaugh, who accompanied Powell on the second voyage down the Colorado River, asked Holmes in 1922: "How is your autobiography progressing? Don't let it slip. It will be an exceedingly valuable book."[4] An autobiography unfortunately never appeared. Yet Holmes did leave posterity a well-organized scrapbook of his life. And as valuable as this source is, the documents it contains are almost entirely professional in nature. Consequently, his private life remains largely concealed from view behind a wall of self-selected records. Thus, in my writing I have had to emphasize Holmes's actions and words over character and motivation.

Holmes's scrapbook, along with his and other papers and notes kept at the Smithsonian Institution, the National Archives, and the Library of Congress; his sketchbooks, located at the United States Geological Survey Field Records Library at the Denver Federal Center; his many published articles; numerous government reports and records; correspondence; and his and A. C. Peale's diaries all formed the basis of my dissertation, which focused on his years in the West. Since finishing graduate school and going into academe, I have had the opportunity to turn my dissertation into a book and expand my study of Holmes to include his later years, which were largely spent in the nation's capital.

Holmes's story is a remarkable one and obviously had there been no vast unknown to explore would have been very different, and, I am tempted to add, probably poorer, too. The richness of Holmes's life, in terms of adventure, discovery, and artistic and scientific accomplishment, was largely made possible by the American West. Just as Meriwether Lewis would have been but another Virginia planter and army officer, his service as private secretary to President Thomas Jefferson notwithstanding, had there been no Louisiana Purchase to provide other fields for his talents, so too would Holmes have probably been a professor in a small Ohio normal school. In either case, the roads not taken were respectable enough, to be sure, but they and the many others who participated in the exploration of frontier America would have lived plainer and no doubt duller lives had there been no West to beckon them thither. And without the West, American culture would have been plainer and duller, too.

Exploration has always been closely associated with opportunity—a fact Americans have always understood, which explains this nation's long-standing commitment to discovery, which has been one of the great constants in U.S. history and rightly a major source of pride. Exploration, after all, has been an affair of the heart and mind that began with Thomas Jefferson's decision to send Lewis and Clark into the wilderness and was again dramatically rekindled more recently with John F. Kennedy's challenge to send a man to the moon. Even in these budget-conscious times, the claim that the space program makes on federal dollars remains impressive. Holmes's life reminds us that exploration is worth the trouble and expense, for in the end we all benefit and are made the greater for it.
Stillwater, Oklahoma

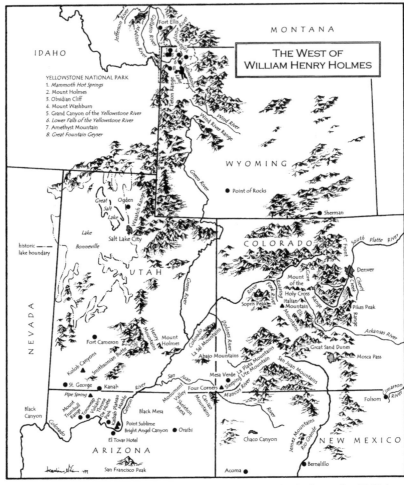

THE WEST OF
WILLIAM HENRY HOLMES

YELLOWSTONE NATIONAL PARK
1. *Mammoth Hot Springs*
2. *Mount Holmes*
3. *Obsidian Cliff*
4. *Mount Washburn*
5. *Grand Canyon of the Yellowstone River*
6. *Lower Falls of the Yellowstone River*
7. *Amethyst Mountain*
8. *Great Fountain Geyser*

historic —·—·—
lake boundary

Map by Jacqueline V. Nolan

WILLIAM HENRY HOLMES
AND THE REDISCOVERY OF
THE AMERICAN WEST

1

"What is the Species of the Bird?"

Ohio

ON DECEMBER 1, 1846, William Henry Holmes was born in a farmhouse on Ohio's Allegheny Plateau. Unlike most of Ohio, which had been leveled by the bulldozer effects of Pleistocene glaciers, the Allegheny Plateau consisted of small picturesque valleys formed by rivers and streams making their way east and south to the Ohio River. Holmes's birthplace was located near the headwaters of Short Creek in Harrison County and fell within the historic region known as the Seven Ranges, a fitting spot for a future surveyor and scientific explorer of the American West.[1] The Seven Ranges were distinguished by being the first part of the Northwest Territory that the newly formed United States had surveyed and opened to settlement. The homestead on which Holmes grew up, in fact, was a subdivision of a tract of Ohio land that his westering grandfather, Joseph Holmes, purchased following the 1795 Indian removal.[2]

Holmes's earliest recollection was of a scene in which his parents, the biblically named Joseph and Mary, took him to the family garden where he tasted the season's first ripened strawberries.[3] Subsequent childhood memories were alike filled with the colors and smells of the rolling Ohio countryside. The brown-haired and hazel-eyed Holmes, who was a lean and vigorous boy, recalled times of play in the surrounding fields, orchards, woodlands, and sloughs, which included daring raids on neighboring watermelon patches. Tongue-in-cheek, he marked these "collecting" forays as the beginning of a career in exploration and museum acquisition. There were also images of an indulgent father who allowed him to hunt squirrels and rabbits or try his luck at the local fishing holes, while his two older brothers stayed behind to work on the farm.

The Boyhood Home of William Henry Holmes in Ohio. This sketch was drawn in 1873, perhaps in a moment of homesickness, while he was in faraway Colorado, probably near the town of Golden.(Holmes, General Sketches, Colorado, 1873, no. 830-A, courtesy USGS Field Records Library, Denver, Colorado).

What set Holmes apart from other children in these early years was a passion for art. At the local common school, which was a small, one-room building situated between the foot of a hill and the edge of an oak forest, Holmes made the exhilarating discovery that he possessed genuine artistic ability. He and his seatmate, Alexander Hammond, began diverting themselves between lessons by using sharp points to trace but not completely cut out the tiny pictures illustrating their primers. In the process, the pupil William realized that he had an exceptionally good eye and steady hand.

After mastering this rather expensive technique, the boy artist went on to sketch in free hand. He found encouragement in these early endeavors from Joseph Thomas, an older and talented student who had his own color kit —a rare item in Short Creek. Not to be outdone, Holmes made do with makeshift brushes and the juices of weeds and berries for green and red colors, respectively, until he eventually managed to acquire his own art materials from the town of Wheeling, Virginia, twenty miles eastward. He took as subjects for his art the features that make up the verdant and rolling landscape of eastern Ohio, including the wildlife, and whiled away many hours content to draw for its own sake. Evidently lacking any formal instruction, knowledge of method, or adequate equipment, Holmes succeeded, through trial and error, in acquiring the artist's basic skills, such as the use of colors and the techniques of perspective and composition.

In 1856, when Holmes was only ten years old, his mother passed away. Under these difficult circumstances, his father thought young William should stay with his mother's parents, with whom the boy got along well. John and Mary Heberling lived in the small village of Georgetown, two and a half miles from the Holmes farm. During this period of emotional adjustment, Holmes made himself useful by helping his grandfather, a blacksmith, whose childhood memories reached back to the eighteenth century.[4]

Unlike the Holmes family, the Heberlings were relative newcomers, second-generation Germans who had not settled in Short Creek Township until 1823. The Holmes family, on the other hand, were among the first Anglo-Americans to open up the Allegheny Plateau west of the Ohio River for settlement and who proudly claimed descent from the Reverend Obadiah Holmes, a Baptist Englishman who immigrated in 1638 and settled in Salem, Massachusetts. Thirteen years later, after being publicly flogged by the Puritans for holding meetings on the Sabbath and expressing heresies, the reverend and his family, like Roger Williams, Ann Hutchinson, and many others, quit the Bay Colony and made Newport, Rhode Island, their home. In the next century, Obadiah's descendants would continue to move south, first to New Jersey and then Virginia, before finally heading west to the newly opened Ohio country.[5] In this move, they went not as colonists but as Americans.

Holmes's father waited a year before deciding that the boy was ready to come home, and waited several years more before remarrying. In 1860, though, the year of Abraham Lincoln's election and South Carolina's secession, the elder Holmes married Sarah I. Moore of Smithfield, Ohio, a small town ten miles and a county away.[6] It was a happy union and all the more so because Sarah Holmes got along well with her stepsons, especially the artist of the family. No doubt, her delight in Holmes's pen sketches and oil paintings and a genuine concern about his artistic progress helped to make the transition easier for all concerned. Four years after his mother's death, Holmes again knew a happy family life with his father.

While many of his relatives fought for the North, Holmes—who was too young to serve the Union—stayed home, attended school, and continued to sketch. By the spring of 1865, as the war was drawing to a close, eighteen-year-old Holmes, like the rest of the nation, began to look to the future. But deciding on a career would vex the young man for several years to come. Farming was out; that much he knew. He loved his father but not his father's way of life.

Since teaching was still the easiest and most common way out and up for a farmer's son, Holmes took advantage of one of the few local avenues of advancement and entered McNeely Normal School to prepare himself for a career in education. At McNeely, Holmes quickly immersed himself in student life and joined the Periclesian Literary Society, the motto of which typified the nineteenth-century belief in progress: "Science Scatters Darkness With A Torch." Outgoing and likable, he participated in theater, among other various school activities and events, performing in now-forgotten plays, such as the "Drama of Handy Andy."[7]

As Holmes began his second term at McNeely in September of 1865, he qualified for a temporary certificate to teach the 3 Rs and geography in the common schools of Harrison County.[8] His cousin, Abram Holmes, who was also a school teacher, needed help and offered Holmes an opportunity to work at Red Hill schoolhouse just outside Cadiz, the county seat. Turnovers among teachers in rural schools were frequent, so Holmes had no difficulty securing a full-time position. He taught at the schools of Science Hill and Beech Spring, both located close to home.[9] Science Hill, in fact, was only half a mile of wood and field from his father's farm.

After a year of disciplining unruly pupils and chopping wood for the schoolhouse stove, Holmes was no more enthusiastic about teaching than he was about farming. The teacher's life offered so few challenges, opportunities for distinction, and chances for improvement — materially or socially — that Holmes turned instead, if gradually, to the idea of becoming a professional artist. This career, he began to realize, was his real desire and ambition in life. In November of 1866, he turned to another cousin, the veteran James T. Holmes of Columbus, for advice.[10]

Colonel Holmes, who had served with the Fifty-second Ohio Volunteer Infantry during the Civil War, suggested in a letter that William contact Lieutenant Moore. Moore was William's uncle and could introduce him to Eliphalet Frazer Andrews of Steubenville, an artist with the "finest studio in the state" and who "stands in the first rank."[11] With great expectations, Holmes left for Steubenville, an agricultural and manufacturing city situated on the west bank of the Ohio River, to see if Andrews would take him as a student. Andrews, already a successful artist at thirty-one and who did not need or want to give lessons, politely turned Holmes away. Crestfallen, Holmes returned to his position in the Harrison County common schools as well as to his studies at McNeely. It would be an especially long and cold winter that year. The dream of becoming an artist had not died in Steubenville, however; it just moved to Cleveland.

In the spring of 1867 Holmes, while telling family and friends of plans to attend a better school, transferred to Willoughby Collegiate Institute in Cleveland. But the real reason behind moving to the Lake Erie city was to start a career in art. His efforts along these lines, as it turned out, again ended in failure. Although Holmes had managed to arrange a meeting with the respected local artist, Caroline Ransome, he made no more progress in becoming her student than he had with Eliphalet Andrews.[12] Frustrated, he retreated homeward to Hopedale and reluctantly renewed his temporary teaching certificate in time for fall classes in 1867. Then he returned to the less distinguished, if familiar, McNeely Normal.

Significantly, Holmes began to develop other interests in addition to art and took courses at McNeely in natural history and mathematics offered by William Brinkerhoff, in which he excelled. Thus, by the time he had graduated from McNeely three years later, he had proven himself proficient, not only in drawing and painting but also in geography and natural history. Although he was considering going on to Yale, when asked to join the small faculty of McNeely to teach art and science subjects in 1870, he accepted.[13] The remarkable symmetry between art and science, the hallmark of Holmes's subsequent career in Washington, D.C., emerged first in his short-lived teaching career in rural Ohio.

But Holmes was not satisfied with his education or the prospect of spending the rest of his life teaching in Harrison County, even at McNeely. After carefully reconsidering his prospects during the spring of 1871, he once again planned to leave family and friends. This time, however, Holmes was less certain about where to go or what to do. He discussed the matter with Edwin Regal, the principal of McNeely, and decided, with some hesitation, to apply to several teachers colleges in the East with "the object of improvement in the teaching of Drawing, Geography, and Natural History."[14] In early April, Holmes made arrangements to attend the State Normal School in Salem, Massachusetts, while Regal wrote letters of introduction. To this end, his father lent him two hundred dollars. Had he gone to Salem, Holmes would have completed a circle of migration that the Reverend Obadiah Holmes had started eight generations before.

That road, however, was not taken. Instead, Holmes chanced to meet John Simmons at Neri Hanna's bookstore in downtown Cadiz. Simmons had recently returned from Washington, D.C., where he had worked as a clerk for the War Department. Holmes discussed with Simmons his plans to attend college in Salem, but also his dream of becoming a professional artist. Simmons, a direct man, told his vacillating new friend to forget about college and go instead to Washington. He knew of a friend and painter there named Theodore Kaufmann under whom Holmes could study. Holmes needed little encouragement in this direction before asking Simmons to write Kaufmann in his behalf.

The year before, Kaufmann, who specialized in portraiture and history painting, had opened an art studio in Washington, D.C., after having recently shown his works at international fairs in Vienna and Munich.[15] Earlier, Kaufmann had participated in the 1848 revolution but, like so many other idealists and reformers, left Germany soon thereafter. For several years, he made a living in New York City teaching art classes. One of his students during this period was the later famous editorial cartoonist Thomas Nast. During the 1850s, Kaufmann adopted the cause of abolition, and after war broke out between the states, he joined the Union army and later celebrated emancipation and other patriotic subjects on canvas. *Westward the Star of Empire* (1867), in which Indians were shown trying to derail a train steaming across the continent, was perhaps the best of this work.

On April 11, 1871, Simmons received Kaufmann's reply. The good news was that the German artist accepted Holmes as a student. The bad news was that Kaufmann warned his prospective student that if he "is coming to Washington expressly for the study of painting, then the regular classes will, I suppose, not be enough for him."[16] Holmes, however, dismissed the warning. After the painful rejections in Steubenville and Cleveland, he saw at last a chance to escape teaching and to pursue a career in art. Besides, there was more to the nation's capital than Kaufmann's studio. The employment prospects that abounded in Washington drew ambitious and talented men like a magnet. In Henry Adams's words, "For young men Washington was in one way paradise, since they were few, and greatly in demand."[17] In mid-April the spring term was over at McNeely, and Holmes packed, said his farewells, and left Ohio with his father's two hundred dollars, if not his blessing, confident that opportunity would present itself at the seat of America's government. However hopeful Holmes may have been of the future, he prudently made sure that his teaching position in Hopedale remained open should the venture bust.

The Capital

Several days later in an art studio on Twelfth Street in downtown Washington, D.C., Holmes introduced himself to Kaufmann and promptly enrolled in an afternoon oil-painting class. Two of the pupils in the class happened to be the daughters of Joseph Henry, the secretary of the Smithsonian Institution. Holmes made their acquaintance and was advised by one of them, Mary, to try sketching at the Smithsonian's Castle. She told him that behind the high red sandstone walls he would discover showcases filled with numerous exotic specimens, any one of which would be a suitable subject for his pencil.[18]

The Smithsonian's Castle, with its landmark spires, was not hard to find. And before Holmes had even stepped fully inside the "north door," he was struck by the sight of a colorful bird on exhibit.[19] He quickly produced a sketchbook and pencil in order to draw the feathered subject. No doubt Holmes recognized that this was an ideal place to practice, meet people, and possibly be discovered. Indeed, on this very occasion, José Zeledon, a Costa Rican ornithologist, passed by and observed a slender artist with a distinguished forehead and prominent nose engrossed in work. Zeledon approached the artist and, on learning that Holmes shared an interest in birds, offered to show him Augustus A. Gould's illustrated study of hummingbirds. He kept the monograph upstairs where certain Smithsonian staff and scientists lived and worked.[20] This encounter was one of the pivots on which Holmes's life would turn. On the second floor of the castle, he met men of closely similar backgrounds who appreciated his talents—Henry Martin Bannister of the Hayden Survey and formerly of the Geological Survey of Illinois; Theodore Nicholas Gill, naturalist with the Smithsonian Institution; and perhaps Henry Wood Elliott, topographical artist with the Hayden Survey.[21] Especially noteworthy in that initial meeting upstairs was Holmes's introduction to Fielding Bradford Meek and William Healey Dall, who would later employ the young artist in drawing shells. These two men would also introduce Holmes to the vast world of American exploration and science and its many possibilities for individuals with talent and ambition.

Meek, an authority on Cretaceous and Tertiary invertebrate faunas, was of

Irish descent and hailed from Madison, Indiana. He was an affable, genuine, and unassuming man who resided quietly in the main tower of the castle. After struggling briefly as a portrait painter, he began a scientific career in the late 1840s working under the geologist and skillful illustrator, David Dale Owen (the middle son of the utopian Robert Owen), who organized the United States Geological Survey of Iowa, Wisconsin, and Minnesota. On finishing his apprenticeship under Owen in 1852, Meek went to Albany where he assisted New York's foremost, if trying, geologist, James Hall. In scientific circles, Meek came to be recognized not only for his vast knowledge of invertebrate fossils but for his ability to draw them as well.

Sickly and suffering gradual deafness, Meek nevertheless refused to permit his poor health to hinder his work. In 1853, Hall sent Meek and the twenty-four-year-old student of Albany Medical College, Ferdinand Vandeveer Hayden, to explore the *Mauvaises Terres* (Bad Lands) of the Upper Missouri for fossils, the existence of which had been made known to the public by the efforts of such men as Owen and John Evans. This scientific adventure into the trans-Mississippi wilderness, which produced one of the West's first stratigraphic columns—a vertical map of deep time—marked the beginning of a long and fruitful collaboration between these two men. Meek went on to write extensively on paleontology, making significant contributions over the years to the state geological surveys of Illinois, Ohio, and California, as well as to the federally funded surveys of Clarence King and Ferdinand Hayden.[22]

Zeledon also introduced Holmes to the zoologist William Healey Dall, whose capacity for work was astounding. Dall specialized in mollusks and brachiopods. Unlike the older Meek, he was Holmes's senior by only a year. But in those brief twenty-six years, Dall had already distinguished himself as a scientific explorer of the only recently acquired Alaska. He had served as head of the Scientific Corps of the Western Union Telegraph Expedition to Russian America, and in 1870 he published *Alaska and Its Resources*, a work that showed skeptical Americans that Alaska was not just an icy haven for polar bears. The faraway land was, according to Dall's account, another frontier rich in possibilities.[23] Holmes must have compared the young Dall's already impressive career with his own and, if not then and there then soon after, determined that he too would make a difference or at least try to force the issue.

In meeting Meek and Dall that spring day in 1871, Holmes came face to face with two representatives of America's grand tradition of exploration that began early in the century with the Lewis and Clark expedition. Moreover, Holmes suddenly had a chance to enter this romantic and exciting world when Meek asked him to draw a rather ordinary looking Carboniferous lamellibranch.[24] In the time that it took Meek to concentrate his eyes and inspect Holmes's work, it happened — that magical moment when opportunity meets talent. A highly experienced and competent judge of artistic talent, Meek found Holmes's quick rendering of the fossilized bivalve shell more than satisfactory and offered Holmes contract work on the spot. Meek needed him to illustrate a monograph that he was preparing based on the antebellum work that he and Hayden had carried out and for the paleontological studies he was doing for the Geological Survey of Ohio.[25] Dall was also eager to share Holmes, for he also had Cenozoic specimens he wanted the talented young artist to illustrate for his own scientific reports. Holmes accepted the joint offer and devoted his mornings to shell drawings, tedious and eye-straining work, while he set the rest of the day aside for art studies under Kaufmann.

While working at the Smithsonian Institution, Holmes fell under the influence of the vertebrate zoologist and assistant secretary Spencer Fullerton Baird, who had started his career in science collecting birds, eggs, nests, reptiles, and fish in his home state of Pennsylvania and ended it as one of America's great museum men. Baird had met Ralph Waldo Emerson and Henry David Thoreau. He had helped direct numerous scientific careers, including Hayden's, and created a vast collecting network for the National Museum that involved numerous private naturalists and anthropologists, Smithsonian-sponsored exploring expeditions, and almost every governmental expedition sent west from 1850 to the 1880s.[26] His protégés were legion. Oddly enough, for a man who did so much to promote the scientific exploration of the trans-Mississippi West, Baird as a young man had turned down an invitation from the great naturalist, John James Audubon, to join an expedition to the Yellowstone River in the Rocky Mountains. Nevertheless, Baird's *Mammals of North America* (1859) and *Birds of North America* (1860), both products of the Pacific Railroad Surveys, brought a new level of sophistication and accuracy to zoological nomenclature, classification, and depiction.[27] This emphasis on empiricism and exactitude marked a turning point in American science as it outgrew its amateur standing, came to embrace higher, professional standards, and strived for Europe's respect.

Soon Holmes ran up against Baird's insistence on precision–in which he measured birds to the hundredths of an inch — and detail in scientific statement, artistic and otherwise. Baird, who had been instructed in drawing by Audubon himself, asked Holmes to illustrate the title page of an ornithological study, a welcome respite from the usual dull fare of brachiopods or echino-derms. The Ohio artist produced, after several attempts, a pretty picture of a bird, as he would later recall, "in flight hovering over a flower." He then con-fidently presented it to Baird, who "glanced at the drawing with a kindly but questioning look and hesitatingly inquired, 'And what is the species of the bird?'"[28] Holmes was mortified. But this incident was crucial in his education as a scientific artist. He learned never again to subordinate facts to aesthetic considerations.

As the summer of 1871 approached, Washington scientists began preparing to go into the field. Holmes's employers were no exception: Meek went to Ohio where he joined John Strong Newberry, the head of that state's geologi-cal survey; Dall returned to Alaska after the seemingly omnipotent Baird had arranged for him to serve as an acting assistant with the U.S. Coast Survey. This annual diaspora to points west left Holmes alone and temporarily out of work, although there was no shortage of specimens to draw. Reluctantly, he honored his commitments and returned to his teaching position in Hopedale.

After the stimulating environment of Washington, Holmes found life in-tolerable back in Ohio. The time had clearly arrived for him to leave. On Sep-tember 9, 1871, he told Meek in a letter that if the illustration work at the Smithsonian could wait "until this term of school ends here, I will gladly re-sign my place and come to you." Holmes also declared that he missed the "good opportunities for studying painting" that the nation's capital provided, and admitted that "draughting is more congenial to my tastes than teaching." Ten days later Holmes wrote another letter to Meek stating that he could come to Washington even sooner if the situation so required. Then, in early October, Holmes received what he had been hoping for—a letter from Meek inviting him to come to Washington. Meek offered him a dollar and fifty cents per figure, "perhaps more." Meek also thought that Baird and others might have additional work for Holmes by wintertime. With the letter that Holmes sent to Meek on October 5, informing the scientist that he would be there in two weeks, and with the resignation that he tendered to Edwin Regal, Holmes had cut his ties to Ohio, and put his career in pedagogy aside.[29]

Holmes thrived in the nation's capital, sharing in the excitement generated by the accounts of American continental and oceanic exploration discussed in such forums as the Philosophical Society of Washington, while at the same time making a reputation for himself as a superb scientific illustrator. Of par-ticular interest that year were reports about the Yellowstone country. The Hayden Survey had explored the area in the summer of 1871, documenting that the Yellowstone was indeed a fantastic and geologically unique area, as Indians and mountain men had long rumored. Nothing more convincingly made this point than Thomas Moran's watercolors and William Henry Jackson's photographs.[30] Congress was so impressed by Hayden's visual record that it established on March 1, 1872, Yellowstone National Park, the country's first such creation. Yellowstone had made Hayden a national celebrity and the nation's most famous explorer. And Hayden's men, who had the appeal of today's astronauts, wintered at the Smithsonian, where Holmes had the chance to mingle daily with them.

Hayden's exploration of the West began in 1853, when he and Meek went on a fossil-hunting trip to the Badlands. Hayden excelled at fieldwork and especially collecting, and quickly learned, according to his biographer, Mike Foster, how to use the expedition as a vehicle to advance his enormous personal ambitions.[31] Until the Civil War intervened, Hayden spent part of every year exploring and geologizing in the "Great West." At first he traveled solo with the traders of the American Fur Company, although with encouragement in the east from scientific men like Baird and Joseph Leidy of Philadelphia. In 1856, Hayden's work earned him an invitation to accompany Lieutenant Gouverneur K. Warren, of the U.S. Corps of Topographical Engineers, to "Sioux country"; and in 1857 he went with the officer and mapmaker again, but this time as the official geologist. The following year Meek rejoined Hayden on another fossil-collecting trip, this time to Kansas Territory. The next two years Hayden served as surgeon and naturalist with Captain William Franklin Reynolds, a pious man who was engaged in the exploration of the Yellowstone country. The Civil War interrupted Hayden's career as an explorer. For much of the conflict, Hayden served as an acting assistant Surgeon of Volunteers. He ran two fifty-bed hospitals in Yankee-held Beaufort, which was situated on Port Royal Island off the coast of South Carolina. Toward the end of the war, Hayden was assigned to the Army of the Shenandoah as chief medical officer.

After Appomattox, Hayden renewed his explorations of the West, but with the advantage of having an institutional base. In 1865, he received an adjunct position in geology and mineralogy at the University of Pennsylvania, and the following year he returned to the Badlands of Dakota. He would come to national attention in 1867 when, with federal funds, he conducted a geological survey of the newly admitted state of Nebraska. In subsequent years, Hayden was able to extend the survey's increasingly more systematic operations to the territories, where in time it would compete with the three other large post–Civil War surveys of the West—the Powell, Clarence King, and George M. Wheeler organizations.

Holmes's artwork came to the attention of Hayden, no doubt through Meek. When Hayden's field artist Henry W. Elliott resigned, after serving for three seasons, Hayden turned to Holmes and offered him the attractive position. Holmes, who only a few months before was a schoolteacher in rural Ohio, probably could not believe his good fortune and he enthusiastically accepted the appointment, which placed him in the national spotlight with Hayden and his other men. Here was an opportunity of a lifetime. The government appointment went into effect on May 1, 1872, at a salary of eighteen hundred dollars.[32] That summer it would be Holmes's turn to share in the high adventure of government science and exploration.

2

Yellowstone Expedition, 1872

H OLMES WENT WEST AN ARTIST, but returned much more than that. By
the end of the 1870s, he enjoyed respect among his peers as a cartographer and geologist, and, in the romantic age of Heinrich Schliemann archaeology, as an expert on the cliff and surface dwellings of southwestern
Colorado.[1] It was Holmes and William Henry Jackson who helped bring
Mesa Verde to the world's attention through their sketches, photographs,
models, and articles. But as Holmes developed into one of America's leading
scientists, his progress as an artist was no less noteworthy. Not surprisingly,
Holmes's scientific interests were reflected in his art, not just in the obvious
sense of the choice of subjects but, more importantly, by the way he represented and interpreted those subjects. Holmes developed a style characterized
by clean lines and subtle composition, in which he purposely avoided classical
or religious allusions, as well as European conventions. Instead, he turned to
the world of science, especially to geology, for ideas and inspiration. He replaced, in effect, one set of aesthetic principles with another. In so doing, he
brought new, scientific meaning to western landscape.

Ever since Titian Peale and Samuel Seymour went west on Stephen H.
Long's "Yellowstone" expedition in 1820, western artists have served in the interest of exploration and science.[2] Alas, no artist accompanied the earlier
Lewis and Clark expedition. The early history of western art, like the history
of the West itself, was closely linked to the exploration and scientific discovery of the region. The ethnographic art of Karl Bodmer and Paul Kane, or the
naturalistic art of John James Audubon serve as cases in point. Holmes was a
direct heir to this artistic tradition—one that ran almost in a straight but
richly embroidered line from Peale to Holmes—in which the need to "report"
was often balanced with aesthetic considerations.[3] But Holmes would go one

A New World. (Photograph, William H. Jackson, no. 695, courtesy USGS Photograph Library, Denver, Colorado.)

step farther and synthesize, rather than simply balance science and art, to produce a genuine scientific art.

After saying good-bye to Professor Meek at the Smithsonian Castle on the evening of May 29, 1872, Holmes, along with the naturalist Campbell Carrington and two other men, entrained for Ogden, Utah.[4] At Omaha, Nebraska, the geologist W. R. Taggart, topographer Thomas W. Jaycox, and W. A. West joined the small party. Before resuming the trip, the men properly outfitted themselves for life in the West at Omaha's Wyoming House. Dressed for high adventure, Holmes and the other men then somewhat anticlimactically took their seats on the train. It was as a spectator, rather than as a participant, that Holmes first saw the West, which he watched roll by his window like an old J. Wesley Jones moving panorama.[5]

Holmes, who was a farmer's son, noted the fertility of the soil in Iowa and observed approvingly the roaming antelope and bustling prairie dog towns. With the predictability of a train schedule, Holmes's praise turned to criticism as the flat, treeless, and arid lands west of the hundredth meridian came into view, lands that made up what Stephen H. Long had decades before called the "Great American Desert." Holmes described these dry and empty plains—the very antipodes of Ohio's verdant hill country—using the farmer's meanest adjectives: "barren," "dreary," "uninviting," and even "sickly." This was not a land for the plow, at least for the foreseeable future.

Toward sunset on June 3, the train stopped at the small railroad town of Sherman, Wyoming, located at the highest point on the Union Pacific main line. There Holmes got his first view of the Rocky Mountains. At that particular moment, a thunderstorm passed over the Front Range, making the already dramatic contrast of the distant peaks with the plains that much sharper. The wide-eyed artist recognized in the startling matrix of plains, mountains, sunset, storm, light, sparkling colors, and vast spaces something that was, in his words, "novel" and "exceedingly splendid." This was the beginning of a long love affair with the lands of the West.

As the train continued westward into the Wyoming Basin, Holmes's wonder of western scenery evaporated into the dry, shimmering air. In this vast physiographic province—which must have seemed like a farmer's hell—short sage grasses, occasional castellated rock formations, and the scattered piles of sun-bleached cattle bones alone competed for the eye's attention. Before the twentieth-century artist Georgia O'Keeffe taught Americans to see animal bones as things of beauty, they were the West's stark symbol of economic failure and environmental collapse. In the face of such aridity and desolation, Holmes, like so many other travelers, was astonished at how "man or beast should have succeeded in crossing such a desert." On reaching the huge sandstone formations of the Green River Valley, however, this vast, broken country finally gave way to lands that Holmes almost gratefully noted were filled with "many curious and interesting scenes." And he waxed poetic about the strange and unfamiliar country that passed into view as the train made its way through the high, angular walls of Echo and Weber canyons on the last leg to Ogden.

Six days after leaving the nation's capital, Holmes arrived at the Ogden depot, greeted by the bearded James Stevenson, Hayden's seasoned assistant director. The following morning Holmes and his traveling companions joined the other men of the United States Geological Survey of the Territories, as Hayden's survey was officially called. Holmes met the sixteen-year-old ornithologist C. Hart Merriam, photographer William Henry Jackson, geologist Albert Charles Peale (who had studied under Hayden at the University of Pennsylvania), and a number of other scientists, general assistants, packers, and cooks. These men, sixty-two in number, were camped along the Wasatch Range, where the Pleistocene waters of Lake Bonneville once lapped. The men of the survey were presently engaged in local fieldwork but were also preparing for the extended trip north into Yellowstone country.

While Hayden and Stevenson organized the expedition, Holmes spent his time sketching, geologizing with the other men, playing tourist in the nearby Mormon capital of Deseret, that is, Salt Lake City, and making the West safe from rattlesnakes. Wherever he found one, he killed it. He seems to have felt that with each rattlesnake dispatched to oblivion, the mission of opening the West to settlement and exploitation moved a step closer to realization. In addition to these activities and diversions, Holmes enjoyed climbing the peaks of the Wasatch for ostensibly artistic and scientific reasons and then sliding down the steep slopes on the loose rocks and debris. On one such occasion, after dusk had already fallen, he narrowly avoided tumbling headlong over a high precipice and joining his rattlesnake victims in the spirit world. The close call fortunately left him unshaken and his fondness of heights happily undiminished.

Holmes also spent this time forming friendships and professional relationships with the members of the survey, some of which turned out to be lifelong. One of these friendships was with the photographer William Henry

Jackson. A restless man with nothing more than an eighth-grade education, Jackson had already mastered the difficult and cumbersome wet-plate process and brought more literal, although carefully composed, western landscapes into eastern drawing rooms via the three-dimensional immediacy of stereographs. Holmes and Jackson, the one with his light pencil and sketchbook; the other with his three hundred pounds of camera equipment, rode together and explored the surrounding country, each influencing the other's work as they went. Although the two image makers were separated into different field parties that year—Holmes went with Hayden, Jackson accompanied Stevenson—they had, in the years to come, many more opportunities to collaborate on various projects.[6]

In hindsight, the relationship between Holmes and Jackson calls to mind the railroad ballad of John Henry, in which man was pitted against machine. Holmes, on the one hand, was an immensely talented topographical artist, accomplishing his work with God-given talent and a pencil. He symbolized, in a sense, the skill and simplicity of a rural and pre-industrial America. Jackson, on the other hand, was one of the West's foremost photographers, an elite company of men that included Carleton E. Watkins, Timothy O'Sullivan, and John K. Hillers. Jackson combined his artistic talent with a rapidly developing technology. He reflected the country's emerging industrial order and growing technical expertise. When the two worked together, Holmes not only held his own with the camera, he even surpassed the machine in its literalism. His sketch work depicted outdoor scenes clearly and accurately, free of the haze and shadow that could obscure photographs. But in the end, photogrammetry, which Jackson's work, in part, anticipated, and the "Kodak" virtually did away with the need for the topographical artist.

On June 22, Hayden ordered Holmes, the twenty-three-year-old Albert Charles Peale, who already had a year with the survey to his credit, and seven other men to take the stage from Ogden to Fort Ellis, Montana, a rough two hundred miles northward. That season Hayden organized his survey into two large divisions: one was to start from Fort Hall, Idaho, under the direction of James Stevenson, with the purpose of exploring the unknown regions of the upper Snake River Valley; the Teton Basin; and the mountain passes in the vicinity of Henry's Lake. Nathaniel Pitt Langford, Yellowstone Park's first superintendent, would, incidentally, accompany Stevenson's Snake River party.[7]

Hayden directed the other division that took as its starting point Fort Ellis, located three miles from the mining town of Bozeman, on the east bank of the Gallatin River. The chief purpose of this division was to survey the rivers of the Yellowstone, Madison, and Gallatin to their respective sources. Among the scientists, assistants, packers, and dignitaries accompanying Hayden and Holmes were Peale; Henry Gannett, a Lawrence Scientific School graduate and later one of the country's top geographers; and Joshua Crissman, a photographer from Bozeman. In addition, the prominent British entrepreneur and land developer Sir William Blackmore and his wife, Lady Blackmore, were present as Hayden's guests.

After nine unforgettable days, Holmes and his traveling companions arrived at Fort Ellis, a small assembly of log and wood-frame buildings.[8] Holmes passed most of the stage trip riding on the outside to escape the heavy smoking of the other passengers. Holding onto his hat and squinting from the sun and wind, Holmes found himself greatly impressed by the driver's stinging oaths and expert horsemanship. The driver, Holmes admiringly wrote, "rush[ed] with the utmost precision through narrow and crooked places[,] over bridges[,] and among rocks." Despite the dangers, Holmes affirmed that he and the other passengers "felt perfectly safe for the art of that man was as sure as science." Between the excitement of negotiating hairpin twists and turns, Holmes managed to study the face of the land, absorbing as best as he could the "strange character of the country."

Half a mile from Fort Ellis—the commander of which was Major Eugene M. Baker, known to his men as the "exterminator," for his role in the massacre of a Piegan village—Holmes and the other rattled and exhausted men pitched camp. Here they waited for Hayden to arrive and outfit the party with animals and supplies. In the meantime, the men busied themselves examining the coal seams located in the region southeast of Bridger Peak, past which the Northern Pacific Railroad would eventually run. (Jim Bridger, incidentally, the famous mountain man after whom Bridger Peak was named, was one of the first Americans to report on the wonders of what became Yellowstone Park.) Later in the season, some of Hayden's men encountered surveyors from the Northern Pacific.[9] The parallel work of these two groups of men showed literally just how close science and technology worked together to open the West.

The local field trips that Hayden's men took in the area surrounding Fort Ellis provided Holmes with perhaps his first lessons in economic geology. Since arriving in Utah, he had undertaken in earnest the study of geology, building on his education at McNeely Normal School. At camp, Holmes shared his white dog tent with his new friend, the shy and modest Peale, who was a descendent of the famous Philadelphia Peales, such as the Revolutionary War portrait painter and museum founder Charles Willson and his scientific artist son Titian.[10] In 1871, Peale graduated from the University of Pennsylvania with a degree in medicine, although his real interests lay in mineralogy and geology. The new friendship of Holmes and Peale was almost immediately tested, for no sooner had they established camp than a Montana snowstorm moved in, catching the two off guard. The other men, who were in town at the time, happily waited out nature's bad temper in the warmth and comfort of a Bozeman hotel, where they drank lager beer and whiskey to the health of their tent-bound colleagues. The surprise storm lasted three days.

In the young Peale, who sported a moustache and bushy sideburns, Holmes found a friend and apparently a good geology teacher as well. Once the weather had cleared, the two went riding together, "[Peale] on a mule and I on a pony," Holmes wrote, sorting out the contorted history of the land and collecting fossils. This saddle-side geology proved to be an invaluable learning experience for Holmes—both as a scientist and as an artist. While realist artists were dissecting animals in order to study their musculature, Holmes was constructing stratigraphic columns. Eventually, he probably understood the earth's own bone and tissue better than any other western landscape artist of his era. He may have supplemented this outdoor education by reading his tent mate's copy of Joseph Beete Jukes's *Student's Manual of Geology*.[11] Holmes's teacher eventually felt comfortable enough with his student's grasp of geology that he included in his published report to Hayden the description Holmes made of Great Fountain Geyser.[12]

In spite of unexpected snowstorms and other hardships, Holmes thrived on life in the open West. In fact, the years he spent with Hayden in the field were in many respects the happiest of his life. Holmes fondly wrote of "riding [with the other Hayden men] . . . from valley to valley and mountain to mountain . . . sketching whatever seemed of particular interest." As an artist, he could have asked little more than to be able to work, virtually undirected, in arguably the most visually arresting place in the world. That Holmes was on an expedition of discovery must have only heightened the immense sense of freedom, adventure, and privilege that he was experiencing.

The high spirits Holmes felt were temporarily quashed when Lady Blackmore took ill and on July 18 suddenly died. Holmes was convinced that the harrowing stage trip had to be partly to blame for her untimely death. This was the second such incident to befall the survey. Several weeks earlier near Ogden, Emma Hayden, Hayden's newly wed wife, was seriously injured in a fall from a wagon.[13] Holmes and the other party members carried out the "melancholy duty" of walking in procession behind the deceased and Sir William Blackmore, who was overcome with emotion. Lady Blackmore was laid to rest in a temporary grave, which Holmes noted in a sketch was a site enclosed by a fence in order to "keep out the wolves."[14] Then in a romantic gesture, which said much about the vigor of Victorian sentiment, Holmes recorded that later "eight days" were devoted "in ascending one of the snow-capped peaks [in the Gallatin Range,] that it might be appropriately and officially named Blackmore Peak."[15] Despite his tragic loss, Blackmore found it in himself to see the expedition through.

On July 20, Hayden ordered his men to form a pack train and head southeast from Fort Ellis to the mountain-rimmed plateau of the Yellowstone. As the train moved in an eastwardly direction toward the Yellowstone Valley, Holmes began to work more closely with Doctor or "Professor" Hayden, as the men variously called him. Hayden was a man of science who also strongly believed in the economic development of the West, although some historians tend to stress the latter.[16] To be sure, Hayden went out of his way to address the concerns of the business world, especially the nascent western tourist industry. So did Clarence King of the Fortieth Parallel Survey, Hayden's contemporary and later rival. But whereas King eventually abandoned his brilliant work in government service to chase after an elusive El Dorado, Hayden never veered from his career in science.[17] And Hayden succeeded in passing on this strong commitment to intellectual discovery to his new artist and young companion, William Holmes.

As the party traveled up the Yellowstone Valley, Hayden explained to Holmes his views on the region's geologic past. The doctor believed that the country was formed as a result of a violent period of "intense volcanic activity" that began as recently as the "Pliocene epoch, reached its greatest power, and then slowly declined, the hot springs and geysers of the present time being the faint departing remnants of these once terrific forces."[18] Taking Yellowstone as a case study, Hayden generalized about the rest of the West. He wrote, "It is most probable that during the Pliocene period hot springs prevailed to a greater or less extent all over the western portion of our continent, and their action may serve to account for many problems which now seem obscure."[19] Predictably, the illustrations that Holmes produced for Hayden's 1872 report focused on the West's fiery origins, and thus included basaltic caps, trachyte dikes, igneous intrusions, columns of breccia, and tuffs.

Pleased with his assistant's work and impressed by his aptitude for geology, Hayden asked Holmes to combine his artistic talents with his growing knowledge of geology to help him produce a colored geologic map of the area.[20] Until now, Hayden's geologizing and mapping had been limited to the traverse method, in which descriptions of the country's features and surveys of the land were confined to the routes of travel, so any geologic map constructed at this point would be provisional. But Hayden planned to return to Yellowstone the following year and conduct a thorough exploration of the region, which would be necessary in order to produce an accurate geologic map.[21] In any event, this work introduced Holmes to cartography, which he discovered was an ideal medium in which to express his artistic and scientific energies.

After stopping to draw and study Cinnabar Mountain, which looked like a giant stratigraphic column lying on its side, Holmes, Hayden, and the main party proceeded southward and reached Mammoth Hot Springs on July 26. For the next couple of days, Holmes sketched the colorful travertine formation, notwithstanding his exclamation that these springs "cannot be described, painted or even recalled by one who has visited them." While working at the springs, Holmes, the government explorer, ran into the health seeker. Up to this point, he had been exposed to the Mormon, the cursing but skilled stagecoach driver, the Indian fighter, the ubiquitous English gentleman, and, in the past couple of weeks, the prospector and rancher of Montana. Hayden's men may have been far from civilization but they were hardly alone. To this list of classic western "types," Holmes could now add the health seeker. Despite the remoteness of the Hot Springs, the site included two bathhouses and nearly thirty bathers seeking cures for their ailments.[22]

Leaving the Hot Springs, the Hayden party rode east to Blacktail Deer Creek and then, on July 30, camped on Elk Creek. The following morning the party temporarily split up: Holmes, Hayden, Blackmore, Adolph Burck, and others headed up the East Fork of the Yellowstone, then up Soda Butte Creek, and finally over to Clark's Fork. Holmes believed the country through which they passed was the equal of Yosemite, which was the yardstick he and other Americans increasingly used to measure scenes of great natural beauty. At one point, Holmes became so engrossed in sketching the "extraordinary scenery" that he got lost. Fortunately, Hayden, realizing that Holmes was still a tenderfoot, ordered one of his men to stay behind to meet the artist and show him the way to camp.

The purpose of the reconnaissance to Clark's Fork, besides exploring new country, was to examine the silver ores that miners had discovered in the area west of Pilot Peak, near present-day Cooke City, Montana. It was not uncommon for Hayden to offer the benefit of his scientific expertise to the local inhabitants. He thought the ore looked good but was too far from a market to be of any value, although he held out the hope that given "the rapidity with which this western country develops under the stimulus of rich mines and railroads . . . that these far-away ores may become valuable sooner than we could anticipate."[23] The party returned by a different route. They headed west via Rose Bud Creek and over to Slough Creek, which the men then followed back to East Fork. After four days, then, the party rejoined Peale, who had stayed behind to collect rock samples in the Tower Falls area. From there, the men continued their journey to the source of the Yellowstone River.

The pack train wound its way past Mount Washburn and on August 5 crossed Cascade Creek, where Crissman was already camped. From there, Holmes and Peale rode the short distance to the Lower Falls of the Grand Canyon of the Yellowstone. Peale had visited the Grand Canyon (of the Yellowstone) the year before and wondered if his recollection of it had become "exaggerated" with time; he duly concluded after the most careful scientific observation that "The canon [*sic*] is still grand."[24] For Holmes, the trip to the Grand Canyon represented a unique opportunity for the student of art. Before leaving Washington, D.C., he had studied a work by one of the great landscape artists of the West, Thomas Moran. The English-born artist had recently unveiled the highly acclaimed, gigantic painting *Grand Cañon of the Yellowstone* (1872).[25] Now, standing at the edge of the canyon, Holmes would be the first artist to see and compare the master's work with the source of his inspiration.

On seeing the Lower Falls, Holmes was deeply impressed with Moran's faithful rendering of the V-shaped canyon and powerful falls. That Moran had altered the details of the scene escaped Holmes's notice. He declared to Peale "that Moran's picture of it is perfectly correct . . . [and] that there is no heightening of anything in it but rather, a softening down of the effects."[26] What deeply impressed Holmes was what he took to be Moran's literalism, which could be used scientifically because a geologist could read the character of the rocks from the painting.[27] Yet in terms of composition, color, and perspective, Moran's *Grand Canyon* was clearly art. What Holmes took away from this experience was that science need not compromise art. Yet Holmes's literalist interpretation of Moran's work differed sharply from Moran's own views of art. The master had written that "I place no value upon literal transcripts from Nature. My general scope is not realistic; all my tendencies are toward idealization." He further declared, "Topography in art is valueless."[28]

Moran's *The Mountain of the Holy Cross*, which was produced several years later in 1875, was a good example of this philosophy put into practice. According to Moran's biographer, Thurman Wilkins, the Mount of the Holy Cross could not be seen from the waterfalls that occupy the lower half of the painting.[29] In regard to *The Grand Cañon of the Yellowstone*, Moran made clear that it was not topographical accuracy that he was trying to convey but rather "the gorgeous display of color."[30] Although Holmes greatly admired Moran's work, his own views of art could not have been more different from Moran's. Ever since Baird had looked quizzically at Holmes's picture of a bird, the young artist had striven to capture, as clearly and as accurately as possible, the topography and geology of the landscape, even though he believed that the artist should treat a grand subject grandly.

After Holmes had finished taking in the Lower Falls of the Yellowstone, he left Peale and joined Hayden and Blackmore to explore the shores of Yellowstone Lake, which sat astride one of North America's most important watersheds. From the perspective of world exploration and empire, Yellowstone Lake was the United States' answer to Great Britain's Lake Victoria, which John Manning Speke claimed to be the source of the mighty Nile River.[31] And just as a great civilization had risen and fallen along the banks of the Nile, so history would gloriously repeat itself, Hayden and his men believed, along the banks of the Yellowstone River, the Three Forks of the Missouri, the Snake River, and the Green.

Holmes occupied himself on this excursion to the aqueous heart of a future empire by exploring, sketching, and geologizing. He took time out from his duties, though, to stop at the southwest arm of the lake to fish for trout with Blackmore. Conveniently located at the shore's edge was a hot spring in which they could boil their catch, without having to remove the fish from the line. Until Yellowstone Park became another Central Park, surrounded on all sides by a vast riparian civilization, it would serve nicely as an out-of-the-way paradise for fishermen.

On August 9, Holmes and the other men joined Peale's group at the Mud Volcanoes south of Crater Hills. After three days of work and swapping fish stories, Holmes left for the Upper Geyser Basin of the Firehole River. This was the site of Old Faithful, Castle Geyser, the Beehive, Giant Geyser as well as numerous other geysers, caldrons, mud pots, hot springs, and fumaroles. In fact, at no other spot in the world was there such an impressive array of hydrothermal phenomena. Here, Hayden's party and Stevenson's Snake River party were to rendezvous, like the fur trappers had done years earlier. At the

Firehole River, Holmes ran into an advance party headed by Jackson, and by the fifteenth the Hayden Survey was reunited.[32] The survey members properly celebrated the occasion, but it was a tame affair by the ribald standards of the mountain men.

At the Upper and Lower Geyser basins, Holmes assisted Peale in measuring, sounding, timing, and taking the temperature of scores of geysers. Holmes and Peale had the privilege of naming many of these exploding wonders that surrounded them. "Great Fountain Geyser" bears the name Holmes gave it, and the geyser was the subject of Holmes's first scientific contribution, which Peale, as mentioned above, published in his annual report.[33] The party spent a week along the Firehole before heading north to its junction with the Madison River. After locating the Firehole's source, they headed down the Madison.

Holmes, Peale, and Henry Gannett then worked their way up the gently terraced Madison Valley, stopping to make a short side-trip to Henry's Lake, located just west of the continental divide. Significantly, this lake lay amidst what cartographers in Jefferson's day called "the Stoney Mountains."[34] According to Hayden, Henry's Lake was

> a remnant, dating back probably to Pliocene times, when all these valleys were filled with water, perhaps connecting the drainage of the Missouri with that of the Columbia, and as the water subsided, formed the vast chain of lake-basins along all the important streams on both sides of the Atlantic and Pacific slopes, of which our present lakes are only insignificant remnants.[35]

Long after the Lewis and Clark expedition had failed to find a water route to India, the search for the Northwest Passage continued, and Hayden believed he had found it in the remote geologic past.

After exploring Henry's Lake, Holmes and the others made their way back to the Madison, which they followed before turning east in the direction of their starting point, Fort Ellis. They reached the fort on September 11, thus completing a large circle.[36] This expedition of the newly created park, which basically followed the present-day highway system through the park, was one of the first of many thousands, indeed, millions of tours to come.

Holmes, Peale, Jackson, and the other Hayden men stayed and worked in the Gallatin Valley area for another month, traversing the remaining unsurveyed sections of the Madison and Gallatin rivers. Hayden settled accounts with his men in Bozeman on October 14, and the party prepared to return home. They left as they had come, although after learning of a recent stagecoach robbery in which several of Hayden's men had lost everything, Holmes and the others took precautions. Peale reported that Holmes, Hayden, Gannett, and the other stagecoach passengers had ready at hand "six revolvers and three derringers, and if we had been attacked there might have been some fighting."[37] Fortunately, the stage reached Corrine, Utah, without incident. After a delay, which was spent playing cards, Holmes and the men boarded the next train and headed for points east.

Holmes expected to return to Yellowstone the following year, but Hayden decided to move the survey operations to the territory of Colorado, citing Indian unrest and the high costs of surveying the Yellowstone region, in terms of "transportation, subsistence, and labor," as reasons for the change in plans.[38] Until Yellowstone Park could be more easily reached by railroad, further government exploration would have to wait. The Kansas Pacific Railroad, however, had connected Colorado to the rest of the nation in 1870. More importantly, with the coming of the railroad, Colorado was clearly going to experience a major economic, political, and social transformation. Yet Americans understood Colorado only slightly better than they understood California on the eve of the 1849 gold rush, in spite of years of American activity in the area. As of 1873, the territory was still inadequately mapped, especially the mountains and the western slope, which made up two-thirds of Colorado. The extent and nature of the territory's resources were largely unknown outside the Rocky Mountain mining towns west of Denver. No territory, Hayden thus successfully argued to Congress, needed a survey more than Colorado.

As for Holmes, whether he went to Colorado with Hayden, explored other new lands, or returned home to Harrison County, he would go as a changed man. His experiences in the West thus far, especially his exposure to geology and cartography—through Peale, Hayden, and his own efforts in the field—as well as his new artistic insights, had broadened him and set the course for the rest of his long, varied, and rich career.

3

Mount of the Ephemeral Cross

A SCORE OF YEARS AFTER THE United States had defeated Mexico and settled the Oregon question with Great Britain, Congress ordered a survey—in all four surveys—of the republic's western territory, including the remaining unsettled lands acquired in the Louisiana Purchase. Besides Hayden's survey, there were Clarence King's Geological Exploration of the Fortieth Parallel, John Wesley Powell's Geographical and Geological Survey of the Rocky Mountain Region, and Lieutenant George Montague Wheeler's Geographical Surveys of West of the One Hundredth Meridian. These surveys published numerous reports, bulletins, atlases, and papers each year, from 1867 to 1879, and every item in some way contributed to the general description of the American West. In 1879, Congress, in the interest of efficiency and economy, consolidated the western surveys into the U.S. Geological Survey. In retrospect, the collective work of the surveys may be seen as the rough equivalent of an earlier post-conquest survey—namely, William the Conqueror's famous *Domesday.*

Hayden had already contributed to this national study by exploring the Yellowstone country and bringing its wonders to attention. Now, in 1873 he began a geological and geographical survey of Colorado Territory. He confidently declared of this land of plains, mountains, and plateaus—even as the U.S. economy fell into depression—"There is no portion of our continent . . . which promises to yield more useful results, both of a practical and scientific character." And Hayden made it clear that his men were prepared, in light of the "prospect" of Colorado's "rapid development," to make the territory's "resources . . . known to the world at as early a date as possible."[1] Hayden was filled with a sense of urgency and purpose. He believed that American civilization was about to wash over the Colorado wilderness like a tidal wave now that the transcontinental railroad had been completed and a line extended to Denver in 1870. Unlike Yellowstone, the infrastructure of expansion in Colorado was in place. Hayden realized, or at least hoped, that his investigations could influence the expected large-scale growth and development of Colorado along rational and efficient lines. The alternative was to watch the territory repeat the costly mistakes of the Pikes Peak gold rush of 1859, when thousands of Argonauts, who knew little of the land and its resources and had little way of knowing, soon found themselves "busted" and forced to return home poorer than when they started. Rather than go through another episode of unplanned economic development, the Hayden Survey intended to furnish enterprising Coloradans and eastern investors with accurate, detailed maps as well as reliable information. At the same time and certainly no less as important, Hayden looked forward to the survey's expanding the many frontiers of science. And finally, in Colorado, it would be even easier for Hayden to stay in the public eye than in the more remote Yellowstone, and publicity helped keep the congressional funding coming, without which there would have been no survey.

Camp Study, 1873, by William H. Jackson. Holmes is seated on the ground at the far right. Presiding over the mess is Ferdinand V. Hayden, the gaunt and care-worn figure in the black hat at the far left. (Photograph, no. 490, courtesy USGS Photographic Library, Denver, Colorado.)

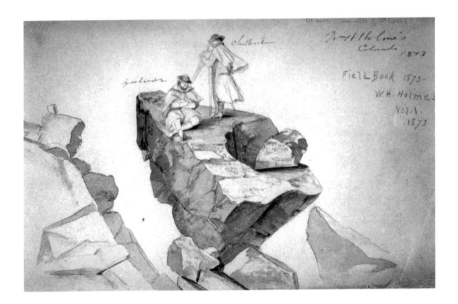

Gardiner and Chittenden Working on the Summit of Mount Evans, Colorado, 1873. This inspired Holmes drawing contains all of the elements of one of the West's most striking images of westward expansion. (Holmes, General Sketches, Colorado, 1873, No-8223 courtesy USGS Field Records Library, Denver, Colorado.)

Holmes shared in this spirit of public service and scientific quest. While in Colorado from 1873 to 1876, he climbed many of the highest peaks in the Rockies, including the Mount of the Holy Cross, a dramatic natural feature consisting of two snow-packed crevices that intersected at right angles to form a brilliant white cross. Providing the viewer was in the right place at the right time, the snowy cross was visible for miles. Atop these commanding heights — many exceeding fourteen thousand feet above sea level — Holmes drew countless topographical sketches and panoramic views, while his partner, George B. Chittenden, measured elevations and horizontal angles. Together, they and the survey's other topographers constructed, in effect, a horizontal and vertical gridwork in which any point in Colorado, whether above timberline or below, could be located with tolerable accuracy. To aid them, Hayden's men measured the height and breadth of the land with transits, compasses, sextants, chronometers, mercurial barometers, gradienters, clinometers, odometers, and that simple and accurate instrument, the steel

Topographical Work, Chittenden and Holmes, 1874, by William H. Jackson.
The following year, Jackson rendered his own version of Holmes idea. Holmes
is the seated figure sketching the landscape. (Photograph, no. 1112, courtesy
USGS Photographic Library, Denver, Colorado.)

tape. American surveying had gone "high tech," especially if compared to the
Jacob's staff, brass compass, and chain and rods technology of the earlier land-
parceling surveys.

Mapmaking, like much else in the United States after the Civil War, had
become a corporate endeavor. Thus, no single individual may take credit for
the work that went into Hayden's *Atlas of Colorado*, although Holmes was
largely responsible for the artistic design and appearance of the maps. Through
Holmes's efforts, along with those of James T. Gardner (also spelled Gardiner),
Henry Gannett, Allen D. Wilson (formerly with King), George Chittenden,
and others, the data thus collected from mountaintops, valleys, parks, and
plains, were transformed into maps at drafting tables in Washington. The

final result was a series of area and thematic maps-topographic, economic, and geologic. The *Atlas*, which the great authority of maps of the American West, Carl I. Wheat, called "magnificent," appeared a year after Colorado—the Centennial State—had achieved statehood in 1876.[2] This masterpiece of cartography was a beautiful example of the many ways in which the federal government assisted the rugged individualist in winning the West.

On finishing the work for the reports of the Yellowstone survey, Holmes left Washington and entrained for Colorado late in spring 1873. He joined the other members of the Hayden Survey at Davis Ranch on Clear Creek, which flows into the South Platte River at a point above the city of Denver. By June 5, the Middle Park, South Park, and San Luis Valley field parties or divisions of the survey were outfitted and ready to go. As artist to the survey, Holmes worked with Hayden, Chittenden, and the other men, but especially James T. Gardner, who had "deserted" Clarence King (the fieldwork of King's organization was completed in 1872) to join Hayden's survey, despite King's Faustian warning to him, "that in this busy materialistic age the greatest danger is that of total absorption in our profession," and that "We give ourselves to the *Juggernaut of the Intellect.*"[3] Whereas King would eventually turn away from science to pursue moneymaking schemes, Gardner presently remained in the field and went on to plan the triangulation of Colorado, in the careful and exacting tradition of William Lambton's and George Everest's Great Trigonometrical Survey of India, although accuracy on occasion was unfortunately sacrificed in the rush to meet Hayden's relentless deadlines.[4] Speed was everything to Hayden. To this ambitious cartographical undertaking, Holmes contributed numerous topographical sketches, a craft he quickly mastered and eventually turned into an unsurpassed art.

During the next several weeks, Gardner and Holmes took the first step in the process of mapping Colorado, an undertaking planned at a scale of four miles to one inch, and at two-hundred-foot contour lines. The first step involved determining the horizontal measurements by running a six-mile baseline near Denver, part of which followed the tracks of the Kansas Pacific Railroad, from which a system of primary and secondary triangles could then be constructed. To check for errors, the baseline was measured twice by steel tape, with due consideration given to tension and temperature. A check base in the San Luis Valley was planned for the following season. In addition, the U.S. Coast Survey established two astronomical stations-one in Denver and the other in Colorado Springs-to determine precisely the lines of latitude and longitude. To serve as a check for the vertical measurements, considerable

Dome Structure of Granite in Estes' Park Looking Nearly
West from Evans' Ranche [Sic], Sketched by Holmes, September 14, [18]73. (Holmes, General Sketches, Colorado,
1873, no. 830-A, courtesy USGS Field Records Library,
Denver, Colorado.)

time and effort was expended to calculate the elevation of Denver.[5] As this
preliminary work was being carried out, Holmes found extra time to assist
the head of the Middle Park division, Archibald R. Marvine, a geologist and
former member of Lieutenant Wheeler's survey.

One of the problems Marvine was working on that season was diagram-
ming the stratigraphy of the plains in eastern Colorado. He discovered that
along the Front Range the plains sediments were "found . . . bent or folded
more or less abruptly upward, their worn edges often rising into the air and
presenting their scarred faces to the mountains."[6] This transitional zone between mountain and plain, argued Marvine, held the "key to a knowledge of
the rocks which underlie the plains, and, by selecting favorable localities for
exposures, we may, in passing from the mountains eastward, pass in succession

across the edges of the beds from the lowest to the uppermost."[7] As Holmes stopped at several points along the Front Range—St. Vrain's Creek, Bear Canyon, Ralston Creek, Bear Creek—he found just such "favorable localities for exposures" and took as the focus of his study the lithological characteristics of a section of Jurassic beds found in each of these areas. Although the Jurassic period was a time when the stegosaur and sauropod thundered across the land and the pterosaur controlled the skies, Holmes's itemized description of this reddish-colored strata, which lay sandwiched between the older Triassic and younger Cretaceous sections, made no references to fossils and instead focused on groups of rocks. He left the paleontology of the survey in the capable hands of Fielding Meek, Leo Lesquereux, and Edward D. Cope. The latter two men were experts on fossil flora and fossil vertebrates, respectively.

Holmes's description of the Jurassic beds appeared in Marvine's report of 1873 to Hayden, along with a sketch that emphasized the basaltic caps of the Table Mountains that overlook Golden City.[8] This illustration and the work Holmes conducted with Hayden on the volcanic dike at Valmont, located south of Boulder Creek, were important in hindsight, especially the dike at Valmont, for they revealed Holmes's continued interest in volcanism, the focus of much of his previous work in Yellowstone Park.[9] His studies of such igneous-rock bodies, e.g., dikes and necks, led two years later, while on the other side of the Rockies, to Holmes's discovery of nothing less than a new mountain-building process based on yet another type of igneous-rock body—the laccolith. Notions of the laccolithic idea were by then clearly in the air, but Holmes arrived at the idea independently.[10]

At June's end, Gardner and the other topographers had finished the baseline and the remaining preliminary work. They now prepared to start weaving a web of primary and secondary triangles that would eventually cover the length and width of the Colorado Rockies. To this project, Holmes contributed his artistic talents and, no less important, his physical strength and stamina. That season he climbed at least eighteen peaks, from the famous Pikes and Longs Peaks to the obscure and unnamed, each in the service of art and science. And as for the unnamed peaks, the Hayden Survey soon remedied that situation. Holmes named personally seven of Colorado's mountains and in one instance showed political astuteness in his choice.[11] In the Gore Range, he christened one of the mountains after John Wesley Powell, who had ascended the same alpine height six years earlier and, incidentally, left a biscuit, rock hard by the time Holmes happened upon it, in a tin can with a note of "dedication of the biscuit to the finder."[12] Powell was the famous one-armed explorer of the Colorado River and its canyons and, significantly, head of one of the rival surveys of the American West. Holmes knew that several of Hayden's men, for instance, Gardner and Marvine, had served on other surveys and that despite his excellent professional relationship with Hayden, he could not dismiss the possibility that one day he too might have to hitch his wagon to another horse. Naming one of the Rocky Mountains after a potential employer was certainly one very dramatic way of placing his application in a favorable light. Holmes would not have been the first explorer to name a natural feature after a potential benefactor. As it turned out, he eventually did work for Powell after Powell succeeded Clarence King as director of the U.S. Geological Survey in 1881.

During the Hayden Survey of Colorado, Holmes claimed a number of first ascents, but his greatest triumph was the conquest of the Mount of the Holy Cross, hidden away in the north end of the Sawatch Range. Gardner had selected the mountain as one of the stations for the primary triangulation.[13] After a rough two-day climb, Holmes, Gardner, Hayden, Yale professor William Dwight Whitney (brother of the famous Josiah), and several others reached the summit on August 23. That same day Jackson, packing two wet-plate cameras, "emerged above timberline and clouds" of neighboring Notch Mountain, and after he "clambered over a vast mass of jagged rocks . . . discovered the great shining cross dead before [him], tilted against the mountainside."[14] On top of Holy Cross, Holmes assisted Gardner and produced the usual series of mountain views.[15] Holmes had obtained his first view of the legendary mountain from atop Grays Peak, near Loveland Pass.[16] According to Hayden, the Mount of the Holy Cross could be seen from other mountain peaks as well, from as far away as fifty to eighty miles.[17] But a sighting of the cross of snow itself depended entirely on favorable atmospheric conditions.[18]

Years later, in 1929, Holmes wrote in a letter to O. D. Randall, chairman of the Mount of Holy Cross Pilgrimage, Inc., that when he, his old friend Jackson, and fourteen other members of the Hayden expedition, first sighted the snow cross up close, it was

By the greatest good luck . . . that our visit was so timed as to find the cross at the particular season when the development of both cross and figure was most perfect. Earlier they were doubtless obscured [*sic*] by the winter snowfall and later reduced indefinitely by melting.[19]

The snow figure to which Holmes referred was of a woman who wore a crown, lifted her hands in prayer, and kneeled to the right of, and slightly below, the snow cross, as seen from the vantage point of Notch Peak. In Holmes's opinion, which was written down long after his ascent, the woman was "really a more wonderful freak of nature than the cross itself."[20] But in a watercolor that he made in 1873 the cross dominated the picture and the woman was barely distinguishable.[21] Jackson, on the other hand, brilliantly captured the woman in his famous 1873 photograph of the Mount of the Holy Cross, and she appears in Thomas Moran's 1875 masterpiece *The Mountain of the Holy Cross*, although in Moran's 1890 version of the mountain she disappeared into the mountain's mists.[22]

The reason why the Mount of the Holy Cross strongly attracted this trinity of image makers—Holmes, Jackson, and Moran—was not hard to find. Scientist and artist alike could view the existence of an enormous snow white cross (the upright stretched 1,500 feet; the arms reached from end to end 750 feet) and a large praying figure, both of which appeared side by side on the somber granite face of Colorado's most remote mountain, as an unmistakable sign to the westward-moving nation that it enjoyed divine approbation. To celebrate in word, image, and deed this powerful sign in the wilderness was to celebrate the manifest destiny of the American nation itself.

The publicity-conscious Hayden was keenly aware of the symbolic importance of the Mount of the Holy Cross and made sure that the world knew that he and his men had found and climbed it. But this activity was only part of the story of the Hayden expedition's conquest of the Mount of the Holy Cross. The other part involved the way in which Holmes and Jackson breathed new life into the older stories about the mountain. The accounts that Jackson and Holmes left behind were based in part on their own experiences, which were extraordinary enough, in part on the familiar story of the quest for the Holy Grail, and, no doubt, in part on the legends of the wandering friar.[23] This romantic mix constituted a new American myth about this legendary mountain.

The storyline of the legends of the wandering priest, who was sometimes known as Father Anselmo, which today have been largely forgotten, went basically like this: the Spanish padre followed Coronado (sometimes it was De Soto or some other conquistador) on his *entrada* into the northern frontier of New Spain. While the conquistador vainly searched for the Seven Cities of Cíbola, the padre looked for the object of an earlier vision that he had experienced—the Mount of the Holy Cross. He believed that finding it was the only way to expiate his sins. The plume-helmeted Coronado, of course, returned to Mexico City without the worldly wealth that he had sought. The padre, however, was rewarded for his faith and patience. One day while kneeling in prayer deep in the mountains, the devoted servant of God opened his eyes, the clouds lifted, and there before him stood the mysterious Holy Cross. At the sight of the cross, his soul was healed at last. It is a good story.

Like the padre, Holmes and Jackson, who placed themselves in the service of knowledge rather than that of God, were no less dedicated to the quest of finding the Mount of the Holy Cross. In his autobiography, *Time Exposure*, Jackson observed the parallel of his own time with that of the romantic past: "In the Middle Ages there was a legend of the Holy Grail. Sixty-seven years ago in Colorado there was the legend of a snowy cross upon a mountain."[24] But Jackson went on to explain that there was a reason for the mountain's legendary status: "As one comes close to the cross it always disappears behind Notch Mountain."[25] What one needed in order to find the cross, Jackson pointed out, was not faith but a good sense of direction. Nevertheless, Holmes and Jackson preserved the element of mystery found in the legends of the mountain by emphasizing—as Holmes put it in the letter to O. D. Randall mentioned above—that they possessed "the greatest good luck," which was the secular equivalent of the padre's miracle, in seeing the cross at one of the rare moments when conditions were ideal.[26] In an article published in 1875, in the religious magazine *The Illustrated Christian Weekly*, Holmes took a leap of faith and suggested that the expedition had been rewarded for putting its "trust [in] Providence to lift the shroud that enveloped the mountain."[27]

On this matter of luck, fate, or Providence, Jackson surpassed everyone. He recalled that as he was preparing to photograph the Holy Cross from the top of Notch Peak (the day after he first caught sight of it), "long flamelike shadows on Holy Cross were rapidly sweeping down into the valley, and . . . [he] had made just eight exposures when they were gone." And to drive home the point that he worked under once-in-a-lifetime conditions, Jackson added: "Since 1873 I have been back four or five times. I have used the best cameras and the most sensitive emulsions on the market. I have snapped my shutter morning, noon, and afternoon. And I have never come close to matching those first plates."[28] As a final touch, on the same day that Holmes was the first man to climb Holy Cross (he evidently reached the top ahead of Hayden and the others) and Jackson was the first man to see the cross from Notch Mountain, both men reported having seen, in the glacier-carved valley below, "a brilliant rainbow; not the arch, as usually seen, but an entire circle, a spectral ring, which, as we still gazed, faded away, and in a minute was gone."[29] This rainbow seemed to be yet another incontrovertible sign that Hayden's errand into the wilderness had enjoyed special sanction.

In the physical acts of locating, climbing, surveying, water-coloring, and photographing the Mount of the Holy Cross, the Hayden Survey took possession of the mountain as well as transformed it from its shadowy existence as a legend into a scientific fact, in much the same way that the survey had transformed the Yellowstone country. And by adding a touch of mystery and romance to the exploration of the mountain, Holmes and Jackson subtly and half-consciously took possession of the mountain in another sense by creating their own myth about it, in which American artists and scientists figured as the heroes rather than medieval knights and padres.

Mountain of the Holy Cross, 1873, by William H. Jackson. At this geological formation, science intersected religion in the American West. (Photograph, William H. Jackson, no. 1276, USGS Photographic Library, Denver, Colorado).

4

Opportunity

Visualizing Geology

THE NOTED HARVARD CARTOGRAPHER Erwin Raisz, appreciated among historians of the West for the handsome, interpretive maps that he made for Bernard DeVoto's classic, *The Course of Empire* (1952), observed: "There is a closer connection between geology and cartography in the United States than elsewhere, perhaps owing to the organization of the U.S. Geological Survey, where many cartographers received their training."[1] Raisz was correct, but if he had looked past the Geological Survey to the four great federal surveys of the American West that preceded it, to Hayden's survey in particular, he would have found that the mapmaker and geologist had already developed a close working relationship.[2]

Since much of the mapping and geological exploration in the West occurred simultaneously, it was hardly surprising that the federal surveyors found ways, sometimes out of necessity, to cooperate with each other. Far from bemoaning this interdisciplinary cooperation, Hayden fully realized the advantages that such an alliance between geology and topography could and did bring to his survey. From the geologist's point of view, he wrote,

> next to entering the field with a finished topographic map of the region to be examined, a thing as yet impossible in our West, the union of topography and geology in one and the same party best furnishes the data for a realization of the full value of the otherwise more or less disconnected observations of the geologist.

And to the topographer,

> equal benefits accrue . . . for mannerism and inexpressive effects are inevitable results when a topographer sees but the surface of a country and understands not its anatomy.[3]

Nowhere was this early collaboration between topography and geology better illustrated than in the work of Holmes. While carrying out his duties as artist-topographer, Holmes worked closely with the survey's geologists, as he had done with Peale and Hayden the year before in Yellowstone country. He took advantage of the opportunity to observe their methods and absorb what he could of their knowledge of an ever-changing earth. Holmes could have attended no better school of geology than this one, which held classes atop rocky, wind-blown summits or along the banks of cold, swiftly running

The Day's Start. Holmes is the man kneeling to the right. (Photograph, "Rolling Up Bedding, Holmes and Chittenden, Rocky Mountains of Colorado, 1874," by William H. Jackson, no. 1292, courtesy USGS Photographic Library, Denver, Colorado.)

streams, some of which flowed to the Gulf of Mexico, others to the Gulf of California.

This continental setting proved to be a continuous source of inspiration to the artist and scientist in Holmes. By the end of the season of 1873, he had developed a double vision of the West. He could see the land with the topographer's eye and with the geologist's insight and imagination; moreover, he acquired the ability to capture both of these perspectives in his art. Holmes's skills and especially his command of structural geology were not lost on

The Day's Finish. (Photograph, "Writing Letters, W. H. Holmes, Rocky Mountains of Colorado, 1874," by William H. Jackson, no. 1291, courtesy USGS Photographic Library, Denver, Colorado.)

Hayden, who probably taught him more about that subject than anyone else. In recognition of Holmes's progress, Hayden saw to it that when Holmes returned to Colorado for the following year, he would do so as an assistant geologist to the survey at a salary of 2,400 dollars, a 600-dollar increase from 1872, when he joined the survey.

Holmes had the chance late in the 1874 field season to combine his artistic talents and his new officially recognized scientific expertise in a topographical and geological study of the rugged Elk Mountains of western Colorado. Hayden had originally planned to do the study, but instead found himself obliged to draw upon his medical training. One of his men, Mr. Shanks, an assistant topographer, fell seriously ill at Capitol Creek, which runs into Roaring Fork River at a point northwest of present-day Aspen, and required close attention. Shanks's illness, which lasted about twenty days, forced Hayden in late August to turn the study and mapping of the Elk Range over to Holmes and topographer George B. Chittenden. Holmes made the most of this unexpected opportunity.

One of the products of this small expedition was Holmes's "Report on the Geology of the Northwestern Portion of the Elk Range," which appeared in 1876. Holmes divided his report into four parts: 1) The Roaring Fork

Showing Intruded, Eruptive Granite, Italian M[oun]t[ain]. This drawing is Holmes's rough field sketch of intruded granite. (Holmes, Sketches, Colorado, 1873, 1876, NO-7448, courtesy USGS Field Records Library, Denver, Colorado.)

Synclinal; 2) Geology of Sopris Peak and Vicinity; 3) Geology of the District Drained by Rock Creek; and 4) The Great Fault Fold of the Elk Range. Here, Holmes leaned heavily on the use of illustration—a rich array of sections, maps, sketches, diagrams, columns, views, and a striking representation of the Great Fault Fold—to make the case for his geological interpretations. It would not be an overstatement to say that the report's text was an extended caption for the artwork.[4]

As topographer and mapmaker, Holmes endeavored to describe, within the limits of technology and time, the shape of the Elk Range's natural features and their relation to other points of interest. From this point of view, Holmes saw the Elk Range as a western "spur of the great continental divide," which zigzagged across Colorado in a north-south direction. But as geologist, Holmes added causation to his study of the mountain range. By looking at causes instead of just physical relationships, Holmes concluded that the Elk Range was "quite independent in origin" of the nearby continental divide, though reading a contour map would suggest otherwise.

In studying the northwestern portion of the Elk Mountains, Holmes used the standard geological method of the day, which consisted of matching rock beds, horizon for horizon, with those delineated in the stratigraphic columns

Italian Mountain, the Polished Product. Once back East, Holmes applied his fine artistic hand to refine and finish his field sketches of western landscapes and geological formations. (Fig 13 from Hayden, "Report," *[Seventh] Annual Report*).

of the West, such as the famous column that Hayden and Meek had laboriously constructed years before.[5] This endeavor was seldom easy—except in areas like the Grand Canyon of the Colorado where the strata was laid bare. On Colorado's Western Slope, where the violent processes of diastrophism had been at work, the job of checking Hayden's columns against strata that had been intruded, faulted, uplifted, folded, warped, or even erased required extensive fieldwork and imagination.

On August 29, Holmes, Chittenden, and an unnamed packer began their expedition into the Elk Mountains by heading down the trough valley of Roaring Fork. Leading their horses and mules along a "well-marked Indian trail," through a forest of pine and scrub oak, Holmes and the small expedition quickly left Dr. Hayden and his patient behind.[6] Before turning west and ascending Sopris Creek, Holmes observed that the course of the Roaring Fork alternated between the bottom of a synclinal valley and a parallel fault line. Then looking up the valley, lying in between the Sawatch Mountains on the east and the Elk Mountains on the west, he noticed that the axes of these two ranges were not parallel but converged, like the two sides of a V, at Italian Mountain. But what led Holmes to the conclusion that the two ranges were geologically distinct, notwithstanding their obvious topographical relationship, was the difference in their respective granite bases. Holmes had discovered earlier in the season, on the summit of Italian Mountain, that the granite in the Sawatch Range was metamorphic. The granite in the Elk Range, on the other hand, was largely eruptive in nature.[7]

This difference was especially noticeable in the geology of Sopris Peak, which stood alone at the far northern extreme of the Elk Range. After Holmes had ascended Sopris Creek for some five miles, he worked his way over to and then up Rock Creek (today's Crystal Creek). He and Chittenden found a promontory that promised a commanding view of Sopris. On this summit, which they called Promontory Point, Chittenden took readings and Holmes sketched. Holmes then turned from the topography to the geology of the cone-shaped mountain in front of him, which he observed shot up like a rocket through the surrounding Carboniferous strata, "in one precipitous, unbroken slope, a rise of 6,800 feet in one and a half miles."

Because of Sopris Peak's isolation from the rest of the range, its eruptive character stood out in sharper relief. But as Holmes observed from a station located farther south, the Elk Mountains—from the Snow Mass group in the north to the White Rock group in the south—were products of the same forces of upheaval that had formed the lone Sopris, except that these two groups of mountains were connected and violently shaped by what he called the Great Fault Fold. This fold, which occurred west of and parallel to the axis of the range, differed markedly from the synclinal fold on the east side of the Elk Mountains that ran in "a gradual and gentle dip from the crest of the range toward the valley of Roaring Fork." The folded slope on the west side, in contradistinction, which was itself divided by four synclinal valleys of sedimentary strata, "drop[ped] off very abruptly" thousands of feet, before reaching the valleys of Rock Creek and East River below.

By September 11, Holmes had completed his fieldwork and prepared to return to Washington where he planned to organize his notes and sketches into a study for Hayden's general report of the 1874 season. The challenge confronting Holmes that winter was how to depict visually the history and structure of the Elk Mountains, in addition to the other projects that Hayden had him working on. The problem was resolved, except for the Great Fault Fold, by using a dual-thematic map and accompanying geologic sections, a multimedia presentation that efficiently conveyed almost the entire sum of the survey's work in the Elk Mountains.

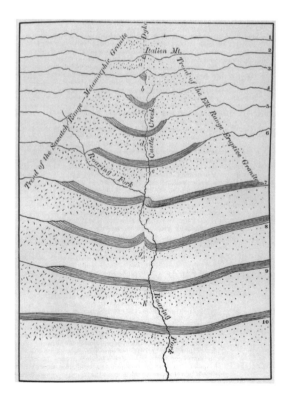

Geology's Superiority to Topography. (Fig. 1 from "Ten Sections Across the Synclinal Valley of the Roaring Fork, Partially in Perspective," by Holmes in his "Report on the Geology of the North-West Portion of the Elk Range," in Hayden, *[Eighth] Annual Report,* opposite p. 60.)

Holmes created the "Map of the Elk Mountains, Colorado" by superimposing a geological map over a topographic map, which he then scored and lettered to indicate where the horizontal sections and one axis section crossed and intersected. The sections themselves—all twelve of them—were presented on a separate sheet. Holmes also marked the vegetation types and trails and roads, and included two attractive insets based on his field sketches. One exhibited "typical sedimentary weathering" found in the Castle group of mountains, the other "typical granite weathering," as Snow Mass Mountain showcased.

This map—scaled at two miles to the inch and contours set at two-hundred-foot intervals—was a collaborative effort. Chittenden and Hayden deserved as much credit for it as Holmes. The sheet of geologic sections, however, was solely Holmes's work. These views were essentially graphic exercises in applied stratigraphy. The horizontal sections of the Elk Mountains, which were arranged vertically and connected to each other by a dotted line marking the axis of the range, were designed to provide an X-ray view of the earth's strata over a large area. Moreover, in showing the changing stratigraphic configurations over the length of each section, and from section to section by means of the axis view, vertical and horizontal scales, and points of reference, Holmes brilliantly succeeded in revealing the internal structure of the entire Elk Range as well as its history. He had learned how to map and draw geologic time.

But what the map and views failed to represent clearly was the Great Fault Fold. Holmes "found," as he put it, "that a very large number of sections, even, could not be made to give a connected idea of so complex a fold." The problem was the fold's "obscur[ity]," which had, Holmes complained, "little apparent effect on the topography." The fold may have been almost imperceptible, but it was nevertheless a geological phenomenon so powerful, he asserted, "that the beds are crushed and shattered and the severed edges shoved past each other."

For the solution of this conundrum of invisible violence, Holmes turned to cartography—quite literally. In illustrating the Great Fault Fold, Holmes took a plain outline map that, with shading and other relief techniques, he made to appear wrinkled and torn in order to dramatize "the peculiar foldings of the broken edges of the strata," represented by the Cretaceous horizon.[8] To focus on this one idea, he omitted the granite masses, in what was a stunning departure from his literal representations of nature. The result was, in effect, a boldly sculptured map that bordered on the abstract. In the sheet of sections, however, Holmes completed the transition from representational illustration to the wholly abstract.[9] In each of the ten sections, which corresponded to the scorings on the outline map, Holmes depicted the Cretaceous horizon as a simple line, drawn to imitate the occurrence of the Great Fault Fold. These highly creative and innovative efforts were well received. One of America's great geologists and Holmes's contemporary (and later good friend), Grove Karl Gilbert, declared that "in the description of [the Elk Mountains] by pen and pencil Mr. Holmes has made an important contribution, not only to dynamical geology, but to the methods of geological illustration."[10]

Holmes's foray into abstract illustration was brief. It was a particular response to a particularly knotty topographical problem. The aberration merits consideration, however, because the exception underscores the rule. Holmes warned that his illustration of the Great Fault Fold was "highly artificial," rather than realistic, as was typical of his art. For the moment, his means differed little from those of Thomas Moran, who placed idealization above everything else.[11] But the ends remained the same for Holmes. His objective in art was still to provide a faithful impression of nature in as representational a language as he could command.[12]

Pogonobogwint

During Holmes's years with Hayden, his life alternated from the sedentary comforts of Washington to the hard round of fieldwork in the West, a yin-yang change that he relished. In a letter to Hayden, written in Pueblo, Colorado, at the start of the 1875 field season, Holmes mentioned that the transition from "office to saddle" was a shock for him and the other men, but after a few days of camp life, "of fierce cold winds—which parched [their] faces fearfully and gave [them] sore eyes also," they were "nicely hardened" and made ready for the season ahead.[13] Caught up in the outdoor and muscular ethos of the day, Holmes—like Theodore Roosevelt, Frederic Remington, and numerous other young men who came of age after Appomattox—saw the West, with its harsh climes, rugged mountains, and trackless wastes, as a perfect field in which to test his manhood. This chance to demonstrate virility was doubly important to Holmes the artist. Male artists, poets, or musicians, unlike men employed in clearly "male" occupations such as business, industry, engineering, politics, and law, ran the risk of being labeled "effete," a devastating charge on either side of the Atlantic in those days, unless they could show by dint of subject matter, productivity, remuneration, or some other means that their masculinity was above question.

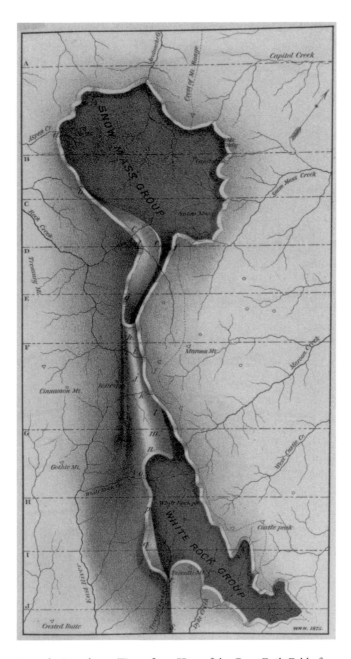

From the Literal. . . . (Fig. 11 from "Part of the Great Fault Fold of the Elk Mountains," by Holmes in his "Report on the Geology of the North-West Portion of the Elk Range," in Hayden, *[Eighth] Annual Report,* following p. 70).

Holmes could not have asked for a rougher assignment to prove himself that year than what Hayden gave him. Pleased with the results of Holmes's brief expedition to the Elk Mountains the preceding summer, Hayden decided to make him head of the southwestern division of the Colorado survey. Holmes would lead a party of men in the geological and archaeological exploration of seventy-four hundred square miles in the Four Corners area of the territories of Colorado, Utah, New Mexico, and Arizona. Here was plenty of room for Holmes's ambitions. The five other members of Holmes's party were Chittenden, topographical engineer; Townsend S. Brandegee, assistant topographer and botanist; "Potato John" Raymond, the cook; and Thomas Cooper and another packer.[14]

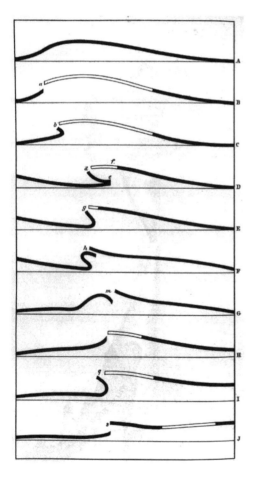

... to the Abstract. This illustration is Holmes's highly stylized rendering of the "Great Fault Fold of the Elk Mountains." (Fig. 10 from Holmes, "Report on the Geology of the North-West Portion of the Elk Range," in Hayden, *[Eighth] Annual Report,* following p. 70.)

To reach the southwestern division or San Juan district of Colorado, as it was also called, Holmes's party left Pueblo, which was situated on the Arkansas River, in mid-June of 1875, dropped south to the Huerfano River, headed west, crossing into the San Luis Valley via Mosca Pass, and briefly stopped to study the Great Sand Dunes situated on the northeastern side of the valley.[15] The expedition got off to a good start and Chittenden confided in a letter to Hayden that Holmes was turning out to be a "first rate Boss."[16] On the nineteenth, the party arrived at Del Norte, on the valley's west side, where it obtained supplies. Holmes then led his men up the Rio Grande, which ran west into the remote but mineral-rich San Juan Mountains. Because of earlier discoveries of gold in the area, the U.S. government had forced the Southern Utes (Capote, Mouache, and Weeminuche bands), under the 1873 Brunot agreement, to cede the San Juans, thereby opening up the range to American miners and settlers.[17]

Holmes's party found itself caught in between the intense resentment that individual Southern Utes felt toward the relentless encroachment of Americans from virtually every direction, on the one hand, and the strong antipathies that land-coveting whites held toward the Utes, on the other. White greed and anger came to be crystallized in the battle cry, "the Utes must go."[18] Over the next couple of weeks, Holmes began to feel the pressure of the situation into which he and his party had entered. At times, in order to work he had to first "stare off" the Indians, who watched his every move.[19] Understandably, Holmes grew worried that his party might become the target of Ute anger. To avoid any misunderstandings, he tried to convince the local inhabitants that his survey party, contrary to appearances, represented no threat to their lands.

Toward this end, he enlisted the aid of Captain John Moss of the mining camp called, in a typical example of frontier exaggeration, La Plata City. Moss was a likable man and one of the few miners who had developed a good rapport with the Utes by having agreed to make an annual payment to them in exchange for the right to mine on their lands.[20] Holmes probably knew the man through Jackson, who, incidentally, was also working in southwestern Colorado before leaving in early August to photograph the Hopi Mesas in northeastern Arizona. The year before, Jackson had called on the services of Moss as guide to Mesa Verde and had been impressed with the captain's grasp of the problems facing the Southern Utes and sympathy for these besieged people.[21]

Moss made it clear to Holmes that the Indian danger was real. The Utes were expecting a boundary survey to arrive and were prepared to stop it from accomplishing its task, "by any means—fair or foul," and Holmes's party risked being confused with this other party, which the General Land Office had promised to send.[22] On July 17, Holmes secured a promise from Moss to explain to the leaders at the main Ute encampment that he had no involvement with the Brunot agreement or any other agreement or purchase between the federal government and the Southern Utes. Technically Holmes was right, but the Utes could certainly see that in a broader, imperial sense Holmes's party as well as the other Hayden parties at work on Colorado's Western Slope were as much a threat to them as was any boundary survey. They no doubt realized, like non-Western peoples all over the world, that making maps and taking inventories of natural resources were activities hardly undertaken for their benefit.

Despite the tensions, Holmes proceeded with the survey, taking pains to avoid the native inhabitants of the valleys of the San Juan and Dolores, and given what seems to have been a predisposition against Indians in general, this course perfectly suited him. Jackson's party, on the other hand, could not remove itself from the locals and, as Jackson explained, accordingly adopted the following precautions:

> At all times we avoided any mention of the Geological Survey; for even the word 'survey' was anathema to all Utes. And I was always especially careful to explain that my camera tripod, despite its telltale legs, was *not* a transit.[23]

Holmes's policy of avoidance worked until July 28, when his party ran out of water and, duly chagrined, was forced to turn to the Utes for help. One of the Indians at the camp of the Ute chief Naraguinnep showed them where to find a spring, which Holmes remarked with disdain was "a very weak and obscure one." Nevertheless, Holmes grudgingly admitted that "without the Indians we should have probably have had a dry camp." In return for the favor, Holmes reluctantly allowed the small camp to board with his party for three days. He complained afterward that they had eaten "like fury."[24]

The lack of water was a constant source of concern whenever the party ventured away from the Dolores or the mud-red flow of the San Juan and its tributaries. The point of the area's aridity was dramatically reinforced on July 30, when Holmes climbed Ute Peak. From that commanding height, Holmes recorded that he

> could trace the course of the San Juan for nearly a hundred miles. Could see the mouths of Mancos, McElmo, and Montezuma. Could see Rough Mountain, Monumental [*sic*] Valley, The Blue and Carriso Mountains, The Needles, The Mesa Verde, The LaPlata [*sic*] Mountains and the Valley of the Dolores.

But, he added,

> Such a country as that to the West I have never seen and never hope to see again. It is dry as a desert, as monotorious [*sic*] as a plain and as complicated as a labyrinth.

Shocked at the vast, red, sun-blasted landscape before him, he nevertheless affirmed, in the noble tradition of discovery and out of Victorian duty, that "it must be explored."

Several days later near Skeleton Mesa, Holmes ran into another Indian group of four men and five women—Navajos—who were herding sheep and goats. The two groups managed to communicate with each other through the medium of Spanish, the same language in which the Utes had some fluency as well. Holmes cared as little for these Navajos as for the Utes he had met, describing two of the younger men as "impudent 'devil-may-care' fellows," and one of the older men as having a "mouth of ungodly width." Seeing that these Indians were making camp at the mouth of Montezuma Creek, Holmes took his party to a site a good four miles farther down the Rio San Juan.

That night, August 4, the shouts of Tom Cooper, the packer, awoke Holmes and the other men. Two Indians had slipped into camp and stolen the horses, which had been tied up across the river on the south bank. Holmes and his men "seized [their] rifles," but while they were bumping into each other, cursing, and stumbling around in the dark, Cooper managed to follow the horses up the valley and recover the animals single-handedly and unarmed. He did not realize that the Indians were behind the plot until he nearly ran headlong into them, after a two-mile chase, believing rather that a coyote or varmint had spooked the horses. Cooper was as surprised as the Indians were at their sudden face-to-face encounter. At this point, the two Indians conceded the game and ran away without the horses. When Cooper returned to camp, the Holmes party issued a collective sigh of relief at not having to postpone the survey and make what would have been a two-hundred-mile trek on foot back to "the nearest habitation."

The incident did not end there, however. The following morning, Cooper and Potato John decided to teach the Indians upriver a lesson. Holmes and Chittenden bravely went to work instead. Cooper and Potato John reported that when they arrived at the Indian camp they found that the four men seen earlier had somehow doubled to eight and they quickly thought better of their intention to impart instruction to the natives. The Indians must have been amused by this abrupt about-face and decided to press the numerical advantage they enjoyed and teach Holmes and his party a lesson of their own. "At noon," Holmes wrote, they "rode coolly down to our camp dismounted and seated themselves in a half circle in the middle of camp and proceeded to scrutinize every object in the outfit, to beg this and pretend to wish to 'swap' for that."

Holmes was clearly galled by this uninvited visitation, especially when, as he put it, "One old scamp had the audacity to nudge me with his elbow and order me to bring a pail of [']Agua[']." The main concern of Holmes and his men was that the Indians did not "steal anything." Taking the Indians at their word that they wanted to trade, Holmes exchanged "matches for some arrows, and gave them some bread to eat," in the hope that this trade would defuse what he regarded as a highly volatile situation. This act seemed effective, or perhaps the Indians simply got bored, for the guests finally took their matches and bread and left, to Holmes's "great relief."

In language that his seventeenth-century ancestor, the Reverend Obadiah Holmes, would have understood, William Holmes recorded in his field notes that "these [Indians] come more nearly up to my notion of what fiends of hell ought to be than any mortals I have seen," a passage that revealed, tough talk aside, real uneasiness. He became convinced, based on the belief that he recognized two of the Indians from a meeting of July 25, that these "thieving pirates" or this "herd of meddlesome and treacherous savages," as he now called them, had been following his party all along and would "perhaps be lying in wait for us until we get out of the South West corner."

Holmes's fears of the "evil intentions" of the Indians were far from groundless. Only days after his encounter with the Indians along the San Juan, near Recapture Creek, named in honor of Cooper's services, nine other Indians, and possibly more, attacked James T. Gardner, Henry Gannett, Albert Peale, and ten other Hayden men, who were at work in the desert country between the Sierra Abajo and the Sierra La Sal.[25] Ouray, the famous Ute chief and diplomat, had warned Gardner on July 11, when the two met at the Los Pinos agency, that there might be trouble with the Indians of that region, who, according to Ouray, had a long history of murdering and robbing whites, especially prospectors, who trespassed through their domain.[26]

The leader of this group was an aged and exceptionally dark-skinned Paiute named Pogonobogwint, who recognized no authority except his own and who apparently attracted the refractory elements of neighboring tribes, including, Holmes believed, the Navajo Indians who tried to take his party's horses.[27] Pogonobogwint had earlier refused to submit to the indignities of reservation life, declaring that "he was not a dog to eat bread from the hands of white men."[28] Despite the danger that the defiant chief and his independent-minded followers posed to Hayden's men, Ouray assured Gardner that as long as he had at least seven armed men and watched the pack mules carefully, he should be able to carry out unmolested his scientific mission to the La Sals.[29] Ouray's intelligence, as it turned out, was dated. Pogonobogwint was stronger than Ouray or anyone else appreciated.

Late in the afternoon on August 15, 1875, Gardner's men learned precisely how strong.[30] On that hot day, at least nine Indians, who had earlier shown the Gardner-Gannett party friendship, opened fire with muzzle-loading rifles from behind a hill—narrowly missing two men. For the next twenty hours, part of which was spent under the bright glare of a full moon, Gardner, Peale, Gannett, and the other men fired their rifles and revolvers in defense as they were forced to make their way up a long, high-walled ravine, at times dangerously exposing themselves, as they looked for a way out. At one point in this deadly game of hide-and-seek, a mule was shot out from underneath a man. An opening in the rocks was finally located, but not before an Indian was picked off the rocks above. While the Indians were apparently regrouping, the men abandoned their packs and instruments (at a loss of well over twenty-five hundred dollars) and climbed a narrow deer trail that led to the tableland and safety above.[31] Amazingly, the men emerged from the ravine unscathed and immediately set out, riding their mules as fast as the nearly worn-out legs of their beasts would carry them. It was two hundred miles and several days to Parrott City. As soon as Gardner's exhausted men arrived at the mining camp, they met a surprised Holmes, who happened to be bringing his party in from the field at the same time, and a happy reunion followed.

The news of the Indian attack generated excitement all over the territory. To Jackson at least, who had his own run-in with Pogonobogwint, the attack on Gardner was not an isolated incident, but rather a manifestation of "the general dissatisfaction among all the Utes."[32] Despite these dangers, Holmes and Gannett resolutely went on with their work, which in Holmes's case required only fifteen more days to complete. While Holmes and Gannett headed north in the direction of the San Miguel Mountains, intending to stay clear of the country west of the Dolores Plateau, Gardner and a party of men succeeded in rescuing two men left in charge of a supply camp on the Dolores River. Each man in the rescue party, including Gardner (who was stung by criticism that it was his bad judgment that had earlier placed his men in danger and therefore felt he had something to prove), carried with him a hundred rounds of ammunition and had every intention of killing any Indians they encountered along the way.[33] Luckily, nothing came of this bloody-minded escapade.[34]

The explanation for Holmes's decision to remain in the field under these hostile conditions, besides the determination to get the job done, may be found in the openly racist attitude, shared by many of his contemporaries, that the Indians were, at bottom, knaves and cowards, and would steal and murder only if the risks were negligible. Gardner summed up this view in a letter to the *Rocky Mountain News*, in which he made the angry assertion that "the whole history of the frontier proves that where the Indian and White come face to face in equal fight his nerve fails before that of the Anglo Saxon."[35] In a similar vein, Holmes believed that the "cowardly scamps [who had tried to steal his party's horses] would not dare to harm [him or the other men] if it were liable to endanger themselves."[36] The only risk, then, as far as Holmes was concerned, lay in either being greatly outnumbered or in failing to observe William Henry Jackson's two commandments—"when in Indian country keep your powder dry—and watch out."[37]

In the larger picture of Indian/white relations, Holmes and the other Hayden men witnessed firsthand one of a series of last acts in the history of Indian armed resistance against the westward advancement of American civilization. This long, troubled period would not be brought to a close for another decade, when Geronimo's Apaches finally surrendered in 1886. The archaeological work that Holmes conducted among the ruins in the Four Corners region, however, along with the ethnological studies of John Wesley Powell in the canyon country to the west, presaged a new role for the federal government to play in Indian affairs, which Powell was instrumental in institutionalizing a few years later, in 1879, as the Bureau of American Ethnology (initially the Bureau of Ethnology). Until the 1870s, the federal government confined its involvement with Native Americans to implementing the various policies of assimilation and removal, both of which often led to tragic results. Now, with the Indian wars on the High Plains and elsewhere along the frontier at their peak but their conclusion never in doubt, Washington, under Powell's growing leadership, began to turn to the scientific study of its former enemies and the civilizations that they and their ancestors had left behind. Holmes was at the center of this change and would one day succeed Powell at its head.

5

Ghosts

IN 1874, WHILE HOLMES WAS AT WORK in the Elk Mountains, Jackson was discovering and photographing the exotic ruins that he and Captain Moss visited in Mancos Canyon, which cuts through the middle of Mesa Verde in a southwesterly direction. Hayden understood at once the scientific interest, to say nothing of the publicity value, of a lost civilization in the American Southwest. The news of the find might even rival, in national attention, the wonders of Yellowstone. As a measure of his confidence in Holmes's abilities, Hayden gave the artist-geologist the job of "making examinations of such ancient remains as might be included in the [San Juan] district surveyed," a charge Holmes welcomed as a "very agreeable task."[1] This assignment came in addition to the geological survey that Holmes was already planning to conduct in the area. In both respects, as we shall see, Holmes realized his superior's expectations and more. In the process, he succeeded in launching himself on yet another career; this time as an archaeologist.[2]

Drawing on the observations, collections, pen drawings, maps, and measurements made during the summers of 1875 and 1876, Holmes prepared his report on the pueblo ruins of the San Juan country. For background information, he turned to the antebellum work of Lieutenant James H. Simpson and Dr. John Strong Newberry.[3] In 1849, Simpson examined the ruins of Chaco Canyon, which lay south of the San Juan in northwestern New Mexico, while in the company of the expeditionary artist Richard H. Kern.[4] Together, they briefly documented the long-abandoned structures and, in the shade of the stone walls, speculated on the original appearance of the lost cities.[5] Ten years later, Dr. Newberry, who constructed the first stratigraphic column of the Grand Canyon of the Colorado, passed by Mesa Verde and described the ruins that he observed in the region. He was a member of Captain John N.

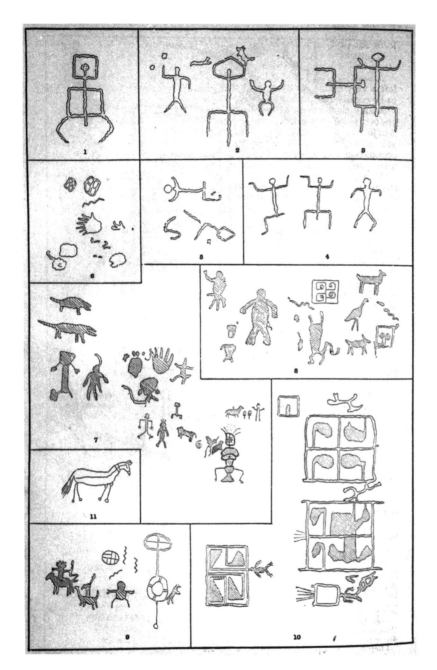

Southwestern Pictographs. (Plate XLII from Holmes, "Report on the Ancient
Ruins of Southwestern Colorado, Examined During the Summers of 1875 and
1876," in Hayden, *Tenth Annual Report,* opposite p. 401.)

Macomb's party that vainly attempted, in the wake of the Mormon War, to find a southern supply route through Utah's rugged canyon country.[6]

Besides the work of Simpson and Newberry, as well as the 1874 report of Jackson (published in 1876), Holmes studied other sources in American archaeology, from the army-engineer reports to the famous study *Ancient Monuments of the Mississippi Valley* (1848), by Ephraim George Squire and Edwin H. Davis. While wintering in Washington, Holmes also took advantage of the National Museum where he was able to compare the artifacts that he had gathered with other southwestern collections. He found Edward Palmer's pottery collection from the Virgin River Valley near Saint George, Utah, particularly useful in suggesting that a large, uniform cultural area at one time existed in the Southwest.[7] In short, Holmes had completed his homework on the science of man before publishing the results of his archaeological survey; his report appeared in 1878 as part of Hayden's *Tenth Annual Report.*

Holmes's approach to the exploration of the open-site ruins, cliff dwellings, and grave sites in the San Juan district was fairly systematic, unlike that of his friend Jackson who relied mainly on his guide Captain John Moss and luck, of which Jackson seemed never in short supply. Holmes, on the other hand, rode down each of the major lines of drainage in the region, checking each of them off in turn. He began with the ruins on the Rio La Plata and eventually visited those of the Rio San Juan, the Rio Mancos, McElmo Creek, Aztec Creek, the south bend of the Rio Dolores, Hovenweep Creek, Montezuma Creek, and lesser water courses, including Caliente Creek in New Mexico. Given the time constraints, the demands of the geological survey, Indian dangers, the complex terrain, and the size of the country, Holmes reluctantly rode past numerous ruins without stopping. Many more escaped his notice entirely, such as the great Cliff Palace, which the cowboys Charlie Mason and Richard Wetherill spotted from the opposite canyon rim in 1888, while they were rounding up strays in Mesa Verde country.[8]

On the basis of Holmes's archaeological investigations, he found that the pre-Columbian ruins of the San Juan country fell into three categories: "(1) lowland or agricultural settlements; (2) cave dwellings; and (3) cliff-houses or fortresses."[9] These classifications added analytical depth to the term *ruin* and provided the first interpretive framework for the study of a civilization that had seemingly evaporated into the pellucid desert air. Holmes illustrated, through his writing and drawing, each of these three categories by closely examining a typical group of ruins. Of special note was the work that he did on the cave dwellings and round towers along the San Juan and the cliff houses

High Tower Rio Mancos. (Plate XXXIV from Holmes, "Report on the Ancient Ruins of Southwestern Colorado, Examined During the Summers of 1875 and 1876," in Hayden, *Tenth Annual Report*, opposite p. 392.)

in Mancos Canyon. According to the early twentieth-century authority on southwestern archaeology, Alfred Vincent Kidder, Holmes made a signal contribution to the field with his keen observations and insights among the San Juan sites.[10]

To the great and fascinating question of who built and occupied the ancient pueblos, Holmes—like Simpson, Newberry, and Jackson before him—offered an answer. In solving the mystery, each of these men used the process of elimination, and concluded that the current possessors of the land—the Navajos, Utes, and Paiutes—were "totally distinct," in Holmes's words, from the former civilized tenants. These contemporary inhabitants were "nomadic savages" and as such incapable of the technology and social organization necessary to have supported the area's once "numerous population."[11] Bluntly put, Holmes stated that the cliff builders were "in many ways superior" to the present-day Pogonobogwints and thus bore no relation to them.[12]

If the modern Indians of the San Juan area did not build the ancient pueblos, the question remained as to who did. Here a consensus was slower to develop. In fact, two schools of thought—the Aztec and Pueblo schools—formed over this question from the beginning. Simpson accepted the local belief that the Aztecs had built the ruins, "when they were on their way from the north towards the south; that after living here and in the vicinity for a while, they dispersed, some of them going east and settling on the Rio Grande, and others south into Old Mexico."[13] In a sense, just the opposite is argued today, although the extent of Mesoamerican influences on the Anasazi (a Navajo term meaning "enemy ancestors" or "ancient ones") remains a topic of lively debate. Simpson based his view in part on the oral tradition of Mexicans as well as those of Pueblo and Navajo Indians; he also referred to Humboldt as a source for his conclusions.[14] His interpretation also had an undeniable logic to it.

Simpson's artist, Richard H. Kern, however, doubted the Aztec hypothesis and with the trained eye of his profession noted that there "can be no doubt [that the Chaco pueblo was erected] by a race living here in long past ages—Its style is so different from anything Spanish & so similar to all the Indian Pueblos."[15] During his expedition to the Four Corners, Newberry arrived independently at the same conclusion. He opined that the former inhabitants of the ruins were "Pueblo Indians." Perhaps thinking in terms of the theory of uniformitarianism, which posits that past geologic events are caused by processes seen to be at work in the present, he argued that the ancestors of the modern Pueblos must have been like the modern Pueblos, namely, "peaceful, industrious, and agricultural."[16]

Holmes's own investigations led him straight to the Kern and Newberry camp.[17] He found that the evidence supported a far less imaginative explanation than what Simpson had advanced for the origins of the ancient ruins. He stated unreservedly: "The ancient peoples of the San Juan country were doubtless the ancestors of the present pueblo tribes of New Mexico and Arizona."[18] This view, which is still largely accepted, ran contrary to those who favored a southern-origins hypothesis for the builders of the ancient pueblos, such as Frederick W. Putnam of Harvard's Peabody Museum of American Archaeology and Ethnology.[19] Looking back in 1928 on Holmes's stand in the debate, Edgar L. Hewett, head of the School of American Research in Santa Fe as well as Holmes's friend, called him "the founder of the science" of southwestern archaeology, a patriarchal honor usually bestowed upon Holmes's contemporary, Adolph Francis Alphonse Bandelier.[20]

The Next Dimension

Holmes found further evidence for his views in the "comparison of the ancient with the modern architecture and a consideration of the geographical relations of the ancient and modern pueblos."[21] Holmes did not cite his sources for, or elaborate on, the similarities that he found between Anasazi and Pueblo building styles in his report of 1875 and 1876 (published in 1878). He apparently felt that he did not have to, for the point had already been so well made at the International Centennial Exhibition in Philadelphia that any further mention of it would have seemed too obvious to belabor. At the Indian exhibit, thousands had the opportunity for the first time to compare — even as they read the shocking news that the Sioux and Cheyenne had annihilated Lieutenant Colonel Custer and his men of the Seventh Cavalry at a site on the Little Big Horn River — the photographs (and positives on glass) of the modern and ancient pueblos by Jackson and John K. Hillers, who served as photographer for the Powell survey.[22] Visitors could also go beyond these two-dimensional representations to inspect the attractive scale models of four ancient ruins, which distinctly resembled their modern counterparts. Ironically, Americans learned about the lifeways of one native people, the Pueblos of the Southwest, while at the same time the U.S. Army was engaged in destroying the horse and hunting culture of the tribes of the Great Plains and the Apaches of the Southwest.

With the help of several assistants, Holmes and Jackson took six months to construct these models and the accompanying details (miniature pottery, utensils). Each of these plaster casts was painted in oil to look lifelike, and one at least included figurine aborigines engaged in carrying water, making pottery, and other routine tasks. The models proved to be an enormously successful and popular experiment in scientific illustration. Jackson recalled with pride that the models "attracted more attention" at the Centennial Exhibition

> than the many photographs and all the rocks and relics of Dr. Hayden's career. [The exhibit] drew almost as many visitors as Dr. Alexander Graham Bell's improbable telephone.[23]

Clearly, science exhibitions could educate as well as entertain. And not forgetting geology, Holmes also prepared a pair of thematic models depicting the Elk Mountains in yet another attempt to illustrate this complex range. These two scale models dramatized the different perspectives of topography and geology, respectively. In the first model, Holmes shaped the lay of the land into bold relief and marked the geological formations through the use of color. He exposed in the second model the internal structure of the range by dividing it into sections.[24]

Of the four models of Indian ruins placed on exhibit in Philadelphia, Holmes was directly responsible for the model of Two Story Cliff House located in Mancos Canyon and another of the Great Triple Walled Tower found near present-day Hovenweep. The Mancos cliff-house model stood forty-six inches high and twenty-eight inches wide and was constructed at a scale of two feet to the inch. The stone building that the model represented, which looked more like an eyrie than a human abode, was anchored to a ledge seven hundred feet above the valley floor and two hundred feet under an overhanging bluff.

Holmes's model of the Great Triple Walled Tower served to correct the general impression that all of the ruins of southwestern Colorado were perched high on the walls of salmon-colored cliffs. This model, built at a scale of four feet to the inch, represented a round tower that was forty-two feet in diameter and twelve feet in height. The inner tower, which enclosed an *estufa* or kiva, a ceremonial chamber that served as the center of the Anasazi's "superstitious" life, loomed above a hundred or so crumbling apartments, all of which overlooked McElmo Creek.[25] In common with other modern pueblos to the south and west, such as the sky cities of Acoma or Walpi, this once prosperous village was situated on a mesa high above the surrounding plain.

Jackson was in charge of building the other two models of Indian ruins. He chose to represent a "cave town," a group of ruins tucked away under the lip of a three-hundred-foot bluff and located in the lower reaches of Canyon de Chelly. The other model was a "reconstruction" of the same cave town. He installed steps in the rock, wooden ladders, roofs that doubled as terraces for the next tier of apartments, and figurine aborigines in natural poses.[26] Jackson's reconstruction bore a strong resemblance to the Hopi pueblos, which he knew well, and served to support Holmes's contention that the Anasazi were the ancestors of the living Puebloans. Jackson was so pleased with the immense popularity of the Indian exhibit that after the Centennial he built several other models, including representations of Tewa and Taos pueblos. Given the wide demand, Jackson's models (and presumably the two Holmes made) were shown in museums all over the world.[27]

Since Peale and Seymour had accompanied the Long expedition to the Rocky Mountains, scientific illustration of the West was largely limited to two-dimensional pictorial images. At the Centennial in Philadelphia, however, Holmes and Jackson broke new ground with their scale models. Moreover, these three-dimensional representations made to scale marked an important step toward Holmes's creation of life-size, realistic, and free-standing dioramas that he unveiled to the public two decades later. Appropriately, the first of these dioramas or "ethnic lay figure groups," which portrayed the quarry methods of Native Americans, was exhibited at another fair—the World's Columbian Exposition in 1893.[28]

The Two Horsemen of the Apocalypse

Holmes's views as to the identity of the cliff builders was eventually accepted by the emerging anthropological profession. In fact, putting questions of popular interest on a scientific basis was an important part of the process of professionalization that the sciences and social sciences underwent in the late nineteenth century. But the question as to why the Anasazi abandoned much of their territory to withdraw southward to the present sites of the Hopi Mesas, the Zuni River, and the Rio Grande and its tributaries remains to this day something of a mystery. Newberry and Holmes put forward two theories as to the fate of the Anasazi that have enjoyed, modifications notwithstanding, considerable staying power. Newberry argued that the climate had deteriorated, whereas Holmes and Jackson believed that a catastrophic war had driven the ancestral Puebloans southward.

Proposed as evidence of this latter theory was Battle Rock of McElmo Canyon, due north of the Sleeping Ute Mountains. On passing this butte late in July of 1875, Holmes recorded in his field notes that "Battle Rock" was "said by tradition to be the site of the last battle between the Ancient Moquis [the Hopi] and the encroaching Utes."[29] Holmes had learned about the legend of Battle Rock from an elderly Hopi man, through the agency of Jackson's amiable guide and friend Captain Moss. Jackson, who was as interested in the source of legends as the legends themselves, visited Battle Rock and described it thus: "The bare floor of nearly white sandstone, upon which the butte stands, is stained in gory streaks and blotches by the action of an iron constituent in the rocks of another portion of the adjoining bluffs, and this feature probably gave rise to the legend."[30] In terms of Native American history, Battle Rock is a significant place, whether the geology gave rise to myth or myth gave meaning to the site. In any event, Holmes believed that the legend had more than a particle of truth to it.

Newberry arrived at his climatic theory after traveling through the Four Corners region in 1859. He argued:

> The surrounding country contains very little animal life, and almost none of it is now cultivable. It is 7,000 feet in altitude, intensely cold in the winter, and very dry throughout the year . . . The arroyos, through which streams seem to have once flowed, are now dry . . . At first sight the difficulties in the way of obtaining a supply of water for any considerable population at this point would seem unsurmountable, and the readiest solution of the problem would be to infer a change of climate, by which this region was made uninhabitable.

Exercising scientific caution, Newberry warned: "Such a conclusion is not *necessary* . . . for the skill and industry of the ancient inhabitants of the arid table-lands of New Mexico and Arizona achieved wonders in the way of procuring a supply of water."[31]

Holmes read closely Newberry's report, but strongly disagreed with the argument "that the climate has grown less moist since the ancient occupation."[32] Holmes's objections, it should be noted, were made after the Civil War, during a period of unusually wet years. This modern climatic change or cycle may well have accounted for Holmes's observations that the majority of the San Juan ruins were located near "running streams, or by springs that furnish a plentiful supply of water during the greater part of the year." Holmes added that the Four Corners region was "by no means an entire desert," that in fact, "a considerable area of rich tillable land" existed there.[33] The land evidently had come to life since Newberry rode through it nineteen years before, although even today some of the northern valleys of the San Juan are no less arable than the lands to which the Anasazi retreated.[34]

Ideological factors may have also shaped Holmes's views on the subject of climatic change. His superior, Ferdinand Hayden, after all, was one of the leading proponents of the "Rain follows the Plow" theory.[35] This theory, of course, would eventually become bitterly discredited, but in the meantime Hayden held firm in his belief that the Great American Desert could be made "to blossom as the rose." To accomplish this mighty imperial feat, he wrote, in 1871,

> that the planting of ten or fifteen acres of forest-trees on each quarter-section will have a most important effect on the climate, equalizing and increasing the moisture and adding greatly to the fertility of the soil.[36]

Clearly, Newberry's climatic theory, which was not published until 1876, was directly at odds with Hayden's beliefs and now those of thousands of farmers preparing to invade the lands beyond the hundredth meridian. The prospect that a large civilization, based on agriculture, perished in the Four Corners region for want of rainfall was about as welcome in the West as John Wesley Powell's *Report on the Lands of the Arid Region of the United States, with a More Detailed Account of the Lands of Utah* (1878), which, according to environmental historian Donald Worster, was "a model of ecological realism in an unsympathetic age of unbounded expectations."[37]

Far less disquieting to the West's boosters was Holmes's theory as to what befell the Anasazi. He was impressed by the defensive appearance of many of the pueblos, especially the cliff dwellings. In his mind's eye, Holmes saw, after years of fighting, that the ancestral Pueblo people were forced, after an apocalyptic battle with presumably the area's present nomads, to flee their homes, "a disheartened and desperate people."[38] This explanation had the advantage of accounting for the remote and hard-to-reach ruins, which were physically separated from fields and sources of water.[39] Such defensive behavior, Holmes suggested, would make little sense in the face of a climate that was growing steadily drier.[40]

In support of this catastrophic-war theory, Holmes used his knowledge of geology to study the age of the cliff dwellings, which were, according to the logic of a protracted war, the last of the three types of structures (the other two were lowland or agricultural settlements and cave dwellings) to have been built. At a dangerously perched cliff house in Mancos Canyon, Holmes had noted that the foundations of the structure were "laid upon and cemented to the sloping and over hanging faces of the ledge." Since the sandstone to which the structure was attached was "coarse and soft, and hence easily disintegrated" (in fact, one of the buttresses had fallen off), and the sandstone was fully exposed to the elements, Holmes concluded that the conditions were close to ideal in determining the relative age of the building, and by extrapolation the age of other buildings of its type. He found

> that since the construction of these foundations no perceptible change has taken place; the thickness of a sheet of paper has hardly been washed away from the surface of the rock, and the mortar, which is of almost equal firmness with the rock, lies upon it as if placed there within a dozen years, and the appearance of the plaster on the outer wall, although somewhat cracked and broken off, does not add greatly to our impressions of their antiquity.[41]

Using these same loose geological methods, which were in themselves a significant contribution to early American archaeology, Holmes observed at another site—the cave dwellings on the San Juan—that the period of time between the first human habitation and the present "would certainly not be inconsiderable."[42] This conclusion provided support for the catastrophic-war theory, for it did suggest a relatively recent construction of the cliff houses, although the cave dwellings and the nearby round towers, like the cliff houses, Holmes believed, may have also served a largely defensive purpose.[43]

Ode on an Anasazi Jar

What fascinated Holmes about the cliff dwellers, however, was not the sense of disaster that befell them, but the success of their artistic efforts. Much of his report was devoted to their pottery and the lively, fanciful, incomprehensible, and mysterious pictographs and petroglyphs with which they had embellished the many different types of rock features of the San Juan area. The rock art and pottery of the Anasazi revealed that whatever may have ultimately happened to these people, they once possessed a vibrant cultural life. More than that, Holmes found in these forms of expression examples of "primitive" art, which were, he signified, "valuable to the historian as records of the grade of civilization reached by the tribes who executed them."[44] According to this view, art, like rock strata, could be given meaning by applying, in effect, the geological principle of superposition, which holds that older rock strata lie beneath younger strata.

Holmes began what would be a long career in American antiquities by studying rock inscriptions in the San Juan Valley. Without a Rosetta stone, he saw that the attempt to decipher the rock art, as written language, was pointless and passed over the hieroglyphical problem to address the questions of attribution and relative dating, where he succeeded in making a

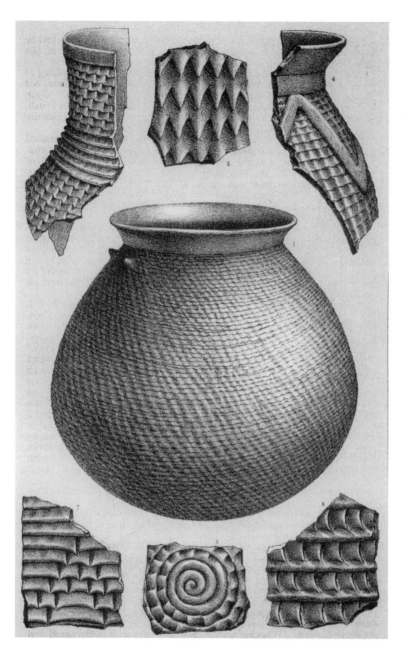

Ancient Pottery. (Plate XLIV from Holmes, "Report on the Ancient Ruins of Southwestern Colorado, Examined During the Summers of 1875 and 1876," Hayden, *Tenth Annual*, opposite p. 404.)

real contribution.[45] Holmes thought it was fairly evident that the cliff builders were the ones who produced much of the region's rock art. He cited the obvious close approximation of the inscriptions to the cliff dwellings and along what would have been routes and places the cliff builders frequented. Holmes made his case stronger by the observations that the pictographs he found in close proximity with a group of ruins in Mancos Canyon were painted with the same clay that the cliff builders used as building material. His best evidence, however, was that some of the rock figures closely resembled designs found on Anasazi pottery.[46]

Turning to the problem of dating, Holmes was able to establish by two means that the Anasazi rock art was inscribed prior to the coming of the Spanish. The first indication of pre-Columbian age was the condition of the figures. New figures could be distinguished by the "freshness of the chipped surfaces," whereas older figures were marked by the dark stains or patina, which gives the appearance of great antiquity. The second means involved looking for signs of the Columbian exchange, notably the horse. Holmes observed:

> It will readily be seen that among all the figures given of the ancient work there is no animal that resembles a horse, and we can hardly suppose that artists who could so cleverly delineate birds and deer and men, would fail in an attempt to represent an animal of so marked a character.

Significantly, on a relatively modern inscription, "done in the manner of the Navajoes [*sic*]," Holmes did find a representation of a horse, which he used as a dividing point between two eras.[47]

Of all the artifacts that Holmes found in the Mesa Verde area—arrowheads, skin-scrapers, rush matting, bundles of sticks, metates, stone axes, ear ornaments, pierced marine shells—the potsherds, besides the pictographs and petroglyphs, proved the most useful in piecing together, as it were, the history of art among the ancient Puebloans. In the first place, potsherds were far more numerous than any other kind of artifact, which allowed the kind of sample base necessary to form meaningful generalizations. Holmes was amazed that near the foot of Mancos Canyon he could collect in an area "10 feet square . . . fragments of fifty-five vessels." Moreover, Holmes was so impressed by the ornamental designs on the pottery that he briefly succumbed to a bout of ethnocentrism and wondered if these people had not somehow come "in contact with Europeans," or were somehow "influenced" by them. After studying the evidence, however, he was forced to conclude that they had developed quite independently their own "art-ideas."[48]

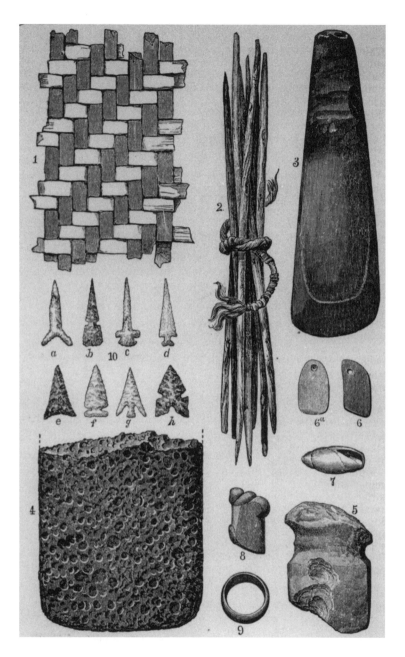

Southwestern Artifacts. (Plate XLVI from Holmes, "Report on the Ancient
Ruins of Southwestern Colorado, Examined During the Summers of 1875
and 1876," Hayden, *Tenth Annual Report*, opposite p. 407.)

The question of outside influences aside, Holmes went on to compare Anasazi pottery with that of the modern Puebloans, thereby showing the influences of the former on the latter and making a strong case for the existence of continuity between the two peoples. Unfortunately, he offered no more support for this comparison than he did for the above-mentioned comparison of architecture. The detailed illustrations that he made and the long descriptions accompanying them were only of Anasazi pottery and not of the modern counterparts. But Holmes's report on the cliff dwellings indicated that he had spent time, whether in the field or in Washington, carefully comparing the pottery of the Anasazi's descendants with that of the Anasazi themselves. Based on this work, he opined:

> The pottery of the ancient tribes of the San Juan Valley is undoubtedly superior in many respects to that of the town-building tribes of to-day. It is especially superior in composition and surface-finish. In form and ornamentation it does not compare well with the highly artistic wares of the Moquois [*sic*] and Zunis. There is great similarity, however, in every respect, and the differences do not seem greater than could be expected in the manufactures of the same people at periods separated by a few generations, or even of related tribes of the same time surrounded by different physical features or by different neighbors.[49]

Implicit in this passage was Holmes's view that the ancient Puebloans had left their homes comparatively recently. The more romantically inclined Jackson, on the other hand, liked to talk about "lost cities," conjecturing that the ruins in the Mesa Verde area were "remnants of a civilization that had died long before the first Spaniards arrived."[50] On one occasion in his report on the cliff builders, Holmes used such evocative language, but only as a means of deflating the romantic aura that some imagined the ruins to possess. While working his way up Mancos Canyon, Holmes discovered:

> In one place in particular . . . as one from below views the ragged, window-pierced crags . . . he is unconsciously led to wonder if they are not the ruins of some ancient castle, behind whose moldering walls are hidden the dread secrets of a long-forgotten people; but a nearer approach quickly dispels such fancies, for the windows prove to be only the door ways to shallow and irregular apartments, hardly sufficiently commodious for a race of pigmies.[51]

Continuing in the spirit of "science" rather than in that of "romance," Holmes concluded—wrongly as further research would indicate—that the "final abandonment of the cliff and cave dwellings has occurred at a comparatively recent date, certainly subsequent to the Spanish conquest," rather than "long before" the first Spanish *entradas* to the Southwest.[52] And Holmes's view that "the differences," as quoted above, between Anasazi and Pueblo pottery "do not seem greater than could be expected in the manufactures of the same people at periods separated by a few generations" perfectly fit an interpretation of a recent abandonment.

Holmes's sketches of rock art and pottery marked a departure from the previous illustration that he produced for Hayden, which had been exclusively on geological subjects.[53] Now he turned his artistic talents in the new directions of archaeology and ethnography, with equal facility and success. This shift was more than a mechanical change in subject matter; it reflected the deeper changes that the West was producing in Holmes as an artist-scientist. Holmes had previously endeavored to capture the West's two sides: its geological complexity and scenic splendor. The ease, in fact, with which Holmes could switch his attention from geological problems to aesthetic concerns was remarkable. This capacity was clearly brought out in the following passage from his 1876 field journal:

> In looking back up . . . [San Miguel] Canon [*sic*] I noticed that the upper 500 or 600 feet of strata were light colored and that the remainder were dull red with a somewhat brighter band, yellow and red at the junction—a contact . . . The great range of the San Miguel as well as the Sneffles group is trachytic with a base of cret[aceous] shales.

And then in the next sentence he abruptly switches from geology to aesthetics with the following observation:

> From the east side of San Miguel Canon [*sic*] I had one of the grandest and most enchanting landscapes possible. The subject is worthy of the brush of Church or Moran.[54]

From either the scientific or artistic perspective, portraying the real West in both word and image remained Holmes's single-minded ambition. But Holmes discovered that the West provided more than unparalleled opportunities to geologize and paint landscape art. As he ran his hands over the chipped and painted surfaces of ancient panels of rock art and picked up half-buried potsherds, he saw that America's newest region also contained the answers to some of the oldest philosophical questions, such as how did art, in the broadest sense of the term, originate and develop. This line of inquiry would eventually take Holmes in entirely new intellectual directions.

6

Laccoliths and Lithographs

Intrusions of Trachyte

LATE IN THE EVENING OF SEPTEMBER 18, 1876, a storm broke that had kept Holmes and Allen D. Wilson cold and confined for nearly two days at the eastern foot of the Sierra Abajo or Blue Mountains in Utah, situated between the Colorado and San Juan rivers. The delay had been costly. Knowing that the season was nearly over and that the time left to conduct fieldwork for the Colorado Survey was drawing to a close, the two men awoke with the sun and rode up to the snow-covered summit of Abajo Peak. Wilson established a topographical station and spent the morning measuring angles and taking barometric readings, while Holmes assisted him in making profile sketches and outlining the drainage. Wilson had taken over the primary triangulation from Gardner and could actually see from the vantage point of Abajo Peak the area where the Indians had attacked and demoralized his predecessor the year before.[1]

With the aid of a pair of field glasses, Holmes surveyed the dazzling country that stretched out below in all directions. To the north, he could see clearly the shining La Sal Mountains; turning eastward, he studied the familiar San Juan Mountains in Colorado; sweeping slowly another ninety degrees to the right, he viewed the country south toward the Sierra Carrizo of Arizona, which lay just to the northwest of Shiprock, New Mexico; and then passing over "the mirage[-]like Monumental [*sic*] Valley,"[2] he looked due west across the canyon country and brought into sharp focus the Henry Mountains, an incredibly remote and rugged range that the indefatigable topographer Almon Harris Thompson (John Wesley Powell's brother-in-law) had first explored and mapped only four years earlier.[3] The "outlines, as well as the detail of form" of the Henry Mountains, led Holmes to suppose that they were akin to the five volcanic mountain groups of the San Juan

The Southwestern Border of Mesa Verde and the Sierra el Late. Plate XLI from
Holmes, "Geological Report on the San Juan District," Hayden, *Ninth Annual
Report*, opposite p. 256.

district—the San Miguel, La Plata, El Late (Sleeping Ute Mountain), the
Carrizo, and Abajo.[4]

Holmes had discovered the previous summer that these igneous mountains
were the result of a new type of mountain-building process, but between wor-
rying about Indians and surveying cliff and other dwellings he had only time
to analyze the Sierra El Late, La Plata Mountains, and the Sierra Carrizo for
his "Geological Report on the San Juan District" for 1875. This summer he
planned to finish his study by examining the two remaining mountain
groups—the Sierra Abajo and the San Miguel Mountains. In addition, he intended to make a broad geological comparison of Colorado's eastern plains
with the Western Slope. As if all that were not enough, he also collected data
for use in preparing Hayden's *Atlas of Colorado*, with special attention given to
the colored maps and sections.

Although the Henry Mountains appeared to have strata with the same
domal dip as that found in the strata of the other five trachytic mountain
groups to the east, which suggested a similar structure, Holmes nevertheless
kept a prudent distance. The Henrys, after all, were in Powell's jurisdiction.
What was more, they were already being investigated by one of his men, the
brilliant Grove Karl Gilbert. After the bitter turf wars had erupted between
the heads of the Great Surveys in 1873, when a Wheeler party camped too
close to one of Hayden's in the upper Arkansas Valley (near Twin Lakes), exposing early on the need for a combined national survey, Holmes and the
other members of the surveys tried to observe the limits of their assigned
areas.

Gilbert had visited the Henrys for a week in 1875 and spent two months there the following year. Familiar with Holmes's work, Gilbert concurred with his friend and colleague that the mountain group was indeed the same type as the mountain groups to the east. In fact, in the appendix that Gilbert added to the second edition of his geological classic, *Report on the Geology of the Henry Mountains*, he quoted at length from Holmes's report for 1875, adding, "All of [his] description [of the Carrizos] could be transferred, with unimportant changes, to the Henry Mountains."[5] Gilbert called this new mountain type a "laccolite" (the modern spelling is *laccolith*) and in recognition of Holmes's prior work, paid tribute to his friend "by naming two of the Henrys after him—the Greater and the Lesser Mount Holmes.[6] Holmes learned about the naming directly from Gilbert. In 1916, Holmes recalled:

> On [Gilbert's] return from the Grand Canyon region away back in the Seventies, he announced with a twinkle in his eye that he had named two mountains after me; one an actual, visible mountain, and the other a mountain as yet unborn. The actual mountain he said was due to the upthrust of a laccolite—a great body of lava which did not reach the surface but lifted the sedimentary strata over it in a great arch or dome, now partly removed by erosion exposing at the summit the conical lava core. It happened that I had been the first to describe this particular form of mountain building, hence this generous recognition on Gilbert's part. The unborn Mt. Holmes was represented, he explained, by a great circle of upturned strata which had been cut down by erosion to the general level of the country making clear, however, the fact that beneath the surface there rests a body of lava which some day, due to its great hardness, will be exposed by erosion, developing in the course of years an actual mountain, the date of whose birth, however, cannot now be determined.[7]

Holmes evidently first grasped the basic structural nature of these eruptive groups in 1875, while studying the northwest side of the Carrizo Mountains. His earlier work in the Elk Mountains, however, had certainly prepared him for the mountain groups on the Colorado Plateau that lay to the west. Holmes had observed in the Elk Mountains, which he had shown to be eruptive in origin as opposed to the ranges to the east, examples of strata arched upward against intrusive igneous masses. Figure 5 in his "Report on the Geology of the Northwestern Portion of the Elk Range," for instance, clearly anticipated the laccolithic idea. Holmes sketched a mountain (known simply as Station 23) in which the Cretaceous strata were shown wedged open by a large

Station 23, Unnamed Mountain in the Elk Range. (Fig. 5 from Holmes, "Report on the Geology of the Northwestern Portion of the Elk Range," in Hayden, *[Eighth] Annual Report*, opposite p. 64.

mass of rhyolite. And in another illustration, entitled "Treasury Mountain" (Figure 7), Holmes sketched the distinguishing features of the laccoliths to the west—a domelike wedge of igneous material, atop a horizontal base of strata, and beneath upturned surrounding sedimentary beds.

But it was not until August 13, 1875, among the Sierra Carrizo, in Navajo country, that Holmes put all of the geological pieces together and, in a moment of inspiration under the hot Arizona sun, realized that the trachytes were intrusive, not extrusive, and thus younger than the country or valley rock. He wrote:

> If a theory were called for to account for the conditions of things in these Mts.; I should say that in the first place the[r]e had been a flow of volcanic matter over a large area of country, resting upon lower cretaceous rocks and forming a table land. That subsequently a large mass of less fluid matter had been forced up from beneath this, ra[is]ing much of the sedimentary strata between it and the lava of the table and arching, both the sediment and the thin (comparatively) bed of trachyte.[8]

In searching for an analogy to describe the mountain's peculiar shape, Holmes turned to the familiar world of art. He likened the arched strata, which consisted primarily of the Middle Cretaceous, to a "mould" that had eroded away, revealing the formerly concealed trachytic "cast."[9] Thus, the geomorphology of the San Juan region was the result, quite literally, of a large-scale sculpturing process.

These insights into the structure of the Carrizos and the relative age of the rock formations came only days before Gilbert arrived at similar conclusions in the Henrys. On August 18, from a distance of twenty miles, Gilbert noticed the unusual shape of Mount Ellsworth. He wrote, "Ellsworth shows no volcanic colors but looks as though built of the valley rocks." On closer examination of Ellsworth and the other mountains of the Henry group, he became impressed by the upturned strata and the underlying igneous material. And like Holmes, it was not long before Gilbert started using descriptive terms, such as "tumor" and "bubble form," to bring meaning to this strange new phenomenon.[10]

To introduce visually to the geological world the structure of a hitherto unknown species of intrusive phenomena, Holmes produced for his report for 1875 a total of three sets of illustrations—plates XXXVI, XLV, and XLVI. "The point of view assumed" in plate XXXVI, Holmes wrote, was "in New Mexico, south of the most southerly bend of the Rio San Juan, and at an elevation of a few thousand feet above the plain."[11] From this Olympian perspective, he could portray all five trachytic mountain groups in his district (including the Henrys to the west) as well as a large portion of the northern drainage system of the San Juan Valley. And the southern border of the view doubled as a section, revealing sedimentary formations and the trachytic structure of the Carrizo Mountains.

The second set of illustrations on plate XLV contained two figures of the La Plata Mountains. The first of these figures was a sketch of the south face of Hesperus Mountain taken from Sentinel Rock, which was a close-up of another sketch from plate XLIV, entitled "Hesperus or Banded Mountain from the West." This close-up allowed Holmes to show in dramatic fashion the succession of trachyte sheets and shales of Hesperus Mountain that alternated like the red and white bands on a barber's pole. No illustration made a stronger case for Holmes's mould-and-cast theory than did this one.

Figure 2 of plate XLV, like the above-mentioned sections, was a rendering of "the supposed method of intrusion of trachyte." As in the other sections, Holmes made the invisible strata appear as if they had been arched, broken, and wedged apart by magma pouring in between the beds. But in addition to this vision of a violently shaped subterranean landscape, Holmes went on to reconstruct the maximum profile of La Plata Mountains and portrayed the repeated wedging of trachyte between layers of Cretaceous shale by the use of imaginary lines—dotted and continuous. This simple but effective artistic device showed how the long since vanished superincumbent strata may have originally appeared.

The final set of illustrations in the 1875 report that Holmes produced were those of Sierra El Late or Sleeping Ute Mountain (plate XLVI), and these were perhaps the most didactically powerful and insightful, especially the diagrammatic section in figure 2. Here, Holmes drew for the purposes of contrast a perfect laccolith, as "if the entire mass [of molten matter] had at once been intruded between the strata at a given horizon arching those above."[12] The result of such a uniform intrusion on top of a level base, Holmes postulated, would be an igneous mass in the form of a dome, with a vent or stock joining it to some deeper pool of magma. (Gilbert used the same ideal form to illustrate the laccoliths of the Henrys.)

In the remaining two sections of Sleeping Ute Mountain, however, Holmes tried in characteristic fashion to show nature's true face. In one, he imagined the "Degree of arching really produced by the irregular intrusions" (figure 3). In the section portraying the "probable method of intrusion of masses of trachyte" (figure 1), Holmes envisioned, correctly as it turned out, not one but a series of asymmetrical intrusions of trachyte stemming from several closely associated stocks. In 1953, Charles B. Hunt examined the Henry Mountains using modern techniques such as aeromagnetic surveys. He found that several adjustments had to be made to bring Gilbert's work up to date. One of those adjustments was based on the discovery "that the laccoliths were satellites injected laterally from the stocks." These "determinations," Hunt remarked with surprise, "accord very well with Holmes's (1877) interpretation of the structure at Ute Mountain in southwest Colorado."[13]

Holmes's follow-up report for 1876, entitled "Report on the Geology of the Sierra Abajo and West San Miguel Mountains," confirmed that these two mountain groups were formed by intrusions of trachyte and contained several panoramas and glimpses that conformed with his high standards of draftsmanship, but otherwise did little to expand on the laccolithic idea. Gilbert put his finger on the report's shortcomings in complaining that Holmes's visit to the Sierra Abajo had been "brief and unsatisfactory" and that his description of it "reports little more than his general impression."[14]

And indeed, Holmes and Wilson had stayed on Abajo Peak that cold September day only until noon before they were "homeward bound," which was hardly enough time to conduct anything close to a detailed investigation. Holmes did not even dismount his mule and "made most of [his] sketches while in the saddle."[15] By keeping up this driving pace, Holmes was able to enjoy the exhilaration and recognition of being involved in a host of projects: mapping, illustration (including modeling), writing scientific reports, preparing for the Centennial, and much else. His life seemed to reflect the terrific

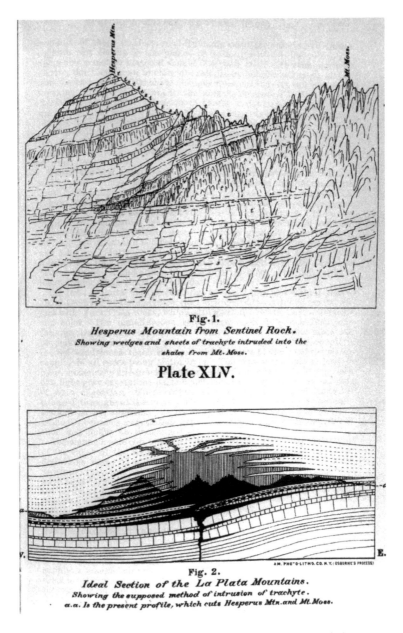

Fig. 1.
Hesperus Mountain from Sentinel Rock.
Showing wedges and sheets of trachyte intruded into the
shales from Mt. Moss.

Plate XLV.

Fig. 2.
Ideal Section of the La Plata Mountains.
Showing the supposed method of intrusion of trachyte.
a.a. Is the present profile, which cuts Hesperus Mtn. and Mt. Moss.

Top, Hesperus Mountain from Sentinel Rock, Showing Wedges and Sheets
of Trachyte Intruded into Shales from M[oun]t Moss"; *bottom*, Ideal Section
of the La Plata Mountains, Showing the Supposed Method of Intrusion of
Trachyte. (Plate XLV from Holmes, "Geological Report on the San Juan
District," Hayden, *Ninth Annual Report*, following p. 270.

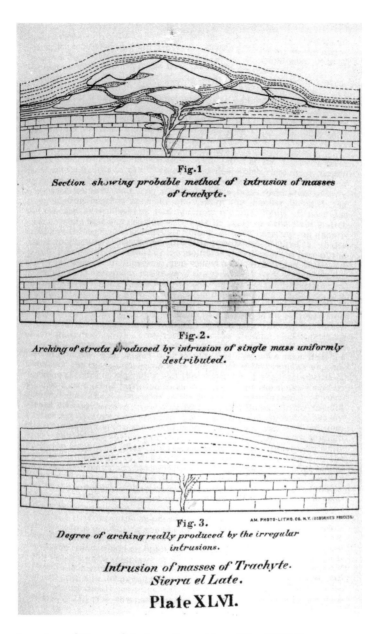

Fig. 1

Section showing probable method of intrusion of masses of trachyte.

Fig. 2.

Arching of strata produced by intrusion of single mass uniformly distributed.

Fig. 3.

AM. PHOTO-LITHO. CO. N.Y. (OSBORNE'S PROCESS)

Degree of arching really produced by the irregular intrusions.

Intrusion of masses of Trachyte.
Sierra el Late.

Plate XLVI.

Intrusions of Masses of Trachyte, Sierra el Late. (Plate XLVI from Holmes, "Geological Report on the San Juan District," Hayden, *Ninth Annual Report*, opposite p. 272.)

energies and excitement of the United States as the relatively young nation in the last part of the nineteenth century frenetically modernized and rushed into world leadership. But there was a cost. To Holmes, scientific discovery was much like mountain climbing—the main thing was being the first to reach the summit. Thus, describing and analyzing the Sierra Abajo and the San Miguels before anyone else could was what really mattered, and never mind how cursory the examination so long as the facts are right and the interpretations sound. The result was that his work, although always filled with keen observations, soon lost its scientific utility. As Charles Hunt politely put it: "Holmes did not provide such complete description of the evidence," as did his contemporary, Gilbert.[16]

The chief reason for this difference was that Gilbert took a more modern, case-study approach. He did not try to perform the equivalent of discussing five structurally related mountain groups and everything in between in just two seasons, along with a dozen other projects and a full workload besides. Instead, he focused on the Henrys and gave this novel mountain type the full attention it deserved, even as he acknowledged the claims of Holmes, Albert C. Peale (who studied the La Sals), and a number of others.[17] Furthermore, Gilbert had his own ideas about laccolithic formation. According to Gilbert's biographer, Stephen J. Pyne, Holmes's vision of the laccolith differed fundamentally from Gilbert's. This was a case, incidentally, containing all of the classic markings of one of Thomas S. Kuhn's paradigm shifts.[18] In Pyne's words:

> The Hayden geologists thought the intrusion was primarily thermal, melting its way up through the rocks and incidentally bulging them, while Gilbert thought the process was determined primarily by pressure, pushing up with little thermal exchange.[19]

But whether laccoliths were primarily formed by heat or pressure was an issue of secondary importance to the far more basic question, as far as Holmes was concerned, of just what this igneous feature looked like. Geologists were quick to accept the laccolithic ideas as advanced by Holmes and Gilbert, but perhaps uncritically. William Morris Davis, one of America's renowned physiographers and topographical artists, stated: "There can be no question that Gilbert determined the general facts of laccolithic structure correctly." But Davis went on to say in the next sentence:

> There may, however, be [*sic*] question whether certain igneous masses which have been in later years explained as laccoliths, after the laccolith idea had been generally accepted, are truly of that nature. For example, Hauthal describes two bold mountains, Payne and Fitzroy, in the southern Andes as lac-

coliths, and explicitly states that they have a partly eroded cover of Cretaceous strata; but he does not give explicit account of any underlying undisturbed strata . . . It is quite possible that the conception of laccoliths has become so popular that masses of other nature have been called laccoliths without sufficient assurance that they have a level base as well as a domed top.[20]

Based on this simple structural criteria, little appreciable difference existed between the descriptions that Holmes and Gilbert offered the scientific world of their respective discoveries.

Holmes's *Atlas of Colorado*

As Holmes crossed the Old Spanish Trail and rode toward the Uncompahgre agency and home in late September 1876, he left southwest Colorado, and it was, he declared, "with considerable confidence that I lay my work . . . before the geologic world."[21] Unlike Hayden, who strove mightily to be everyman's geologist and who expected errors due to haste to be outweighed by the benefits of speedy delivery of new knowledge, Holmes hoped that his writings and art, however rooted in the older, sweeping reconnaissance style and methods, would make a more lasting impression on the American scientific community. In 1876, this body of men was small, elite, yet growing in influence. He intended that his cartographical work, in contrast, be received by the widest possible audience, but without compromising on accuracy or aesthetic appeal. With these twin objectives in mind, Holmes supervised the publication of the folio-sized *Geological and Geographical Atlas of Colorado and Portions of Adjacent Territory*, which appeared in 1877 and was updated in 1881.[22]

Holmes's personal contributions to the *Atlas* consisted of preparing the colored sheets and, in addition, drawing seven panoramic views of the Colorado Rockies. To work on the *Atlas*, Holmes remained in Washington during the summer of 1877, while the rest of Hayden's men began to survey the territories of Idaho and Wyoming now that Colorado was finished (and no longer a territory), although the tragic flight of Chief Joseph and his band of Nez Percé Indians from General Oliver O. Howard interrupted some of that year's operations. By mid-July, a considerable portion of the Colorado mapwork had been completed, and Holmes spent a week in New York City at the famed chromolithographic firm of Julius Bien, who, like Holmes's Washington art teacher, Theodore Kaufmann, had fled to New York after the German revolution of 1848. In the following years, Bien had become a highly skilled lithographer, producing numerous maps of the West, including Lieutenant Gouverneur K. Warren's celebrated map of 1857.[23]

Despite Bien's reputation, or perhaps because of it, the two men's working relationship was far from harmonious. No doubt Holmes's insistence on perfection added to the tensions. Nevertheless, the two men did eventually reach an agreement. In a letter to Hayden, who was out west at the time, Holmes made clear that he had taken care of the situation. In a tone that was markedly condescending toward Bien, he reported: "Mr. Bien is doing his best, and by our somewhat lengthy consultations we have come to such a mutual understanding of *our* (the Survey's) wants and *his* capacity to fill them that there will, hereafter, be no trouble." In fact, Holmes left New York confident that his "colored maps [and panoramas would] be inferior to none."[24]

The colored maps that Holmes constructed fell into two categories: land-use maps and geological maps, with accompanying sections. The chromatic schemes that Holmes employed, which reflected the growing trend toward a common usage, were based on the colors either found in or suggested by nature—when possible. Hence, pine forests were expressed in green, whereas placer deposits were depicted as yellow, and eruptive formations were shown in red. (In a happy coincidence, the color that Holmes used to represent the rocks formed during the Cretaceous age was green. Since Mesa Verde—Spanish for "Green Table"—was largely composed of Cretaceous formations, especially the Foxhills sedimentary formation, this famous archaeological site was colored appropriately.) Holmes's fidelity to nature and his ability to present an enormous quantity of information with economy, taste, and elegance help account for why the *Atlas* has long been regarded as a masterpiece of cartographic art.[25]

It is tempting to see the panoramic views that Holmes produced as harkening back to the mapmaker's ancient practice of adorning maps with figures of diving porpoises, sea monsters, exotic beasts, minarets half-buried in drifts of sand, and ships in full sail or turbaned men seated in a brilliantly colored howdah on top of an elephant. In the same spirit of adornment, the mapmaker embellished the cartouches with fruits and flowers, goddesses, escutcheons, or instruments such as the sextant or a pair of opened calipers. Perhaps the number of these fanciful or real figures, idyllic or local-color scenes, and the size of the cartouche was in direct proportion to the mapmaker's geographical ignorance. In which case, the less that was known, the more that was adorned. Since the Hayden Survey had explored practically every foot of Colorado's high country, the only room to spare on the *Atlas* maps themselves was for the legend, with which Holmes covered a culturally empty portion of the eastern plains. Thus, he would have to find another

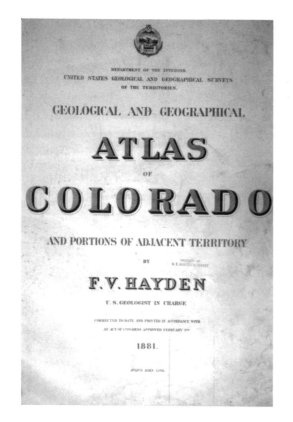

DEPARTMENT OF THE INTERIOR.
UNITED STATES GEOLOGICAL AND GEOGRAPHICAL SURVEYS
OF THE TERRITORIES.

GEOLOGICAL AND GEOGRAPHICAL

ATLAS
OF
COLORADO

AND PORTIONS OF ADJACENT TERRITORY

BY

F. V. HAYDEN

U. S. GEOLOGIST IN CHARGE

CORRECTED TO DATE AND PRINTED IN ACCORDANCE WITH
AN ACT OF CONGRESS APPROVED FEBRUARY 9th

1881.

Title Page of the *Atlas of Colorado*. (Hayden, *Geological and Geographical Atlas of Colorado and Portions of Adjacent Territory*.)

place off the map for his illustrations. Accordingly, Holmes presented them on separate sheets at the end of the *Atlas* and in so doing elevated their importance and at the same time enjoyed having the final "word."

But beyond this seeming bow to tradition, the panoramic views that Holmes chose to present were carefully selected to supplement the maps and bring attention to his accomplishments as a field artist. He also used them to highlight his major scientific contributions. Holmes based this artwork on his topographical sketches and in one instance on a Jackson photograph. And because most of the views were of Colorado's high country, they provided familiar representational images to balance the abstraction of contour lines of the six black-and-white maps contained in the *Atlas*. As government mapmakers made the transition from hachures to contours during the 1870s, Holmes's panoramic views served to help preserve in maps a sense of three-dimensional reality that might otherwise have been lost.[26] King's geologic mappers (Samuel F. Emmons and Arnold Hague), on the other hand, found that the new technique of plastic shading could also effectively retain the illusion of relief.[27]

The use of the views as map aids aside, Holmes intended that his panoramic views portray an untamed land, celebrate the scientific exploration of the American West, and above all increase the body of pure knowledge. This latter aim certainly exceeded the more practical instructions of the secretary of the interior (probably Zachariah Chandler), who informed Hayden

> that the ultimate design to be accomplished by these surveys is the preparation of suitable maps of the country surveyed for the use of the government and nation, which will afford information concerning the agricultural and mineral resources, and other important characteristics of the unexplored regions of our Territorial domain.[28]

Holmes's views, however, portrayed a Colorado that consisted almost entirely of endless ranges of mountains and waterless mesas—hardly a usable land. Outside of tourist retreats and health resorts, here was a country that seemed to invite little of the economic activity, except maybe for high-altitude mining, that the secretary had in mind. The maps, of course, corrected this impression and precisely because of that fact they freed Holmes to express his own vision of the West. For the first time, he enjoyed the same license and the forum in which to show his work that previously had only been the due of Hayden's other two artists—Jackson and Moran. Holmes had come a long way since drawing fossil shells at the Smithsonian for Meek and Dall.

Of the seven panoramas that Holmes exhibited in the *Atlas* on two sets of facing sheets, five were of mountain ranges: *The Pike's Pike Group: from Bluff east of Monument Creek* (1874), *View of Sawatch Range, from Buffalo Peak* (1873), *Central Portion of the Elk Mountains, Looking West* (1874), *The Quartzite Group—San Juan Mountains, Looking South West from the Rio Grande Pyramid* (1876), and finally *The La Plata Mountains, View Looking East from Mt. Hesperus, Showing the Trachyte Mass and Its Relations to the Surrounding Sedimentary Formations* (1876). The two other panoramas, which in size were only half the length of the mountain panoramas, were of the *South-western Border of the Mesa Verde, Showing the Sierra El Late in the Distance Looking West Across the cañon of the Rio Mancos* (1875) and *The Twin Lakes-Lake Fork of the Arkansas, Showing the Great Moraines* (1874).[29] The latter view was a more subtle and picturesque rendering of the same moraines that Holmes had illustrated with exacting detail in Hayden's geological report for 1874.[30]

Like a good musician, Holmes began his repertoire of panoramas with something familiar to the audience. In this case, there was probably no other mountain west of the Mississippi better known to Americans than Pike's Peak—a Januslike symbol that represented hope, on the one hand, and failure or "bust," on the other. The other views introduced largely new material, however. The two that appeared on the same sheet below *The Pike's Peak Group* showcased the Sawatch and Elk Mountains, respectively. For those familiar with Holmes's scientific work, these drawings reinforced in a grand manner his contention that these ranges were the products of different mountain-building processes. Likewise, in *The La Plata Mountains*, Holmes showed with great effect the intrusions of trachyte, thus adding in his inimitable way the artist's touch to scientific insight.

Included in the foreground of *The La Plata Mountains* view were two figures based on Jackson's tightly composed photograph of Allen Wilson and Franklin Rhoda atop of Sultan Mountain in which the forms of the two surveyors harmoniously paralleled the distant mountain range behind them.[31] Holmes moved the two men to the top of Mount Hesperus, but he retained their action poses: Wilson measuring angles with a theodolite and Rhoda sitting on the ground in front of him sketching. From Humboldt and Bonpland's exploration of the Andes at the turn of the nineteenth century to Hayden's survey of the southern Rockies, the image of scientists at work in the rarefied air of mountain summits had a strong appeal to the romantic imagination. Holmes understood that appeal, and his art clearly alluded to it.

The romantic spirit was even more forcefully, although just as selectively, evoked in the view entitled *South Western Border of the Mesa Verde*. The elements of tragedy and mystery were present in the depiction of a ruined Anasazi tower situated in the right foreground, conjuring up the classic romantic image of a vanished race. And in the far left foreground, Holmes placed a man, tiny and insignificant in relation to the rest of the picture, but nevertheless contemplative, maybe even in awe of the landscape spread wide before him. The focus of this view, however, was not the tower nor the man but the timeless geological struggle between the contending forces of upheaval and erosion. In the top half of the picture was the distant Sleeping Ute Mountain, the result of nature's creative forces of uplift. Mesa Verde, on the other hand, which occupied the view's bottom half, was a portrait, complete unto itself, of the destructive forces wearing down the land.

In view of the art of his day, Holmes's panoramas stood alone. Despite his intense admiration for America's landscapists—Thomas Moran, Frederic E. Church, and his favorite, Sanford Robinson Gifford—the only thing that he shared in common with these men was a love of the nation's open spaces.[32] Holmes's work neither expressed the fashionable themes of progress nor the romantic emphasis on the observer—his inner emotions, intuition, individuality—that occur throughout the writings of New England Transcendentalists, the reports and artwork of the Topographical Engineers, and the paintings of the Hudson River as well as Rocky Mountain schools of art. Instead, Holmes focused on the observed, on nature herself, independent of the interior needs and desires of the individual. Holmes's landscapes reveal, in short, an artist possessed by the confidence that his work, informed by science, could achieve nothing less than an exact picture of the physical world. Perhaps the work of no other artist exists that better illustrates the famous unbridled optimism of the American West.

Holmes' Panoramic Views of Colorado. (Sheet XX from Hayden, *Geological and Geographical Atlas of Colorado and Portions of Adjacent Territory*.)

7

New Wests

The Eclipse

THE TEMPERATURES IN WASHINGTON throughout February 1878 were warm, leading Holmes and the men of the other surveys to turn their thoughts westward earlier than usual. The good weather, however, was only one of the reasons why Holmes looked forward to another season outdoors. At the urging of the administration of Rutherford B. Hayes, Congress was once again considering the question of reforming the western surveys and had not appropriated any funds for Hayden's survey—and would not until July of that year.[1] Consequently, Holmes was becoming increasingly anxious about meeting his personal expenses. He enjoyed a decent return on his investments ("D.C. 3-6s Bonds") and had the benefit of good credit, but the last time Holmes had received any payment for services rendered at the Washington office was in mid-November.[2]

Although Holmes continued to conduct faithfully the general business of the survey, he nevertheless began to complain that his office was "getting very 'hard up' for money." In January, to pay for his board he apparently had to collect old debts from his friends, including five dollars from the young, lanky ethnologist Frank Hamilton Cushing. (Cushing, whose name is now strongly associated with the Zuñi Indians, with whom he later lived and studied, was another one of Spencer F. Baird's many protégés.) Holmes would hardly starve that winter, but he found himself obliged to borrow "small sums" from William H. Jackson, who roomed with him at the Waverly House.

Holmes's straitened circumstances did not stop him from living fully. He continued to pursue his art studies, which included taking classes three times a week; to work in the studio; to show his work at the Art Club; to socialize with his friends; to entertain "handsome young ladies" who came by to see his sketches and watercolors of the West, some of which were of ethnological subjects; and to attend Washington parties and receptions. On one such occasion, Holmes was invited to the office of John Wesley Powell for a private exhibition of one of Thomas Moran's oils. Later, Moran called while Holmes was at work on a panorama of the Elk Mountains and showed him a few "tricks" on finishing and scumbling.

On another occasion, fellow Ohioan President Hayes, in the company of Albert Bierstadt (presumably the great western landscape artist), paid a visit and spent over an hour inspecting the survey's collections and works. Holmes also found time to take up the genteel sport of boating, and he even acquired a taste for opera. He set two weeks aside for a vacation to Avoca, North Carolina, where he availed himself of the hospitality of his friend, James W. Milner of the U.S. Fish Commission. So that no one could accuse him of wasting time—the great bourgeois sin of the age—Holmes arranged through Baird to have photographic equipment sent ahead so that he could make an archaeological study of local Indian ruins.

William Henry Holmes, Thirty-two years old, Self-Confident, and Brilliant. (Photograph courtesy Smithsonian Institution Archives, George P. Merrill Collection, Record Unit 7177.)

But above all Holmes relished his social standing as one of the leading members of the Hayden Survey, which in the 1870s was *the* western survey. What was more, he had distinguished himself in the worlds of art and science and had proved over the past year to be an able administrator. His accomplishments were underscored when issues of the *Atlas of Colorado* were distributed around the country. It may be true that one cannot go home again, but Holmes made sure that copies of the *Atlas* were sent to schools in Harrison County. He noted in his diary that "many people say it is the finest atlas ever published in this country," and he added, in a colloquialism of the day, "It does me proud."

By any standard, Holmes had, at the age of thirty-one, achieved the Victorian ideal of "respectability," which he perfectly reflected in his faultless personal appearance, in speech that was as correct and clear as one of his drawings, and in the increasingly firm, maybe even stiff manner in which he held himself. In later years, the gravitas in his deportment, which he had long and carefully cultivated, was forcefully expressed in a sharply pointed beard. And Holmes's enormous energy, drive, and devotion to science, which the intensity of his eyes revealed, made this otherwise stainless steel bearing of self-control seem, to those who were not familiar or close to him, even more austere and formidable.[3]

Here was a man who had become confident of his prospects, although clear signs existed that a major political struggle was in the making over the mission and leadership of government exploration that would have no small effect on him. For months, senators, congressmen, and scientists filed through the survey office "by the score" to gather facts in preparation for the debate over reorganization, putting Holmes and the other survey members under intense public scrutiny. Holmes no doubt believed, like most observers at the time, that Hayden, who enjoyed strong support from western politicians and businessmen, would emerge in a strong, if not commanding, position in the new survey. But however things turned, Holmes's reputation as a scientist and his enormous artistic talent would stand him in good stead.

By late May of 1878, however, Holmes confided in his diary with some alarm that the "Survey matters are in a most uncertain state." This was the time of year, after all, when he usually prepared to enter the field, an event beginning to look less and less likely. Delay followed delay, but finally Congress appropriated to Hayden a budget of seventy-five thousand dollars, so that the survey could continue its work for another season. The exploration of the West would not be placed on a permanent basis until March of the following year.

But as Holmes, Jackson, and the other men readied themselves to head west in July, something this time was different. They were not heading into the great unknown as before; Holmes's destination, in fact, was none other than Yellowstone National Park, the point where he had started his adventures in the West six years before. Except that this time around, Holmes would enter the park from the south after stopping to sketch the Wind River and Teton Mountains, side excursions that resulted in some of his finest panoramic views, such as *Glacial Lake and Moraines, on New Fork of Green River, Wind River Mountains; The Teton Range from Upper Grosventre Butte, Looking West with the Valley of Snake River in the Foreground*; and particularly *The Glaciers of Fremont's Peak, Wind River Mountains, Wyoming*.[4] The novelty was thus gone, and the Yellowstone expedition of 1878 had more of the feel of an encore about it than a first act. And as if to dramatize this denouement, Holmes happened to observe on July 29, 1878, from a site northwest of Point of Rocks Station (on the Union Pacific main line in Wyoming), the darkening of the western sky as the moon passed completely before the sun to form a spectacular solar eclipse. Holmes used watercolors to capture this ancient symbol of change, complete with a dazzling corona, in his sketchbook.[5]

This astronomical phenomenon may be seen to have marked two important transitions in the history of the American West: on the one hand, it represented the end of the great surveys; and, on the other, it indicated the change in the exploration of the West from general reconnaissance to special investigation, which was less obvious and had been gradually taking place throughout the 1870s. Grove Karl Gilbert's study of the Henry Mountains, as Stephen Pyne has pointed out, is a good example of this growing intensification of scientific research. But it was not until Hayden's men began preparing their reports for the summer of 1878 that they themselves began to recognize clearly the limitations of the old ways. Henry Gannett expressed this turning point in thinking about scientific exploration perhaps better than anyone by using a metaphor that resonated with the region's colorful mining past:

> The explorations in this region [Wyoming, Montana, and Idaho] by this Survey, in 1871 and 1872, were singularly prolific of facts, geological, physical and geographical, and little that was new was evolved from numerous expeditions that followed. The big nuggets had been taken, and nothing but a careful, scientific, reworking of the tailings would extract from them the wealth of fine gold which they still held.[6]

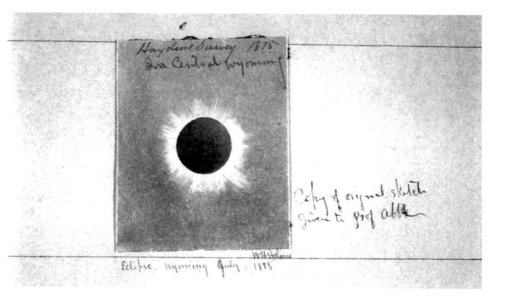

New Alignments. (Illustration, "Eclipse, Wyoming, July 1878," no. 830-E, in Holmes, Sketches Made on a Trip from Point of Rocks to Yellowstone Park, Wyoming, U.S.G.S. Field Records Library, Denver, Colorado.)

Similarly, Holmes found

> that up to this time geologists have but glanced at the surface features of the country, and that the more profound and intricate problems remain almost untouched.[7]

The pursuit of knowledge, like after-the-rush gold mining, had now entered a more intensive phase. The pan and pick days were over.

Several important, even ironic, consequences followed from this new way of looking at science in the West. The most startling result, from the perspective of American exploration, was the fragmentation of the West into smaller and smaller subregions, which were defined by a particular line of inquiry or some order of classification. The West as an identifiable region was becoming more and more of an abstraction. Gone were the older continental visions of Lewis and Clark, Stephen H. Long, John Frémont, or Holmes's contemporaries—Hayden and Powell. To these generalists, the West had encompassed all of the richly varied lands between the Mississippi River and the Pacific

Ocean. Moreover, their missions differed little from the encyclopedic instructions that Thomas Jefferson had issued to Captain Meriwether Lewis in 1803 in which almost everything of scientific interest was to be recorded.[8]

Holmes's "Report on the Geology of the Yellowstone National Park" for 1878, which was not published until 1883, inaugurated this change in American exploration as much as any of the more specialized works beginning to appear. In the introduction, he noted that several other reports had already addressed the geology of the Yellowstone region. Then Holmes pointed out the shortcomings of the old science. The park and its environs, he wrote, "over which the early explorations were carried, comprises an area of not less that 10,000 square miles." For the kind of detailed and exacting work that science now demanded, this area would require lifetimes to study fully, to say nothing of the greater West beyond.

Suddenly, the once endless western horizon of myth and song had been compartmentalized and subdivided into smaller and smaller but more and more manageable units, as scientists traded their field glasses for microscopes, a trend with parallels in the areas of politics, economics, society, and culture. Since then, science has developed a multitude of new ways of seeing the world that includes everything from satellite images to the Richter scale. These relatively new technologies have helped partially to restore the Jeffersonian vision of the West as a global region. What modern scientists are learning, however, is largely at odds with the traditional view that the West is a land of promise and hope; instead, they are finding it beset by a legion of environmental problems.

Thus, by the end of the 1870s, the scope, methods, and purpose of scientific exploration had changed. As long as American explorers of the West of the first three-quarters of the nineteenth century were propelled by the Humboldtian belief that every fact collected, no matter how small or insignificant, would somehow find its way into a master system of knowledge, their exertions had meaning. But by 1878, as a practical matter, the old faith in the unity and hierarchy of knowledge, along with universal laws, was rapidly giving way to the realities and demands of the growing and relentless movement toward specialization that eventually affected all aspects of American life, as the nation modernized and became a world power. The reconnaissance methods and the scientific view that they implied had become, as Holmes admitted, inadequate, if not obsolete. In the same introduction mentioned above, he all but apologized to the reader for once again conducting saddle-side geology: "if I could have consumed years instead of months in the study of the

The Heroic Age of American Geology. (Detail of "The Glaciers of Frémont's Peak, Wind River Mountains, Wyoming," by Holmes, sheet 7, from "Panoramic Views in the Wind River and Teton Mountains," in Hayden, *Twelfth Annual Report.*)

3,400 square miles comprising the Park, I might justify myself in putting my observations on paper."[9]

The park would not receive that kind of commitment in time and resources until 1883, when Arnold Hague of the U.S. Geological Survey visited the park and initiated twenty years of surveys that produced scores of publications, including the mammoth work, *Geology of the Yellowstone National Park* (1899). Holmes, in contrast, spent less than three months in the field, from July 21 to October 13, 1878, and part of that time he was grounded on account of heavy rains and snowstorms. The result of these constraints was that Holmes's geological report read much like one, as he put it, "of the twenty-five-mile-a-day kind."[10]

The Last Reconnaissance

Holmes organized his Yellowstone report into a dozen short sections, each of which discussed notable geological features along a route that ran counterclockwise through the northwest portion of the park, but ended at Yellowstone

Lake. Rather than adhere to his own erratic route of travel, Holmes arranged the sections "such as would naturally be adopted by the observer who approaches the Park from the North by way of the Yellowstone Valley."[11]

After briefly reviewing Yellowstone's general surface features, Holmes opened his richly illustrated account by pointing to the existence of a great displacement or a large fault. He showed, with the aid of a scored map and six sections, that this rupture in the earth's surface paralleled in a rough manner the Yellowstone River as it flowed northwest along the foot of the northern highland, before exiting the park. This fault line served as a natural park boundary, for the many geological wonders of Yellowstone were located south of this break. The first of these features was the low-lying Mount Evarts, which stood below the great displacement at a point east of Gardiner's River.

As Holmes led his mule up to the flat summit of Mount Evarts, he discovered masses of basalt "bearing the strongest evidence" that they were intrusive in character.[12] This was a phenomenon he was uniquely qualified to study. By applying the lessons that he had learned about intrusives in southwestern Colorado, Holmes imaginatively solved the problem of where the masses of basalt originated. He theorized that the fault in the valley below was the source of the basalt. From there, he reasoned, the sheets of igneous material had wedged their way between and along the mountain's strata to form long, lateral arms or sills. These intrusions occasionally ballooned at weak spots, arched the overlying rocks, and at points nearly penetrated the surface.

Before moving to the subject of the East Gallatin Mountains, Holmes included a section on Sepulchre Mountain. He had to admit, however, in a grim reference to the mountain's name: "So far as I know it, the most important thing buried beneath its dark mass is the secret of its structure."[13] He had better luck in the adjacent range of mountains. To the northeast of Sepulchre Mountain rose Electric Peak, where, in 1872, Peale and Gannett had been caught in a terrifying lightning storm.[14] Electric Peak formed the head of the East Gallatins, which ran north to south some fifteen miles and terminated at an eminence known as Mount Madison, west of Obsidian Cliff. Earlier, this mountain was known as "Mount Gallatin."[15]

On October 8, Holmes and Gannett climbed the namesake of the great Virginian and established a topographical station. From this lofty summit that loomed 10,336 feet into the clear Yellowstone sky, these two men quietly carried out a little-known coup d'état in the cold alpine air. After questioning "on what authority or for what reason" the mountain was called "Madison," they renamed it Mount Holmes. Holmes, however, made clear that Gannett, not he, proposed the name change. Thus, today two mountains in the West bear Holmes's name: the laccolithic Mount Holmes of the Henry Mountains in Utah and the bysmalithic Mount Holmes of the Gallatin Range in Yellowstone National Park.[16]

Midway between Mount Holmes and Electric Peak lay the "Great Laccolite" of Indian Creek. From a distance, the laccolith looked like the head of a crocodile in the act of devouring its prey. The elevated jaw consisted of Carboniferous strata, whereas the lower jaw, which rested in a horizontal position, was made up of Silurian limestone. Caught in this titanic maw, Holmes discovered, were masses of hornblendic trachyte, which resembled the trachytes that he had studied in Colorado and Utah. To describe this feature, Holmes adopted Gilbert's term *laccolite* and referred readers to Gilbert's study of the Henry Mountains for the best description of the phenomenon. Whatever his personal beliefs were about the priority of discovery, Holmes modestly acknowledged the superiority of Gilbert's work in this matter.

In the next section of the report, entitled "Upper Gardiner River," Holmes took issue with one of Hayden's catastrophic interpretations. To Hayden, the "hot springs and geysers of the present time" were the smoldering embers of a once mighty conflagration.[17] On investigating the hot springs at Gardiner River, Holmes, with characteristic astuteness, observed:

> They existed before the valleys of Gardiner River and the Yellowstone were laid out, and built their heavy sheets of deposit upon the level floor of the unbroken sheet of rhyolite that bridged the future valley. As erosion went on and the bed of the river sank, the springs sank and have followed step by step until now they issue from the hills, a thousand feet below their old level.

Then, in an oblique reference to his mentor, Holmes overturned Hayden by framing his evidence in terms of uniformitarian theory:

> The geyser and hot-spring action has been spoken of frequently as the last stage of the great volcanic activity of the later Tertiary age. Here we trace the hot-spring terraces far back as so many links that connect the far-distant past with the present without a break.[18]

This criticism should be seen in light of the fact that Hayden himself during the 1870s came to adopt a more gradualist outlook.[19]

In a brief archaeological interlude, Holmes turned his attention to the quarry located at Obsidian Cliff. In addition to finding "an old but quite distinct trail" leading to the site, he found man-made piles of dark "glistening flakes." What was more, Holmes identified a number of implements, mostly arrowheads, among the thousands of glasslike fragments. Hence, the evidence

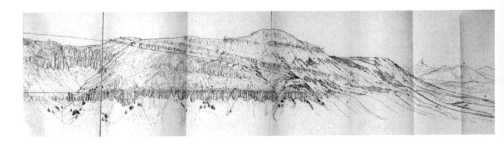

Part of Indian Creek Laccolite. (Plate XIII from Holmes, "Report on the Geology of the Yellowstone National Park," in Hayden, *Twelfth Annual Report . . . Part II*, opposite p. 24.)

was strong that this was an Indian mine—and an old one. In later years, Holmes would be drawn to many such quarries by the controversy over the antiquity of early man in North America. After examining several of the obsidian specimens, three of which he illustrated for the report, Holmes concluded that they were "nearly all . . . imperfect, as if broken or unfinished."[20] In other words, they were discards and constituted mere refuse, not prototypes of more advanced tools. One day this insight would take on important new meaning and form the basis of much of his later archaeological work.[21]

East of Obsidian Cliff on the summit of Mount Washburn, which protruded high above a frozen sea of rhyolite, Holmes absorbed the broad, unobstructed landscape stretching out in every direction of the compass. From here, he declared, one could unlock the secret of the park's geology. Yet what he saw as a scientist he could not draw as an artist. The landscape seemed to possess everything but what Holmes required to render it on paper—"strong lines." As an artist, he found the "broad expanses of the great plateau with its lakes, canons [*sic*], and poorly defined forest-hidden drainage" to be "an unintelligible maze."[22] In few other men could such a conflicted intellectual vision exist.

The next stop on Holmes's itinerary was the Grand Canyon of the Yellowstone. Today the canyon is recognized as the product of a number of forces, including that of an enormous caldera, the outer circle of which enclosed the first five miles below Lower Falls. In fact, F. R. Boyd's discovery of the Yellowstone Caldera in the late 1950s has so fundamentally altered the geological interpretations of the park that it stands out like a large fault line in the history of the literature.[23] Holmes's work, one of the first drafts of the canyon's history, identified erosion as the sole author of this extraordinarily complex feature. And with that problem seemingly well in hand, Holmes assured the reader in an outburst of optimism of near Paul Bunyanesque dimensions that only if he had been granted a little more time, a few days or a week, he would also "have been able to solve the whole problem of the relative ages of all the canon [*sic*] rocks."[24] Given the standards of the day, he no doubt would have succeeded, and brilliantly at that.

Completing his study of the Grand Canyon, Holmes then turned to the fossil forests of Amethyst Mountain.[25] These remarkable features were located downriver and through Junction Valley, where "the very perplexing events of the 'Volcanic Tertiary'" stood exposed on every side. At this place, he found the "strong lines" that were wanting in the view from Mount Washburn. Riding up to the north face of Amethyst Mountain, Holmes positioned himself to draw the extraordinary scene before him (see plate XXVII of Holmes's Yellowstone report for 1878). The succession of fossil forests, twenty-five in all, rose tier after tier up the side of Amethyst Mountain. At the summit, Holmes included in the drawing a few living trees from the present Yellowstone forest, suggesting a disquieting link with the present. For illustrative purposes, Holmes felt obliged to alter the lay of the mountain. But he was careful to explain this tampering with Mother Nature:

> The North face of Amethyst Mountain does not present as abrupt a profile as that given in the section, the middle part only being so precipitous. At the base and top there are comparatively gentle slopes; nevertheless the actual stratigraphical conditions are truthfully represented.[26]

In a separately published article, Holmes attempted to explain how forest after forest could be overlain one on top of the other. He speculated that after a "great oscillation" in which the mountain peaks of the Yellowstone region soared to the heights of "20,000 feet," there followed, during the Tertiary age, an equally great period of erosion and, more importantly, "subsidence." Eventually, the mountains were "submerged" beneath a sea or lake, but before undergoing a "frequent alternation between land and sea," and all of this during a time of "intense volcanic action." When the land was above water or the water was filled with "accumulating ejecta," then "forests grew and matured." Conversely, when the land was inundated with water or with airborne volcanic debris, the forests were buried in the "succeeding stratum."[27] As a geologist, Holmes usually confined himself to discussing the immediate problem at hand, which included describing features, defining topographical relationships, sorting out the relative ages of rocks, or engaging in structural analysis. On this occasion, however, Holmes stepped back and explicitly worked aeons of time into his account of the feature.

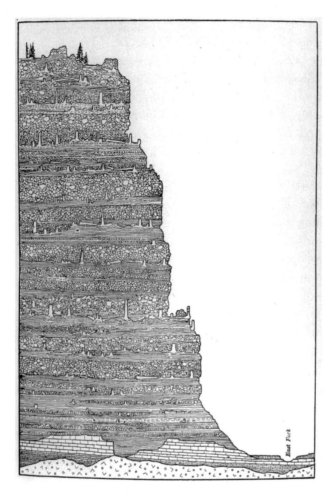

Section of Amethyst Mountain, Showing Fossil Forests. (Plate XXVII from Holmes, "Report on the Geology of the Yellowstone National Park," in Hayden, *Twelfth Annual Report . . . Part II*, opposite p. 48).

In the penultimate section of his Yellowstone report, entitled "Glacial Phenomena," Holmes departed from the roadside format to consider a single problem that affected a wide area of the park.[28] Seven years before, John Muir had discovered a living glacier in the High Sierras. This proof that the Creation was not over led Muir to consider, in a series of seven articles for the

Overland Monthly, the role that glaciation had played in the formation of the Yosemite region.[29] Likewise, glaciers had been very much on Holmes's mind since climbing and sketching in the Wind River and Teton Mountains earlier in the season, where he had observed the existence of living glaciers and the drifts left behind by dead ones.[30] Subsequently, he looked for evidence of glaciation in Yellowstone Park, but there were few of the usual telltale signs, especially on the central plateau. Yet Holmes found—quite unexpectedly—indications that great ice sheets had covered the lowlands of the park that were just as compelling as terminal moraines or scoured rocks.

While riding along the west rim of the Grand Canyon of the Yellowstone, Holmes got caught in a cold rain. He sought refuge from the elements under the ledge of a large, isolated boulder. In the meantime, he inspected his surroundings and was surprised to find that his shelter was composed of a "coarsely crystalline feldspathic granite," whereas the plateau supporting the boulder was made up of rhyolite.[31] Looking for the boulder's point of origin, Holmes surmised that it had been abandoned by an ice sheet that had issued from the north, either from the East Gallatins or the Great Highland of the Yellowstone Mountains (today's eastern Absarokas that lay north of the park). Both ranges were separated from the boulder by a distance of twenty miles.

Holmes had first hypothesized that the glacier started from the south because that was the direction of the upper drainage of the Yellowstone River and thus the path of least resistance. But after failing to find any evidence that granite existed in the ranges to the south and east, he was obliged to reject that idea. In the ranges to the north, on the other hand, he found the granite exposures that he was looking for. Holmes also found and documented the location of other glacial erratics. Using an outline map, he then proceeded to plot their distribution.[32] Many of these loose boulders were located either along or south of the line formed by the valleys of the Yellowstone and East Fork rivers. The pattern of occurrence that emerged strongly suggested that one or more glaciers had, indeed, slowly advanced southward across the park, at least as far as the Lower Falls. Having persuasively argued that much, Holmes then went on to generalize from the established facts:

> It takes no great effort of the imagination to picture the whole Park Plateau covered with a mass of snow and ice—a great *neve* field fed by the accumulating snows from the surrounding highland, and extending its numerous ice tongues far out to the south and west, forcing them across the ocean divide into the Snake River Valley, or into the headwaters of the Missouri.[33]

At the time that Holmes wrote, geologists were absorbed in the highly abstract debate over what caused a glacier or glaciers to descend across the landmasses of the Northern Hemisphere. A range of theories were advanced, including a highly imaginative one in which the earth passed through a cold patch of space.[34] Whether out of caution or wisdom, Holmes avoided such speculations and addressed the far more limited but answerable question of the degree of glacial extent in the Yellowstone region. Accordingly, his findings, like Muir's, have survived the test of time tolerably well.[35]

Holmes closed the report and thus his work as a member of the Hayden Survey with a section on Yellowstone Lake. In a basic study of change over time, Holmes contrasted the ancient Yellowstone Lake with its modern counterpart. His views were directly at variance with those that Hayden had advanced on the subject in 1872. Holmes argued that the old shoreline was not as high; that the old lake had expanded north and east of its present borders, rather than to the south and west toward the Pacific Slope. Moreover, Holmes found "no indications" that Yellowstone Lake had ever been connected to the Columbia River through the drainage of the Snake. The "Northwest Passage" that Hayden thought may have existed during the late Tertiary, or rather a "chain" of freshwater lakes covering vast areas of the West, was a chimera after all.[36] An era of exploration was indeed over.

Holmes officially submitted his report on the geology of Yellowstone National Park on August 2, 1879. Since Congress had consolidated the surveys into the Geological Survey under the direction of Clarence King six months before, this item was in a sense the unfinished business of an earlier period in American exploration. With the establishment of the Geological Survey and, concurrently, the Bureau of American Ethnology, knowledge had become organized along clear institutional lines. In the process, the old omnibus surveys were replaced by single-purpose field parties. And the government was no longer the principal sponsor of scientific exploration. Private museums and societies, individual benefactors, and the universities would assume an ever greater role in the acquisition of facts and artifacts.

In the last few years, however, the relentless destruction of the earth's biological diversity, especially in South America, has set the stage for another great, if final, reconnaissance. The Smithsonian Institution, the Missouri Botanical Garden, the Nature Conservancy, and other museums and universities have organized so-called SWAT teams to perform rapid inventories of plant and animal species in the Andes and Amazonia before it is too late.[37]

Holmes and the other members of the nineteenth-century surveys would have understood the aims and methods of their modern counterparts, but not the reasons for their urgency.

An American in Munich

While government science was undergoing a bureaucratic revolution, Holmes elected to spend a year in Europe, away from the politics and the struggles for positions in the new organizations. He left the United States on August 2, 1879, the same day that he officially submitted the Yellowstone report. He returned home the following July. Although he traveled widely, he was not in Europe as a tourist or a pilgrim. Holmes went there with two specific purposes in mind: 1) to visit and learn about Europe's museums and galleries; and 2) to study art. He was clearly preparing himself for another career, one that perfectly symbolized the closing of what Goetzmann has called the "Second Age of Discovery."[38] Holmes the explorer, who had spent years collecting information on the frontier, was getting ready to become a museum builder dedicated to presenting the new knowledge to the world.

But if Holmes stayed away from Washington for a year, he nevertheless made sure that the head of the Bureau of American Ethnology, John Wesley Powell—who wrote to Professor A. Bastian, president of the Ethnological Society of Berlin, introducing Holmes as an "earnest and skillful investigator"—knew of Holmes's activities in Europe, and Powell was no doubt aware of how they might be helpful to his new organization.[39] In a letter to Kate Clifton Osgood, Holmes referred to one of these many museum visits.[40] Osgood was a twenty-two-year-old artist whom he had apparently met in Washington and would eventually marry in 1883. In Dresden, he met with Adolphe B. Meyer of the Anthropology Museum and received "a great lesson in Museum making." Holmes explained to the woman who would one day be his wife and mother of his two sons—Osgood and William Heberling—that Professor Meyer was "the great authority on museums and installation." And indeed, Meyer would later become the director of the Royal Zoological, Anthropological, and Ethnographical Museum of Dresden.

On another occasion while at London's Crystal Palace, Holmes was notably impressed by several of the exhibits, which no doubt reminded him of his earlier model work for the Centennial Exhibition. He "observed . . . groups of plaster casts representing various savage tribes, life size; they are very fine; also

View in the Green River Basin, Looking West from Green River Towards Granger.
(Holmes illustration from Peale, "Report on the Geology of the Green River District,"
in Hayden, *Eleventh Annual Report*, opposite p. 516).

a group of Tartars in rich costume."[41] Years later Holmes would design similar
life-size dioramas (indoor as well as outdoor) for the Smithsonian Institution.
Even today, in spite of a growing range of competing media, the diorama or
lay group concept remains a popular form of documentary art.

Holmes also devoted time to his art studies and even briefly joined the
American art colony in Munich. Many of his subjects, such as Stonehenge,
Vesuvius, or the glaciers in the Swiss Alps, marked a continuation of his scientific interests. But he also made sketches using pencil and pen, as well as
watercolors (but not oils, which he tended to avoid) of human figures—several directly from hired models.[42] As Holmes acknowledged, his pencil and
watercolor sketches—*An Amalfi Woman at the Well* (1880), *A Monk, Ravello,
Italy* (1880), or the *Young Faggot Gatherer, Ravello, Italy* (1880)—all owed a
debt to the naturalist Frank Duveneck.[43] Holmes briefly studied under this
large, blond-haired artist, whom John Singer Sargent called "the greatest talent of the brush of this generation."[44] Duveneck, who was one year Holmes's
junior, looked to the Dutch masters rather than the French impressionists for
sources of inspiration. He is best known for *The Whistling Boy* (1872). Duveneck taught scores of American artists in Munich, Florence, and Venice from
1878 to 1888. Duveneck, known as the "Old Man," and his students, the
"Duveneck Boys," had as their motto the directive: "work."[45] This latter fact
alone would explain Duveneck's appeal to Holmes. While in Venice, the Duve-

neck Boys with whom Holmes had a chance to associate included Louis Ritter, Charles Abel Corwin, Charles E. Mills, and Ross Turner (the latter of whom was a "Washington boy" and "good friend"). Incidentally, Duveneck returned to the United States in 1888 and twelve years later took a position at the Art Academy in Cincinnati, Ohio.[46]

Significantly, Holmes was far less receptive to new ideas from European artists than he was from European museum builders. The reason for this difference lay in the way he saw American art, at least when it depicted non-European models, such as the landscapes of the West, viewing it as being on an equal basis with that of Europe. As early as 1876, Holmes had formed the opinion, after viewing the fine art exhibit of American artists at the Centennial, that "Americans are not so far behind other nations."[47] Holmes no doubt was as affected by the heady patriotism in Philadelphia at that time as were many of his fellow citizens, but his belief that American landscapists could render American landscapes with Europe's best survived well beyond the morning after.

Holmes's views on art were based in large part on his unique experience as an active participant in both the artistic and scientific openings of America's western frontier. Out there, where the land and its people were being recorded, often for the first time, his emphasis and that of his contemporaries was naturally on the subject rather than the artist or his technique; and on representation rather than abstraction. The experimentation in light and color that was sweeping France and preparing the way for the modern art movement thus held little appeal to Holmes, or to other artists of the frontier for that matter.[48] In this sense, America's new lands and the primary need to document them visually acted to perpetuate the realist movement in the United States long after it had lost its sway in Europe.

8

"The Great Innovation"

The Toroweap

O N JULY 9, 1880, HOLMES RETURNED TO Washington, D.C., after completing his year-long Grand Tour of Europe. He had little doubt that his unique talents would soon be in demand by Clarence King's new organization — the United States Geological Survey. Holmes was, after all, the best scientific illustrator in the country, and he knew it. So did King who hired Holmes as a temporary assistant geologist at $200 per month on August 1, 1880 and sent him to Utah to join Captain Clarence Edward Dutton of the Ordnance Corps, U.S. Army. Holmes and Dutton already knew each other well. The world of Washington science was a small one. And this was not the first time the two men had worked together. Holmes had turned over the volcanic rocks that he collected on his last expedition to Yellowstone National Park to Dutton for examination and included the results of Dutton's work in his report for 1878. Given the common interests and previous association of the two men, it seems very likely that they had reached an agreement to collaborate well before Holmes had returned from Europe.

Dutton, who came to science after first studying for the ministry at Yale and fighting for the Union in the Civil War, belonged to that famous troika of American geologists, which included John Wesley Powell and Grove Karl Gilbert. Dutton arrived in Washington, D.C., in 1871, the same year Holmes did. In 1875, while Holmes was in Colorado, Dutton went west as a member of Powell's survey of the Colorado Plateau. From 1880 to 1880, he was in charge of the USGS Division of the Colorado. Today, Dutton remains the poet laureate of American geology because of his brilliant word pictures of the West found in the geology classics *Report on the Geology of the High Plateaus of Utah* (1880), and *The Tertiary History of the Grand Cañon District* (1882).

Dutton had left Washington in early July 1880, for Salt Lake City. After

The Grand Cañon from Toroweap Cone, Looking East. (Two sheet panorama, from
Holmes, Sketches of the Grand Cañon and Vicinity, Arizona and Utah, 1880, NO-8202,
courtesy U.S.G.S. Field Archives, Denver, Colorado.

outfitting his small party there, which included the topographers Richard U.
Goode and Sumner H. Bodfish, two assistants, and eight hired hands, he proceeded southward to Kanab, on the Arizona-Utah border. Centrally located at
the foot of the Vermilion Cliffs, this tiny Mormon settlement would serve as
the base of operations, as it had for government surveys in the past. From
Kanab, Goode rode on to the San Francisco Peaks via Lee's Ferry to begin
mapping, while Bodfish's destination was the nearby Kaibab Plateau.[1]
Meanwhile, Dutton devoted himself to studying the geology of the Grand
Canyon district. This rectangular area was bound on the north by the Mark-
agunt, Paunsagunt, and Kaiparowits plateaus; on the south by the Colorado
River; on the east by the Echo Cliffs; and on the west by Shivwits Plateau.
Dutton knew this country well. Since 1875, he had worked on the geology of
Utah's high plateaus as a member of the Powell Survey. Although at times, he
confessed,

> I . . . found the temptation irresistible to wander far outside of the limits of
> my prescribed field; and whither should the errant geologist turn his footsteps
> so eagerly as towards the wonder-land of the south?[2]

Holmes, on the other hand, had never seen the Grand Canyon and had
only penetrated the Colorado Plateau from the east as far as Comb Ridge. He
nevertheless fully expected to discover a "land of marvels." After some initial
confusion and delay in St. George, he finally caught up with Dutton on August 18, at a camp ten or so miles outside Pipe Spring—a lonely Mormon
fort built of cut stone and known locally as "Winsor Castle."[3] Over supper

that evening, the two men discussed the work ahead. Dutton planned to consider a number of problems—volcanism, faulting, and, above all, erosion—but he made clear that he had only one guiding theme: the natural history of the Grand Canyon district through Tertiary and Quaternary times. Although Dutton expected Holmes to assist in "working out geological details," illustration was to be his chief responsibility.[4] In a sense, Holmes had come full circle since 1872, when he had the time and freedom to devote himself almost entirely to art. But now he had the benefit of years of field experience, scientific writing, and artistic study, including time abroad visiting Europe's great cultural centers. Holmes was seasoned in every way, and as his art would subsequently prove, his eye, skill, and scientific understanding had become an even match for the scenic grandeur of the Grand Canyon of the Colorado River.

The following morning the two men rode in a southwesterly direction toward Mount Trumbull, situated on the Arizona Strip north of the canyon, where they spent the next four weeks. Soon the large 19- x 13-inch sheets of Holmes's sketchbook began to fill up with the likenesses of Mounts Trumbull, Logan, Emma, and Dellenbaugh; the Uinkaret and Kanab plateaus; Toroweap and Queantoweap valleys; Hurricane Ledge, and other features such as cinder cones and lava flows. Besides geological subjects, Holmes turned his "magical pencil," as Dutton called it, to sketching the variety of local vegetation—aspen, oak, pine, prickly pear, yucca, grasses, and, above all, the ubiquitous juniper.[5] The latter tree he mastered and used with fine effect in the foregrounds of his finished drawings, notably the Point Sublime triptych. Although Holmes worked largely in pencil, he did make use of watercolors and even paused to take photographs to serve as *aides-mémoire.*[6]

Among the many sketches Holmes produced in the Mount Trumbull area, none stood out like the dizzying masterpiece *Grand Cañon at the Foot of the Toroweap, Looking East.*[7] For an artist who worked best when nature presented herself in "strong lines," here was the perfect landscape. The Grand Canyon's distinct and multiple layers of strata, clearly defined slopes of talus, sharp cliff recessions, eye-arresting buttes, jutting promontories, all of which were exposed to view, given the nearly complete absence of vegetation, provided an endless number of subjects for Holmes's pencil.

He drew the *Toroweap* from the seat of Vulcan's Throne, a 567-foot-high basaltic cinder cone situated on the Great Esplanade and towering above the Toroweap and the inner gorge far below. If Holmes had drawn the view to the west, the most noteworthy features would have been the recently cooled lava

Grand Cañon at the Foot of the Toroweap, Looking East. (Holmes illustration, sheet 4, in Dutton, *Atlas to Accompany the Monograph on the Tertiary History of the Grand Cañon District.*)

flows that had poured past the foot of Vulcan's Throne, covering the Esplanade and cascading over the brink of the inner gorge down to the Colorado River.[8] On his famous boat trip through the Canyon in 1869, Powell observed the points where the lava met the river's edge and exclaimed:

> What a conflict of water and fire there must have been here. . . . Just imagine a river of molten rock, running down about 2,500 feet into a river of melted snow. What a seething and boiling of the waters; what clouds of steam rolled into the heavens![9]

Instead of rendering this fiery episode in the natural history of the Grand Canyon, Holmes faced east where erosion, not volcanism, was the undisputed agent of geological change. In fact, from his vantage point atop Vulcan's Throne, he had a central view of both the outer and inner "chasms" of the Grand Canyon. At one level, the *Toroweap* that emerged in this sketch was pure illustration, little different from the hundreds of other drawings Holmes had made of the West. This carefully composed picture, which was redrawn in the studio, depicted the images of these two monuments of erosion, with almost perfect—indeed "stunning"—clarity and scientific rigor, to use Stegner's term.

But at a deeper and more subtle level, Holmes's picture went beyond faithfully delineating the landscape to suggesting the effect or impression that the landscape had on the viewer. On this point, Dutton strongly influenced Holmes and anticipated a more modern sensibility. Dutton devoted entire sections of the *Tertiary History* to the problems of comprehending the Grand Canyon, which he argued was a "great innovation in modern ideas of scenery, and in . . . conceptions of the grandeur, beauty, and power of nature."[10] The disposition of the explorer's mind, in other words, was as important to Dutton as what was explored. Along these lines, he warned that the "observer"

> who visits its commanding points with expectation of experiencing forthwith a rapturous exaltation, an ecstasy arising from the realization of a degree of grandeur and sublimity never felt before, is doomed to disappointment. Supposing him to be but little familiar with plateau scenery, he will be simply bewildered.

To appreciate the Grand Canyon, Dutton declared, the observer needed a "special culture, requiring time, patience, and long familiarity for its consummation."[11] Holmes's paradoxical task was to express visually this psychological idea, and yet report as well.

This call for a "special culture" was an early manifestation of the specialization that brought an era of American exploration to a close and transformed government science. It was also the beginning of something more. For Dutton insisted that the Grand Canyon must be "dwelt upon and studied, and the study must comprise the slow acquisition of the meaning and spirit of that marvelous scenery." This demand to take one part of the West on its own terms, rather than in reference to something else, played its part in influencing the regionalism, attachment to place, and environmentalism that became so pervasive in the work of modern western writers and artists, from Georgia O'Keeffe to William Kittredge. Edward Abbey's advice to the automobile tourist in the canyon country, for instance, possessed a clear "Duttonian" ring to it:

> you can't see *anything* from a car; you've got to get out of the goddamned contraption and walk, better yet crawl, on hands and knees, over the sandstone and through the thornbush and cactus. When traces of blood begin to mark your trail you'll see something, maybe. Probably not.[12]

Holmes was far more subtle on this point than Abbey, but he was able, through the adroit use of space and a hard-won sense of geologic time, to convey a similar idea in his canyon art of the *Toroweap* and the Point Sublime triptych. In short, Holmes's Grand Canyon was unique and incomparable and defied easy comprehension. His work, moreover, is unequaled.

At the level of reporting, Holmes's main challenge was, in effect, negative. That is, he had to capture what was not there, namely, vast, empty space. What was most striking about the Grand Canyon, in terms of erosion, was the staggering amount of earth that had been washed away by the Colorado River and its tributaries. Many of these tributaries existed only after a thunderstorm filled their usually dry arroyos and channels with a boulder-moving flood of chocolate-colored water that then stair-stepped its relentless way to the main river thousands of feet below. To impress upon the viewer the immensity of the Grand Canyon, Holmes used the effective devices of scale and juxtaposition. In the left foreground of the *Toroweap*, he drew in a handful of tiny figures, representing Dutton's party, who were about to reach the brink of an almost bottomless and shadow-darkened inner gorge. In reference to this scene, Dutton wrote in the *Tertiary History*:

> We feel like mere insects crawling along the street of a city flanked with immense temples, or as Lemuel Gulliver might have felt in revisiting the capital of Brobdingnag, and finding it deserted.[13]

Besides showing that the Grand Canyon was in large part the product of erosional forces, Holmes's line drawings also made it clear that the Grand Canyon would require years, perhaps a lifetime, to come to know and truly understand. He made this same point, if not nearly as well, in his study of Yellowstone National Park.

Besides space, time was important to Holmes's work in another, more profound respect. The *Toroweap* was not just a study of the awesome effects of erosion, but also of the endless stretches of time necessary to achieve such a spectacular result. To make time an almost tangible presence, Holmes contrasted the vastness of excavated space with the barely visible excavator — the Colorado River, which represented a small fraction of the overall picture. The visual effect of this grossly disproportionate ratio of canyon to river was initially that of shock. As intended, the picture, like the Grand Canyon itself, required time to study and absorb. And in the Archean depths of the inner gorge, the oldest part of the Canyon, where the very roots of the earth lay exposed, Holmes hinted at the meaning of geologic time, or rather, eternity. Here, in the canyon country, Holmes and Dutton had discovered the "great antiquity" of America that Nathaniel Hawthorne and the other romantics of an earlier generation had searched for in vain.

Point Sublime

By September 17, the work at and around Mount Trumbull was completed, and Holmes, Dutton, and the other men headed east toward the Kaibab Plateau. In marked contrast to the rock and sage that Holmes had grown accustomed to seeing—except in the vicinity of the Uinkaret Mountains—the Kaibab, which was considerably higher in elevation, was covered with pine, aspen, swales, and grassy parks adorned with flowers. Moreover, the forests abounded in wildlife, especially deer and fowl. The Mormons found the Kaibab (a Paiute word that meant "mountain-lying-down") a hunter's paradise and called the place Buckskin Mountain.[14]

The following day the party reached De Motte Park, where Bodfish and his men were camped. In the morning, Holmes rode out to the eastern edge of the plateau where he could get a commanding view of that great crack in the earth's surface, Marble Canyon. He spent a leisurely two days making sketches of the scene stretching endlessly before him, which included the Henry Mountains in the far distance. Holmes returned to De Motte Park late on September 20 and set aside the next day to draw aspens. He had become taken with these trees and at one point described their yellow leaves as "like gold" and playing "about the white branches and trunks like the golden head dress of a Trojan queen about her shoulders."

During the next several days, Holmes toured the North Rim, making sketches of the Canyon and examining Indian ruins and pottery. (Since arriving in St. George, he had taken note of the numerous points of archaeological interest that he found across the length and width of the Arizona Strip.) On the evening of September 25, Holmes had worked his way west to Point Sublime, one of the longest promontories of either rim of the Grand Canyon. From there, Holmes watched the sun set behind what he called the "grandest" and one of the "most extraordinary panoramas in the wide world." Like his companion Clarence Dutton, Holmes was deeply impressed with the 270-degree view obtainable from this point in geologic space. Inspired, Holmes devoted the next three days to sketching this wide-angle view, "from sunrise to sunset except while at meals and until nine o'clock the morning after." The result was his best work—the three-part continuous panorama from Point Sublime, looking east, south, and west.[15] The West's greatest draughtsman had found the West's greatest view.

Holmes, of course, was not the first artist of the Grand Canyon and plateau country. Others had come before—F. W. von Egloffstein, Heinrich B. Möll-

"Panorama from Point Sublime: Part I, Looking East; Part II, Looking
South; Part III, Looking West." (Holmes illustrations from Dutton,
*Atlas to Accompany the Monograph on the Tertiary History of the Grand
Cañon District.*)

hausen, Gilbert Munger, John E. Weyss, and Thomas Moran. Of these artists, Egloffstein seems to have had the most influence on the popular conception of the Grand Canyon. His illustrations, which appeared in Lt. Joseph C. Ives's report of his 1857 expedition up the Colorado River, were actually of Black Canyon, a feature that lies well to the west of Grand Canyon proper. From these views of one part of the canyon country, and not a representative part at that, the public generalized about the whole. "Never was a great subject," Dutton charged, "more artistically misrepresented or more charmingly belittled."[16] Wallace Stegner suggested that Egloffstein was unable to overcome his preconceived notion that canyons had high and narrow walls, thus distorting the Grand Canyon's real appearance. In other words, Egloffstein was captive to the culture of the civilized centers from which he came.[17]

William H. Goetzmann has pointed out that "Egloffstein's vertical rendering of Black Canyon," as opposed to the Grand Canyon, was actually quite accurate.[18] A fact that explains why in 1930 engineers selected Black Canyon as the ideal site for Hoover Dam (originally named Boulder Dam). At the heart of Dutton's criticism, however, was not Egloffstein's fidelity to nature, but what he took to be the artist's notion of grandeur, or lack thereof. Dutton rejected the idea that "in some way an essential part of the grandeur of the Grand Cañon is the narrowness of its defiles," which was the impression left by Egloffstein's views. "In truth," Dutton maintained, "a little reflection will show that such a character would be inconsistent with the highest and strongest effects." Only the Kaibab section of the Colorado River, according to Dutton, measured up to this rather subjective formula of grandeur in which the "distance [between the walls] must bear some ratio to the magnitude." Here, then, an observer could see the Grand Canyon's "vast proportions," as well as "its intricate plan, the nobility of its architecture, its wealth of ornamentation, the splendor of its colors, and its wonderful atmosphere."[19] All of these attributes taken as a whole, Dutton argued, made the Grand Canyon grand.

Holmes understood what Dutton meant. In the three panoramas he drew from Point Sublime, his aim was to capture the Grand Canyon in its totality, or in Dutton's words, "its ensemble." Other works such as Thomas Moran's *The Chasm of the Colorado* (1874) showed only a part of the awesome spectacle.[20] But what Moran did show or rather illustrate in this celebrated painting was the power of cause and effect. In the left half of the painting, the Chasm was shown drenched in a downpour—a major agent of erosion; the remainder of the Chasm was depicted in bright colors brought out by the Arizona sun. The scientific lesson was clear: the Chasm was the result of millions of such rainstorms, and would continue to be changed by millions more. If the objective, then, was to show the Grand Canyon's full ensemble, the canyon art up to that point, including Moran's other canyon art, some of which appeared in both Dutton's monograph and atlas, was similarly circumscribed or suggestive. Moran's *Transept*, for instance, based, incidentally, on one of Holmes's sketches, depicted a side canyon of Bright Angel Canyon and thus was thrice removed from the main canyon. So only indirectly did Moran expose the viewer to the sheer enormity of the Grand Canyon. This was a common shortcoming, according to Dutton's standard, of all the previous visual representations of this geological wonder.

Holmes, on the other hand, attempted to provide the world with its first comprehensive view of the Grand Canyon in Dutton's exacting and aesthetic terms. To underscore the close relationship between the artist and the scientist, Holmes drew himself at work in the foreground of the Point Sublime panorama (see "Looking East"), with the figure of Dutton literally standing over his shoulder. Not surprisingly, their interpretation of the vast scene before them showed no trace of Egloffstein's narrow and darkly shadowed defile, an idea that had so clearly influenced Moran's *Chasm*. Instead, Holmes presented the Grand Canyon in its true dimensions—wide, open, and long. Even his inner gorge, shown in the distance through an opening between two intervening ridges (the East and West Cloisters), was wider than it was deep. Through this collaboration of artist and scientist, made possible only by the unique and complementary qualities of these two men, the scientific world was presented with its first accurate image of the Grand Canyon in its entirety.

To portray the Canyon any differently, of course, would have marked a departure from the literalism that informed all of Holmes's scientific art. In fact, his near-photographic views caused a critic like the naturalist John Muir, who at one point wrote that it was "impossible to learn what the cañon is like from descriptions and pictures," to praise Holmes's work as "wonderfully good." "Surely," he admitted, "faithful and loving skill can go no farther in putting the multitudinous decorated forms on paper." His only complaint was that Holmes's pictures, which Julius Bien reproduced in earth-toned lithographs, lacked the Canyon's "living, rejoicing *colors.. . .* Whose brush or pencil, however lovingly inspired, can give us these? And if paint is of no effect, what

Holmes and Dutton, Each Other's Muse. (Detail from "Panorama from Point Sublime, Part I, Looking East" by Holmes, sheet XV, in Dutton, *Atlas to Accompany the Monograph on the Tertiary History of the Grand Cañon District*.)

hope lies in pen-work? Only this: some may be incited by it to go and see for themselves."[21] Emmanuel de Margerie, one of Holmes's French admirers, was effusive in his praise of the illustrations in the Dutton atlas. He wrote to Holmes commenting, "How geology would quickly progress & would be quickly learned by students, if every geologist could know the handling of pencil as you do it."[22] The great physiographer William Morris Davis, another one of America's great scientific artists, visited the Grand Canyon. He came away in awe of Holmes's artistic achievements, a sense he shared with Holmes in 1901.

> I hope you will not be severe with my efforts to follow your drawings; indeed, I should like very much to know if you find some success in my apprenticeship, for truly I labored over those things, especially the landslides, the "wedge" and the view down the Canyon. But your manner of generalizing is beyond me, far away. I cannot pick out the right lines, as you seem to do instinctively.[23]

But what was important about Holmes's Point Sublime triptych was not how he drew, but what he drew—and for whom. In these panoramas, the

The Temples and Towers of the Virgin. (Holmes illustration, sheet IV, in Dutton, *Atlas to Accompany the Monograph on the Tertiary History of the Grand Cañon District.*)

Grand Canyon of the Colorado emerged for the first time as a fully articulated idea. And this bold conceptualization pointed in a direct line twenty-eight years later to Theodore Roosevelt's creation of Grand Canyon National Monument. There was a long delay between the Canyon's exploration, documentation, and conceptualization and the public recognition that it was a unique area that merited preservation, a lag sharply contrasted with the exploration of Yellowstone and the quick establishment of the geyser country as a national park. This difference can be explained in large part because Dutton and Holmes directed their work to a select audience, unlike Hayden who had cast his net widely. Dutton's monograph and atlas were intended for the scientists at the Geological Survey, and consequently only one edition of three thousand copies was issued (it was republished in 1977).[24] Nevertheless, in time readers outside the survey, such as John Muir and George Wharton James, fell under the influence of Dutton's prose and Holmes's art and, in turn, helped promote the idea of setting the Grand Canyon aside as a national treasure to be enjoyed by future generations.[25]

Before returning to Salt Lake City, Holmes and Dutton tarried close to another month in southern Utah. The two men headed back to Kanab, then passed along the Vermilion Cliffs, camped along the Rio Virgin, and worked their way up the Hurricane Cliffs, and from there rode on to Fort Cameron, located at Beaver, Utah. Holmes thus had ample time to draw and photograph the country of Zion, including the Towers of Short Creek, Smithsonian Butte, the Pink Cliffs of the Paunsagunt, Rock Rover's Land, the Domes of Little Zion Valley, and the unusual rock formations on the aptly named Kolob, a large terrace cut by canyons.[26] (Kolob-Holmes spelled it with a "c" — was a Mormon term from *The Pearl of Great Price*, which meant a place close to where God lives.)

From the town of Beaver, Holmes traveled to Milford in what was apparently a horse-drawn conveyance called a "jerky," and then on to Salt Lake City by train. He arrived in the Mormon capital on October 19. Although Holmes had parted company with Dutton, his business in Utah was not finished. He had been corresponding with Gilbert, who now headed the Geological Survey's Great Basin division, based in Salt Lake.[27] Gilbert was involved in a long-running investigation of Lake Bonneville. Unlike his report of the Henry Mountains, however, Gilbert's Lake Bonneville study took years to finish. (The monograph was finally published in 1890.) Before Holmes left, Gilbert wanted him to illustrate various types of terraces. Holmes happily agreed and spent the next three days in the field with Gilbert. Gilbert would have preferred that Holmes had been more closely "associated" with his lake study, but recognized that Lake Bonneville, even in all of its Pleistocene glory, could not compete in terms of geologic and aesthetic interest with the Grand Canyon.[28]

Grand Canyon Postscript

Twenty-nine years after Holmes and Dutton's scientific and artistic triumph on the edge of the North Rim, which, incidentally, was a high point in the intellectual history of American exploration, Holmes returned to the Grand Canyon in May of 1909. This time, however, he came not as an explorer and artist, but as a tourist and dignitary. And this time he came by train, not horse; he stayed at the sumptuous El Tovar Hotel (where he dined with the railroad hosteler Ford F. Harvey), not in a dog tent that flapped in the wind all night. But more importantly, since the official reason for Holmes's second visit was to help locate a suitable site for a monument to the explorer of the Grand Canyon, John Wesley Powell, this 1909 trip was, in effect, a nostalgic look at the past, instead of one filled with the excitement of discovery, as was the case with the expedition of 1880.[29]

Terms of Embellishment

Holmes arrived in Washington by early November of 1880, with plans to start work on the Dutton atlas and to attend to numerous other illustration projects for the Geological Survey and the Bureau of American Ethnology. On October 30, Dutton had written a very strong letter of recommendation to Clarence King on Holmes's behalf urging that Holmes's temporary position in the organization be made permanent. Dutton wrote that Holmes's "geological knowledge and skill" were "of a high order" and that "his ability as an illustrator is well known to you." He went on to say that "Holmes's assistance [in preparing the report on the Grand Canyon] will be indispensable." Dutton also recommended that "a salary of $3,000 per annum would be the most reasonable and just measure of the value of his services."[30] At the same time that Holmes was securing a position at the Geological Survey, Hayden—who was syphilitic and slowly wasting away—was trying to bring his own survey to a close.[31] To settle the outstanding financial and editorial matters, Hayden decided to place Holmes as head, thereby replacing Elliot Coues, the noted ornithologist, who was out west at the time. Coues did not take this news well. But Holmes took charge on his birthday, December 1, 1880; seven months and ten thousand dollars later, he finished the job.[32]

In the fight over the directorship of the USGS, Hayden had all but been destroyed by his enemies, a determined group that included King, Powell, Othniel Charles Marsh, president of the National Academy of Sciences, and many others. He had been reduced from his former commanding position in American explorationand science to something of an embarrassment in King's organization. Although Hayden retreated from Washington to the City of Brotherly Love, he continued to serve as a field geologist at the more than respectable annual salary of four thousand dollars. And he was still perceived, initially, at least, as a threat. After King resigned from the USGS, Holmes advised Hayden to stay out of politics. Based on his own very good Washington connections, Holmes no doubt knew where the political winds were blowing. In March of 1881, Hayden stated his position to Holmes clearly: "I have not written a word or inspired a word of criticism against Powell or King since I have been in Phila. but I have prevented it when I could." Moreover, he wrote the next day, "I resolve to support [Powell], and I propose to do so now absolutely and fully." Hayden admitted that "even if I could defeat Maj. Powell," no one would take up his name with the U.S. Senate. And Hayden realized that he would probably be treated better by

Powell than by a "new man." Clearly, Hayden, famous for his explorations of the wonders of Yellowstone, had resigned himself to working, in a condition of growing obscurity, for Powell, whose fame was the result of his explorations of the canyons of the Colorado. "The idea," as Hayden put it, "of some field work is most pleasant to me." Hayden went on to tell Holmes to assure Powell of Hayden's support, adding, "Should you or Maj. Powell hear of any Senator opposing on my account, telegraph me and I will telegraph him at once my status toward Powell." Hayden declared, "You can assure the Major I have not in thought, word or deed, made a motion against him. I have not written one word to any official, and I shall not, unless it is necessary *to quiet opposition* and I know of none," although he acknowledged "[Edward Drinker] Cope may kick a little."[33]

Meanwhile, in one of Clarence King's last duties before leaving the survey on March 6, 1881, the great raconteur re-appointed Holmes on January 1, 1881, to the temporary position of assistant geologist at two hundred dollars a month. On March 1, this position was made permanent, and Holmes was placed on a yearly salary of twenty-four hundred dollars (six hundred less than what Dutton had requested, but nevertheless a decent income).[34] Holmes had thus survived the reorganization and was now officially with the new survey under the direction of the highly capable John Wesley Powell. Holmes divided his schedule with the Smithsonian's National Museum, where he worked under the auspices of the Bureau of American Ethnology, which remained under Powell's control. Holmes was drawn to the museum's prehistoric pottery collection and set to work labeling, cataloging, classifying, arranging, exhibiting—at the museum as well as at fairs, such as the World's Industrial and Cotton Centennial Exposition in New Orleans—and studying these antiquities. This was unsung work, but Holmes developed a love for it. In 1883, at Powell's direction and with Spencer F. Baird's support, he went on to become honorary curator of pottery at the National Museum.[35] Since Powell was director of both organizations, this dual arrangement was not only tolerated but encouraged. Powell, in short, knew how to get the most out of his men and stay within budget.

While Holmes's double duties were another testimony to his multifarious talents, in the area of illustration his connection to both the survey and the bureau was largely a practical matter and provided Powell with the advantages of a single management. As the uses for, and methods of, illustration, which included photography, proliferated throughout the 1880s, standardization, specialization, economy, and efficiency became an ever-increasing concern. By 1885, these forces, which were transforming the American economy, led

Holmes and Powell to institutionalize scientific illustration, a development that had broad implications for the history of western American art.[36]

In 1884, the division of illustrations was created at the survey with Holmes in charge. In the report Holmes submitted that year, he announced a number of changes, such as the hiring of a permanent staff of draughtsmen, instead of farming out the work, as had been done in the past.[37] But no change was so important as the adoption of what was essentially a new definition of scientific art. In Holmes's words: "Illustrations are no longer to be treated chiefly as a means of embellishment; they are expected to express facts with a clearness and accuracy not surpassed by the language of the letter press."[38] Holmes thus resolved in a simple statement of policy the often ambiguous relationship between "embellishment" and "documentation" that had characterized so much of the art of America's new lands since the surveys of the early nineteenth century. This was the man, after all, who was seared years ago by Baird's almost taunting question: pretty picture, but what species of bird is it? Henceforth, he declared, art and illustration, which he himself had learned how to combine successfully, if not uniquely, were to be two separate and distinct endeavors.

Holmes's position in exploration had clearly changed. He was now writing the instructions as to what to see and how to see it, rather than carrying out someone else's agenda in the field. In Goetzmann's terms, he had become a "programmer." And having drawn the distinction between art and illustration, he directed his energies toward the latter, although Holmes remained informed about the ever-changing art market and made his wonderful watercolors of genteel themes, which were never overstated, available for purchase as well as for exhibition.[39]

The key to understanding the changes in illustration that Holmes instituted during these years lies in analyzing the relationship of the picture to the text. In the extreme instance when a picture bore little or no relationship to the text, the term *embellishment* was appropriate. In Holmes's case, his illustrations rarely fell into this category. On the contrary, his artwork often lay at the other extreme. One of his pictures would express the content of several pages of text, as if to verify the old saying that a picture was worth a thousand words. As scientific publication became an industry, a work that contained both graphic and written descriptions of the same phenomenon was seen as a luxury. Accordingly, the survey's policy toward illustration was changed to reflect these new realities.

In the report for 1887 that Holmes no doubt outlined or worked up, Powell, in a section entitled "The Illustration System," announced that "one of

the most satisfactory methods for diminishing the volume of scientific trea-
tises on general or special subjects is that of substituting graphic representation for verbal statement." Illustrations were to stand on their own, not as
embellishment, but as scientific statement. In addition, illustration, or as it
was now called, the "graphic method," was also to serve as an "instrument of
research," when "graphic representation is essential to the comprehension of
relation."[40]

Interestingly, freeing illustration from art was, for Holmes, one thing. Freeing art from illustration was quite another, and abstraction was something he
was never able to accept. In fact, Holmes's attitudes toward art, especially
landscape art, remained remarkably unchanged over the years, an inflexibil-
ity that did not prevent him from becoming, in the words of Charles C.
Glover, president of the Corcoran Gallery of Art, the honored "dean of all of
the painters of Washington."[41] As far as Holmes was concerned, it did not
follow that artists were free to experiment in new directions now that scientific illustration had assumed full responsibility for realistic representation, although that was precisely what happened. Instead, from 1907 until Holmes's
retirement in 1932, first as curator, then as director of the Smithsonian's National Gallery of Art, Holmes strongly resisted the new art movements from
Europe.[42] As late as 1928, long after the 1913 Armory Show in New York had
changed American art forever, Holmes complained bitterly:

> In this degenerate day in art the people pass by [Thomas Moran's *Grand
> Canyon of the Yellowstone* (1901), which Holmes had acquired for the National
> Gallery] giving it a mere glance because perhaps it represents one of Amer-
> ica's grandest landscape wonders. As a landscape it is without doubt the great-
> est masterpiece of landscape by an American, if not by the painters of any
> people or age. This will doubtless come to be recognized by critics when the
> lunacy of impressionism has passed, as it must if the painter's art is ever to be
> resuscitated.[43]

What impressed Holmes about Moran's work in 1928 was the same thing
that had impressed him in August 1872, when he compared in his mind's eye
the Lower Falls of the Yellowstone with Moran's famous earlier version of this
subject, that is, the artist's literalism. According to Holmes, Moran's 1901
painting was "executed with a skill bordering on the marvelous and is realized
in forms, colors and effects as exquisitely beautiful as can be conceived without," he added in the highest of praise, "transcending the verities of earthly
landscape."[44] In the world of art, Holmes's views were drawn very much from
the old, genteel school, views that did not conflict with his views of scientific

illustration. The aesthetic was identical for both, even if the aims and purposes differed for the respective audiences.

Genesis II

Holmes's views on the high art of his day were as deeply held as those he expressed on the primitive art of the prehistoric Indians of the Americas. Since he had surveyed the Anasazi ruins of the Southwest in 1875, Holmes had been a student of primitive decorative art. His main interests were in pottery, stone implements, textiles, and shellwork. And the materials that he examined came from a wide range of places: Mexico, Peru, the Chiriqui Isthmus of Darien (Columbia), the Potomac Valley, the Mississippi Valley, the mounds of Ohio, and countless other sites in the southwestern and eastern United States. By virtue of his positions in the government, he enjoyed unlimited access to all of the collections of the Smithsonian Institution.

Holmes, like most anthropologists in the late nineteenth century, was influenced by the evolutionary thinking of the time, in particular by the writings of Lewis Henry Morgan, author of *Systems of Consanguinity and Affinity of the Human Family* (1871) and *Ancient Society* (1877). Indeed, in 1909 it fell to Holmes, as chief of the Bureau of American Ethnology, a position that placed him at the top of the anthropology profession, to write Morgan's biographical memoir for the National Academy of Sciences. He greatly admired Morgan's *Systems of Consanguinity*, calling it "a model of inductive research." Evaluating the work as a whole, Holmes was impressed with Morgan's pioneering achievements, noting that Morgan had "found the vast domain of American ethnology practically unexplored." In light of this fact, Holmes observed that it was understandable that this "first hasty survey should have failed to reveal to him in their true relations and full significance all the diversified phenomena with which he had to deal."[45] More critically, and especially revealing about Holmes's own cautious approach to science as well as his own sense of place in the history of anthropology, he pointed to what he believed was Morgan's "tendency to generalize too broadly on incomplete observations," and that while Morgan deserved credit as "an heroic figure" for reaching "the threshold of the dawning science of primitive institutions," it was Holmes and the men and women of his generation, by implication, who successfully crossed that divide.[46]

In 1909, Holmes was in a position to look back on his own career as well as on the history of anthropology, which became a profession during his lifetime, a development with which he was at the very center. During the 1880s, the first decade of the Bureau of American Ethnology's existence, Holmes began to work hard, with Powell's complete support if not insistence, to make anthropology more than a pleasant way to divert a gentleman's time. Morgan was more important in this regard than Holmes's biographical assessment would suggest, for Powell all but made Morgan's ideas the official platform of BAE anthropology, except that he added "enlightenment" as a fourth stage of human development to Morgan's famous scheme of "savagery, barbarism, and civilization."[47] Holmes, whose interests lay at the other end of the evolutionary scale, introduced a stage preceding that of savagery, which he called "pre-art."[48]

The cultural evolutionary thought of Morgan, in fact, was evident in the stream of papers that Holmes wrote during the 1880s on the subject of primitive decorative art, as seen in Holmes's concern with determining the "pathway of progress," a phrase he used in reference to the development of aesthetic ideas. What was more, while he studied primarily American materials, "the principles involved," he declared, were "applicable to all times, as they are based upon the laws of nature." But he added an important qualification: none of the artistic ideas along the pathway of progress, in the advance to higher and higher "planes of culture," "retain a uniform expression . . . as they are subject to modification by environment just as are the forms of living organisms."[49] As Holmes even more succinctly put it in 1893: "Arts change with change of place and consequent change of environment."[50] Significantly, although Holmes drew on biology for analogies in his analysis of cultural difference, he stressed environmental influences. He all but ignored race as a factor.[51]

Holmes attempted to demonstrate through logic and empiricism the ways in which primitive art gradually advanced, step by step, from instinct to conscious embellishment. This inquiry led him to consider carefully and perceptively a number of factors, including accident or "adventition," suggestions from nature, changing technique, intention, methods of construction, and the tendency toward convention. In addition, he argued, counter-intuitively, that the symbolism associated with a given figure, such as the sea with the scroll, followed rather than preceded the development of the ornament. Holmes's theoretical work on the subject of primitive art was required reading for fifty years, and his 1887 paper, entitled the "Origin and Development of Form and Ornament in Ceramic Art," has become a classic in the field.

Holmes's article "On the Evolution of Ornament—An American Lesson," published in *The American Anthropologist* in 1890, in which he refines and adjusts some of his ideas on the origin of art, is written in a less abbreviated, less formal, and more accessible style. Here he states that the "artistic sense is in some degree developed in the minds of all men, and through its intuitive and

constant exercise has become a rival of nature in the realm of the beautiful."
And although he admitted that it was "impossible to trace back the idea of
embellishment to its inception, for the presumption is that it came up from
the shadows of the pre-human stage of our existence," Holmes did speculate
that art was probably first practiced on "man's own person," but "was later extended" to familiar objects. What was possible to reconstruct, according to
Holmes, was the mental process by which the "first steps" of decoration were
taken in the "early stages" of culture, when art was not "intellectual," but
rather "an instinctive act." As Holmes explained:

> The desires of the mind constitute the motive power, the force that induces
> all progress in art; the appreciation of embellishment and the desire to elabo-
> rate it are the cause of all progress in purely decorative evolution. It appears
> . . . that there is in the mind no preconceived idea of what that elaboration
> should be; the mind is a growing thing and pushes forward along the lines
> laid out by environment. Seeking in art aesthetic gratification, it follows the
> lead of technique *along the channels* [italics are mine] opened by such of the
> useful arts as offer suggestions of embellishment. The results reached vary
> with the particular art [textile or fictile] and are important in direct propor-
> tion to the facilities furnished by it. In this respect the textile art possesses vast
> advantage over all the other arts, as it is first in the field, is of widest applica-
> tion, is full of suggestions of embellishment, and is inexorably fixed in its
> methods of expression. The mind in its primitive, mobile condition is as clay
> in the grasp of such forces.

In his analysis of Indian decoration, Holmes took as the starting point, then,
the "inherent tendencies of the art." Pure embellishment was something that
developed later, much later. Technique, in short, preceded decoration by an
indefinite number of generations. In Holmes, there is no sense that art occasionally advances through periodic bursts of creative insight and energy that
occur in a single Kubrickian moment. Instead, art is something that is slowly
"transformed by imperceptible steps."[52]

In a paper entitled "Order of Development of the Primal Shaping Arts,"
read before an audience at the American Association for the Advancement of
Science probably in 1893, Holmes left little doubt as to what set of ideas informed his thinking on the subject of primitive art. He said:

> Modern Science has gone far toward establishing the proposition that the
> human race . . . is the product of evolutionary processes, and the student of
> history has added the corollary that human culture has likewise developed
> through a long series of progressive stages from infinitesimal germs up to the

present complex and wonderful conditions. The history of culture can not, therefore, be complete until the course of its development has been traced back to the remotest beginnings.

Holmes then went on to explain the significance of archaeology, specifically the artifacts of American peoples, to the general understanding of the origins of humanity: "The phenomena of art are the tangible representatives of human progress and achievement, and upon these we are almost wholly dependent for an insight into the initial stages of history." And he added in tones strongly reminiscent of *Genesis*:

Assuming the general uniformity of nature's genetic processes, we conclude that in the beginning there was a period of rudimentary or instinctive use of materials during which our race carried on its activities much as the bird builds her nest of sticks and grass and the badger burrows a home in the ground. But the time must have come when the hand of this creature, man, was so developed and his brain so matured that articles supplied by nature, such as sticks and stones, were held in the hand for throwing, striking, and rubbing. These things became implements, multiplying the powers of the hand and finally giving man dominion over nature.[53]

Here was a new creation story, courtesy of government science. A story in which the artifacts of America's aboriginal peoples helped illuminate the larger story of all humanity.

Mexico: Old and New

During the 1880s, Holmes punctuated his museum work on reconstructing the origins of art by making a number of collecting trips, the two most notable of which were to old Mexico and New Mexico. In May and June of 1884, Holmes went to Mexico as the guest of his good friend William Henry Jackson and J. A. Chain, Jackson's friend and business partner in Denver. Holmes and Jackson left their wives behind, but Chain's wife, who was a landscape painter, accompanied the party as it made its way south in the comfort of a private railway car. Jackson's objective for the trip was to photograph and climb Popocatépetl, a dormant volcano, which nevertheless occasionally emitted a plume of smoke.[54] Although Holmes was no less desirous to see Popocatépetl and its twin Ixtaccíhuatl, as well as to take in the other sights and sounds of Mexico, he was more interested in visiting that country's museums and ruins, including the great pyramids of San Juan Teotihuacán. He was especially anxious to calculate the relative ages of Mexico's native pottery. In the process, Holmes collected "several hundred pieces of ancient ware," which he presented to the National Museum.[55] The most important outcome of this trip was Holmes's apparently extemporaneous study of pottery at the open pits of an adobe brick factory, located near the Central Railway Station in Mexico City. By applying the geological method of stratigraphy to archaeology—the principle of which was that the lowest level of undisturbed layers of habitation were the oldest—he was able to establish two culturally distinct periods of occupation in the *Valle de México* and thus introduce the concept of relative dating to American archaeology. As Joan Mark has pointed out, Holmes's work in Mexico predated the use of stratigraphical excavation by Adolph F. A. Bandelier, Max Uhle, Manuel Gamio, Franz Boas, Alfred L. Kroeber, Nels C. Nelson, and Leslie Spier. By the 1920s, stratigraphy enjoyed widespread acceptance.[56]

While taking the trains to San Juan Teotihuacán, Holmes also had occasion to learn about the counterfeit art of making "antiquities." He had already observed that it "was very easy . . . for the native artisan to imitate any of the older forms of ware; and there is no doubt that in many cases he has done so for the purpose of deceiving." But it was during his stops at train stations that he observed firsthand the traffic in "spurious" antiquities. To quote from an article that he wrote for *Science: An Illustrated Journal,*

> This ware may be purchased at any of the relic shops in the city of Mexico; but San Juan Teotihuacan [*sic*] seems to be the headquarters of the traffic. In passing back and forth by the railway, I found that each train was met by one or more of the venders [*sic*], who were careful to expose but a limited number of pieces, and that this method of sale was systematically practised [*sic*]. Wishing to secure a piece, I waited until the train was about to move off, when I held out a silver dollar, and the vase shown in the accompanying figure was quickly in my possession. The price asked was five dollars, and in the city of Mexico would have been three times that amount. At the rate of purchase indicated by my experience at San Juan, at least one piece per day was carried away by tourists, making hundreds each year. It is not wonderful, therefore, that museums in all parts of the world are becoming well stocked with this class of Mexican antiquities. Oddly enough, no such ware is found among the antiquities of the locality; and none, so far as I know, occur on the site of any ancient Aztec or Toltec settlement. Notwithstanding this fact, the venders [*sic*] do not hesitate to assign definite localities to the relics, and to give full accounts of their discovery.[57]

Holmes was aware that his "present" was a "museum-making era" and understood the importance of guarding against fraud. His real concern was that while "in time most of the spurious pieces will be detected and thrown out

. . . in the mean time they will have made an impression upon literature, and upon the receptive mind of the public, that is most difficult to eradicate."⁵⁸ The stakes, in other words, were high indeed and nothing less than the curator's credibility was at issue.

Several years later in the summer of 1887, Holmes, along with Powell and Samuel P. Langley, secretary of the Smithsonian Institution, made another major trip.⁵⁹ The purpose of this excursion was to visit the pueblos and ruins located near the village of Jemez, New Mexico. Holmes, however, was forced to cut short the trip to the Jemez because he sustained an incapacitating, as well as embarrassing, back injury from a rough, jarring pony ride as he tried to keep up with Major Powell, who was mounted on a horse. James Stevenson (Holmes's old friend from the Hayden Survey) and his wife and fellow ethnologist, Matilda Coxe Stevenson, who had come up from the Rio Grande town of Bernalillo to join the party, cared for him. James managed to take Holmes to a railway station by means of a "docile" mule that pulled his prostrate form in a litter stretched between two long poles.⁶⁰ He was evidently no longer in the same prime physical condition that he had been during the Hayden years, subsequent field trips here and there notwithstanding. Nor was James Stevenson for that matter. He was suffering from a "peculiar and distressing" illness known as "mountain fever," which he contracted in 1885. Stevenson died the following year in New York City.⁶¹

The back injury aside, this trip allowed Holmes to resume and extend his studies of the pueblos in the region south of Abiquiu, the southernmost point he had reached in 1875, as well as add further to the Smithsonian's already impressive collection of pottery remains. However, his sketch map of the upper Jemez Valley and descriptions of the pueblo ruins in the area would not appear in print for another eighteen years. Holmes's original intention was to return to the Jemez Valley for more intensive study. But when that proved impossible owing to other commitments, he finally made his notes available in order to "place them on record for convenience of reference in connection with the preparation of measures for the preservation of antiquities by the departments of the Government having control of the public lands."⁶² By this time, the preservation movement, led, in part, by Edgar Lee Hewett of the Archaeological Institute of America, was in full swing. In fact, in 1906, Theodore Roosevelt signed the Antiquities Bill into law. The period between the exploration of the West's archaeological treasures and the move to preserve them from a civilization that was moving in on every front—a time that Holmes's career fully encompassed as well as highlighted—was, in hindsight, remarkably brief.

9

The Death and Rebirth of Pleistocene Man

THE TRANSITION FROM EXPLORATION to preservation was but one of many developments that occurred during America's modernization from 1877 to 1920, signifying a movement that historian Robert Wiebe has called the "search for order."[1] Another important theme of this time was the professionalization of the sciences. This was an involved process that among other things established scientific authority in a democratic culture. Holmes, who was particularly zealous in this endeavor, took on the Herculean task of trying to rid American archaeology of the fanciful, bizarre, and decidedly unscientific explanations for the ruins and monuments found throughout the Americas. A good example of Holmes's efforts along these lines was the article he prepared on the Great Serpent Mound in his native Ohio that appeared in December 1886 in the weekly *Science, An Illustrated Journal*. He visited the famous site in the company of the bureau's mound expert, Cyrus Thomas, probably earlier that year. After dismissing the classic work of Ephraim George Squire and Edwin Hamilton Davis and writers such as F. W. Putnam for their "omissions," "over-elaboration," and unwarranted speculations, Holmes proceeded to offer his own highly reductionist interpretation of the "origin and significance" of the mound and its peculiar features.[2]

Noting that the religious "use of the serpent by our aboriginal races has been well-nigh universal," Holmes concluded that the serpent mound was yet another, if extraordinary, example of these "superstitious delineations."[3] Hence, to learn what the serpent probably meant to the mound builders, one had to look no further than the religion, symbolism, and myths of the ancient or modern Indians, rather than to more exotic sources of symbolism such as Oriental philosophy, as some had argued. Since it was a matter of degree, the choice did not seem to matter particularly. Holmes believed, in good unifor-mitarian fashion, that until it could be proven otherwise the mound builders of Ohio, like the cliff builders of the Southwest, were the ancestors of the modern Indians of the area—a view Thomas shared and one that Powell's bureau would, by 1892, officially adopt.[4] The increasingly outspoken role that the federal government assumed, incidentally, in arbitrating scientific "truth" in the closing years of the nineteenth century was impressive and prepared the way for a much more expansive role in the next century. Powell's failure to place the settling of the American West on a scientific basis is known better than his successes in other areas.

Holmes also argued that the idea for the serpent mound was probably sug-gested to an ancient "Sylvan prophet" by the topography of the headland (overlooking Brush Creek) on which it was built. "Having the idea of a great serpent in the mind," Holmes observed, "one is at once struck with the re-markable contour of rock, which readily assumes the appearance of a colossal reptile lifting its front from the bed of the stream."[5] He sketched the head-land, omitting the trees that obscured the view, to reveal the outline of a great serpent, although not without effort of the imagination. Through these means, Holmes was able to demonstrate to the world of science that there was nothing mysterious about the Great Serpent Mound. The site was simply an unusually large outdoor shrine, that nature herself had suggested, to the "great serpent manito."[6] In flawless symmetry, Holmes's separation of embel-lishment from illustration mirrored his denigration of grand theorizing and amateur speculations unless they were solidly grounded in scientific fact.

This strong tendency to correct errors of fact and disabuse fanciful notions, which crept into Holmes's writings during the 1880s, had its origin in his mu-seum work. One of the vexing problems with which he had to contend as honorary curator of pottery at the National Museum, at least since his trip to Mexico in 1884, was the passing of forgeries or what he called "spurious an-tiquities" as genuine articles. It was not a big step from this crusade to clean up the trade in fake artifacts to undertake another crusade to put an end to the uncritical acceptance of stone implements as "paleolithic."

A growing number of American scientists and museum men, including Thomas Wilson, who was also a curator at the National Museum, accepted the existence of an Old Stone Age in the Americas that paralleled the Old Stone Age in Europe. This group was not about to give Europe a monopoly on the world's cavemen. They therefore used the term *paleolith* to identify crudely made stone artifacts that appeared to resemble the paleolithic artifacts uncovered in the lands across the water. Unlike the makers of fake artifacts, however, these individuals were not trying to deceive the public, or anybody else for that matter.[7] They came to their conclusions honestly. But not everyone agreed with them.

In the great debate over the existence of an American paleolithic man, Powell turned to Holmes in 1889 to settle the matter, just as he charged Cyrus Thomas with the task of refuting the theory that the mound builders were a "lost" race, instead of the ancestors of modern Native Americans. Indeed, Powell thought that the problem was so important to the credibility of American anthropology that he assigned Holmes to work on the problem full time.[8] Accordingly, Holmes resigned his position on June 20, 1889 as assistant geologist and illustrator at the USGS and assumed the position of archaeologist at the Bureau of American Ethnology.[9] Intent on focusing much of his formidable energies on the problem, Holmes took over the archaeological fieldwork of the bureau and, over the next three years, became the foremost authority in the country on the antiquity of humans in North America.[10]

One of the hallmarks of Holmes's work was the effective use he made of geology in solving the paleolithic problem. In his discussion of sites ranging from New Jersey to California, which appeared in a number of papers, Holmes demonstrated how important it was to take into account the plastic and mutable nature of the earth's surface before drawing any conclusions about the antiquity of tools found at a given site. Holmes warned:

> The superficial formations from which the evidence has been and must be derived are treacherous custodians of the records intrusted to their keeping. The waters uncover, transport, intermingle, and redeposit the traces of man's presence; ice scores deeply into the surface, likewise destroying the normal sequence; the winds sweep the sands into deceptive semblance of stratification, burying and uncovering and burying again the relics of all periods, imposing thus on the unwary student false and confusing chronologies; gravity with persistent activity carries down and ever down, rearranging in utmost disorder; forests are uprooted, dragging up the deeply buried records and letting down the superficial into their place; and man and beast are ever at work digging and boring and preparing the ground for abundant crops of misleading observations and erroneous interpretations.[11]

Also, making "analogies of form," in which New World tools were compared with their supposedly Old World and glacial age counterparts, was by itself, Holmes persuasively argued, not compelling evidence. He insisted that "paleoliths" be considered in geological context and that the evidence advanced by the proponents of a glacial man in America pass "competent tests of verity."[12] Although the question at hand was the age of stone tools, Holmes used this controversy to push American archaeology to establish very conservative standards of evidence. He also broke down the kinds of data acceptable to archaeology—a broadly conceived subfield of anthropology—into nine categories: historical, traditional, biological, cultural, geological, paleontological, mineralogical, geographical, and astronomical. In determining the antiquity of man in the Americas, Holmes deemed the geological category, an area in which he was a recognized expert, the most important.[13]

Outside government science and from the vantage point of the Peabody Museum of Archaeology and Ethnology at Harvard, the scientist and museum builder Frederick W. Putnam, who was a cautious believer in the great antiquity of early man, watched with dismay Holmes's progress on the paleolithic problem. In a letter written on July 5, 1892, Putnam summed up his observations to Holmes with the opening remark: "You seem to be annihilating Paleolithic man."[14] This view was widely shared in the scientific community, if not so forcefully expressed. Indeed, Holmes became almost obsessed with his investigations, yet he never opposed the possibility of a Pleistocene, or even Tertiary, man in America, just the evidence to date in support thereof.

Holmes may have been assigned the paleolithic problem, but over the next ten years he made it his own. His criticisms of those with whom he disagreed could be pointed, even severe, although Holmes's behavior remained perfectly civil and courteous during face-to-face encounters with his opponents, such as Thomas Wilson of the National Museum; George Frederick Wright, professor of the relations of science and religion at the Oberlin Theological Seminary; and Charles C. Abbott, a physician and amateur naturalist and archaeologist who enjoyed Putnam's encouragement and support. Wright wrote to Holmes that "I wish all the controversialists would be as courteous as you and I have been; and we owe it to truth to take some pains to secure respectful treatment in the discussion of such weighty questions as are before us."[15] William John McGee, a close friend of Powell who, like Holmes, came to ethnology by way of geology, was not so courteous and, in taking sides with Holmes, could apparently make things unpleasantly personal—behavior that was altogether unprofessional.[16] McGee, incidentally, initially supported Charles C. Abbott's work on "paleoliths," which Abbott had found in the gravels near Trenton, New Jersey, in the Delaware Valley; but in the late 1880s McGee started having reservations, and then went on the attack against proponents of the idea that peoples were in the Americas before the end of the last Ice Age or in paleolithic times.[17]

After 1899, when skeletal evidence received greater attention, Holmes was joined by the Czech-born scientist Aleš Hrdlička, a much more effective ally than McGee. Aleš Hrdlička, who was known in Washington, according to archaeologist Alfred Vincent Kidder, as "Ales and Hardliquor," had a reputation for meanness but was greatly respected. He also evidently had a sense of humor. As head of the National Museum's division of physical anthropology, Hrdlička once reported that "we have more than 15,000 skulls, but no brains," to which Holmes penciled in the margin, "Of this, I've regretfully been aware for many years."[18] Holmes and Hrdlička became as close to each other over the years as they became intimidating to others. They would form a formidable team and dominate the antiquity debate from the nation's capital until the Folsom discovery in 1927.

The Piney Branch of Washington, D.C.

For a man used to traveling to the western territories every summer to conduct fieldwork, Holmes found that his study of early man required that he walk no farther than the slopes of Piney Branch, about a mile and a quarter from his Washington residence. Piney Branch, a small stream, made its way through a lovely little valley, green and thickly wooded, just off Rock Creek, which ran south through the District of Columbia before emptying into the Potomac River. Here, in September of 1889, Holmes began a major excavation of the old quarry workshops that he had identified in this vicinity. Despite the extensive time and effort that he put into this archaeological work, his conclusion differed little from what he had already concluded over a decade earlier, after visiting the quarry site at Obsidian Cliff in Yellowstone National Park. That is, the crude hand-shaped tools were not finished tools marking a paleolithic era in American prehistory, but rather instances of numerous failed attempts of native workmen to chip obsidian into more sophisticated tools. And what was true of the volcanic glass rejects of the Yellowstone toolmakers, Holmes argued, was true of the flint, quartz, novaculite, argillite, quartzite, slate, jasper, pipestone, steatite, chert, mica, and other stone counterparts of toolmakers not only at Piney Branch but at many other eastern quarry *and* manufacturing sites.

In 1878, Holmes's observation at Obsidian Cliff was a disconnected fact that was interesting but not meaningful. Now, the idea of rejectage took its place at the center of one of the most persistent and divisive questions in American archaeology—that is, when did humans first arrive in the New World? Holmes used rejectage, in addition to other evidence, as we shall see, to prove that the stone implements being labeled "paleolithic" were, in fact, nothing more than discards of relatively modern Indian workmen, not finished tools of a much earlier, paleolithic stage of cultural development. In this way, it should be noted, Holmes's work on paleoliths had transformed him, by the early 1890s, into America's premier authority on Indian mining—a subject in which his interests in geology and archaeology were joined in perfect matrimony.

To make the case against an American paleolithic man, however, Holmes turned not only to the familiar fields of archaeology and geology, but also to history and to a bold, new method that he, Frank Cushing, and others were developing, that is, the attempt to rediscover the aboriginal methods and techniques through a trial-and-error process of reenactment. By trying to duplicate how ancient stone tools or pottery were originally made, they believed they could unlock the secrets of a forgotten time. They were trying, as W J McGee put it, to "think as the Indian thinks."[19] In so doing, Holmes helped open up another exciting new world, this time of the imagined past, to scientific exploration.

But while Holmes may have tried to think like an Indian, this did not mean he stopped thinking like an American. Indeed, it is remarkable how the Native American miners seemed to share the contemporary qualities of Americans living in the midst of a nation undergoing rapid modernization. Thus, these people were, according to Holmes, industrial and hardworking. Perhaps the best example of this kind of projection or transference is seen in Holmes's article "An Ancient Quarry in Indian Territory." The article was based on field notes, drawings, and photographs, one of which he believed was "the first representation of an aboriginal flaking shop ever brought out." The quarry that he visited in October of 1891 was located seven miles northwest of Seneca, Missouri, on the Peoria reservation, at a site the locals called the "old Spanish mines."[20]

Throughout this piece, Holmes used the language of an industrializing and modernizing America to make sense of what he saw. He therefore referred to "evidences of manufacture," to "mines," "pits," and "shops"; to "management and manipulation" and "work in reduction and manufacture"; to buckhorn "picks," stone "hammers," and to the application of such agencies as fire and water to the production process; to "workmen" and "skilled specialists." And to what end? To the production, he believed, of a wide variety of tools to meet the needs of a clearly industrious people. The New World may not be able to boast of cavemen, but it did produce a race, according to Holmes, who were worthy predecessors of the American people. Interestingly, Holmes noted that frontier whites supposed that this mine must have been operated by the Spanish, rather than by local indigenous peoples, and thus began digs of their own until discovering that there were no precious metals present.[21]

As for the paleolithic problem, Holmes did allow that at the quarry in Indian Territory "occasional specimens, by a semblance of specialization accidentally acquired, have assumed forms characterizing some of the well known types of European paleolithic implements." He convincingly argued, however, that these forms were produced in the shaping process and were "not themselves the subject of the shaping operations." He would make this point repeatedly over the years. As to the question of the age of the artifacts produced at this particular site, Holmes pointed to evidence of recent occupation, such as the light degree of weathering found on the deposits and rejectage and the relatively new forest growth on the site, and then concluded: "Having considered all points, I am strongly impressed with the belief that the period of occupation was not very remote, and that the last work done may come to or very nearly to the occupation of the region by the white man."[22]

Holmes's work on aboriginal mining, however, in which an image of a proto-industrial people emerged, did little to change the image of the Indian as a nomad and hunter and above all as warrior, which was being deeply ingrained in American and European popular culture in the 1880s and 1890s by such entertainments and diversions as the Wild West Shows of Buffalo Bill or Pawnee Bill. And the disconnection between anthropological perspectives and popular views—both products, to be sure, of the same culture—would only widen during the twentieth century with the advent of the cinematic western. As late as the 1960s, American historians still did little to help correct these popular notions. They only refined the point: the historical significance of America's "savages" was not that they were important actors with their own contributions to the broader story of humankind's general ascent. Rather, they posed a flesh-and-blood barrier, which required centuries to overcome, to the westward advance of a supposedly more deserving people. To this day, the image of Native Americans as a people who possessed and physically altered the land to meet their needs, however modestly by modern standards, has yet to replace entirely the very colorful and tragic stereotypes of the past.[23]

If Holmes was unsuccessful in capturing the public imagination with his archaeology, it was not by want of tireless effort or failure to seize opportunities to express his ideas. One such opportunity was the Columbian Exposition in Chicago held in 1893. It allowed him to exhibit "systematically" and for the "first time the arts of mining and quarrying and the manufacture of stone implements by the aborigines."[24] Holmes tried to show scholars as well as the general public that Indian mining was a widespread and, in some cases, an impressive activity. In his words—which appeared in an article the year before the fair, entitled "Modern Quarry Refuse and the Palaeolithic Theory"—although the means were simple (stone tools, wood, bone utensils, and fire) the aborigines were able to penetrate solid beds of rock "to depths often reaching twenty-five feet, and extensive areas were worked over, changing the appearance of valleys and remodeling hills and mountains." At one site in Arkansas, Holmes exclaimed in "astonishment" that "upwards of 100,000 cubic yards of stone had been removed and worked over."[25] Like everything else in America by the 1890s, Indian mining had become a big business.

Holmes's point regarding how unappreciated the magnitude of some of the aboriginal mines received reinforcement during another trip to Mexico that he made in 1899 in the company of his old friends, Clarence E. Dutton and Grove K. Gilbert.[26] At the site of obsidian mines located on the pine-covered *Sierra de las Navajas* or "Mountain of Knives" in the state of Hidalgo, located twelve miles northeast of the city of Pachuca, Holmes was struck by the extensiveness of the native operations. This large site recalled to mind the great quarries at Newark, Ohio and Hot Springs, Arkansas.[27] He wrote:

> The enterprising peoples of the valleys below must have operated the mines vigorously for centuries to have thus worked over hundreds of acres of the mountain side, and so fully and profoundly, moreover, that the deep pittings and heavy ridges of excavated débris are practically continuous for a mile or two in length and cover a width reaching in places possibly half a mile.[28]

His work on Indian quarrying and mining was scientifically significant, Holmes believed, because it would establish "the most important achievements of the native races." Moreover, it was "a work claiming precedence over nearly all others, lying as it does at the very threshold of art and constituting the foundations upon which the superstructure of human culture is built."[29]

Besides Indian Territory and Mexico, Holmes's work on the paleolithic problem, which was the main task at hand, and on the related subject of Indian mining would take him to many other sites far from the nation's capital. During the 1890s, he stopped at sites along a circuit that wound through states located east of the Appalachians in the tidewater province, along the Ohio and Mississippi valleys, around the Great Lakes, and down to the Southwest. The result of this extensive fieldwork was that Holmes was able to shift the terms of the great debate over human antiquity in the New World.

Clearly Holmes enjoyed the funding and resources available to him as a member of the Bureau of American Ethnology, advantages few possessed who were outside of the government. The BAE could render the scientific community and the public a great service; it also had the potential to overwhelm those whose views differed from official policy. This unhealthy situation would soon change with the rise of universities and museums at the end of the nineteenth century, but as of the early 1890s the BAE was a powerful institution that was hard to challenge.

The question, Holmes said in 1892, was not whether a stone implement, if indeed it was a stone implement and not a stone whose tool-like shape occurred naturally, was produced by humans during the Ice Age. The question was whether the artifact was neolithic or post-glacial, which Holmes maintained was far more likely for a variety of reasons, including the fact that several ancient sites continued to be used into historic times. The burden of proof, according to Holmes, was on the supporters of the paleolithic theory to demonstrate that an artifact was *not* neolithic.[30] As he put it, "it must still be shown that they [rude flaked stones] are not neolithic before it can be safely asserted that they are palaeolithic, for the exclusively rude period of flaked art observed in Europe is so extraordinary that its repetition in other countries would approach the marvellous." On reading this article in San Antonio, Texas, Clarence Dutton shot off a letter to him, stating:

> It strikes me as the most level headed article in the anthropologic "racket" I have seen for many a year. Your simple statement of the facts is such as to carry conviction with it by the sheer force of good sense and to resist it looks like "biting a file." I wonder I never thought of that view of the situation before. We always do wonder when a simple sensible explanation comes forward to take the place of a complex overloaded hypothesis and no better evidence is wanted of the strength of a hypothesis than its perfect simplicity and naturalness.

He ended the letter on a high note of support: "Keep the ball a-rolling my dear fellow; you have made a good strike here and I rejoice to see it."[31]

Holmes kept the ball "a-rolling." The next year he stressed the importance of having an expert command of field geology in order to interpret a site correctly. This was especially true, Holmes declared, now that he had separated the paleolithic problem into two very different questions: 1) "Is there evidence of a glacial man in eastern America?" and 2) "Is there evidence of a palaeolithic or primal stage or period of culture?" Holmes thought you could have either one without necessarily having the other. Given these two areas of concern, Holmes asserted that "it would appear that until students of the great questions of chronology and culture acquire a thorough scientific knowledge of geology as well as early phases of human art the discussions in which they indulge can be of little real value."[32] This left a person with Holmes's background, by Holmes's own definition—as Joan Mark has noted—as the only one fully qualified to study the matter.[33]

Holmes put these words into practice and prepared two major papers: "Natural History of Flaked Stone Implements" (1894) and "Stone Implements of the Potomac-Chesapeake Tidewater Province (1897)," the latter of which won the Loubat Quinquennial Prize for 1898 that was worth one thousand dollars in cash. These century-old "lithic papers" were, according to anthropology professors David J. Meltzer and Robert C. Dunnell, "surprisingly modern works."[34] The second-place prize went to Franz Boas for his 1897 study "The Social Organization and Secret Society of the Kwakiutl Indians." Educated in Germany and with a face scarred by dueling, Boas was a brilliant anthropologist with a talent for feuding.[35] He would one day become one of America's great anthropologists and in the meantime, as we shall see, would cross swords with Holmes on several occasions.

Meltzer and Dunnell found that in "Natural History of Flaked Stone Implements" Holmes "grappled with problems of equifinality, of differentiating artificial from naturally flaked stone tools and patterns of wear . . . of sorting finished from unfinished implements." These men also noted that Holmes "appreciated and detailed the effects of different raw material types on stone tool production." In "Stone Implements of the Potomac-Chesapeake of the Tidewater Province," Meltzer and Dunnell noted that Holmes had "distinguished between local and exotic sources of stone . . . the movement of stone by direct acquisition, exchange, or natural processes . . . the differential 'distribution' (we would term it curation) of 'domestic' and 'chase' implements by type of site in relation to distance from the stone source . . . [he] spoke of direct percussion, indirect percussion, and pressure flaking . . . of refitting cores . . . [and] of what we now term the 'Frison effect' . . . and, of preform ('blade') caches."[36]

Holmes's anticipation of modern archaeological issues aside, what is particularly striking about Holmes's "Natural History" paper from a historical perspective is the way in which he treats stone implements as living "things" that are virtually independent from the agency of man. In stating his purpose, Holmes wrote:

> An analysis, not yet fully perfected, of flaked stone art has been attempted, in which much weight is given to the idea that art should be studied as natural

history is studied, that objects of art must not be treated as independent individuals merely, or as groups of individuals associated by superficial characters for convenience of description, but as phenomena to be rightly understood only through their relationships with the whole scheme of nature, viewed in the light of evolution.

In a diagram, he illustrated the point by showing the "Steps in the Evolution of Species," in this case inanimate arrowheads, both in terms of "progress in time and culture" and in the "Development of Individual of highest type," complete with missing links. Rows of arrowheads were depicted in ascending morphological order, starting from the unshaped boulder. Man was, of course, implied in this scheme, but little more.

In form as well as content, Holmes was at his best in "Stone Implements of the Potomac-Chesapeake Tidewater Province." This 1897 work was a monograph rather than a paper. It was well organized; clearly written in his lean, vigorous style; brilliantly, even lavishly, illustrated, not only with drawings but numerous photographs as well; and, finally, thoroughly researched. Holmes examined every facet of the stone-tool industry—from quarrying to manufacture, and finally to distribution. He also conducted personal experiments replicating the processes of boulder flaking that went even further to support his contention that American "paleoliths" were nothing more than rejects. The results of these experiments were important, Holmes claimed, because he was able to determine

> that every implement resembling the final form here described, and every blade-shaped projectile point made from a boulder or similar bit of rock not already approximate in shape, must pass through the same or nearly same stages of development, leaving the same wasters, whether shaped today, yesterday, or a million years ago; whether in the hands of the civilized, the barbarous, or the savage man.[37]

Holmes paid a physical price, however, in learning to "think as the Indian thinks." In his words, "I was unfortunately prevented from carrying out these experiments as fully as desirable by permanently disabling my left arm in attempting to flake a bowlder [*sic*] of very large size."[38] It would be hard to find a better example of the seriousness with which Holmes and his contemporaries took the scientific enterprise.

Holmes's scholarship and dedication aside, what stands out about Holmes's "Stone Implements" was his success in establishing the guidelines for future exploration and in providing the basis on which discoveries could be deemed significant. This was Holmes's real contribution to the antiquity controversy and it dramatically illustrated the position of power he had assumed in the scientific community, even if his views were never completely accepted by the "experts." "The main question at issue," he wrote, was: "Do these rude objects form part of the remains left by the peoples of the region known to us historically—the Algonquian tribes and their neighbors—as their associations in a general way indicate; or do they belong to an earlier race of much lower culture as suggested by the fact that somewhat analogous forms, found in other parts of the world, characterize the art of very ancient and primitive peoples?"[39] Holmes had already answered this question, but now had a prize-winning study to back up his position.

In addition to asking the questions and establishing "competent tests of verity," Holmes had for several years been serving notice to those outside or on the edges of the scientific community, to Miss Franc E. Babbitt, a teacher who collected relics in the vicinity of Little Falls, Minnesota, and hundreds of other such amateur arrowhead collectors like her.[40] He made it clear that the day of the amateur in American science had passed. "The fact is," he wrote, "that the field has, up to this time, been occupied mainly by amateurs who have not mastered the necessary fundamental branches of the science. The work done is mainly their work, the literature produced is mainly their literature, and the world has received its impression from this source." At the same time that he was distancing himself from amateurs he condescended to allow that it was "necessary that all departments of investigation should pass through this novitiate or formative stage and the world of science must look with lenience upon the mistakes of the period." In 1893, the same year that Frederick Jackson Turner read a paper at the Columbian Exposition in which he declared that the American frontier had closed, Holmes, in a like-minded manner, declared that

> the time has now come for a change—for the opening of an era when scientific acquirements of the highest possible order shall be brought to bear upon these questions. Anthropologists are now to unite with geologists in investigating the early history of man and his culture, just as the geologist has been for years assisting the biologist in unfolding the history of living things.[41]

Change was in the air and Holmes brilliantly used the controversy over early man to separate laymen from professionals. The role Holmes assumed here was perhaps necessary, but not very attractive. That he had received his scientific credentials in a western saddle, however, rather than in an eastern classroom never seems to have been an issue.

For all of that, Holmes did grant that a number of those on the other side of the early-man controversy were "competent and reputable observers." In the fall of 1898, he went with McGee to the old gold fields or auriferous gravels of California, where the celebrated relic known as "Calaveras Skull" was discovered. The skull was claimed to have been found under 132 feet of volcanic ash, a story accepted by Josiah Dwight Whitney, director of the State Geological Survey of California, after he personally investigated the matter and interviewed the miners who were at the scene. Whitney then proposed a theory that during Tertiary times California had been the home of an ancient race of men. Clarence King's discovery of a pestle found in situ in "the tufaceous deposits under the lava cap" of Tuolumne Table Mountain in 1869 added considerable weight to Whitney's Tertiary Man. For the previous thirty-three years, the Calaveras Skull had been kept in Cambridge, Massachusetts, under the care of Frederick W. Putnam. In Holmes's published review of California's Tertiary Man, he judiciously listed the arguments for and against great antiquity, but believed that Whitney, King, and Putnam had the weaker case.[42]

Holmes's position on the early-man question did not come without cost. He found himself the object of criticism from the "defenders of the faith," as he called them, who took issue with his characterization of their work as amateurish or belonging to what he referred to as the "old archaeology." But almost from the beginning of the debate Holmes took a rather smug position:

> If my "rash" assertions, hitherto made, respecting the nature of the testimony relied upon to establish a glacial, paleolithic man in America, lead finally to a just estimate of the real evidence and to the establishment of a firm basis for future operations in this great field, I shall feel amply repaid, notwithstanding the storms of sharp words and the streamlets of doggerel the publication of these views seems destined to call forth.[43]

Holmes, in fact, relished his appointed role as keeper of standards, and over the years his position on this point only hardened. In 1918, twenty-nine years after he entered the fray, he wrote in the journal *Science,* as he had on many other occasions:

> It is manifestly a serious duty of the archaeologist and the historian of man to continue to challenge every reported discovery suggesting the geological antiquity of the race in America, and to expose the dangerous ventures of little experienced or biased students in a field which they have not made fully their own.[44]

In short, Holmes became an imposing force, and in his campaign against the use of the term *paleolith,* his use of geology was particularly effective, indeed devastating. The use of history was no less important to his line of argument. Holmes drew on the writings of the Jamestown colonist John Smith to help him locate Indian village sites in the early 1890s, just as Heinrich Schliemann had turned to Homer's *Iliad* to guide him to the ancient city of Troy.[45] Holmes found that John Smith had actually observed a Powhatan toolmaker at work. Smith wrote: "His arrow-head he quickly maketh with a little bone which he ever weareth at his brasert."[46] Moreover, Holmes discovered that historical documents and the art of first or early encounters between Europeans and Indians were not only treasure maps to archaeological sites but also rich sources of ethnological detail.

In an explanatory text for a diorama of quarrymen at work in Piney Branch, installed at the National Museum years later in 1911, Holmes indicated that he had based the costumes on one such source of ethnological information—the illustrations of John White, the English artist of the short-lived Roanoke Colony.[47] Holmes, however, had referred to the work of White, Joseph Francois Lafitau, George Catlin, and many others much earlier than 1911, and probably drew on such sources when he was designing a diorama representing a similar, if not largely identical, scene for the Chicago Exposition of 1893. Although Holmes's use of history in archaeology was not new, he was one of the first scientists to recognize the ethnological value of colonial and early American illustration and to treat art as memory.

Holmes's success in using documents and art to guide him to, and inform him about, abandoned Indian villages and quarries led him to contend that the so-called paleoliths found at these historic sites might be only three hundred years old. If that were so, Thomas Wilson asked sarcastically in 1894, why stop at the time of contact? Why not argue that the quarry at Piney Branch was even of more recent origin, "that [it] might have . . . been made while digging boulders with which to pave Pennsylvania Avenue."[48] Holmes—who came to believe that man had arrived in the New World probably no more than several millennia ago, although he granted the possibility of a period of human occupancy dating back to "the closing stages of the glacial period in the northern United States"—was undeterred by such questions. He knew that the opposition was on the defensive and that henceforth he would largely control the debate. As he half-mockingly put it years later, in 1919:

A Japanese teapot from the alluvial deposits of a Virginia valley found at a depth of 25 feet may not prove, in the hands of even the most inexpert and credulous, an element of danger, since its origin and period are not liable to misinterpretation, but a rudely shaped implement or a reject of manufacture of recent origin found at an equal depth may in incompetent hands take its place in the literature of archaeology as proof of great antiquity and an unknown race low in the culture scale.[49]

Of greater significance, the triumph of Holmes's views influenced an entire generation of anthropologists to focus their undivided attention on the modern Indian, rather than on what Holmes called the "antiquity phantom." So complete, in fact, was Holmes's victory that by 1925, the year of the famous Scopes Trial (or Monkey Trial), he included the question of early man along with those other dubious "theories" that proposed

numerous pre-Columbian discoveries of America; ancient races preceding the Indians; of civilizations antedating those of the Nile and the Euphrates; of glyphic inscriptions miles in length that await a translator; of skeletons of men twelve feet in length; of dinosaurs and ibexes engraved on rock surfaces; of the ruins of a Chinese city; of America as the probable birthplace of humanity; and so on, *ad infinitum*.[50]

In a letter dated June 6, 1925, to Edgar L. Hewett, now director of the San Diego Museum, Holmes complained about the increasing volume of what he labeled "archaeological jazz." Hewett was in full sympathy and thought that given what was being passed off as science, William Jennings Bryan, John T. Scope's prosecutor in the Monkey Trial and three-time Democratic nominee for the U.S. presidency, was beginning to sound more like an ally of sober-minded science than an enemy of the theory of evolution. Hewett then suggested that if shysters could be disbarred and quacks could be turned out of medicine, why should not scientific fabricators be treated in a similar manner.[51]

In a like vein, F. W. Sardeson, a geologist from Minneapolis wrote Holmes: "Among my friends here in the City is the Rev. W. B. Riley who with the Hon. W. J. Bryan has been giving the Evolutionists a thoughtful hour. My suspiceons [sic] are that most of the irritation to the Fundimentalists [sic] comes from this notariety [sic] humbug and commercialized exageration [sic] and not from the kind of science that you and I stand for."[52] Holmes could not have agreed more. He had been fighting bad science and popular fancies dressed up as science for decades, attacking those who built grand edifices on "faulty observations and unwarranted conclusions," as he put the matter in 1910. But he always had faith that with enough persistence and patience, reason and good science would ultimately prevail.[53]

Without creditable evidence to the contrary, Holmes understandably became convinced that glacial man was nothing more than a "phantom" conjured up by the overheated imaginations of romantics or, more than likely in his estimation, crackpots. So convinced was he of the rightness of his views that in the spring of 1925 he became involved in a campaign to have Piney Branch set aside as a monument, before the forces of suburbanization obliterated the site. Holmes hoped to adorn a section of the Piney Branch with a bronze statue based on a life-sized plaster group that he had made of five quarrymen and toolmakers at work.

In letters dated April 6 and April 29 to Clarence O. Sherrill, director of the Federal Office of Public Buildings and Public Parks of the National Capital, Holmes made the following case for a monument. He explained that the site was significant because of its importance as a quarry to the Indians who had dwelled in the Washington area long before the arrival of "foreign and merciless invaders," who drove the Indians out of the area by the late seventeenth century. Holmes made an uncharacteristically impassioned plea to Sherrill:

> shall we go on selling and buying and selling again the hills and valleys of their birthright, amassing fortunes upon fortunes, without thought of their former existence or their sacrifice? In the world's history races have succeeded races in possession of the garden spots of the world, and are we to follow the example of the barbarians of the past? Are we the barbarians of the present? Or shall we preserve the Piney Branch site, erecting thereon a monument, a memorial, to show the world that we are not utter ingrates?

Worked up, Holmes went on to claim, rather brazenly, that Piney Branch was also the site of his own greatest scientific triumph—the explosion of the theory that man existed in America during late Pleistocene times. In his words:

> When, forty years ago, I began the study of the ancient remains of the eastern states, the archeologists of Washington, New York, Boston and other cities were gathering rudely chipped stones such as are found on the slopes of Piney Branch. They filled museum cases with them and labelled "American Paleolithic Implements," and the archeologists of the world accepted without hesitation the view that these chipped stones were the implements of a race preceding the Indian, a race of glacial age, that, in the scale of culture had never risen above the use of rude stone tools. I examined carefully these spec-

imens and visited the Piney Branch sites and soon reached the conclusion that this was all wrong, and that these chipped stones were not implements at all, but rejectage of the difficult chipping process, the failures of the Indian blade maker. The successful blades, not one in twenty attempts, were carried to the villages and finished to serve as weapons of war and the chase, and in the various primitive arts. For a score of years controversy over this interpretation raged, but there is today, so far as I know, not in any museum of the world, a single American shaped stone of any kind labelled as belonging to the glacial period or to a stone age culture corresponding with that of the Old World.[54]

Thus, Holmes's argument broke down into two parts: Washington should have a monument because it was the right thing to do; and in this long controversy over human antiquity, he was right all along. Sherrill was apparently sympathetic to the idea, but the monument to the Indians' industry and to Holmes's scientific achievement was not meant to be. Congressional action was delayed and by 1928 the attractiveness of the areas surrounding the site and Holmes's hopes were ruined, buried as they were under piles of yellow clay and debris deposited on a daily basis by truckers who pulled up their huge vehicles to the edge of the slopes above.[55] According to Meltzer and Dunnell, the Piney Branch quarry itself, however, was spared and still exists in Rock Creek Park.[56]

Folsom, New Mexico

In his late seventies, Holmes was clearly a man trying to secure his place in history. His work on paleoliths had profoundly influenced the study of man in the Americas. As of 1925, despite one challenge after another, especially the claims made at Vero, Florida, on the Atlantic Coast, which he answered without even bothering to investigate the matter firsthand, fully trusting the judgment of his good friend and colleague at the Smithsonian, Aleš Hrdlička, who did. The Vero finds (human skeletal remains in association with extinct Pleistocene fauna), which were announced in July 1916, had engaged not amateurs, but precisely the kind of professional men on whom Holmes had always insisted, like geologists Elias Howard Sellards, Rollin T. Chamberlain, and T. Wayland Vaughan; archaeologist George Grant MacCurdy; paleontologist Oliver P. Hay; and physical anthropologist Hrdlička. (Oliver P. Hay, incidentally, had served as assistant curator of ichthyology at the Field Columbian Museum while Holmes was there.) The only thing lacking in the debate over this site was agreement over the meaning of the evidence.[57] Holmes was not surprised at the lack of consensus and went on believing that his stand on the question of early man would withstand the test of time, despite the renewed defense of the Florida finds in 1925 by Frederic B. Loomis, a geologist at Amherst College.[58]

In 1925, the same year that Holmes wrote to Sherrill about turning the Piney Branch site into a monument, Fred J. Howarth, a cattle inspector, and Carl Schwachheim, a blacksmith, both of Raton, New Mexico, found animal fossils exposed in the bank of an arroyo on the upper sources of the Cimarron River, near the small town of Folsom.[59] They notified Jesse Dade Figgins, the director of the Colorado Museum of Natural History in Denver's City Park, of their find and then sent him samples of bone. Figgins and his staff determined that the bones were from the *Bison antiquus* (*occidentalis*) and a "large deerlike member of the *Cervidae*."[60] Figgins was so impressed with what he saw and hopeful that "evidence of man's antiquity in America might be uncovered" that he and Harold J. Cook, a part-time paleontologist who was an honorary curator at Colorado Museum, visited the arroyo in April 1926.[61] Excited by the possibilities the site offered, they organized an excavation party under the supervision of Figgins's son, Frank. The party took to the field that summer. During the course of the season, several arrowheads were found, resembling other arrowheads, deemed to be older, located in the bank of Lone Wolf Creek, near Colorado, Texas. But these points at Folsom had "been dislodged from the matrix," and thus Jesse Figgins knew that these specimens would fail to pass the rigorous standards imposed by Holmes and Hrdlička, whom he referred to in his correspondence as the "anthropologists." Toward the close of the 1926 season, however, another point had been uncovered. As Figgins described the discovery in *Natural History* (submitted on February 22, 1927):

> This artifact, too, had been dislodged before its presence was suspected, but at the spot from which it came, the tool struck a hard substance, which, upon being exposed, proved to be a wedge-shaped fragment of flint, approximately one-quarter of an inch in width by three-quarters of an inch in length, lying in a fixed position, adjacent to a bison rib. This was removed without being disturbed.[62]

Oliver P. Hay, a strong advocate of human antiquity in America, believed that Figgins's evidence would at long last "clinch the subject of Pleistocene man." Moreover, Hay thought the Folsom finds would lead to a "showdown" with Holmes and Hrdlička, the prospect of which he personally relished given their earlier dismissal of his views in regard to the Vero finds.[63] Figgins, on the other hand, was nervous about taking on the archaeological establishment, that is, Holmes and Hrdlička. But with Hay's strong support and armed, after all, with the same weapons that had brought down a Pleistocene megafauna, Figgins braced himself for an onslaught of criticism following the publication of his article in *Natural History*. Expressing his concerns, if not fears, to Barnum Brown of New York's American Museum of Natural History, he wrote, on February 16, 1927:

> From what I gather, Hrdlicka is waiting and preparing for an attack on what I have to say. He has made some comments suggestive of his purpose to attack on the grounds that a scientist was not present when the artifacts were uncovered . . . I have no patience whatever with that type of man and my comments in the introduction are, of course, directed at him with the wilful purpose of stirring up all the venom in his system.[64]

The person to whom Figgins referred in his article "The Antiquity of Man in America" was indeed a thinly veiled Hrdlička. Figgins opened the piece with the statement:

> When we analyze the technical opposition to the belief that man has inhabited America over an enormous period of time, we find it is not only restricted to an individual minority, but it also appears to be traceable to the results of a too circumscribed viewpoint, — a failure to appreciate properly *all* the evidence, and a seeming unwillingness to accept the conclusions of authorities engaged in related branches of investigation.

And lest there be any question as to the identity of the individual minority, Figgins added:

> This appears to be very well illustrated by individuals learned in physical anthropology, comparative craniology and racial relationships. The chief denials of man's antiquity in America appear to have their origin in those sources of investigation.[65]

Figgins went on in the same letter to Brown: "Naturally, Hrdlička would select me for attack and since I tried my best to push as far under his hide as I am hopeful *Natural History* will permit, it is obvious he will dig me as deep as he is capable of and I am suffering for just that. Of course, I would not ask *Natural History* to publish the reply, as it does not make use of asbestos paper and case-hardened type—something that will be needed."[66]

Several months later, in another letter to Brown dated June 8, 1927, Figgins referred to a series of meetings he had that winter in Washington, D.C., with the "anthropologists, ethnologists, archaeologists and anarchists of the National Museum," meetings that included face-to-face encounters with

Hrdliçka and Holmes. But as a result of these dramatic encounters, Figgins "came away with the belief that they will not attack the accounts of our finds."[67] Moreover, Figgins's defensiveness regarding rumors that Hrdlička would attack him on the grounds that a scientist was not present at the Folsom excavations had changed to one of agreement. He wrote that Hrdlička's "sole complaint was that we did not call in outside scientists to study the artifacts in situ . . . I have no complaint to make regarding such a belief. Rather, I agree with it, had the artifacts been reported before they were removed." Figgins's estimation of Hrdlička had also changed: "Altogether, my interview with Dr. Hrdlička was very satisfactory though I did not get the impression he had changed his opinions."[68]

If Hrdlička "retained" Figgins's "respect," the scientists at the National Museum, especially Holmes, "excited" his "disgust." According to Figgins, after meeting with Hrdlička, Hrdlička "suggested that we take the artifacts," which Figgins had brought with him in a box, "into Dr. Holmes and omit introducing" Figgins as the Colorado Museum director. Hrdlička also suggested that the two men "say nothing regarding the locality from which the artifacts were taken." Figgins then reported to Brown and to Hay what happened next:

> Dr. Holmes took a brief look and declared they were "undoubtedly foreign— European—both in material and workmanship." He got no farther, as Dr. Hrdlicka [*sic*] broke in with an introduction of myself and the statement that they were the artifacts from Texas and New Mexico. I managed to retain a fairly straight face and dignified demeanor. So much for the great Dr. Holmes and all his hedging failed to overcome the effect of his first statement. Dr. Hrdlicka [*sic*] was no[t] happy.. . . Holmes finally declared he would never believe man and these prehistoric materials were contemporaneous,—that man hunted these mammals—until arrowheads were found embedded in the bones of the latter in such manner as to prohibit question that they were shot into them while the animal was living. Not having arrowheads so embedded, I left Dr. Holmes happy in his determination to oppose any and all evidence likely to interfere with his personal theories.. . . I had expected an aggressive attitude [in Washington] but found one of defense—pitiful in its weakness.[69]

As it turned out, Figgins met Holmes and Hrdlička's criteria, namely, that a scientist, rather than a collector or amateur, oversee the excavation and that an arrowhead be found "embedded in the bones."

On September 29, 1927, Figgins wrote to Hay telling him that when a party from the Colorado Museum discovered another arrowhead at Folsom, it was left undisturbed and Hrdlička himself was invited by telegram to inspect the find personally and in situ.[70] The BAE archaeologist Frank H. H. Roberts Jr., who was attending the first Southwest Archaeological Conference in nearby Pecos, New Mexico, was directed to come in his stead. This is Roberts's account of what transpired:

> Arriving at the fossil pit, on September 2, [the writer] found Director Figgins, several members of the Colorado Museum board, and Dr. Barnum Brown, of the American Museum of Natural History, New York, on the ground. The point, which became the pattern and furnished the name for the type, had just been uncovered by Dr. Brown. There was no question but that here was the evidence of an authentic association. The point was still embedded in the matrix between two of the ribs of the animal skeleton.[71]

A. V. Kidder, who was also attending the Pecos conference, came two days later and "agreed that the association could not be questioned."[72]

In December, Roberts and Barnum Brown presented their findings at the meeting of the American Anthropological Association, which was held in Andover, Massachusetts. After nearly forty years, it was not surprising that Holmes's influence was still in evidence. Roberts reported that "doubt" and skepticism prevailed, that "numerous explanations were offered to show that the points might have gotten into such an association without actually being contemporaneous with the bison remains," that "several mentioned that points of that type were numerous in collections from certain mound sites, from village sites in New York State, and elsewhere, and for that reason could not be very old," and "others insisted that, although they accepted the conclusions on the genuineness of the finds, there must be some mistake about the antiquity of the animal remains."[73]

Roberts reported that not until 1928 did skepticism turn into belief. During that summer, another party was at work at Folsom, which included Barnum Brown, Clark Wissler, and a number of graduate students. When more points were found in situ with bison bones, more telegrams were sent. By now everyone knew the drill. According to Roberts:

> This time numerous specialists—archaeologists, paleontologists, and geologists—rushed to see the evidence. The consensus of the informal conference held at the site was that this constituted the most important contribution yet made to American archeology. Some of the most skeptical critics of the year before became enthusiastic converts. The Folsom find was accepted as a reliable indication that man was present in the Southwest at an earlier period than was previously supposed.[74]

The Folsom discoveries predictably created a stir, but eventually led to the legitimization of a new field of inquiry—paleo-Indian studies.[75] Historians, however, were slow to recognize the revolutionary significance of Folsom Man; their disciplinary blinders were firmly fixed and in place. Walter Prescott Webb's treatment of Indians in *The Great Plains* (1931), for instance, which was an otherwise innovative study, remained fixed in the older historiographical tradition that assumed a relatively recent arrival of humans in the New World; a tradition that would inform historical writing for decades to follow as well.[76] Thus, Webb made no mention in the chapter "The Plains Indians" that the meat served at the first Texas Bar-B-Q was probably mammoth, musk oxen, or some other late Pleistocene mammal. Instead, Webb's story began with modern Indians whom he discussed as a "barrier" to European advancement, and in this view, of course, he was hardly alone. Webb also discussed Native Americans in the equally static—and again generally accepted—terms of linguistics, race, and cultural regions. These classifications had been firmly established by the BAE and codified in Frederick Webb Hodge's two-part *Handbook of American Indians North of Mexico* (1907, 1910), a highly influential work that Holmes oversaw after he became chief of the BAE in 1902, following Powell's death. As a result, Webb missed the opportunity to include the Folsom point in his otherwise exhaustive discussion of technological responses to the environment of the Great Plains.[77]

At the same time that Webb was preparing to go to press, a fellow University of Texas faculty member, Elias Howard Sellards, wrote to Holmes on March 6, 1930. Sellards, was an economic geologist who, along with Oliver Hay, had been involved in the Vero controversy as an advocate that humans were present in Florida in Pleistocene times. What Sellards wanted to know now was where Holmes stood on the question of the antiquity of man in light of the recent discoveries "in this part of the country."[78] To which Holmes, who was now eighty-four, responded:

> I have now dropped the matter entirely, and am perfectly willing to accept the conclusions of the skilled men who are carrying on researches with the full knowledge of the problems and the dangers. I wish them all every possible success, and have no trace whatever of the vigorous antagonism that arose from my early battles with the advocates of a paleolithic man and culture in the Eastern United States.[79]

In a narrow but important sense, Holmes had won. His insistence on method and evidence, be it scientific or historical, had prevailed. As he wrote more than a decade before in 1919, in the then authoritative *Handbook of Aboriginal American Antiquities*:

> [I] favor the view . . . that the continent was probably not reached and occupied until after the final retreat of the glacial ice from middle North America. At the same time it must be granted that there is no apparent reason why, if already occupying northern Asia, man should not have reached American shores by way of Bering Strait during any of the periods of mild climate which preceded and interrupted the Ice Age; yet we may wisely await the results of further research and provide for the application to these of the severest tests that science can devise.[80]

Seven years later, the Folsom site passed these very tests. But by identifying himself so closely for nearly forty years with the results obtained by such methods and severe tests—namely, that there existed no acceptable evidence for humans in the Americas in Pleistocene times—the Folsom and later Clovis discoveries damaged rather than enhanced his reputation.

Still, it needs to be stressed here that Holmes was not dogmatic on the point of post-glacial antiquity, although his contemporaries might be forgiven for having drawn a different conclusion. Holmes did, in fact, allow "that the peopling of America with the present race was accomplished in *late Glacial* [italics mine] or post-Glacial time rather than early Glacial or Tertiary time."[81] His position, then, is largely in line with modern views. But given the way Holmes chose to handle his end of the debate, he was not vindicated by the discoveries at Folsom. On the contrary, Holmes sadly and unfairly looked like he had forced American archaeology to make a detour that required nearly four decades to negotiate.[82]

10

"On the Ragged Edge of Uncertainty"

Chicago

As holmes prepared to attend the World's Columbian Exposition in Chicago during the summer of 1893, his position on the antiquity of man in America seemed unassailable and made him one of the foremost archaeologists of his day—and, we have just seen, for years to come. In 1893, Holmes's stature in the scientific community rose only higher after reading the paper "Natural History of Flaked Stone Implements" to a large audience of anthropologists at the exposition.[1] In addition, he was responsible for the exhibit of the Bureau of American Ethnology. Frank Hamilton Cushing, James Mooney, and Matilda Coxe Stevenson rendered valuable assistance. Holmes was able to use the exhibit to illustrate his ideas on the antiquity question through the bold and innovative use of life-size dioramas, which were presented in conjunction with the Smithsonian Institution's many other displays, including a stone age exhibit by Thomas Wilson.[2] Holmes's figures portrayed the "domestic life, arts, and industries" of Native Americans, including aboriginal quarrying methods.[3]

This close relationship between research and exhibition, incidentally, was crucial, for it distinguished scientific representation from freak shows and circus attractions, which was a real concern at the time. For over forty years, Holmes was a regular participant in the national expositions, "on account," he said, "of my artistic skill" and by virtue of his positions with the Hayden Survey and the Smithsonian Institution.[4] The expositions he attended were held in major cities around the country and included the Centennial Exposition in 1876, the Southern Exposition in 1884, the World's Columbian Exposition in 1893, the Trans-Mississippi and International Exposition in 1898, the Pan-American Exposition in 1901 (President William McKinley was assassinated during this event); the Louisiana Purchase Exposition in 1903, the

Lewis and Clark Centennial and American Pacific Exposition and Oriental Fair in 1905, the Jamestown Ter-Centennial Exposition in 1907, the Alaska-Yukon-Pacific Exposition in 1909, the Appalachian Exposition in 1910, and the Panama-Pacific International Exposition and the San Diego Exposition, both in 1915.[5] At each of these popular events, he insisted that scholarship take precedence over showmanship, although it is clear from the diplomas and medals he won for his exhibits that Holmes's work still pleased the eye. Holmes's insistence on accuracy first guided him in his museum presentations as well. Indeed, the exposition exhibits—part or all—were often the "forerunners" of permanent museum installations, not only at the National Museum but "in collections preserved in other Museums throughout the country."[6] At the exposition in Chicago in 1893, the most famous of these great affairs, Holmes even served as an honorary judge in the department of ethnology, which was yet another way he worked to ensure that education was not sacrificed for entertainment.

While in Chicago, Holmes also found himself supervising his supervisor, John Wesley Powell. Holmes wrote to his wife Kate, "I took charge of the Major and for four days did nothing but take care of him and pilot him around. We saw all the anthropology exhibits and studied them with care and naturally landed occasionally in Old Vienna which place the Major enjoyed very much. He is quite weak and I had to take great care not to let him get tired out. He expects to go on to California in a few days."[7] Clearly, Powell was not the man he used to be; but he could rely on Holmes, McGee, and others close to him for protection. And they did their job well. Few outside of a small circle in government service were aware of the major's steadily deteriorating condition and he was thus able to hold on to his directorship of the BAE until the end.[8]

Holmes had been to Chicago before. In 1872, on his first trip west, he stopped long enough to marvel at the city's fast and furious recovery from the great conflagration of the preceding year. His subsequent career thus coincided with the city's Phoenix-like rise out of the ashes. And Holmes may have returned again in 1892, when he was elected on August 31 to the geology department of the University of Chicago as a nonresident professor of archaeologic geology.[9] Holmes accepted the position, largely at the urging of the chair of the geology department, Thomas C. Chamberlain, formerly with the Geological Survey as chief of the glacial division and one of Holmes's allies in the antiquity debate.[10]

Chamberlain's goal was to build the best department in the country. He saw in Holmes precisely the type of man whom he wanted: original, broad-minded, hardworking, accomplished, and experienced in museum work. Moreover, Chamberlain appreciated the authority that Holmes brought to the antiquity debate. The Washington scientist was setting new standards by which American archaeology would be judged. Here was a man for the University of Chicago, an institution widely touted as the next great intellectual center of America, as the country moved west and developed its great inland empire.[11]

In the University of Chicago's Programme of Courses in Geology, for the 1892–93 academic year, Holmes was listed as offering courses in Anthropic Geology—"A course of special lectures on the critical relations of Geology to Archaeology, with collateral readings"—and Graphic Methods—"A course of special lectures and illustrative exercises on the applications of sketching and other graphic methods to geological subjects."[12] These courses, however, were evidently withdrawn because Holmes appears to have remained in Washington until the summer of 1893, at which time he definitely came to Chicago to work on the Smithsonian Institution's anthropology installations at the world's fair.

Besides the teaching appointment, Chamberlain also helped persuade the Columbian Museum, established in 1893 (also known as the Field Columbian Museum and renamed the Field Museum of Natural History in 1906), to offer Holmes the position as curator of the anthropological department.[13] Chamberlain hoped ultimately to see the museum under the codirectorship of Holmes and Charles Doolittle Walcott, another Washington man who was also made a nonresident member of the department of geology at the University of Chicago.[14] Walcott, incidentally, remained in Washington and, from 1894 to 1907, directed Powell's old Geological Survey. "You would make a glorious team," Chamberlain wrote of Holmes and Walcott, "and no similar opportunity has ever presented itself in this country." At the same time, Holmes was offered a position at the New York Museum, but the Chicago offers, he wrote, were far more attractive. And after discussing the matter over with Powell, he decided to go to Chicago.

Holmes's decision to go to Chicago came at a time when he was at the height of his powers and very much in demand. The Bureau of American Ethnology, which reluctantly accepted his resignation, observed: "To him science is indebted for a consistent method of interpreting primitive art products through the study of the arts of primitive peoples cognate to those whose relics have come down to us from prehistoric times."[15] In other words, Holmes helped establish a uniformitarian method, already widely accepted in geology, for American archaeology. Moreover, he developed a rigorous evolutionary approach to the subject of primitive art as well. Unfortunately for this pioneering archaeologist, moving to the Windy City in 1894 was the biggest mistake of his life, and three years later he managed—to his great relief—to return to Washington as head curator of the U.S. Museum's department of anthropology.

There were serious problems from the very beginning. First of all, Holmes was not offered an entirely vacant position. A thirty-six-year-old anthropologist, the German-born Franz Boas, was already temporarily in charge of the museum's anthropology department, a position Boas held by virtue of his connections with Frederick W. Putnam.[16] Boas would eventually become the dominant figure in American anthropology, and his ideas on cultural relativism would all but replace evolutionism. But in late February 1894, this intellectual combatant and revolutionary was trying hard to secure a position in the new profession of anthropology in his newly adopted country (Boas became a U.S. citizen in 1891), a struggle that would pit him against Holmes. When Boas found out that Frederick J. V. Skiff, the director of the Columbian Museum, was going to offer "his" position to a "Washington man," that is, to Holmes, to take effect June 30, 1894, instead of making him permanent, and that he would be offered a subordinate job in ethnology, he wrote an angry letter to Putnam calling Chamberlain "a most shrewd politician" and reporting that Putnam's own "administrative ability was assailed in every way."[17] Actually, Holmes's position was not confirmed until October 27, 1894 at a salary of $333.22 per month, or $4,000.00 annually.[18]

According to Boas, Chamberlain was attempting by various "intrigues" to make the museum subservient to the University of Chicago. In Boas's view, Holmes was a means to this greater end. On February 18, 1894, Boas wrote Putnam that he intended to fight Chamberlain even as he conceded that his "chances of success" were "very slim."[19] The next day Boas submitted his resignation when Skiff, whom he had accused of "prevarication," was unable to assure him that "nobody besides myself has been or is being considered in connection with the position of Director of Anthropology."[20] Several weeks earlier, Chamberlain had written to Holmes to say, "My private information regarding the organization of the Museum staff is to the effect that 'the plan proposed by Chamberlain will be adopted,'" but given the "delicate relations" between the museum, on the one hand, and Putnam and Boas, on the other, the "proposed arrangement with you will best be kept confidential for a time."[21] Chamberlain went further to reveal that he had "set [his] heart on having the great museum under the scientific directorship of yourself [Holmes] and Professor [Charles] Walcott".[22] Chamberlain's caution was fully warranted given Boas's strong reaction to the news of the museum's offer to Holmes—which must have been particularly galling to Boas since, as early as August, Boas had discussed with Holmes his "general plans and prospects" and the possibility of moving to the Bureau of American Ethnology.[23]

In trying to piece together what had happened behind the scenes, Boas approached Holmes and W J McGee directly. In his reply, which he made known to Skiff, Holmes indicated that he was led to believe that he was being offered, in effect, a new position and thus had no reason to believe that Boas would be injured if he accepted it. On February 27, Skiff wrote to Holmes that he had

> received your letter enclosing correspondence in the matter of the inquisitiveness of Dr. Boas, which I will preserve until you are in the city, or will return it to you if you desire. I was aware of the knowledge which the Doctor had obtained, and now that it has all transpired do not regret in the least that he knows what he does. With a full knowledge that he will not continue in charge of the Department, I have arranged with him to complete the installation. I prefer, however, that you should consider this confidential. Your treatment of the case was judicious and dignified, and I dropped your communication in the letter box myself, after reading the copy.[24]

In any event, there was never a question of Boas's ability, for in the same letter Skiff went on to say that "Dr. Boas is handling the installation of the material entrusted to his care superbly. His methods are economical, intelligent, and to an extent artistic . . . "[25]

By March 21, McGee had acquired a basic understanding of what had taken place, although his version of events, which was based in part on his own conversations with Holmes, nevertheless differed from Holmes's version to Boas. According to McGee, Holmes was quite aware that Boas would be affected by his appointment, but made every effort to provide a meaningful role for Boas if he should decide to remain at the museum. Boas's resignation, however, settled the issue. He remained unemployed for more than a year until eventually he was able to establish himself in New York City at the American Museum of Natural History as an assistant curator and, with the help of his uncle Dr. Abraham Jacobi at Columbia University, as a lecturer in physical anthropology there. Accepting this lectureship was a critical move in

Boas's career, as it turned out, for it gave him the opportunity to develop an outstanding and highly influential anthropology program.[26]

After the unpleasant Boas incident, things only became worse for Holmes, despite the good start he got with a farewell banquet at which sixty-four scientists and artists honored his Washington years.[27] The source of the problems from Holmes's standpoint was Skiff, who may have learned about Chamberlain's plans.[28] According to Holmes, trouble was in the air from the moment he arrived in Chicago, despite earlier "glowing" promises, namely, that a "salary of $5000 was in sight, along with free and untrammeled control of the [Anthropology] Department to carry out my ideals of what such a Department should be."[29] Instead, Skiff, "acting with innate cunning—the outstanding features [*sic*] of his character," began to indicate through third parties that Holmes's appointment was only for one year, and that he "better hold on to [his] old place in Washington tentatively, accepting the position for a year on trial."[30] This threat kept Holmes, as he put it, "on the ragged edge of uncertainty."[31] Crisis followed crisis and Holmes soon found his situation intolerable. Holmes believed that Skiff was gradually, and deliberately, making the industrial arts division of the department of anthropology more important than the anthropology division, a shift in emphasis and resources that Holmes said was depriving him "of the very features of the work—the development of the features illustrating the various branches of human progress from the point of view of evolution."[32] At one point, events, or rather Skiff, pushed Holmes to the point where he uncharacteristically led the scientific staff "in rebellion" against Skiff, a business man who was set on running things his way, heedless, Holmes claimed, of scientific needs and concerns.[33] Things had to be bad indeed to push Holmes this far. Given months of conflict, it is not surprising that a deep personal antipathy had developed between Holmes and Skiff that would eventually result in a break between the two men.

The Voyage of the *Ituna*

But one good thing did come out of the Chicago episode: Allison V. Armour of Chicago (and patron of the Field Columbian Museum) invited Holmes and other scientists to explore the Yucatán and southern Mexico during the winter of 1894, on board his yacht the *Ituna*. The notes and drawings that Holmes produced on this three-month trip formed the basis of his two-part classic *Archaeological Studies among the Ancient Cities of Mexico*. The first part appeared in December 1895 and was devoted to the "Monuments of Yucatan," including the great ruins of Uxmal and Chichén Itzá, whereas the second part was published in February 1897 and discussed the ancient cities of Palenque in Chiapas, Mitla and Monte Albán in Oaxaca, and Tenochitlán and San Juan Teotihuacán in the Valley of Mexico.

Holmes was hardly the first white man to explore these ancient ruins. In fact, he himself had already had the opportunity to visit the Temples of the Moon, the Sun, and other monuments at Teotihuacán in 1884, on his trip to Mexico with William Henry Jackson. And of course, centuries before, the Spanish conquistadors and missionaries had either visited these and other ruins or at least had been aware of their existence. In 1839, the American lawyer-turned-explorer John L. Stephens and the English artist and archaeologist Frederick Catherwood, after a series of hardships and dangers, discovered the ancient city of Copán in Honduras, which Stephens purchased for the small sum of fifty dollars.[34] The work of these two men at this and other sites in Middle America led to the publication of first the *Incidents of Travel in Central America, Chiapas, and Yucatan* (1841), and then two years later the *Incidents of Travel in Yucatan* (1843), both of which quickly became classics in the literature of exploration and served Holmes, along with the works of Hubert Howe Bancroft, Claude Joseph Désiré Charnay, and other authorities, as valuable sources.[35]

In 1894, the same year that Holmes boarded the *Ituna* at Jacksonville, Florida, and sailed for the port city of Progreso, Yucatán, the English archaeologist Alfred Percival Maudslay concluded fifteen years of exploration on the Mexican peninsula. During that period, Maudslay succeeded in, among other things, clearing the thick vegetation that had hidden many of the ruins of Palenque from view. This feat was no small achievement and one to which Holmes later acknowledged a "great indebtedness."[36] The American amateur archaeologist Edward H. Thompson, the U.S. consul at Mérida, had been an enthusiastic student of Mayan civilization since the late 1870s and would gain renown for his work at Chichén Itzá, especially for the dangerous underwater excavation that he carried out with a dredge and diving equipment at the Sacred Well of Chichén Itzá, which was a deep cenote.[37] This unusually dedicated man of science joined the Armour expedition and provided Holmes with a highly knowledgeable guide and companion. In return for his help, Holmes wrote to McGee requesting that he send Thompson a number of Smithsonian publications.[38]

Not until the mid-1890s, however, did the archaeology of Middle America finally receive the attention that it deserved. Just in the short time between

Panorama of Chichén-Itzá. (Plate XVIII from Holmes, *Archaeological Studies Among the Ancient Cities of Mexico, Part I: Monuments of Yucatan,* opposite p. 138.

the publication of the first and second parts of the *Archaeological Studies among the Ancient Cities of Mexico,* Holmes found himself at pains to keep up with the "numerous publications" appearing on the subject.[39] Perhaps to protect himself, he called his work nothing more than a "sketch of limited portions of a great subject" and cautioned that "years of patient study, excavation, comparison, and literary research are necessary to the elucidation of each great site."[40]

Such statements call to mind the last days of the Great Surveys of the American West, when Holmes and others recognized that a new era of specialization was about to replace the reconnaissance tradition. But the Armour expedition of 1894–95 bore only a superficial resemblance to the surveys of the 1870s. True, in terms of ground covered, there existed room for comparison. In not quite three months, Holmes visited a number of major sites, from the east coast of Yucatán — and the islands just off Yucatán: Contoy, Blanca, Mujeres, Cancún, and Cozumel (now popular tourist spots) — to Mitla in Oaxaca and San Juan Teotihuacán, north of Mexico City, as well as to many lesser known sites. Even Hayden would have been impressed with the miles logged.

Holmes covered this ground by foot, horse, steamer, rail, stage, and by "volans," an animal-powered vehicle that could make fifty miles in one day. In a letter to McGee, he explained that this vehicle was "a boxbed on two high heavy wheels drawn by three mules abreast."[41] This was how Holmes made his way over the Yucatán's rough limestone roads. At least on one occasion, he crossed a lagoon in a canoe, a single mahogany log twenty-eight-feet long, three feet wide, and six feet deep. Occasional use was found for a gasoline launch that had been brought on the *Ituna*, as when the party negotiated the Rio Usumacinta on their way to Palenque in Chiapas. To aid the expedition, *cargadores* were employed to carry supplies, including Holmes's awkward camera equipment. And the party was also able to enjoy the warm and generous hospitality of various gentlemen along the way, such as Don José Dolores Peréz of San Miguel, Don Carlos Díaz of Las Playas, and other Mexican notables, including President Díaz's brother in-law.[42] The trip was largely uneventful, but, as Holmes's letters home to his wife Kate make clear, exacted a physical toll. Weeks of bad weather, rough roads, sleeping in hammocks, enduring ticks, a diet that alternated from princely fare aboard the *Ituna* to a local and unfamiliar cuisine, which included chocolate and bread for breakfast, all left Holmes feeling sick a good part of the time. In fact, he lost about twenty pounds. Still, he did not slow down.[43]

The personnel of the expedition itself resembled the omnibus character of the Great Surveys. Between Holmes, Thompson, Charles F. Millspaugh, and Allan Marquand, the broad range of subjects of anthropology, botany, natural history, and geology were represented. There were even "hostile natives" whom the expedition took care to avoid. Plans to visit the ruins of Tuloom on the east coast of Yucatán, which Stephens had described in 1840, were abandoned (to Maudslay's great disappointment) because the site was now held by a tribe of Maya Indians at war with the Mexican government. The party had to content itself with a view at sea.[44] Four hundred years may have passed since Columbus's arrival and the start of the conquest, when wooden caravels plied the Caribbean waters now parted by Armour's yacht, but the peoples of Middle America were still not entirely subdued.

These similarities aside, the contrasts between the Armour expedition of 1894 and the surveys of the 1870s were clear. One of the differences was the source of sponsorship. The members of the Great Surveys, of course, were supported by the federal government, while Holmes, Thompson, and the others enjoyed the financial backing of a private benefactor. That private citizens, such as Armour, now possessed the princely sums to back scientific enterprises was in itself an indication of the enormous economic and social changes that the United States had undergone since the 1870s. And Armour's expedition paled before the extravaganza organized by the railroad magnate Edward H. Harriman in 1899, when he took a party of 126 of some of the country's top scientists and artists to Alaska, entirely at his own expense, for a period of two months.[45]

But what really distinguished Holmes's work from what he did under Hayden was that his *Archaeological Studies among the Ancient Cities of Mexico* was anything but a "sketch" or general treatment.[46] This was a 328-page, detailed monograph on Middle American architecture, which established him as an authority on yet another subject.[47] He could now add aboriginal architecture to the list of his archaeological specialties, which already included mining, lithics, and ceramics. At each of the major sites that Holmes visited, he systematically examined the orientation and assemblage of the buildings, ground plans, styles, substructures and superstructures, building materials, stone cutting and sculpture, masonry, arches, pillars, stairways, roofs, and so on. He also was careful to note unique buildings and distinguishing features.

Although Holmes helped break new ground in the study of aboriginal architecture, he not surprisingly framed his discussion in largely the same theoretical terms that he had used in his interpretation of the origin and development of form and ornament in the ceramic arts. In both cases, he tried to determine the laws of evolution that govern art. In a lecture that he gave in 1895 at the Field Columbian Museum, he stated emphatically that "the growth of art is as systematic and well regulated a process as the development of the various forms of life that go to make up the vegetable and animal kingdoms."[48] The "pathway of progress" followed, according to Holmes, a clear, but not universally uniform, line of genetic development. Here, he was allowing for variations. As he pointed out in his discussion of ornament in 1886: "New ideas are acquired . . . all along the pathway of progress. None of these ideas retain a uniform expression, however, as they are subject to modification by environment just as are the forms of living organisms."[49] Thus, different people in different places—specifically the Mayas (Yucatán, Chiapas), the Zapotecas (Oaxaca), and the Nahuas (Valley of Mexico)—produced different art. He stressed that factors such as a people's religion and cultural development, as well as their material resources, must be considered in any appraisal of their art and art in general.

But Holmes was less certain about determining what inspired art in the first place than he was in 1886. Then, he thought that the since the "dawn of art" in America evidently occurred much later than it had in Europe and Asia, and since the prehistoric and historic periods overlapped here, it would be possible to reconstruct the origins of art, indeed "to penetrate deeply into the secrets of the past," and thus gain insight into the development of art generally. In other words, American archaeology provided opportunities long since lost in the Old World.[50] But in his discussion of ornament in the *Archaeological Studies among the Ancient Cities of Mexico*, he cautioned: "It is impossible to say of the ornamental art of any primitive people just what causes have operated to bring it into existence, or what ideas underlie its varied phenomena."

But if conception remained a mystery, the stages of art's pregnancy and childhood could still be worked out to satisfaction. In studying the aboriginal architecture of Yucatán, Holmes announced:

> We discover in the non-essential elaborations of these ancient buildings numerous elements surely traceable to constructive sources, but further perceive that most of the motives employed in embellishment have their origin in religion, that their use in art was first significant and second aesthetic. It is probably safe to say that in Maya ornament nine-tenths of the elements used are, or were, present on account of their significance, or because of some associated thought, although we cannot say just how much of the original meanings were retained by the advanced peoples who continued to employ them in their buildings. . . . We may go further and premise that very many of the purely conventional designs, the scrolls, the frets, the meanders and the zigzags had meanings, hidden to the uninitiated, coming down from their less conventional phases of development.[51]

Holmes thus found his earlier ideas on primitive art helpful in interpreting Middle American architecture. Conversely, he was able to use in a somewhat oblique but shrewd way the ancient cities of Mexico, particularly those in Yucatán, as further evidence to support his already well-established position on the antiquity question. He began with the theory, advanced by Thompson in 1879, that the Yucatán peninsula was settled by people from the lost continent of Atlantis, an idea Holmes referred to but politely dismissed. He looked for a point of origin possibly as far north as the Rio Grande. Holmes then turned around the image of Atlantis sinking into the watery realm of Poseidon so that he had the Yucatán rising from the sea at approximately the same time that Atlantis was reputed to have disappeared, that is, "eleven or twelve thousand years ago." These events occurred, he significantly added, "not far from the period that witnessed the oscillations attending the close of the glacial period." He used geological evidence to support this theory, pointing out that the Yucatán, which is essentially a great limestone platform, contains fossils of living species and therefore the peninsula was no older than "late Pliocene or early Pleistocene."[52]

If the Yucatán did not exist much before the end of the last Ice Age, then supporters of the paleolithic-man theory had no ground, quite literally, on which to stand. This good argument was made even better by Holmes's proposal that the "pioneers of the red race" entered this land "some thousand or more years ago," and, in that relatively short period of time (ending with the arrival of the Spaniards in the early sixteenth century), managed to construct the most elaborate stone structures in the Americas.[53] Placed in this context, Holmes's discussion of the monuments of Middle America strongly buttressed his position on the antiquity of humans in the Americas.

Perhaps the most important contribution that Holmes made to Middle American archaeology was the foldout panoramic views and maps that he produced of each of the major cities that he visited—Uxmal, Chichén Itzá, Palenque, Monte Albán, Mitla, and San Juan Teotihuacán. To produce these now historically valuable visual aids, which required a great deal of labor, he drew on the skills that he had learned in Yellowstone National park twenty-three years before as well on the aid of photographs. The Armour party carried a large camera into Yucatán's tick and mosquito-infested jungles and lagoons. What was striking, however, was the change in his views toward this line of work. Gone, of course, was the notion that field art was in any sense to be used as a "means of embellishment." During his years as director of illustrations at the Geological Survey, Holmes had institutionalized that change and in the process drained the romance and color out of scientific art, leaving nothing but illustrated facts. Holmes reserved his artistic impulses, in the larger sense, for his watercolors, a medium in which he later succeeded in making a name for himself in the local Washington art scene.[54]

Accompanying this sharp separation between illustration and art was a corresponding demotion in the status of the expeditionary artist. Holmes, in fact, would have left the drawing to someone else if he had been able "to secure," in his words, "a skilled draughtsman." This failure to find someone was, however, not too surprising. He was, after all, one of America's great field artists, and doubtless few could meet his high and exacting standards. After reluctantly assuming the role of artist, or rather, "draughtsman," he went on to complain disingenuously that "haste and lack of skill in architectural work have left me with the merest sketches." Holmes's panoramas of the ancient cities of Mexico, however, were anything but mere sketches. But they were not "art," either. They were technical masterpieces.

These panoramic views were the result not only of a great deal of work involving the compass and tapeline, by means of which he carefully determined the location of each ruin and its relationship to the whole. They were also the product of Holmes's imagination, for in many cases the ruins were so overgrown with jungle foliage that clear views of individual buildings, to say nothing of a city in toto, were simply impossible. To surmount this physical obstacle, Holmes settled on drawing the cities as if "a fire had recently swept the country leaving the various buildings exposed."[55] The total effect of the illustrations was as dramatic as it was important. For as accurate, beautiful, and

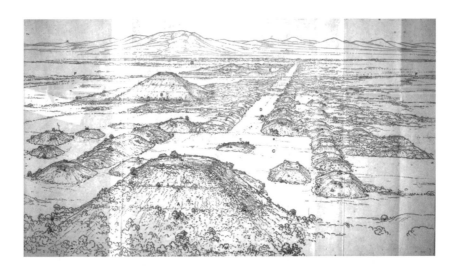

Panoramic View of San Juan Teotihuacan. (Illustration from Holmes, *Archaeological Studies Among the Ancient Cities of Mexico, Part II: Monuments of Chiapas, Oaxaca and the Valley of Mexico*, opposite page 298.)

even haunting as Frederick Catherwood's famous illustrations were of the ruins of Middle America, his work nevertheless captured only particular buildings and monuments. Holmes's art, on the other hand, taken from an imaginary perspective high above the jungle and ruins below, rendered Uxmal, Palenque, and the other sites in their entirety. In other words, he was the first to articulate visually these cities as cities, and not just depict individual or random scenes from these ancient centers of population. In a sense, Holmes did the same thing for Mexico's ancient cities that he had done for the Grand Canyon's natural architecture, except this time he confined himself to illustration, avoiding embellishment altogether. The difference shows. If Holmes's views were not artistic, they were nevertheless models of scientific reporting and it was not until the advent of aerial photography in the 1920s, which introduced a new era in scientific exploration, that science acquired bird's-eye views that surpassed his panoramas in accuracy and content.

"The Washington Idea"

After Holmes returned to Chicago, he devoted himself to working up his notes, sketches, and photographs into a two-part manuscript on Mexico's ancient cities, even while his relationship with Skiff steadily deteriorated. His work on the antiquity question in the eastern United States had established his reputation at the Bureau of American Ethnology; and now he hoped that his study of aboriginal architecture in Mexico would perform the same service at the Field Columbian Museum. His expectations were largely realized as the work was well received. Holmes also resumed his museum responsibilities, at the expense apparently of his course on archaeological geology at the University of Chicago. Ever since his Ohio days at Science Hill, Beech Spring, and McNeely, Holmes showed little real interest in teaching. His interests were clearly elsewhere.

Holmes's troubles with Skiff, however, probably convinced him sometime fairly early in 1896 that things had to change. In a letter to Walcott, who was now acting assistant secretary of the Smithsonian Institution, Holmes identified the ongoing problem as principally one of control. "The trouble developed out of the Chicago idea," he explained, "that only a business man, and a business man only, can conduct the business of an institution—museum or otherwise—which," Holmes allowed, "would have been well enough had the man chosen as director been qualified for the work." Thus, the "difficulty was due not only to the business direction which extended over the scientific work, but to the personality embodying more unfortunate elements than I have ever known assembled in one individual."[56]

After leading a rebellion against the tyrant, the situation apparently improved but Holmes still was ready to leave, and, as he made clear to Walcott, "if an opening should develop for me in Washington, the possibility of which Mr. McGee has indicated in a recent letter, an opening suited for the display of my particular talents, I should be deeply gratified, but I beg that you will not feel for a moment that you must provide for me, and especially"—as if he recalled the unpleasant Franz Boas affair—"would stipulate that whatever is done, other worthy people should not suffer on account of my ambition." Holmes then revealed his true feelings in the matter when he went on to say, "That my thoughts frequently turn *homeward* [italics mine] and the picture of settled conditions, congenial associations fully in sympathy with scientific work comes before me cannot be denied." After three years, Chicago was still not home; Washington was and Holmes wanted nothing more than to return there. Especially as he reflected that in Chicago, "the field here is a great one and promises much for the future, but I fear that years of crudeness, struggle and uncertainty must follow notwithstanding the fact that we have in the Museum management some of the best and most appreciative men I have ever known."[57] Chicago, in other words, was not a great cultural center yet, and Holmes was no longer attracted by the challenge of making it into one, not when a position might be beckoning in the nation's more civilized capital. Being in a position to choose, he found the idea of returning to Washington decidedly more appealing than remaining in Chicago.

Finding a position in the world of government science had become more complicated since Holmes was offered a position on the spot in 1871, after José Zeledon casually discovered he possessed artistic talent. Since then, Congress had passed the Pendleton Act in 1883, which established the Civil Service Commission. As a result, government jobs would increasingly be filled on the basis of competitive examinations instead of through political patronage, as had been the case at least since the Andrew Jackson administration. In 1897, Holmes learned that the position Walcott and Smithsonian secretary Langley were prepared to offer him, the head curatorship of the division of anthropology in the U.S. Museum, was among those that now required testing. In a letter of April 7, 1897, Walcott assured Holmes, who was "disturbed" by the matter, that "I shall recommend that it be mainly the presentation of evidence of ability, as shown by works published, and positions filled." On May 11, he added that Holmes write "an essay on the administration of the division of Anthropology in order that it might bring out your views in relation to the same." Holmes's anxieties on the point proved groundless. On June 11, Walcott was happy to report that he had passed, adding that the grading "committee consisted of Major Powell, an officer of the commission, and myself."[58] A friendly group, to be sure. Times may have changed, but not by that much. Holmes was officially notified by Langley on June 17, and on the twenty-second he accepted the offer and stated that he would "close [his] engagement with the Field Columbian Museum at the earliest possible date — not later I hope than the first day of September."[59] He would maintain his nonresident teaching position in Chamberlain's department of geology at the University of Chicago, however, for another three years.

The Chicago interlude, then, was all but over. It had been marked by accomplishment, disappointment, and anxiety. It was with relief as much as with a sense of great things yet to be done that Holmes looked once again upon the familiar towers of the Smithsonian Castle, which was indeed the very center of his world, and where he knew he belonged.

11

The Significance of the "Frigid Gateway" in American Anthropology

HOLMES RECEIVED A WARM WELCOME in Washington. The Washington *Star* favorably reported on his return, as did Alfred R. Calhoun of *Monumental Records*. Calhoun observed on this noteworthy occasion in Washington's cultural life:

> Professor Holmes's life has been a busy and undoubtedly happy one, for he early found that his life-calling and its pursuits brought him happiness. He has published fifty-four papers, many of them voluminous, and all of them crammed with valuable additions to those sciences which he has studied so carefully and continuously.

Calhoun went on to note that the former Washingtonian was a

> graceful speaker, and he has mastered a style that is a surprise and a delight to the purely literary man. His illustrations made, it is said, with marvelous rapidity, are the very best we have seen. They are not simply superior as works of art, but they illustrate his text in a way that make his reports clear to the veriest novice.

And finally:

> Professor Holmes is in the midst of his great work, and, as it proceeds, it is our hope that the readers of *Monumental Records* will know more and more of this scholarly and gifted American.[1]

These words were, as Holmes was fond of saying, "gratifying" indeed, and augured well for the return to Washington of the fifty-one-year-old artist, scientist, and curator.

The Great Work

The reference Calhoun made to Holmes's great work was not specific, and no doubt what came to mind for many readers was the antiquity debate. Less well known to readers, however, was Holmes's work on aboriginal pottery, which had consumed much of his time and attention in the 1880s, before he became embroiled in the paleolithic question and was diverted in Chicago by the study of Middle American architecture. It was as early as 1883 when Powell "detailed" Holmes to begin the study of the National Museum's aboriginal pottery collection, although he had shown interest in the subject dating back to the Hayden years. Now that he was once again among the familiar and ever growing collections of the National Museum, Holmes devoted more and more time to what Meltzer and Dunnell rightly call Holmes's magnum opus, "Aboriginal Pottery of the Eastern United States," published in 1903 in John Wesley Powell's *Twentieth Annual Report of the Bureau of American Ethnology, 1898–1899.*[2]

Holmes explained in the preface of "Aboriginal Pottery" that he had started work on the monograph in 1890 with the intention that it would be limited to the fictile arts of the mound builders and would accompany Cyrus Thomas's "Report of the Mound Explorations," which appeared in 1894 in the *Twelfth Annual Report of the Bureau of Ethnology*. Plans changed, however. In the meantime, Holmes expanded the study's parameters to include the "entire region," or rather regions, "east of the Rocky Mountains." These provinces, or "culture areas," included the South Appalachian province, the middle and lower Mississippi valleys, the Gulf Coast, the Florida Peninsula, the Middle Atlantic province, the Iroquoian province, the New Jersey-New England province, Apalachee-Ohio province, the Ohio Valley, and the Northwest, which encompasses the upper Mississippi Valley, the Missouri Valley, the region of the western Great Lakes, and the Red River valley of the North. To illustrate these vast divisions, Holmes provided a color-coded distributional map of aboriginal pottery clearly marking the five major pottery groupings: Middle Mississippi Valley, South Appalachian, Middle and Northern Atlantic Slope, Iroquois, and the North Western. As usual, the printing was done by the old and trusted company of Julius Bien.[3]

Besides the collections of the Bureau of American Ethnology on which Holmes based his study, he also turned for materials as well as assistance to the Davenport Academy of Sciences (Iowa), the Peabody Museum (Cambridge), the American Museum of Natural History (New York), the Academy of Sciences and the Free Museum of Science and Art (both of Philadelphia), the Museum of Art (Cincinnati), and the Canadian Institute (Toronto), as well as to private collections. And as collaborators, Holmes acknowledged W J McGee; William Dinwiddie (photographer); John L. Ridgeway, Mary M. Mitchell, H. C. Hunter (illustrators); and DeLancy Gill (illustrator, engraver, and printing illustrator); and members of the Smithsonian Institution, Bureau of American Ethnology, the Geological Survey, and the National Museum—a group of individuals that included the sickly Frank Hamilton Cushing and James Mooney.

Clearly by the end of the nineteenth century, America could take pride in its collection of museums and growing scientific expertise. And Holmes's own curatorial work at the National Museum and the Field Columbian Museum, along with his formidable scholarly production—especially his pottery papers—showed that he was as important as a museum builder as he was skilled in the use of this ever-expanding institutional network of knowledge, which would prove to have a lasting and significant influence in shaping the study of Native Americans in this country. Indeed, Holmes was perhaps unequaled in his understanding of collecting, on the one hand, and classifying, on the other, as his "Aboriginal Pottery" brilliantly demonstrated.

Unlike Holmes's prize-winning work on stone implements, "Aboriginal Pottery" dealt with a relatively new art, springing into "existence," Holmes believed, "long after other arts had been well perfected." In fact, according to Holmes, "pottery naturally fell heir to duties previously performed by vessels of bark, wicker, shell, fruit shells, horn, stone, or more archaic receptacles for boiling, serving, containing, and transporting." In the Morgan scheme of evolutionary development, Holmes placed the rise of pottery somewhere between "the upper savage and barbarian stages of progress." But since Indians on the Atlantic slope had reached the "middle status of barbarism" by the time of contact, the art was "not new, having probably extended through all of the first stage of barbarism." But as far as what these relative determinations meant in terms of years, Holmes thought that it was "impossible" to say.[4]

Holmes believed he was on firmer ground in discussing the relationship between aboriginal textile art and ceramics. Holmes believed that there was "no doubt" that the textile art was the older of the two arts. But more importantly, "the potter, working always with textile appliances and with textile models before him, has borrowed many elements of form and ornament from them."[5] To make the case for the transference of "technic" and other actions from one medium of art to another, Holmes noted that pottery often bore the impressions from different classes of textiles, such as baskets, cloths, nets, woven textures, and tools wrapped with cords. And in pointing out that the use of baskets in molding and modeling pottery was "overestimated," he went on to make the startling discovery that their use in molding the base of earthen vessels gave the potter support as well as a "pivot" on which to turn the vessel during manufacture. Thus, the basket used in this fashion was nothing less than "an incipient form of the wheel."[6] Cultural history in anthropology would eventually be replaced by the relativistic concept of culture groups, each with its own unique history, but not before evolutionists like Holmes provided science with valuable insights into the intricate workings of human progress.[7]

As in the study of stone implements, Holmes based his study of pottery, in part, on efforts to replicate aboriginal methods in order to test his theories. For example, he demonstrated that certain earthenware surfaces had been finished with cord-wrapped paddles. In these experiments, however, he apparently escaped any disabling injuries, as had occurred during his knapping experiments. Powell called this method "experimental reproduction" and in 1900 credited Cushing with laying the "foundation of a system of investigation which has since proved of marvelous efficiency and which has been successfully developed by other laborers."[8] Cushing justified this "thinking like an Indian" approach, which was yet another application of uniformitarian theory to anthropology, by arguing that the

> *things* of the past were personal . . . They must, therefore, be both treated and worked at, not solely according to ordinary methods of procedure or rules of logic, or to any given canons of learning, but in a profoundly personal mood and way.

And Cushing explained away the ahistorical tendency here by stating, in the first person, that since he was physically and mentally "virtually" the same as primitive men then it followed that if

> I dominate myself with their needs, surround myself with their material conditions, aim to do as they did, the chances are that I shall restore their acts and their arts, however lost or hidden, rediscovering what they discovered precisely as they discovered it. Thus may I reproduce an art in all its stages; see how it began, grew, developed into, and affected other arts and things.[9]

To this remarkable position, Holmes added the idea of a natural "force." He maintained that there existed a force or "esthetic influence" that could be found even "during the earliest practices of the art."[10] It followed that the effect of this influence could be replicated in pottery or any other art for that matter.

In "Aboriginal Pottery," Holmes was very clear about the general significance of this subject to universal history. He demonstrated that in America the earliest stages of art were still in evidence. Because of this fact, Holmes maintained that the study of aboriginal pottery gave students opportunities denied those of the early ware of classical Greece and Rome, for the latter "represents mainly the stages of culture rising above the level of the wheel, of pictorial art, and of writing." Early pottery in America, on the other hand, was "entirely below this level, and thus illustrates the substratum out of which the higher phases spring." Only in the New World, in other words, could scientists step onto the escalator of progress and enjoy a ride from the earliest beginnings all the way to the "very verge of civilization."[11] Holmes's parallelism made possible a sense of national pride in the advantages of American anthropology over its European counterpart—one example of an attitude that was common enough among intellectuals at the turn of the century, from Theodore Roosevelt to Frederick Jackson Turner. This was a time, after all, of rising nationalism all over the world, an irrational and highly destructive set of beliefs that were greatly bolstered in the United States with the successful war against Spain and the subsequent acquisition of an overseas empire.

This universalism or belief in an *ideal* progress aside, Holmes saw any number of reasons—"climatic conditions, degree of sedentation, nature of food supply, and availability of material"—for why the peoples of America had reached so many different levels of artistic progress. In short, the environment, according to Holmes, largely determined the differences found in the peoples of the Americas, differences that could be produced very rapidly. As he explained:

> The art that flourishes on the Gulf coast with a prosperous people may be undeveloped or entirely neglected by a people wandering from place to place in the barren, icy regions of the North; yet, could we for a generation exchange the environments of these peoples, the potter's art would still be found practiced and flourishing in the more salubrious climate and neglected and disused in the rigorous one.[12]

To turn this idea around, Holmes contended that similar environmental conditions produced similar artistic results.

Interestingly, Holmes's emphasis on the environment led him to a cultural relativism, but one still set squarely within the qualified framework of Morgan's evolutionary stages and thus distinguishing it from the cultural relativism and pluralism being developed by Franz Boas. Holmes noted that the arts were not "symmetrically and equally developed" among peoples, that "the inferior ware of one locality does not indicate that the people of that locality were inferior in culture, for the reverse may be the case." These views led Holmes to the brilliantly articulated position that "the culture status of a given people must be determined by a consideration of the sum of the planes of all the arts and not by the plane of any one art."[13] Profound insights such as this one were the result of many years of field and museum work.

By 1914, the year when many of the world's most advanced civilizations plunged into four years of slaughter and destruction on a scale hitherto unknown to history, Holmes's growing environmentalism—reinforced almost daily by museum work in which classification and arrangement of antiquities were paramount concerns—led him to adopt what he called "culture characterization areas," of which he identified eleven separate geographical regions in North America. This idea remains fundamental to the anthropology of the Americas. Perhaps given Holmes's belief in a relatively recent human occupation of the New World, his growing appreciation of the environment as a crucial agent of change was inevitable.[14]

California

In 1898, a year after Holmes had returned to the Bureau of American Ethnology, he and W J McGee spent six weeks in California during the summer of 1898—while the United States was at war with Spain—engaged in archaeological and ethnological studies of the state's Indians. As Holmes pointed out: "One of the principal objects of the journey was to look into evidence relating to the antiquity of man in the Auriferous Gravel region of the Sierra Nevada."[15] Visiting Tuoloume and Calaveras counties and other locations on the western slope "made classic in science by [James D.] Whitney and in song by Bret Harte," Holmes gathered more evidence in his dogged and decades-long campaign against the existence of a "Tertiary Man" in America.[16] Unlike the previous battles against amateurs, this one pitted Holmes against the great Whitney himself, who had visited the gravels in the early 1860s and, in Holmes's words, had concluded in 1879

> that many of the relics of man and his arts came from those portions of the gravels that with reasonable certainty be assigned to the Pliocene; that these finds were associated with the remains of extinct species of animals and plants; that they represented a race of ordinary physical characters, though having a culture of the lowest range compatible with the human status.[17]

But much of Whitney's evidence was based on the testimony of amateurs, namely the miners, or "inexpert observers," as Holmes called them, who worked the gold-bearing gravels and in the process discovered human relics and bones, such as the famous Calaveras Skull, which was kept in Cambridge, Massachusetts, in the care of Professor Putnam.[18] Holmes noted that no less an authority than Clarence King, of the Fortieth Parallel Survey, "found a pestle in the tufaceous deposits under the lava cap of Tuolumne table mountain and removed it from the matrix with his own hands," a fact that lent credence to the claims of the miners.[19]

But in the papers Holmes produced on the subject, which appeared in the *American Anthropologist*, he judiciously examined the arguments for and against Tertiary Man in a manner that would have impressed another Holmes contemporary, Sir Arthur Conan Doyle's fictional character, the master sleuth Sherlock Holmes. After visiting the mines to which Whitney referred and interviewing pioneer miners still living in the area, Holmes found that the explanation for the widely reported occurrence of ancient relics buried in the Tertiary gravels was obvious, if not elementary, once the matter was put into the proper light.

On inspecting a mining site where stone implements were uncovered in 1864, Holmes noted that the spot had once been occupied by native peoples; that specimens were abundant but scattered about because of the topography of the site, which consisted of steep slopes and gullies; and that stone implements in the mine itself had quite evidently simply "rolled in." In fact, Holmes went on, "it is no wonder that collectors were able to secure from [the mine] the flat dish or platter of granite referred to by Whitney, for a dozen of these objects were still scattered along the brink above ready to fall in as the work of the miner advanced." Holmes allowed that the artifacts were different from modern Indian sites, but answered this particular objection to the "theory of recent origin"[20] by remarking that this fact "does not necessarily indicate different peoples, but probably results from changes in habits due to contact with the whites and the degeneracy of aboriginal work in general." At another site, Holmes found gravel mines "in intimate association" with native settlements.[21]

Beyond the "Frigid Gateway"

Holmes was not completely consumed by his interest in the antiquity question, although it sometimes seemed that way. His ongoing work on pottery and his work on aboriginal architecture in Mexico demonstrated clearly that other subjects did engage his attention. His paper "Anthropological Studies in California" was but another case in point. It too refers at length to his investigations in the auriferous gravels on the western slope of the Sierra Nevada, but Holmes nevertheless stated that "in considering the archaeology of a great region like California, it is proper that the present aborigines and their culture should be studied, and that the knowledge thus acquired utilized in discussing the prehistoric monuments and artifacts of the region."22 Like a good uniformitarian, Holmes always believed, in his words: "There is nothing in the past of culture that is not comprised in the present."23

Nevertheless, Holmes's study of "present aborigines" rarely involved direct contact with Native Americans. Holmes was no Frank Hamilton Cushing, James Mooney, or Matilda Coxe Stevenson, BAE ethnologists who had distinguished themselves in their work with living Indians. Just why Holmes showed such limited interest in contemporary Native Americans is unclear. Perhaps his negative experience with a group of Indians in the Four Corners region in 1875 as a member of the Hayden Survey, which was discussed earlier, had a lasting impact on him. Perhaps he was more comfortable with things or artifacts than he was with people. In his paper "Anthropological Studies," he discusses an incident with an elderly Native American woman, which revealed more than he no doubt intended about his attitude toward Native Americans. He identified her as "Susan," because he did not know her native name. Having exhausted all other means, he said that he failed to learn what she was really called. Evidently, the one source he did not pursue was the woman herself. In any event, it was McGee who worked "securing vocabularies and hints of the customs and history of the people," activities typical of ethnology under Powell, while Holmes devoted his energies to investigating their arts, that is, the things they made, at least when he was not gathering information relating to the antiquity question.24

In dealing with the broader issues and concerns of American anthropology, Holmes was much stronger, and reviewing the anthropology of California elicited a particularly clear articulation of his views on the general development of aboriginal culture. What was especially striking here was his emphasis on environmental forces. Indeed, Holmes advanced a "frontier hypothesis," not unlike the one Frederick Jackson Turner—a young historian from Wisconsin—presented to an audience at the Columbian Exposition in Chicago several years earlier in 1893. Turner's famous paper, "The Significance of the Frontier in American History," stated the simple but powerful idea that the frontier was what made Americans American. In the move west, Turner suggested, Americans lost their cultural baggage, which they had inherited from Europe, and acquired a rough but dynamic set of traits that made them a new and different people. Holmes's faith in the transforming effects of the American environment, or rather environments, was no less strong than Turner's.

Holmes observed that among the native peoples of California there existed great linguistic diversity, which he thought was "largely due to the arrival of tribes already speaking diversified tongues rather than to differentiation within present habitats."[25] Holmes dismissed the idea of a "very ancient autochthonic people," and even if such a people had existed "they must now be merged fully into the Asiatic populations of the present period."[26] But despite the linguistic diversity of native California, there existed, Holmes wrote, a "marked uniformity in the physical characteristics of the people, and culture in general is diversified only in details." And "all those elements of culture dependent upon immediate environment and readily modified by it have been remodeled into a homogeneous whole." Holmes also noted "that in its ensemble Californian culture is sharply marked off even from that of most of the neighboring peoples—as, for example, the Pueblos, the Mound-Builders, and the Mexicans."[27]

Holmes believed that the native peoples of California were of "Asiatic" ancestry, but, he warned, "to speak of them as Chinese, Malay, or Tartar in origin, without very considerable qualification, is a great mistake."[28] He thought Asiatic languages, arts, and industries had all but been lost in the intervening "centuries of migration and struggle" as various peoples made their way down from the shores of the Bering sea to California far to the south. These peoples were changed by the move and ultimately by the place where they moved to. As Holmes declared:

> Every art save the most elementary, would be lost or transformed in passing the frigid gateway. Religion, social institutions, government, industries, all would change with changing conditions and be remodeled in each of the numerous distinctive environments encountered between Tartary and California. Agriculture, pastoral arts, metallurgy, ceramics, and all forms of domestic art would be obliterated, and other activities, such as weaving, stone-shaping, house-building, hunting, and fishing, would be so completely modified that no knowledge of original practices would remain in the mind of any individual or be preserved in any tradition.[29]

In other words, despite the Asiatic origins of the native peoples of America, they were now, and had long since become, American.

Holmes was certainly not the first anthropologist to stress the importance of the environment in ethnology. As Curtis M. Hinsley, Jr. points out, Otis Mason, also of the BAE, whose ideas on museum exhibition no doubt influenced Holmes's own work in this area, drew attention at the Columbian Exposition in Chicago to the "role of the physical environment in influencing cultural behavior."[30] Indeed, as Turner's essay made clear, which was also delivered in 1893, such ideas were very much in the air. What seems to have escaped the notice of Holmes, Turner, and many other professionals in the 1890s, however, was how much the United States' own coming of age—symbolized, in fact, by the World's Fair in 1893—came to influence an entire generation. The heady nationalism of fin de siècle America, which produced a war with Spain and an overseas empire, led to a perhaps stronger than usual cultural bias in which national distinctiveness was stressed over universalism. Evidence of ethnocentrism—or, stated in scientific terms, of not taking into account the role of the observer's biases in his or her results—is not hard to find. And it is easy to overstate the importance of this perspective. But in the flush of America's triumphs abroad and the jingoism of the day, Holmes's conclusion, "What is now found, old or new, in the culture of California, is America's own, if not, indeed, fully and absolutely Californian," was an idea containing a sense of possession that no doubt resonated strongly with his contemporaries.[31]

Powell, Cuba, and the Flight of the Turkey Buzzard

In 1900 Holmes made another noteworthy field trip, this time to newly independent Cuba. Holmes had left the country only the year before when a banker from San Antonio had invited Clarence Dutton, who also resided in the Texas city, on a trip to Mexico. Dutton, in turn, invited Holmes and Grove K. Gilbert along. The two men both happily accepted the offer and Holmes took advantage of the opportunity, as we have seen, to further his study of aboriginal mining at the Sierra de las Navajas in the state of Hidalgo.[32] But the trip to the Caribbean Islands in the wake of the Spanish-American War, where the exploration of the Americas began, was an event of special interest in its foreshadowing of the new directions American exploration would take in the twentieth century.

Holmes went to Cuba in early 1900 to accompany John Wesley Powell. Powell, who lost his right arm to a minié ball at Shiloh in 1862, should probably have retired after undergoing an operation on what was left of the amputated limb in 1895. After that, his health steadily deteriorated until his death in 1902. During this twilight period, W J McGee claimed—as bad as the pun is—to have been Powell's right hand, and not just in the literal sense. As McGee stated: "I drafted every plan of operations, and wrote every report, and drafted every important letter, letters from Major Powell as well as from myself."[33] McGee went even further and claimed: "In his office I knew the condition better than anyone else, and sought in every way to have his best side kept outward."[34] Others, of course, were also privy to the facts. Holmes certainly knew the truth of Powell's condition. He knew the major well, after all, had worked for him for years, had helped take care of the him in Chicago during the World's Fair, and was now traveling with him in Cuba—reporting back, in fact, to the Smithsonian Institution on Powell's health.[35] And happily, with the exception of a bout of sea sickness and a cold, the major's health turned decidedly for the better, if temporarily.[36] Holmes mentioned in a letter home to his wife, Kate, that at the Institute of Jamaica, in Kingston, Powell gave a lecture on his heroic exploration of the Grand Canyon, which, he wrote, was "first-rate and the old man is so full of enterprise and vigor that it is impossible to keep him in check."[37] Notwithstanding McGee's account, evidently there were times well after 1895 when the major was in full possession of his faculties. But that the incident was something to write home about suggests that the exception proved the rule.

There was more to this trip than sight-seeing or rest and relaxation. Holmes, after all, did find time away from watching the major to visit museum collections, to go into the field, and to give thought to the problems of West Indian archaeology, namely, as Powell (or was it McGee?) expressed it: to the "tracing of the lines of cultural migration between the great continents of the Western Hemisphere." Powell went on to explain that he and Holmes confirmed the "researches of the past two decades," which "have shown clearly that the customs of the aborigines in what is now southeastern United States were affected by extraneous motives," originating from South America via the Antilles.[38] The timing of their trip was owed to the consequences of the Spanish-American War; or, in Powell's words, "it was thought desirable to seize the opportunity offered by recent political changes for special studies in the Antillean islands."[39] And indeed their trip, at least their transportation, was facilitated by the quartermaster general's office of the U.S. War Department.[40]

In effect, Holmes and Powell, as agents of the U.S. government, that is, the Smithsonian Institution, conducted a "reconnaissance" (Powell's word) of the post-Spanish Caribbean, in much the same spirit as the two had participated in the Great Surveys of the American West.[41] A feat that was, of course, an important step in that region's rapid incorporation into the U.S. economy. The sense of conquest was very much in evidence as Holmes's own account of his travels in the Caribbean attests. He wrote that he and Powell were "armed" with letters of introduction and, although commenting that Havana was a "great wonderful city," hoped that "we can do something to put it under civilized government."[42] The Platt Amendment, incidentally, was still a year away. Holmes had an interview with the Nordic-looking warrior Leonard Wood, governor-general and good friend of Rough Rider and soon to be president Theodore Roosevelt. Holmes admiringly described Wood as "a strong man."[43] In the course of his stay in Cuba, Holmes met a number of U.S. officers, "most of whom," he noted, "have been over the Rocky Mountain country and we had many stories and a very jolly time."[44] Powell's retelling of his exploits in the Grand Canyon in Jamaica, a crown colony (which Holmes described as "black—awfully black—600,000 colored to 14,000 white, and one sees little but Africa on the streets" and where the language spoken was "a funny Cockney dialect modified by the thick lips of the African"), further reinforced the already strong mutually justifying relationship between exploration and empire.[45] A relationship that would be worked out again in this part of the world, which the United States clearly planned to dominate and control into the indefinite future.

As the nineteenth century closed and the light of a new century streamed in through the dense tropical foliage of the Caribbean Islands, Holmes found himself, almost as an afterthought, engaged in an enterprise with profound implications. Secretary Samuel Pierpoint Langley, a self-taught astronomer from Roxbury, Massachusetts, served as director of the Allegheny Observatory and professor of physics at Western University of Pennsylvania (today's University of Pittsburgh) before becoming secretary of the Smithsonian Institution in 1887. In 1891, Langley published the treatise "Experiments in Aerodynamics." In the ensuing years, he put his ideas on this subject of heavier-than-air flight to the test and, at one point, two of his model airplanes—steam-powered, pilotless, and with thirteen-foot wingspans—achieved flights of several thousand feet before alighting on the waters of the Potomac. Other attempts, however, met with less success.[46]

Present at one of these trials was Theodore Roosevelt, who was a friend of Langley and knew him through the Cosmos Club.[47] This organization, incidentally, was Washington's answer to New York's Century Club. It was founded in Powell's parlor in 1878 and was where Washington's intellectual elite, including, of course, Holmes, who was a cofounder and later president, met to discuss, in comfort and informally, the great scientific issues of the day.[48] Roosevelt quickly grasped the military advantages of mechanical flight and, as assistant secretary of the navy, persuaded his superior, John D. Long, that given the fact of Langley's limited success in this area "it seems to me worth while for this Government to try whether it will not work on a large enough scale to be of use in the event of war."[49] General Adolphus W. Greely of the U.S. Signal Service was no less supportive of Langley, and between the urgings of the two men a scientific board was established, headed by Charles H. Davis, and fifty thousand dollars was appropriated by Congress to fund Langley's work.[50]

The Spanish-American War was over before Langley could develop the technology that Roosevelt and Greely had in mind. Langley nevertheless continued with his research in aerodynamics, and like the two brothers from Dayton, Ohio, Wilbur and Orville Wright, took a special interest in the flight of the buzzard.[51] Early in 1900, Langley made arrangements to study Jamaica's turkey buzzard and planned to visit the island at the same time that Holmes and Powell were in the Greater Antilles. Langley then enlisted Holmes's cooperation. "Having your camera always with you," Langley wrote to Holmes, "I should value any pictures you might take of a buzzard near enough to show the disposition of the wings and the end feathers which lie separated when soaring. Any will be welcome, more especially those taken near to when the bird is in the act of turning or swinging round, which it does every other minute."[52] The purpose of these photographs was to determine the bird's center of gravity. With the skilled help of the residents of Port Antonio, located in northeastern Jamaica, Holmes captured the birds.[53] There, Holmes met Langley, who arrived in the company of Arnold Hague, the geologist of Yellowstone National Park, and Hague's wife. Holmes warmed to the task at hand, rendering Langley assistance in Jamaica and continued to work on the problem once he was back in Washington, D.C.

In 1901, Langley built a gasoline-driven airplane, the first of its kind. And it worked. He then proceeded to construct a full-scale airplane, or "Aerodrome," as he called it, capable of carrying a man. The wingspan of the Aerodrome, which was not finished until 1903, was forty-eight feet and was powered by a fifty-two horsepower gasoline engine that Stephen M. Balzer and Charles M. Manley designed. Interestingly, the plane was to be launched into the air by a catapult, a device situated on top of a houseboat. This plane was tested twice: once on October 7 and again two months later, on December 8. In both cases, the result was the same: the plane plunged directly into the wide waters of the Potomac River. Fortunately, the pilot, Charles M. Manly, was not hurt in either incident. Six days later on December 14, Wilbur Wright, at Kill Devil Hills, North Carolina, ploughed his engine-powered aircraft into the sand immediately after takeoff. But on December 17, 1903, Orville took off and kept the Flyer I in the air for a very long twelve seconds during which 120 feet of ground was covered. Three more historic flights were made that morning, the last one by Wilbur. On that occasion, he stayed in the air almost one minute and covered 852 feet of ground.[54]

Holmes was not there to see the Wright brothers make aviation history in North Carolina, but was present with his pencil and sketchbook at a dock on the Potomac to watch the Langley launches, in which he felt he had a small personal stake in the outcome. The dotted line that Holmes drew in one of the sketches from the catapult to the water immediately below recorded as accurately as possible the "flight" of the Aerodrome.[55] On December 9, the day after the second crash, Washington's *The Evening Star* published a mocking editorial cartoon of the event. In the top half of the cartoon several different kind of birds—a parrot, an owl, stork, and several others—watch the crash of the Aerodrome depicted in the picture's bottom half by a dotted line (except unlike the more dignified downward arc Holmes drew, this line loop-de-looped). The birds in the cartoon say to each other: "Wonder Which of Us Was the Model!" The answer was written on a sign above the houseboat, which said, "Home of the Buzzard," and on another sign above the sinking aircraft were the words "The Buzzard." Holmes no doubt saw the cartoon, but his reaction to these taunts can only be imagined.[56] Langley was devastated and died three years later believing all of his efforts in aviation had been for naught.[57] For their part, the Wright brothers would go on and develop an improved aircraft, which the U.S. Army Signal Corps agreed to purchase in 1908.

12

The Racial Frontier

The Succession

ON SEPTEMBER 23, 1902, John Wesley Powell passed away in Haven, Maine. The timing of his departure was fitting. Late September was a time when American explorers of the Far West typically brought their field-work to a close before the weather turned. When Holmes heard the sad news, he was in Kimmswick, Missouri, which was located south of St. Louis in Jefferson County, on the west side of the Mississippi River. He and Gerard Fowke of the Smithsonian Institution were in the field investigating fossil-bone beds where human artifacts were found in association with mammoth fossils. Holmes again found insufficient evidence to establish a direct link, however.[1] On learning of the demise of "the grand old man," Holmes dropped everything and "repaired at once to Washington."[2] W J McGee was the "ethnologist-in-charge" and had been Powell's second-in-command for years. Many in the scientific community, including Franz Boas, who was emerging as one of the most influential men in American anthropology, ex-pected the directorship to go to McGee, a former farmboy from eastern Iowa.

Secretary Langley, however, had developed a strong dislike for McGee and was determined that he should not succeed Powell. In Holmes's words, McGee "had in some way antagonized" and gained the "ill-will" of the secre-tary. Indeed, Langley made it clear as early as 1893 that he did not want McGee to serve as director of the BAE and only because of his deference to Powell did he allow McGee to run the bureau as "ethnologist-in-charge."[3] Beyond personal differences, Langley had prepared a list of reasons why he believed McGee was unsuitable to succeed Powell as director. In "strict confi-dence," Langley told Holmes on February 13, 1902, that with Powell's immi-nent demise the bureau would be "placed in great danger" because "Mr. McGee was not regarded with confidence by the Senators and Members responsible for appropriations." According to Langley, McGee was regarded as a "poor financial manager." Langley also explained that McGee had "enemies," not least of whom, apparently, was Langley. Holmes reported that he spoke up for McGee, made it clear that "his present place" as head curator of anthropology at the National Museum "was [his] choice of all places," and that he was concerned about his health given the pressures of the position.[4] He clearly did not want the job. The upshot of this and subsequent private conversations with Langley, however, was that when the time came Holmes understood that he, not McGee, would replace Powell, although Holmes would be allowed to keep a place at the National Museum. That is, in carrying out Langley's orders, he was allowing himself to be used at the expense of McGee. Holmes understood the ethical quandary involved in this situation, but justified acceptance of the position by citing that he was only following his superior's orders, and thus had no other choice in the matter.[5] Institutional loyalty was for him paramount, and it overrode any other considerations.

When the major died, then, things moved very quickly. On October 11, 1902, just eighteen days after the fact, Langley named Holmes as Powell's successor and two days later Holmes officially "took charge" of the bureau, the offices of which were located in the Adams Building on Washington's F Street.[6] Holmes made it clear early that he would try to bring "conservatism and modesty" to the old bureau, noting with pride that he enjoyed a reputation for the same. He was entirely successful in achieving this less than inspiring goal, as the next eight years would show. To set the right tone for his administration, Holmes insisted on the more modest title of "chief" instead of "director," and asked that his salary be reduced from forty-five hundred dollars to the more modest four thousand dollars. The dynamic and expansive Theodore Roosevelt may have been president at this time, but not every executive in Washington was Rooseveltian.[7]

These changes, of course, were in strict accord with Langley's wishes and represented the subordination of Powell's maverick bureau to the secretary of the Smithsonian Institution. Powell's stature in government science had been so commanding that he was able to do things—or get away with things—that no else could dream of doing. According to the historian of the BAE, Curtis M. Hinsley, Jr., "Langley wanted, in short, to return the Bureau to its original role of 1879, as an information arm of the Congress and the people."[8] It was Holmes's mission as chief to see to it that the BAE's activist days were over.

For Powell, science without reform was useless. In fact, Powell, as his own career richly illustrated, believed that one of the responsibilities of the scientist was to work for the betterment of society by actively exposing truths that were pertinent to current issues and concerns. The best example of this position was his insistence on the rational, even planned, development of the country's arid lands—a view soundly rejected. Holmes's own work on aggressively correcting the erroneous beliefs concerning the existence of a Pleistocene man in the Americas was another case in point. Cyrus Thomas's work on the identity of the mound builders was yet another. What Langley wanted was a passive bureau, one that avoided rather than stirred up controversy. And it was for that reason, again to quote Hinsley, that "Langley concentrated all BAE resources on the long-awaited *Handbook of American Indians* (formerly the *Cyclopedia*), which he intended as a practical manual for congressmen and constituents."[9] It was not to be a blueprint for reform. The bureau should be in the job of fact-gathering, Langley believed, not of reform, of policymaking, or of concocting grand visions for American society. All that was best left to others.

McGee was bitterly disappointed and humiliated by this turn of events and by his subsequent treatment at the Smithsonian Institution. Indeed, when McGee finally resigned on July 31, 1903, Holmes "promptly" and no doubt gladly forwarded it to the secretary.[10] It was understandable that McGee should have felt wronged. He had been virtually running the BAE for years. Langley's appointment of Holmes, then, was very much a repudiation of his service. Under the circumstances, there was no other way to view the matter. Given the new direction Langley intended for the bureau, it is hard to see how things could have been managed in any way that would have pleased all sides.

Initially, McGee acquiesced in Holmes's appointment, but according to Holmes's account, this acceptance of things was painfully brief. Holmes recounted:

> I hoped that [McGee] would have settled down for a time to his scientific work and wait until his turn should come and it might have come soon, but he broke over all bounds and assumed an attitude toward the Secretary that could not do otherwise than lead to his separation from the Bureau. In seeking revenge himself on the Secretary he has not hesitated at any act fair or foul that promised advantage, howsoever temporary over the Administration of the Bureau. I appreciated fully his claims to the Directorship and his deep disappointment at failure, but I have lost faith in his discretion and honesty. His criticisms are ill-judged and trivial or utterly false. He has stooped to misrepresentation and falsehood which will fully appear from a study of his statements.

If all of this was not enough, Holmes went further to state for the record:

> My work was hard because of the enmity of McGee and his constant attacks. He antagonized the Secretary and was in every way disloyal and harmful. He should have been dismissed at once for the good of the service.

These were hard words and summed up what Holmes felt after months of dispute with McGee. Holmes seemed sincere in his belief that McGee would finally be made director, all evidence to the contrary. McGee, however, seems to have had a clearer understanding of what to expect from the organization. Thus, for him it was a matter of when to fight his demotion: now or later. It did not take him long to choose the former course. In a letter to Franz Boas, whom he had turned to almost immediately for support, McGee wrote on Cosmos Club letterhead: Holmes "has adopted the Langley policy of fair words and foul acts."[11] McGee expressed himself even more melodramatically when he told Boas that "you saw Holmes's cloven foot at Chicago," a reference to when Holmes had vied with Boas for the same job at the Field Columbian Museum, "but I see both of them and the forked tail as well."[12] The sympathies Boas and McGee felt for each other brought the two men together in this time of crisis in McGee's life. So had the intense criticism the two men weathered when McGee, as ethnologist-in-charge, worked out a plan with Boas to share the resources of the bureau and the American Museum of Natural History. The agreement involved the American Museum putting up funds for fieldwork and the bureau the personnel, namely John R. Swanton, who was to conduct ethnological research among the native peoples of the Pacific Northwest.[13] As far as the critics were concerned, inside and out of Washington, the potential for abuse of this arrangement outweighed any possible benefits.

That there was so much acrimony is hardly surprising given the stakes. At issue was nothing less than the directorship of the BAE—the premier position in American anthropology. McGee fought hard for the directorship but, in the end, lost. Boas warned him that "the possible result [of fighting] might be to make [McGee's] relations with Holmes impossible, and," Boas went on, "I believe that after you once begin to attack the Secretary, it will be practically impossible to undo the action that has been taken."[14] Boas had advised Langley directly to reconsider, but Langley responded on October 13, 1902, that it was time to "alter the method of administration."[15]

Despite Boas's advice, McGee decided to fight. Unlike Hayden many years before, McGee was not content to simply disappear in the bureaucracy. His ambition was too great. But he was unable to gain any support inside the

Smithsonian Institution and his attempts to get friends outside to intervene, with the major exception of Boas, proved just as ineffective. His case was even argued in the press, with letters of support from Boas appearing in the November 1902 issues of *The Popular Science Monthly* and *Science,* but again to no avail.[16] Holmes, however, did enjoy support—and not just inside the Smithsonian Institution. From faraway California, Holmes's friend Charles Fletcher Lummis, the editor of *Out West,* wrote: "Your fault certainly would never lie in the direction of grasping, or of trying to elbow anyone else out . . . . I sincerely trust that McGee will not break away. He is certainly too good and strong a man to let even a great disappointment sour him."[17] Lummis had met Holmes and McGee in 1898, when both men had come to California to do fieldwork, and while he may have been right about Holmes, he completely misread what McGee would do in this situation.

The Boas Critique

Boas was more than willing to help McGee, who had "gained" his "esteem and friendship," he recalled years later, "by the courage he showed at the time of [his] troubles in Chicago, in which I found him the only person who had the courage to speak the truth."[18] Boas believed that Holmes had lied to him in 1894 and had been part of a conspiracy with the other Washington men to take his place in Chicago in order to make room for Powell at the bureau. As Boas explained the situation:

> While I was at work there, I learned that Mr. Holmes had been engaged behind my back, and under the condition of secrecy from me, to take my place as soon as I should have done the work of installation, which, owing to my knowledge of the material, nobody else could do. This move was, as I understand it, part of the general attempt at re-adjustment in Washington. Major Powell was to be transferred to the Bureau of Ethnology from the Geological Survey, and some one had to get out of the Bureau to make room for Powell. This whole negotiation was largely carried on . . . by [Charles D.] Walcott, who was one of the candidates for the position of Director of the Geological Survey. I was in their way, and, owing to their influence in Chicago, I was simply turned out. When I learned about these moves, I tried to protect my interests. Among the Washington people concerned I heard nothing but prevarication except from McGee, who had the courage to shoulder his part of the responsibility.[19]

McGee was no doubt behind Powell's subsequent offer of a job to Boas in 1895 to edit bureau reports at a salary of eighteen hundred dollars. He personally tried to get Boas to accept the position. But Boas turned that job down, in part, on the advice of Frederick W. Putnam, and accepted a position at the American Museum of Natural History instead at almost twice the salary.[20] Thus, Boas's decision to help McGee in 1902 was complicated. Friendship and a sense of loyalty to McGee was certainly one reason. Another reason was that he believed that Langley's decision to pass over McGee for the directorship was a great "injustice," since McGee had been "shouldering," in Boas's words, "the whole responsibility for Major Powell, who, during the last few years of his life, was practically incapacitated."[21]

Boas also saw several larger issues at stake here for American science. One was his fear that under Holmes the BAE would become subordinated to the National Museum. Since Holmes kept a place at the National Museum and served as chief of the bureau, Boas could not see how Holmes could do justice to both institutions, and feared that the bureau would be the institution to suffer. Moreover, Boas thought the bureau would, given the combination of the two positions under one person, lose the independence it had enjoyed under Major Powell. "It seems to my mind fundamentally wrong," Boas wrote in a letter to the famous German émigré, former secretary of the interior, and chairman of the executive committee of the Smithsonian Institution, Carl Schurz, "to combine the work of the museum with that of a survey, because the methods and aims of the two are entirely distinct, and because they require men of quite different training and bent of mind. That this is true, is best shown by the fact that the Biological and Geological Surveys are entirely independent of the National Museum."[22]

Boas made it clear in another letter, this one to the inventor and Smithsonian regent Alexander Graham Bell, what he thought of Holmes. "Without casting any reflection on the ability of Mr. Holmes," Boas wrote, "whose work on prehistoric art and the geologic aspect of archaeology I greatly admire, I judge that his natural gifts lead him to a thorough appreciation of visual objects, but that his interest in that part of anthropology which deals with ideas alone is slight."[23] In short, it was Boas's opinion that Langley "considered the Bureau primarily as a personal affair of Major Powell, the independent life of which was to end with his life, not as a public institution capable of expanding and of becoming a useful member of our Government institutions."[24]

What troubled Boas even more was that he believed the time had come for the bureau to adopt an ambitious new agenda; one that went beyond the old charge of studying Indian peoples before they were completely overwhelmed by American civilization, as important as that charge was. In the summer of 1903, he offered such an agenda to Carl Schurz in the form of a critique of the bureau's twenty-three-year history. First, Boas said, the bureau's "purely scientific work ought to have been directed to a reconstruction of the earliest history of our country, the records of which will have vanished with the disappearance of Indian culture and Indian languages"; second, "it should have investigated the influence of education upon the Indian"; third, "the Bureau should have trained intelligent teachers for Indian schools"; fourth, "it should have studied the physical and social effect of mixture between White and Indian, and between Negro and Indian"; and fifth, the "practicability of an economic development of native industries might have been investigated." In addition, Boas thought the "Bureau should have been given authority to extend its work over the Negro and White races," thereby transforming it into an "Anthropological Survey of the country." This survey "would have furnished information of no less importance to Congress and to the Administration than that collected by the Biological and Geological Surveys."[25]

After observing Holmes's conservative administration as chief of the BAE for little over a year, Boas had very little to say that was positive. Holmes may have been a Powell man, but he was no Powell. And even if he had been, he would have been at odds with Langley. In another letter to Alexander Graham Bell, Boas concluded that Holmes was doing little more than bringing to a close projects that had been started under Major Powell. "From what I know about the work of the Bureau," he wrote:

> I gain the impression that the whole policy is directed at the present time to giving final reports of work that has been carried on during previous years. The "Cyclopedia of Indian Tribes" [*Handbook of American Indians North of Mexico*], which is under way, is put forward as a final report on the work of this class. A "Handbook of North American Languages," which is in my charge, seems to find encouragement from the same point of view, as being a final presentation of the linguistic results of the Bureau. I fear that the strong emphasis laid upon these summaries may create the impression that the work of the Bureau may be closed within a reasonable time. This of course is an impression which would be exceedingly unfortunate, because no scientific work of the magnitude of the work of the Bureau can be expected to be closed, but ought to develop constantly in depth and usefulness.[26]

Thus, in Boas's estimation Holmes lacked vision and leadership, which not only hurt the bureau in particular but American anthropology in general. The profession, after all, had looked to the bureau to help set the terms of scientific debate. As chief of the bureau, however, it is fair to say that Holmes acted more like an executor of Powell's estate rather than as a prime beneficiary who had the freedom to invest the bureau's wealth in new scientific ventures. In sum, the head of the bureau worked for Langley now, and everybody knew it. Still, there was more to Holmes's administration of the BAE than Boas's critical evaluation would suggest.

Holmes's Vision

Indeed, Boas's criticisms miss an important point. The bureau was formed, after all, in order to study the Native American population of the United States before it was too late; for it was widely believed in 1879 that the days of these people—culturally or genetically—were numbered. That the bureau under Langley and Holmes would go on to concentrate on bringing the results of years of work together in a series of useful, popular handbooks, then, is entirely consistent with its original mission. Accordingly, Holmes made the two-volume, labor-intensive *Handbook of American Indians North of Mexico* (1907, 1910), which Frederick Webb Hodge edited, the bureau's first priority. This work was designed to "represent the latest views of ethnologists on the subjects treated" and to be a "history of the past work of the Bureau."[27] At one point, the bureau referred to the handbook as nothing less than "a résumé of all that is known regarding aborigines of the United States, based on information from every possible source, including unpublished records of the Bureau."[28] Holmes called it "the most important single achievement of the Bureau of Ethnology."[29]

Holmes, in fact, wrote a number of the handbook entries, including those entitled "Arrows, Bows, and Quivers," "Chisels," "Antiquity," which succinctly reviewed the history of the paleolithic question, "Cache disks and blades," "Knives," and "Mortars." This work became an invaluable reference, and no doubt Holmes's entries in it enjoyed many more readers over the years than did any of his other published works. Boas himself was responsible for the *Handbook of American Indian Languages*, which appeared in 1911, the year after Holmes stepped down as chief. And in 1919, Holmes would finally go on to present to the public his *Handbook of Aboriginal American Antiquities*, which helped solidify his position as the foremost authority on the subject of Indian mining, and for a few years anyway, as the expert on the antiquity question.[30] While the absorbing work on the handbooks went forward, time was found to receive delegations of Indians who were then photographed, in the same last-chance spirit that canyons in the American West were later photographed before being dammed and turned into reservoirs.

Holmes did not push to turn the bureau into a United States Anthropological Survey, as Boas proposed, but he did have similar, even Powellian ideas. At one point, Holmes prepared for a plan in which he called for the establishment of a physical anthropological fund.[31] The purpose of this fund, which would have the "requisite laboratory facilities," was to provide for a "comprehensive biological study of the many and diversified racial elements of the American nation, and the application of the results to promoting the welfare of the nation." Thus, the fund's purview would extend far beyond the bureau's study of America's aboriginal peoples. More specifically, Holmes wanted the fund to pursue the following six broad "lines of work," which were

One:

A determination of the character and potentiality of the physical, intellectual and social elements which the nation should control, direct, and assimilate.

Two:

A determination of the results of the intermingling of the white, black, and other races, on physical development, longevity, fecundity, vigor, and liability to disease, as well as on the intellectual and social attributes, and an elucidation of the operation of heredity and the effects of changing social and climatic conditions, so that a firm base of knowledge may be provided for those who are to frame and administer laws relating to these objects, and those who direct the policy of thousands of institutions that deal directly or indirectly with the physical and intellectual and social welfare of the nation.

Three:

Physical, physiological and pathological investigations on the living, and physical studies of such remains of man as may be essential in carrying out the purposes of this foundation.

Four:

Cooperation as far as possible with all agencies, now existing or hereafter established, engaged in collecting data relating to the physical, mental and social man, in such manner as to encourage in the broadest and most liberal way investigation, research and discovery in the field specified.

Five:

The utilization of existing collections of anatomical material, and the supplementing of such collections, so far as necessary or feasible, by procuring and maintaining the laboratories necessary to the purposes herein defined.

Six:

The publication of reports, memoirs, etc., and the distribution by means of lectures and publication of the results of the activities of the proposed establishment.

And finally:

In general, to do all and everything that may be requisite to the fulfilment [*sic*] of the purposes of this Fund.[32]

In short, Holmes's proposed fund or department of physical anthropology under the Smithsonian Institution would have collected and interpreted data—if it had been established—that would have allowed it to advise the government and inform legislation on race matters. Holmes did not attach a dollar figure to his plan. His thinking along these lines apparently did not get much beyond the preliminary stage. But Boas estimated that his own, similar five-year plan for the bureau would require an 800,000-dollar budget, in contrast to the bureau's contemporary annual budget that varied between 30,000 dollars and 40,000 dollars.[33]

Nothing came of Boas's grand plan, which Boas presented to the regents of the Smithsonian Institution, or of Holmes's fund. In other words, there would be no powerful federal agency, imbued with the Progressive era's faith in scientific expertise, dedicated to an applied anthropology based on racist classifications of human groups. This was probably a very good thing, for while Boas and his students would try to disentangle race and culture, it is far from clear whether students of this relatively liberal and egalitarian school of anthropological thought would have been the ones to prevail in either Boas's survey or Holmes's fund.[34] Indeed, even Boas himself, as the historian Vernon J. Williams, Jr., has pointed out, never entirely escaped the racism of nineteenth-century physical anthropology. As late as 1915, Boas was still "torn between his commitment to physical anthropological assumptions, which suggested that the races were not equal, and his commitment to cultural anthropology, which suggested that white prejudice was an obvious obstacle to black progress."[35]

Holmes did succeed, however, in making the case for the establishment of the much more modest division of physical anthropology in the National Museum, which was to study the mental and physical characteristics of Native Americans. Holmes saw to it, then, that the science of anthropometry was added to the other categories of bureau investigation, such as aboriginal arts and industries, languages, religious and social customs, and forms of government. With the death of Thomas Wilson and his own acceptance of the chief job, Holmes knew that the means, in the amount of fifty-seven hundred dollars, were presently at hand for such an undertaking.[36] All that was needed, then, was a collection and a curator to oversee it. And Holmes deftly acquired both. He arranged to have the collection of twenty-two hundred human crania stored at the Army Medical Museum transferred to the National Museum and he secured Aleš Hrdlička's appointment as curator, which turned out to be a major coup for the Smithsonian Institution. Hrdlička took charge of the new division on May 1, 1903, after finishing a four-year expedition to the Southwest and Mexico, sponsored by the American Museum of Natural History in New York. In his new capacity as chief, then, Holmes created—simply and economically—a division of physical anthropology, headed by one of this country's great physical anthropologists.[37] Hrdlička, in fact, founded *The American Journal of Physical Anthropology* in 1918. And the authorities C. Loring Brace and Ashley Montagu referred to Hrdlička's 1930 work, *The Skeletal Remains of Early Man*, as "fundamental."[38] These accomplishments were much less than what Boas had called for or what was envisioned in Holmes's own proposed fund, but it did mark a significant, new departure for the National Museum. And Holmes did so with Secretary Langley's full support.[39]

A New People?

Holmes's enthusiasm for physical anthropology carried over into his own work and indeed preceded his appointment as chief of the bureau. On February 11, 1902, as retiring president of the Anthropological Society of Washington, he gave the annual address, entitled "The Origin, Development, and Probable Destiny of the Races of Man," under the auspices of the Washington Academy of Science and in the Hall of Columbian University. The address subsequently appeared as the lead article in the July–September issue of the *American Anthropologist*.[40] In a talk illustrated by a series of lantern slides and illuminated by metaphors drawn from the more familiar worlds of art and geology, Holmes emphasized that the racial distinctions among members of the human family were the "most striking and important that can be made, and the races naturally become the subject of special study." This is the traditional view. Today, of course, physical anthropologists hold precisely the opposite position. In the words of Frank B. Livingston author of the article "On the Non-Existence of Human Races," which appeared in *Current Anthropology* in 1962, "There are no races, only clines."[41] A cline, incidentally, in

C. Loring Brace's succinct definition, is "simply the gradient in the response of a trait [such as skin color] to the graded intensity of the selective force [such as ultraviolet intensity].[42] Moreover, in the words of the anthropologist, Mark Nathan Cohen, "one cannot predict other traits by knowing one trait that a person possesses."[43] Ashley Montagu is perhaps even more clear than Cohen: "there is absolutely no genetic linkage between genes for physical traits, mental capacities, or civilization-building abilities."[44] Thus, the concept of race, according to contemporary views, no longer has any biological meaning because human traits cannot be linked in racially specific ways.

This was certainly not how science saw the matter in 1902. In a panoramic sweep, Holmes described the human family as being separated on various land areas and divided up into "nations, tribes, and families." "At the right," he wrote of the spectrum of human skin color,

> the assemblage is white, and at the left it is black, while between are varying shades of yellow and brown connecting the extremes by insensible gradations. Along with the difference in tint and tone go certain dissimilarities of form, stature, proportion, and physiognomy, emphasizing the distinctions due to color and thus blocking out the groups called races—the Caucasian, the African, the Mongolian, and the American.[45]

The linking of traits, as Holmes does here, is typical of the traditional view on human race; his observation of "insensible gradations," on the other hand, which he extended to other "divergent characters" besides skin color, has a modern ring to it, if for different biological reasons.

Holmes's main argument, however, was that racial differences aside, there was a "general physical unity" of the races, and to make the point he contrasted slides (slides in his lecture; figures in his article) of humans with slides of apes—chimpanzees, orangs, and gorillas—noting that even the Australian, although "a debased savage," is "still distinctly a man."[46] Debased or not, Holmes went on to note to his audience that there were few differences between the Caucasian and the Australian, "except in minor features," which in any event are "difficult to express by graphic means." Holmes did call attention to the "wide distinctions between black and the white," such as "color, physiognomy, hair, etc."; however, he came back to his point that "in all elements that go to make up the physical type of *Homo sapiens* there is practical unity."[47]

The stress on the "general physical unity" of the races also served Holmes's larger point that the races of man diverged from a common stock in post-Tertiary times as early "pioneers" broke away from the original homogeneous group and slowly spread out from the tropics to every corner of the globe. He called this view *monogenesis,* a "term . . . used to signify origin in a common stem or ancestral group, and is thus contrasted with the word polygenesis, which signifies origin in a number of stems or widely variant ancestral groups."[48] Racial differentiation, then, according to Holmes, occurred as a result of the subsequent long "occupancy of isolated continental areas of the earth by primitive man." Environment or geography was the crucial agent of divergence.

Holmes went on to say: "I prefer to think of the present races as representing in their diversified types the fullest degree of divergence by the human species at any period in its history."[49] But he did not believe that this situation would remain static for very long. There existed, in his judgement, only a "brief opportunity to witness and record the intermingling of the racial elements of the world, and the resultant physical, mental, moral, and pathological manifestations in all stages and in every phase."[50] Holmes boldly declared:

> Man has spread and occupied the world, and the resulting isolations and partial isolations on continent and island of peoples having meager artificial means of transportation, have brought about, directly or indirectly, the variations called races; but the period of group isolation and consequent race specialization is at an end. In the last few hundred years the sea-going ship and the railway have been invented and the extremes of the world are no farther apart than were the opposite shores of good-sized islands when, a little while ago, all men went afoot. The period of differentiation is closed forever and the period of universal integration is upon us. . . . The continent of America has changed its inhabitants in the twinkling of an eye, and Asia, Africa, Australia, and the islands of the Pacific are in the throes of race disintegration.[51]

As an anthropologist turned prophet, Holmes believed that it was inevitable that "the races will fade out and disappear as the combined result of miscegenation and the blotting out of the weaker branches." The whole world, in other words, would not only become one great racial melting pot, it was becoming one. And to reassure his no doubt largely white audience of their place in this future, he predicted, "The world will be filled to over flowing with a generalized race in which the dominating blood will be that of the race that today has the strongest claim physically and intellectually to take possession of all the resources of the land and sea."[52] At the beginning of the twentieth century, there was no question what race that would be.

Reading this statement today, it sounds like another example of the "survival of the fittest" ideology that led the West straight toward the epic disaster of the Great War. It clearly represented Holmes's own indirect embrace of America's successful bid for empire as a consequence of the recent victory of the United States over Spain. Certainly, there was no question in Holmes's mind what people would and should dominate in any new racial ordering of the world—although he was far less clear on how this result would actually work in a real biological or genetic sense. Many of his assimilationist contemporaries, including President Theodore Roosevelt, were equally fuzzy on this point. But it was an article of faith, if not of science, that the races or "somatic groups" of the world would somehow be integrated into one, but the blood of whites, specifically Anglo-Saxons, would somehow continue to flow supreme in the veins of this new people.

Perhaps one explanation for the ambiguity in Holmes's thinking here is that he personally took part in the exploration and scientific conquest of the American West—an endeavor that helped facilitate the region's rapid peopling by whites and its integration into the rest of the nation's capitalist economy. Thus, Holmes's racial predictions were based on more than just scientific speculation; they were also, in effect, projections derived from his own personal experience in a part of the country where by 1902 the future he saw for the world had already become the past for the American West. For that region was a place where religious visions of "Manifest Destiny" had rapidly given way to the secular reality of a white-dominated society, in which Native Americans had been confined to reservations and subjected to assimilationist policies; and where other non-Anglo-American groups, from the Hispanic inhabitants of Texas to the Asian populations in California, were subordinated just as effectively as the black minority in the Jim Crow South. From this historical and biographical perspective, Holmes's words, "The world will be filled to over flowing with a generalized race in which the dominating blood will be that of the race that today has the strongest claim physically and intellectually to take possession of all the resources of the land and sea," make more sense. They conform perfectly with the pervasive racist and Social Darwinist thinking of his day; they also seemed to validate America's very recent frontier and imperial experiences in which he played a part.[53]

In 1910, Holmes published another article on race in the *American Anthropologist*, entitled "Some Problems of the American Race." He read an earlier version of this piece on December 28, 1909, at the Boston meeting of the American Anthropological Association. As chief of the BAE, Holmes was one of the U.S. government's most recognized authorities on Native Americans.

His views on the subject of race, therefore, were especially noteworthy, and they provide an official window into American race relations on the eve of World War I. The piece also brought up to date the state of research on Native Americans, which was still concerned with answering such fundamental questions as "the *how*, the *when*, the *whence*, and the *who* of aboriginal inhabitants."[54]

Holmes expanded on the idea he had raised earlier of a great racial mixing. The peoples of the world had entered, he argued, irreversibly into a period of "rapid integration" and "race comminglings."[55] Holmes pointed out that this development was "especially pronounced between the black and red races in the United States, between white and red in Mexico, among all three in middle and South America, and among the yellow, white, and black races in various parts of the Old World." And looking ahead, he forecast "successive somatic changes." The driving force in bringing about the integration of the races, Holmes believed, was that the "barriers of land and sea are almost wholly broken down." He went on to note, interestingly, that the "only remaining barrier of the races is race prejudice, which attitude will retard the progress of integration but not prevent its final triumph."[56] Thus, Holmes, like Boas, if for different reasons, also noted what he believed to be the temporary importance of racial discrimination.

At first glance, Holmes's ideas seem consistent with fairly modern views and, taken together, form an early model of racial tolerance and acceptance of intermarriage or "amalgamation." However, Holmes went on to reveal that he believed that the process of racial blending might not proceed peacefully and, in fact, would definitely involve winners and losers. Indeed, Holmes was chillingly clear on this point:

> The complete absorption or blotting out of the red race will be quickly accomplished, and beyond this, though still far away, we foresee a final reduction of all peoples to a common race type. If peaceful amalgamation fails, extinction of the weaker by less gentle means will do the work. No other result can be anticipated unless the wonder-working agencies of transportation should make possible migration to other worlds other than ours. The final battle of the races for possession of the world is already on.[57]

Holmes was even more blunt several years earlier in a newspaper interview he gave for Washington's *The Evening Star*. In response to the reporter John E. Watkins's question, "What, professor, will be the Indians' future?" Holmes answered:

> In the great crucible of our civilization so many elements are now being mixed together a racial strain so numerically weak as the Indian will not only amalgamate with the other race, but disappear . . . As diagrammed by the ethnologist of the far future the career of the Indian will appear as a lenticular figure—beginning in nothing, ending in nothing—a figure of perhaps universal application by the historian of mundane things."[58]

Holmes's vision of integration, or rather obliteration, carried a very dark undertone, which is hard to avoid given how he and his contemporaries confused race and culture. As a consequence of this huge intellectual muddle, it is not surprising that Holmes's views on "the American race" was what turned out to be destined for "total oblivion," rather than the American race itself.[59]

Holmes's acceptance of the concept of race as an organizing principle and category of analysis signaled the direction in which the rest of the anthropology profession was moving in the early years of the twentieth century. However problematic *race* would become as a useful scientific term, during the years that Holmes was chief of the BAE, that is, from October 11, 1902, to June 10, 1909, racial theory was viewed as a new and supposedly more precise way of studying human physical and cultural differences. In the years preceding the human disasters of the First and Second World Wars, racial distinctions, which somehow always involved invidious comparisons, could and were justified in the name of science and progress as a matter of course. In retrospect, however, this was a dangerous period of relative innocence; a prologue to Holocaust.

13

History and Prophecy

For holmes, the history of Native Americans was far more interesting and rich than was the future of these peoples, the latter of which he and many of his generation thought looked bleak indeed. Indians were literally seen as buffaloes in a world where cattle either was becoming or was already king. Indeed, the history of the movement to preserve endangered species in this country should begin with this nation's callous willingness, although almost always expressed in terms of dutiful regret, to allow not only numerous animal species to disappear, but an entire people, the American "race" to disappear from the face of the earth as well. It was precisely this dire and degrading outlook, of course, all of the interest expressed in studying language and culture notwithstanding, which provided the BAE with its raison d'être and informed the government's policies of assimilation.

These policies — such as land allotment, citizenship, and education, which the self-proclaimed "Friends of the Indians" advocated in the 1880s — were based on the brutal idea that Native Americans, who were estimated to number ten million at the time of contact, but whose numbers had drastically dwindled to several hundred thousand by 1900, had only two choices: they could change, that is, assimilate or, in effect, cease being Indian; or they could die off.[1] Either way, the result was the same in the long term — the obliteration of an entire people. The poverty of imagination displayed by Anglo-Americans when it came to the "Indian question," or to race questions in general, in the early twentieth century is remarkable given what was otherwise an enormously creative and dynamic period in the nation's history. It would be another generation before the country would finally be prepared to entertain other possibilities in regard to Native Americans, such as those advanced by John Collier, New Deal reformer and advocate of cultural pluralism.

Holmes, as we have seen, devoted much more of his time and energy to the fundamental questions of Native American antiquity than to the present well-being or future of Indian peoples. In fact, he personally seemed uncomfortable with Indian people, alive anyway. It was to the questions—"the *how*, the *when*, the *whence*, and the *who* of the aboriginal inhabitants"—that Holmes devoted the rest of the article on "Some Problems of the American Race," discussed in the preceding chapter, which is key to much of his thinking on these subjects.

As to the questions of *who* and *whence*, Holmes's summary of the conclusions that the scientific community had reached as of 1910 differ little, in the main, from modern views. Holmes distinguished the Indian tribes throughout North and South America from the "Eskimo" or Innuit people of the far north. Holmes wrote: "When we observe that the Eskimo are manifestly more closely allied with the boreal peoples of the Old World than are the Indian tribes, and take into account the fact that they occupy the northern margin of the continent including the ferry and the bridge to Asia, we conclude that they represent late intercontinental movements and that they may be comparatively recent arrivals in America." On the other hand, Holmes noted that Indian peoples showed "wide divergence" in "secondary racial characters and especially in cultural achievements, a condition indicating a prolonged period of well-localized yet not wholly isolated occupancy."[2]

Holmes also observed, "In a large percentage of their characters the American aborigines distinctly approximate the Asiatic type of man." Hrdlička, incidentally, was a strong advocate of the Asian origin theory and Holmes, who was deeply impressed with "evidence furnished by osseous human remains," clearly agreed with it. However, Holmes was also unwilling to close the door to other possibilities. As he put it two years later, in another piece entitled "Bearing of Archeological Evidence on the Place of Origin and on the Question of the Unity or Plurality of the American Race," which also appeared in the *American Anthropologist*, "it seems to me highly probable, considering the nature of the archeological evidence, that the Western World has not been always and wholly beyond the reach of members of the white, Polynesian, and perhaps even black races."[3] Such reservations have tantalized students of the Americas ever since. At the same time that Holmes agreed with the Asian-origin hypothesis, he dismissed the now largely forgotten North Atlantic land-bridge theory, which held, on the basis of differences in crania types, that paleolithic Europeans beat the ancestors of Indians to the Americas; he believed that the arguments for an "autochthonous origin of American man" would wither away under the "sharp fire of criticism"; and he thought, for a host of reasons, that it was in "the highest degree improbable" that America was the birthplace of the human race and that the peoples of the world migrated from the New to the Old World, instead of the other way around.[4]

And as for the questions of the *when* and *how*, that is, "the problems of antiquity and distribution," Holmes showed a particular interest, especially in regard to the first of the two, since here, after all, his prodigious archaeological work over the past twenty years made him the premier authority on the subject. Holmes restated his oft-stated position that he thought that the case for glacial man had yet to be proven and he thought that new claims for a glacial-era man based on evidence found in Brazil and Argentina would no more hold up to scrutiny than did those made in North America. Interestingly, he discussed the matter in terms of absolute years instead of in relative geological terms, as was more typical. As a result, at least from the standpoint of the chronology in use as of 1910, Holmes's position and the modern view suddenly and ironically coincided with each other. Today, it is generally accepted that humans were present in North America at least twelve thousand years ago or more, if not as early as twenty thousand years ago, that is, sometime during the end of the last Ice Age. According to the chronology Holmes used, however, "the Recent or post-Glacial" period was estimated to cover the past twenty-five thousand years.[5] In an earlier newspaper interview he gave for *The Evening Star*, Holmes told the reporter, John E. Watkins, "I should say that we as yet have no satisfactory proof that man existed on this continent until about the close of the glacial period, which might be eight to ten thousand years ago, but the figures must not to be [*sic*] taken too seriously."[6] So the timing of the two positions roughly overlapped. But the great debate centered, as we have seen, on Holmes's argument for a post-glacial arrival, which today means that the event had to have occurred within the past ten thousand years. So in retrospect Holmes was wrong on both counts, if right, as was pointed out above, in terms of the science of the day. Holmes did include, at this time, an important refinement to his argument for a late occupancy of the Americas, which complemented his view on *how* the first inhabitants reached the Western Hemisphere, namely by crossing the Bering Strait—literally, by sea or by seasonable ice bridges. Beringia, incidentally, still awaited discovery. By equating the ability to settle harsh northern climes, which separated the temperate climes of the Old World from the those in the New, with advanced intelligence, Holmes was then able to argue the point that the peopling of the New World must have occurred relatively late in human evolution.

Since the European discovery of the Americas, native peoples have been the subject of a great deal of scientific and popular curiosity, especially in regard to who they were and where they come from. Native peoples could answer these and related questions, but Europeans and their descendants never took Indians or their myths seriously. By the early twentieth century, however, science had finally succeeded in providing a basic framework for understanding, at least to the satisfaction of European Americans, the fundamental questions associated with the indigenous people of the Americas. And what should be clear by now is that Holmes played no small role in the intellectual progress that the scientific community had achieved in this area of knowledge. What is more, in a world of rapidly growing specialization, Holmes continued to call for a very broad interdisciplinary approach, which he declared to be indispensable to the writing of "the history of the American race."

Exhibiting Science

For decades the Smithsonian Institution had participated in the international expositions hosted by various U.S. cities, notably Philadelphia's Centennial Exhibition and Chicago's Columbian extravaganza. The Smithsonian Institution's exhibits at these events, which Holmes had helped to organize over the years, were invaluable public-relations events and as such were taken very seriously. The expositions also provided periodic opportunities to rethink and redesign museum displays and were as important in this regard as were the international congresses and exhibit exchanges with the world's other leading museums, such as the Field Columbian, the Carnegie, the American Museum of Natural History, the Peabody, the Trocadero in Paris, the British Museum in London, the Royal Ethnological Museum in Berlin, and the National Museum of Mexico. The expositions, congresses, and exchanges help explain the enormous creativity in exhibition during this great international museum-building era.

As chief of the BAE from 1902 to 1909, with strong ties to the National Museum, Holmes was directly and sometimes personally involved in the supervision of the Smithsonian Institution exhibits, work that he was exceptionally well prepared to do given his previous exposition work. As chief he was involved with the Louisiana Purchase Exposition in St. Louis in 1904; the subsequent Lewis and Clark Exposition in Portland; the Jamestown Ter-Centennial Exposition in Norfolk in 1907; and the Alaska-Yukon-Pacific Exposition in Seattle in 1909. For instance, Holmes, with the assistance of De Lancy Gill, H. W. Hendley, W. H. Gill, and others, prepared plaster casts of over a hundred archaeological objects, including five replicas of building ruins from Mexico and Yucatán, in a reprise of the model work of Southwest cliff dwellings that he and William Henry Jackson had displayed at the Centennial Exhibition in Philadelphia. These models, which were shown at the museum and loaned to other institutions, depicted the "Temple of the Cross" at Palenque, Chiapas; the "Temple of the Columns" at Mitla, Oaxaca; the "Pyramid Temple" at Xochicalco, Morales; the "Castle" at Chichén Itzá, Yucatán; and the "House of the Governor" at Uxmal, Yucatán.[7] The theme of the St. Louis exhibit was "the mythic symbolism of various tribes as embodied in their decorative arts."[8] At the end of the St. Louis Exposition in 1904, a portion of the Smithsonian exhibit was broken down and sent to Portland for the Lewis and Clark Exposition, a process of recycling that was not at all uncommon.

Holmes, A. Howard Clark, and Cyrus Adler served on an advisory committee to W. De C. Ravenel, the administrative assistant of the U.S. National Museum and representative of the Smithsonian Institution at the Jamestown Exposition. Holmes personally designed the Jamestown exhibit, a hall lined with statuary and walls adorned with frieze, rows of historic portraits (for example, Raleigh, Smith, Pocahontas), pictures, and maps.[9] Holmes reprised the lay-figure idea, including one depicting the historical subject of "John Smith Trading with the Indians."[10] The exhibit was largely historical rather than archeological in emphasis, although Holmes did see to it that the stone tools of the Virginia Indians were on display, as examples of aboriginal technology.

The Alaska-Yukon-Pacific Exposition in Seattle in 1909 was, among other things, an important imperialistic ritual intended, in part, to "illustrate our national history, especially with reference to Alaska, Hawaii, the Philippine Islands, and the United State west of the Rocky Mountains."[11] To reach Seattle and this grand demonstration of U.S. incorporation, Holmes took the long way around. He stopped at the Grand Canyon to select a site at Sentinel Point to commemorate John Wesley Powell's feats of exploration and, indirectly, the scientific conquest of the American West (the monument was dedicated on May 20, 1918); and he visited a number of museums along the West Coast, from Los Angeles to Victoria.[12] He also stopped long enough in Santa Barbara to study the mission establishment there in order to build to scale a model of a Spanish mission for the Seattle exposition, a display which, in effect, nationalized the mission-revival movement already under way in California; this display was also another example of the growing awakening of the nation to its rich Spanish heritage. In addition to the mission model, Holmes also designed Eskimo lay-figure family groups. This was yet another illustration of the ethnological richness of the United States and at the same time, with unintended irony, a form of imperial celebration.

Holmes's interest in Spanish missions may very well have been a result of his friendship with Charles Fletcher Lummis—the likely inventor of the term *Southwest* and one of the founders of the Landmarks Club, an organization dedicated to historic preservation.[13] Prior to reaching Santa Barbara, Holmes stopped in Los Angeles where he probably visited Lummis, whose many regional involvements included preserving California's missions. And interestingly enough, Holmes also knew Dr. Herbert E. Bolton, who would eventually become the nation's greatest Borderlands historian. Bolton, who was then at the University of Texas before moving on to the University of California at Berkeley, had offered his services to the bureau in January 1906. Since then, Bolton had contributed close to a hundred articles on the Texas Indians for the second part of F. W. Hodges's *Handbook of American Indians North of Mexico*.[14] While it is not clear how familiar Holmes was with Bolton, he knew him well enough to ask him to join the bureau's editorial staff and to try to solicit from him a monograph on the Texas Indians. Bolton did not produce this proposed work, but he did publish a piece on the Hasinai.[15] In any event, Holmes's life intersected with two generations of Anglo intellectuals whose work on the country's Hispanic heritage would ramify American culture and scholarship for the rest of the century.

Stuttgart and Santiago

Holmes's activities as chief of the BAE were important from the standpoint of the complex, dialectical relationship between America's rapidly evolving national culture and its established (or newly discovered, or perhaps invented) regional traditions. In addition, there was a growing appreciation for the ethnological diversity of the country's "savage" past, which the BAE had done so much to capture for posterity and the awareness of which further defined in many subtle and not so subtle ways the country's "civilized" present. The Smithsonian Institution shared this information through its exposition exhibits, its many publications, and, of course, through its vast Washington collections. In 1905, the National Museum averaged 753 visitors a day, which added up to an impressive annual total of 235,000 persons.[16] To accommodate the growing collections and the museum's swelling popularity, Congress authorized in 1903 the construction of a new museum building (today's massively magnificent National Museum of Natural History, which sits on the north side of the Mall directly across from the Smithsonian Castle and the

Arts and Industries Building (the old National Museum building). That Native Americans did not disappear according to script did not take away from the richness of the ethnological record that the bureau had laboriously collected since 1879 and which was constantly being expanded and revised. In a deeply ironic way, the bureau's work actually helped prepare the country for a time when cultural pluralism and even Indian self-determination would not only be generally accepted, but considered a "national" good—within limits, of course.

As important as was Holmes's bureau to the internal cultural development of the United States, Holmes's bureau activities also included participation in the broader museum-building movement that had swept the entire Western world. On August 18–23, 1904, Holmes represented the Smithsonian Institution and the U.S. government at the Fourteenth International Congress of Americanists in Stuttgart, Germany. There he gave an address entitled "Contributions of American Archeology to Human History." Other American scientists who were accredited by the U.S. State Department to serve as delegates were Franz Boas of the American Museum of Natural History, Marshall H. Saville of Columbia University, George Dorsey of the Field Columbian Museum, and Charles W. Currier of the Catholic University of America.[17]

What was significant about this meeting was Holmes's commission to visit "the principal museums of Europe for the purpose of acquiring information to be utilized in the erection of and furnishing of the new National Museum building." It would have been hard to find someone more qualified and experienced in museology than Holmes. To carry out this task, Holmes sailed from New York for Plymouth, England, on July 26, 1904, in the company of J. R. Marshall of the firm Hornblower and Marshall.[18] This firm was responsible for drawing up the building plans for the new museum. By September 25, Holmes had visited no less than fifty-three museums in Europe. Of those, the most useful for Holmes's purposes were the British Museum and the Natural History Museum in London; the Classical and Natural History museums in Cambridge; the Natural History and Anatomical museums in Paris; the Ethnographical and University museums of Berlin; the Natural History Museum and the Art Gallery in Hamburg; the Natural History Museum in Bremen; the Reiks Museum in Amsterdam; and especially the recently constructed Natural History Museum in Brussels, which Holmes observed "was built to accommodate particular collections," rather than starting out as an older building that was converted to the purpose, "and is the most perfect example of its kind perhaps in existence at the present time." From the notes he took during this "hasty review," he prepared the internal document "Report of Studies of European Museums Made During the Summer of 1904."[19]

Holmes opened the report with the pointed criticism: "A not unusual shortcoming of the more ambitious modern museum building is that although designed for collections and in general adapted to purposes of exhibition, the architect has been unduly influenced by his desire to produce a building that would be imposing and beautiful, making of it an architectural monument first and a repository for collections to be displayed, second."[20] Holmes then went on to state what he believed was "the ideal museum building." In his opinion, the "chief essentials" for a museum of general rather than specialized collections included 1) "simplicity of plan"; 2) "large spaces of proper height"; and 3) good lighting. On the first point, Holmes called to mind his experience in the British Museum, which he said required of the visitor a "geographical genius" to enjoy fully, a biting comment coming from one of the noted explorers of the western frontier. As for spaces, Holmes's rule was straightforward and incontrovertible: "larger exhibits should occupy the larger spaces, the smaller exhibits or minor subdivisions of large exhibits the smaller spaces." There should be "convenience of access" and the "visitor should be able to pass connectedly through halls occupied by particular exhibits." Holmes spent the rest of the report on the subject of lighting and the technical complications that must be carefully considered from quite literally all angles. The new museum on the Mall was completed on June 20, 1911, six years after breaking ground. There was obviously a good deal of agreement at the Smithsonian Institution in regard to Holmes's basic museum principles. The floor plan was simple and the building was spacious. Of the Natural History museum's no less than ten acres of floor space, half were devoted to exhibits and public education, the rest of the area being held for reserve collections, laboratories, offices, and maintenance. And the vast structure, with its airy rotunda, was amply lighted.[21]

As chief, Holmes also attended the First Pan-American Scientific Congress in Santiago, Chile, which was held in late December of 1908. In light of the lingering suspicions and sensitive feelings toward the United States throughout Latin America, as a result of Roosevelt's high-handed Panama policy, the State Department saw the congress as an excellent opportunity to mend fences.[22] Holmes delivered the address "The Peopling of America," and presented a paper on behalf of Charles E. Munroe of George Washington University, who could not attend the South American meeting. Holmes clearly enjoyed complaining about dining with Chile's president, Pedro Montt, and fulfilling his other formal obligations as a designee of the U.S. State Department to represent the Smithsonian Institution. He also, incidentally, represented George Washington University at the meeting. Holmes certainly looked the part. Photographs of him during this period show a man of impeccable dress, stainless-steel manner, and distinguished character. Holmes left no room for doubt; he was superbly respectable.

Although impressed by the attention that South America's scholars were devoting to the study of the continent's indigenous peoples, he was nevertheless critical of the "sporadic" quality of this work. He attributed this failing in large part to the lack of government support. "Individual initiative" was not enough. He complained that with the exception of Argentina, which he noted "alone provided liberally for systematic research and the publication of results," the other nations in the region were neglecting the study of their aboriginal peoples. Holmes warned, "One of the four great races of mankind is rapidly disappearing from the face of the continent—which but recently was wholly its own—and unless vigorous measures are taken it will have vanished along with its interesting culture . . . The failure to preserve such a record will be lamented by future generations."[23] In short, according to Holmes, what Chile, Bolivia, Peru, Columbia, Brazil, and other Latin American nations required was their own version of the Bureau of American Ethnology and National Museum. But this was a point on which there was Pan-American agreement. What is more, the Americanists gathered in Santiago resolved to memorialize the Chilean congress to adopt, in effect, the U.S. model and the belief in aboriginal extinction or assimilation that it implied.[24]

As was the case with Holmes's trip to Stuttgart in 1904, Holmes combined the conference with an international survey of museums. The route Holmes followed to Santiago provided him with opportunities to visit a number of institutions. The Hamburg steamer *Amerika* took him first to Plymouth, England, where he then made his way to London. These trips were hard on the sixty-three-year-old Holmes and he complained to his wife about "the depressing lonesomeness of a journey in a strange land."[25] In London, he visited the National Gallery and the Tate. He then went to Salisbury to see the Blackmore Museum, which was "kept by Dr. Blackmore the brother of Wm. Blackmore with whom [he] traveled in the Yellowstone Country in '72."[26] The cold wind, unfortunately, kept him from visiting Stonehenge. He returned to London and already found himself short on funds. He had to have his wife Kate "look up more money" for him. He then set sail for Argentina, with port calls in Vigo, Spain, and Lisbon, Portugal. After a twelve-day voyage, he reached Buenos Aires, where he stayed ten days and was joined by other delegates heading to the conference. While in the capital, he visited the University of La Plata Museum, the Faculty of Philosophy and Letters Museum, and the National Museum. He then crossed the Pampas by rail to Mendoza, then went up the Mendoza River by boat to Las Cuevas, and then crossed the Andes by coach to Santiago on the Pacific side of the mountains.

In Santiago, he took full advantage of Chile's National Museum. And on the return home, he stopped at the national museums of Bolivia and Peru. While Holmes was in Peru, he made a special trip to the ancient city of Tiahuanaco on the south shore of Lake Titicaca. He called the site the "most remarkable of the prehistoric South American cities, if not all aboriginal America."[27] Holmes's visit to western South America strengthened his tendency toward environmental determinism. As he put it:

> The remarkable contrast of the plateau peoples and their civilization with the peoples and culture of the eastern slopes of the Cordillera and the vast lowland region drained by the Orinoco, Amazon and La Plata was pointed out as a matter of exceptional scientific interest. A more striking example could hardly be recalled of the profound influence of environment upon peoples, for it is seen that the tribes occupying a land rich in natural resources remained nomads and savages gathering the plentiful fruits of the forest, while those whose lives were cast in the bleak plateaus where there was a constant struggle for existence, acquired habits of industry and thrift, developed social and political systems of a very high order and built temples, fortresses and tombs of surpassing grandeur.[28]

Holmes finally reached Washington via Panama on February 11, 1909, which ended a remarkable trip abroad. On May 4, he turned around and headed west to the exposition in Seattle, mentioned above.

Since Holmes had become chief, his fieldwork had shrunk as his administrative duties and responsibilities expanded. The year 1909, as we have just seen, was an exception. That year (actually beginning in October of 1908), Holmes made a trip to Santiago for a congress and then to Seattle for an exposition; he also made a number of side excursions to museums and points of archaeological interest along the way. The glory days of bureau exploration, however, were behind it. This field activity was now referred to in bureau reports as "systematic researches," which did not have the same aura of romance as the older term *exploration*. The bureau's "regular force"—in distinction to its many "collaborators" inside and out of the Smithsonian Institution (including Franz Boas, as honorary philologist)—consisted of Matilda Coxe

Stevenson (the Pueblo tribes), Gerard Fowke (archaeology), James Mooney (the Great Plains tribes), J. N. B. Hewitt (the Iroquoian tribes), John Swanton (the Pacific Northwest and the Southern tribes), Frederick Webb Hodge (the Handbook of the Indians), Jesse Walter Fewkes (the Caribbean and the Southwest), Cyrus Thomas (the Handbook of the Indians and a bibliography of Hawaii), and, of course, Holmes (Indian technology and mining).

Although Stevenson, Mooney, Swanton, Fewkes, and Holmes were dedicated field researchers, they nevertheless found themselves increasingly diverted from fieldwork to office work because of the growing demands of Hodge's Handbook. In James Mooney's case, for example, according to the 1905 bureau report:

> At the end October Mr. Mooney returned to Washington and was engaged in writing a preliminary paper on Kiowa heraldry until about the end of the calendar year, when he was called on to cooperate in the preparation of the Handbook on the Indians, for which work the following articles were furnished [in alphabetical order]: Arawakan colony, Calusa tribe, Cheyenne tribe, Kiowa tribe, military societies, peyote, population, shields, skin-dressing, signals, sign language, Timucua Tribe. Besides these about 100 minor articles were prepared, treating of tribes, biographies of noted Indians, and other subjects. In connection with this work the available information relating to the ancient tribes of Florida and the Gulf States generally was found to be so deficient and confused that Mr. Mooney undertook an investigation of the subject from original resources. A part of the results has been embodied in the Handbook of the Indians, and the foundation has been laid for an extended paper on the ethnology of this region to form a complement to his previous studies of the Siouan tribes of the east and the Cherokee.[29]

As Mooney's situation makes clear, Holmes's bureau was in the "summarizing" or desk-work business now, not exploration.

There were other factors besides the Handbook and normal administrative cares that limited Holmes's fieldwork during his years as chief. In addition to his regular duties, he continued on at the National Museum as honorary curator of the section of prehistoric archaeology; and beginning in 1906, Holmes assumed responsibility as curator for the Smithsonian's new National Gallery of Art, which he did without financial compensation. Richard Rathbun, the acting secretary of the Smithsonian Institution (following Langley's death in 1906), formalized this arrangement on August 10, 1906.[30]

Until 1905, the Smithsonian's art collection was a modest affair (there was a fire in the Smithsonian building in 1865) and over the years the pieces in its possession, including the George Catlin collection of Indian paintings (given to the Institution in 1879), had been entrusted to the Library of Congress and the Corcoran Gallery of Art. But in 1905 everything changed. In that year the Smithsonian was bequeathed the Charles L. Freer and Harriet Lane Johnston collections, the former of which was particularly large and valuable (2,250 objects). These gifts were followed by the William T. Evans collection of 150 paintings by contemporary American artists. The Smithsonian Institution, which hitherto had been largely a scientific organization, now found itself custodian of the fine arts. The Smithsonian's regents, were, in Holmes's words, in a "quandary" as to how to properly care for these collections, and they appealed to President Roosevelt. He "emphatically advised 'acceptance whether you can care for it or not.'"[31] The regents did, and stated in the annual report for 1907: "there seems no reason why the principles which have for years guided the Institution in administering upon scientific matters should not be applied with equal success to the fine arts."[32]

It is hardly surprising that Holmes, given his long interest in art and in his own impressive portfolio, which now included many watercolors of local subjects, would be directly involved in the organization of the new gallery. Indeed, in the years to come the gallery would consume more and more of his time and energy until he would leave science almost entirely to devote himself full time to the gallery as director for the remainder of his years in Washington.

In addition to these demands, Holmes was also responsible, as chief of the BAE, for helping to implement the Act for the Preservation of American Antiquities, which President Roosevelt had signed into law on June 8, 1906. Holmes had even been involved in the politicking that had preceded the passage of the bill. In fact, he had written the bill, which the senator (and Smithsonian regent) Shelby Cullom sponsored in the Senate and Representative Robert Hilt introduced in the House (both men were from Illinois). The question was over who would be responsible for preserving antiquities on the public lands. Holmes's bill placed the responsibility in the hands of the secretary of the Smithsonian, while a competing bill, the Lodge-Rodenberg bill, made the secretary of the interior the responsible party.[33] In the end, responsibility was to be shared by all of the secretaries of governmental departments with jurisdiction over the public lands, namely, Agriculture, War, and Interior.

In this new era of conservation and preservation, the Smithsonian Institution still had an important role to play, as was evident in the government's new rules and regulations, which Holmes helped to write. Interior, Agriculture, and War prepared—in cooperation with the Smithsonian Institution

and the Archeological Institute of America—guidelines, which were then fi-
nalized and made public on December 28, 1906. Accordingly, the Smithsonian Institution was given the responsibility to ensure that archaeological
fieldwork on public land was conducted by appropriate parties. To that end,
field-workers were now required to obtain permits, and all applications for
such permits "shall be referred to the Smithsonian Institution for recommendation." The idea here was to protect America's archaeological treasures from
amateurs, pot hunters, and vandals. In addition, "every permit shall be in
writing and copies shall be transmitted to the Smithsonian Institution and
the field officer in charge of the land involved." Moreover, "at the close of
each season's field work the permittee shall report in duplicate to the Smithsonian Institution, in such form as its Secretary may prescribe, and shall prepare in duplicate a catalogue of the collections and of the photographs made
during the season."[34]

Actually, even before the signing of the Antiquities Act, the government
started to restrict access to the public lands. In the fall of 1905, Charles
Fletcher Lummis, for instance, went through Holmes and Gifford Pinchot
and Francis E. Leupp in order to obtain a conditional permit for the Southwest Society of the Archeological Institute of America. Without that permit,
Gifford Pinchot, forester and chief of the Bureau of Forestry and one of the
leading conservationists of the day, and Francis Leupp, commissioner of Indian Affairs, would not have allowed the institute to conduct explorations in
the U.S. forest reserves in Arizona's Apache and Navajo counties or the Indian
reservation in Gila County, respectively.[35] As Holmes's BAE made the transition from exploration of antiquities to their preservation, it was clear that the
freedom of the frontier was over and the modern era of bureaucracy and governmental red tape had officially arrived.

Hand in hand with the movement to preserve the country's numerous archaeological sites, were President Roosevelt's actions in setting aside sites of
exceptional archaeological interest as national monuments. These sites (all of
which have become an essential part of America's cultural landscape) were located largely in the Southwest. In New Mexico Territory, there were the cliff
dwellings in the Gila National Forest, the ruins in Chaco Canyon, and the
ruins and famous rock inscriptions at El Moro; in Arizona Territory, there
were the cliff dwellings at the Tonto National Monument, the ruins and cliff
dwellings at the Grand Canyon, and Montezuma Castle in the Verde Valley.
In addition, the BAE's Jesse Walter Fewkes was involved in the restoration of
Casa Grande, in southern Arizona, and Spruce-Tree House and Cliff Palace,
both located in Mesa Verde National Park in Colorado.

Less directly than making actual repairs but perhaps more importantly, Holmes's bureau rendered signal service during this crucial time when sites were being selected for protection by making available the wealth of information on antiquities that it had collected over the years to the departments of the Interior, Agriculture, and War. Holmes did so by starting work on compiling an archaeological map and catalogue of the Southwest. Edgar Lee Hewitt, founder of the School of American Research in Santa Fe, collected and collated data, which were then platted on USGS topographical maps, for sites in Colorado and New Mexico, while Joseph D. McGuire did the same thing for Utah and Arizona.[36] Holmes's commitment to preservation went beyond his government work. He also found time to serve as chairman of the Joint Committee of the Archeological Institution of America and the American Anthropological Association for the Preservation of Antiquities.

The movement to preserve America's archaeological treasures in the early twentieth century simply would not have been successful had it not been for the years of government exploration in the American West, which had done so much to draw the nation's attention to the sites in the first place. Holmes's involvement in both the exploration and preservation of America's antiquities helps us understand the close relationship between these two cultural activities. Specifically, it helps us understand why generations of Americans, who explore the parks and monuments of the American West by the millions every summer in their air-conditioned sport utility vehicles, approach their country's archaeological and natural heritage in the spirit of discovery; it also helps us to understand why this celebrated family vacation has become an important nationalizing experience or process. "Seeing America" is really a subtle form of conquest or way of taking possession—just as it was in Holmes's day.

Given all of these activities, it is not surprising that during his years as bureau chief, Holmes did not make it into the field very often. But he did not seem to mind. His daily motto, after all, was "Let's get on with the job." Besides, there were other compensations. His explorations of the West and Latin America may have declined while serving as chief, but he nevertheless continued to enjoy the company of explorers and notices of recognition for his work in the field. As already noted, he was a co-founder and member of the famous Cosmos Club, which served as a very selective and privileged "home away from home."[37] Not all of the members, however, of this elite social club were explorers, as Holmes himself noted in 1904 at the Cosmos Club's twenty-fifth-anniversary dinner. On that occasion, he wryly observed that club membership was composed of the following eleven types: "1) Geologists, Biologists, Anthropologists, Chemists, and Astronomers—including many scientific men; 2) Writers of prose, poetry, and editorials—mostly literary men; 3) Painters, Engravers, and Sculptors—all men of genius; 4) Doctors, Dentists, Physicians, and Specialists—but no quacks; 5) Lawyers—but no shysters; 6) Army and Naval Officers—all heroes; 7) Teachers, and Professors, and some Educators; 8) Preachers and Ministers—and Divines; 9) Bankers and Financiers; 10) Designers of buildings—all Architects; 11) Statesmen, Diplomats, Secretaries, Directors, Chiefs, Superintendents, Chief Clerks, office holders, and others; 400 in all, and absolutely select."[38] In 1905 and 1906, Holmes served as the club's vice president, and in 1907 as president.[39] But membership had its price, and to help pay dues Holmes adopted the practice observed on occasion by several of the other members who were artists, which was to donate paintings in lieu thereof. In 1900, for instance, he gave the painting *Orizaba from the Gulf* to meet his obligation.[40]

Besides the offices he held at the Cosmos Club, many other honors came Holmes's way as well, including the great honor of being elected to the National Academy of Sciences on April 20, 1905, for his geological and archaeological work that he produced during his years in the West with the Hayden Survey.[41] Apparently, Holmes had been considered for this coveted honor before, but, as William Dall explained in his letter of congratulations, he was not elected due to "circumstances which [he] had no responsibility for, and which should have had no weight"; moreover, Dall continued, "There is more or less human nature mixed up with all the affairs of men, and pure justice is strictly supernatural and not to be counted on here below."[42]

As the new National Museum building was nearing completion, Holmes decided to resign as chief on June 10, 1909, and resume his old position as head curator of anthropology at the National Museum, a position he would hold until 1920. Frederick Webb Hodge took over the bureau as "Ethnologist-in-Charge," which was W J McGee's old title. At sixty-four, Holmes had no thought of retirement. Indeed, he would continue at the Smithsonian Institution for another two decades. Apparently, his personal finances were such that he could not afford to leave government service. As he explained in a letter to Hrdlička, written the year he died and sent from the home of his son William, who lived in Royal Oak, Michigan: "I have proved myself an average idiot—by not saving from year to year when money was plenty."[43] (His son William, incidentally, had three daughters by Mary Herbert; they were Barbara, Mary, and Kathryn. His other son, Osgood, an architect, remained a bachelor and at the home of his parents in Washington. Tragically, Osgood was made an invalid by a bad fall down the basement stairs.)

Holmes lived well though. His home on 1454 Belmont Street in Washington was lovely. Built of Seneca sandstone with hardwood floors of Georgia Redpine, the home commanded a panoramic view of the city—at the cost of a yard that sloped steeply away. It was perfect for entertaining guests and was known "to intimates for its gracious hospitality, wit, and wisdom."[44] Holmes and his wife Kate also enjoyed their summer retreat, a charming little farm they called "Holmescroft," located not so far away in Rockville, Maryland. Here the two artists were able to indulge themselves in what they loved to do best. His life was a good life and the very *beau ideal* of genteel America.

14

The Great Dragon of Quirigua

A Monumental Occasion for Science and Art

WITH THE NEW NATIONAL MUSEUM building nearing completion (although the structural work was not finished on June 20, 1911, parts of the building were opened to the public before then), the Smithsonian Institution was preparing for its greatest show on earth, although Holmes and his associates would have been loath to put it that way. The process was necessarily a huge undertaking. The staff had to clear out one attic (the old National Museum) and move everything into another (the new National Museum of Natural History). During this transition, Holmes, starting on January 1, 1910, served as head of the department of anthropology. Under him were the following divisional curators: Walter Hough (ethnology), Aleš Hrdlička (physical anthropology), I. M. Casanowicz (historic archaeology), George C. Maynard (technology), J. M. Flint (medicine), and A. Howard Clark (history). Holmes was his own assistant curator for the division of prehistoric archaeology.[1]

The move presented Holmes with the opportunity, as he put it, to subject the "entire body of the collections . . . to systematic scientific scrutiny," a process that involved comparing and studying, as well as moving, sorting, classifying, arranging, labeling, and, of course, installing items for public display.[2] Installation was actually another matter entirely and involved Holmes in the design and construction of his always popular lay-figure groups as well as the upright cases and display tables. Unlike his situation before, in the old museum, he now had plenty of room to move. The "three large halls on the second floor of the new building," he wrote, "were at my disposal."[3] Otis Tufton Mason—author of *Aboriginal American Basketry* (1902)—and Walter Hough were also involved in this work. Holmes believed that what he did here was essential. Looking back, he saw "the classification and installation of [the archaeological and ethnological] collections, although still far from complete," as "probably the most important single achievement of my archaeological career." And looking ahead, he said, "it can not be expected that those who follow and criticize me will have any conception of the condition of these collections before I took charge."[4]

Perhaps the most important idea to emerge out of Holmes's museum work was his decision to exhibit archaeological and ethnological materials at the Smithsonian by culture areas—an idea that had begun with Otis Mason after the Chicago fair in 1893 and developed further by Alfred. L. Kroeber and Clark Wissler.[5] This museum presentation proved very influential and popular, especially when combined with lay figures or life-size models—an idea Holmes had originated and introduced at the Chicago fair.[6] As a result of his years of "practical work" in "museum classification and arrangement," Holmes had become deeply impressed by the fact that "environment has had a large share in determining the course" of cultural evolution. And he believed it was inevitable that when the archaeologist "examines the antiquities and finds that analogous geographical distinctions characterize the material culture of the past," he will then arrive at "the conclusion that the relations of environment to man and culture must play an important part in the prosecution of his researches and in the analysis of aboriginal history."[7] Holmes went on to make the point that "certain characteristics of achievement or groups of culture traits within each area will be found to separate it from its neighbors and afford effective means of comparison with other culture groups."[8] By means of delimiting the "areas of culture characterization," he was literally able to map the cultures of man in the Americas.[9]

For the museum visitor, this approach to museum presentation meant a powerful visual experience where he or she could survey cultural areas of the Americas one display at a time. The visitor, in effect, became an explorer and could enjoy the experience of exploration in a highly condensed, concentrated, if interpreted form. The culture areas that Holmes identified for North America were: 1) the North Atlantic area; 2) the Georgia-Florida area; 3) the Middle and Lower Mississippi Valley Region; 4) the Upper Mississippi and Lakes Region; 5) the Plains and Rocky Mountains; 6) the Arid Region; 7) the California area; 8) the Columbia-Fraser area; 9) the Northwest Coast area; 10) the Arctic Coastal area; and 11) the Great Northern-Central area. In a bow to America's expanding empire, Holmes added the Hawaiian Islands and the West Indies to this list. For Middle and South America, Holmes marked off the following areas: 1) Northern Mexico; 2) Middle Mexico; 3) Southern Mexico; 4) the Maya Provinces; 5) the Central American or Isthmian Region;

6) the North Andean-Pacific area; the Middle Andean Pacific or Incan area; the South Andean-Pacific or Chilean area; 9) the Amazon Delta area; 10) Primitive South America, northern division; and 11) Primitive South America, southern division.[10]

Holmes was careful to make the point, however, that the culture-area concept was not meant to flatten out the history of aboriginal America into environmentally determined but relatively equal parts of a greater whole. As he put it, "These areas in all cases are based on the clearly manifested phases of their culture content" and "haste must be made slowly as the utmost acumen of the student is called for in making areal *and* [italics mine] chronological discriminations."[11] Moreover, Holmes noted, culture areas were

> merely intended to cultivate familiarity with the vast field as a whole and to lay out its great features tentatively as an aid in describing and comparing the antiquities and the cultures they represent. It is by no means assumed that the culture phenomena of any considerable area are uniform throughout. There may be much diversity, possibly great complexity of conditions. There may be a number of somewhat independent centers of development of nearly equal importance, or a single center may have spread its influence over a wide area.[12]

These important caveats aside, the cultural-area concept that Holmes helped pioneer has endured as a popular heuristic device, and has been the way millions of museum-going Americans across the country have been introduced to the continent's rich native heritage.

At the same time that Holmes was installing the Smithsonian Institution's archaeological and ethnological materials, he was also responsible as curator for setting up the national gallery of art, which was now an independent division of the National Museum. The displays were located in the middle of the large central hall of the new building—an area illuminated by skylight. Holmes divided this space by screens into nine different rooms. The new gallery was informally opened on March 17, 1910, to a large gathering.[13] As well as things went, it was clear that eventually a gallery of art befitting the nation would require its own building and independence—a point heard more often as the collection expanded in size and value over the years.

Holmes derived a great deal of pleasure and satisfaction in his responsibility for showcasing the nation's fine art, estimated to be worth a million dollars. But he was not only involved in how things would be shown; as member of the gallery's permanent honorary committee, he also participated in the decisions as to what art the gallery would accept in the first place. Holmes,

Francis Millet (president of the advisory committee), Frederick Crownin-shield (of the Fine Arts Federation), Edwin H. Blashfield (of the National Academy of Design), Herbert Adams (of the National Sculpture Society) were men "so identified," according to the Smithsonian Institution's own report, "with the art interests of the country as to assure to the public and especially to the lovers and patrons of art the wholly worthy purpose of this movement on behalf of the nation." Holmes had come a long way since he first arrived in Washington to study under Theodore Kaufmann. He was now a member of America's growing but already powerful art establishment. This fact was reinforced by his talent, on the one hand, as an illustrator, water-colorist, and painter of growing distinction (his paintings, such as *The Ox Team on a Dusty Road,* received favorable reviews, and they won prizes at exhibitions, such as *The Wanderluster's Rest*—which took second place at the Poland Springs' Art Exhibition); and by his leadership, on the other, in such genteel organizations as the Society of the Fine Arts, the Water Color Club, the Society of Washington Artists, and the Cosmos Club Art Committee. He also found time to serve as art editor of, and even contribute to, the Archaeological Institute of America's journal, *Art and Archaeology.*[14]

Free of his many responsibilities as chief, Holmes had hoped to publish his Handbook of Aboriginal American Antiquities soon after he took over as head of anthropology. Other matters intervened, however. There were his "exacting" duties at the museum; his tending to the national gallery; his continuing involvement in the early-man controversy (he and Bailey Willis of the Geological Survey, and Frederick Eugene Wright and Clarence N. Fenner, both of the Geophysical Laboratory of the Carnegie Institution of Washington, all collaborated with Hrdlička on his article "Early Man in South America," which appeared in 1912 in a BAE bulletin); a trip to the jungle ruins of Guatemala and Honduras with Sylvanus Griswold Morley in 1916; his service on the National Research Council (a war-preparedness measure); and various other and sundry duties and activities, including attending congresses, touring museums, and serving on Woodrow Wilson's inaugural committee (he also had the honor of serving on Theodore Roosevelt's). There were, of course, the summers at "Holmescroft" painting with his wife as well. As a result, Part 1 of the Handbook was kept out of type until 1919, and Part 2, although reported to be in various stages of progress, was never finished. The many delays, however, did not work to the detriment of the Handbook, for in 1923 Holmes received the second award of the Loubat Prize for it.

In the years before the war, Holmes's fieldwork was limited. In 1913, he did make two collecting trips on behalf of the museum. He visited the pre-Columbian mica mines in western North Carolina, a number of mounds and village sites in South Carolina and Georgia; he also made a trip to a flint quarry in southern Illinois. He reported that the "old workings" in western North Carolina were

> found to be very numerous and extensive; some of the excavations, traces of which still remain, extended to a depth of nearly a hundred feet, and the amount of mica extracted and carried away by the aborigines may be estimated at many hundreds of tons. By digging in the ancient pittings, many specimens of the mica and of the stone implements employed by the natives in their mining work were secured.[15]

Again, Holmes's work in uncovering the mining history of pre-contact America has not been fully appreciated.

The Fall of the Maya

In terms of exploration, the main event in these years was without question Holmes's trip to Middle America with Sylvanus Griswold Morley, from February 16 to April 12, 1916. The Smithsonian Institution had published Morley's classic *An Introduction to the Study of Maya Hieroglyphs* (it was issued as Bulletin 57 of the Bureau of American Ethnology) only the year before. Morley, who owed, in part, his position as head of the Carnegie Institution's Mayan project to Holmes's influence, invited the author of the *Archaeological Studies among the Ancient Cities of Mexico* to join the Carnegie Institution's archeological expedition to Central America, which included a tour of the ancient Mayan cities of Antigua, Iximache, Quirigua (in Guatemala), and Copán (in Honduras).[16] The objective of the trip was to study Mayan culture—specifically to discover "additional inscriptions embodying glyphic dates—for it is the dates now read with facility which furnish the skeleton of Mayan history." Along the way, Holmes, who received a grant to accompany Morley from the Smithsonian Institution, could not help but observe the magnificence of Spanish colonial architecture, as especially evidenced in the earthquake-plagued capital of Antigua, which was eventually abandoned. Of the ruins of some fifty churches Holmes visited in Antigua, he commented that they "were the most wonderful structures I have ever seen." Perhaps Holmes's model work of the Santa Barbara mission complex for the Seattle exposition in 1909, and the general interest in Latin America with the opening of the Panama Canal during the summer of 1914 and the Panama-California Exposition the following year, led him to an appreciation and awareness of things Spanish that he apparently did not possess earlier in his career.

The trip to Guatemala and Honduras, particularly to the ancient Mayan city of Quirigua, reinvigorated Holmes's archaeological imagination. Holmes was not the first explorer, of course, to visit the site. Alfred P. Maudslay and Edgar L. Hewett had already been there. In fact, when Holmes arrived he found the illustrator Joseph Lindon Smith—the "master portrayer of ancient monuments"—at work on a platform atop twenty feet of scaffolding. Smith was capturing on canvas a large sculptured stela for the Peabody Museum of Ethnology and Archaeology in Cambridge. On returning home, Holmes began to work up his notes into an article on the Great Dragon of Quirigua—a brilliantly and intricately embellished "ovoid mass of coarse-grained sandstone of warmish grey color weighing about 20 tons," in which he used with singular effect the theory of social evolution to explain and give meaning to this masterpiece of aboriginal art. Incidentally, Hewett had cleaned off the piece in 1910, so Holmes was able to devote his entire time to the study rather than the excavation of this extraordinary Mayan artifact.[17]

Holmes was deeply impressed by the piece's esthetic qualities—the "form, line, color, and arrangement," which give "pleasure to the eye." He declared that "the great dragon of Quirigua may be regarded as representing the culminating stage of religious art in aboriginal America." In Holmes's view of the laws of cultural evolution and in his theory on the origin of art, the "religious motive was the strong dynamic force which, more than all other agencies combined, carried culture forward through the prolonged stages of savagery and barbarism to the borderland of civilization." He claimed that "it was not until religious symbolism gave special significance to the subject matter of representative art, that particular advance was made toward the higher esthetic expression." The Maya, according to Holmes, as evidenced by their outstanding cultural achievements, came closer than any other aboriginal people in the Americas, including the Aztec and Inca, to reaching the crowning stage of civilization. Indeed, Holmes went so far in his praise as to assert: "It is doubtful if any people at a corresponding stage of cultural evolution," which would presumably include his own ancestors, "was more highly gifted with artistic genius and appreciation and gave more attention to its application to all forms of art than the Mayan race. Every plastic form and every line of the dragon bear testimony to this fact." He eloquently went on to say:

It was not religion that stipulated that no straight line and no right angle should appear in the image of the dragon; it was not religious restriction that provided that no curve should be the arc of a circle, that every curve should be subtle, and that all outlines of glyphs and cartouches should take roundish, calculiform character. Every feature of design had complete esthetic supervision. Throughout America plastic freehand methods always prevailed over the mechanical. In the creation of the monument the great motor force was religion, but the ever-watchful esthetic impulse joined hands with that force in making it a masterpiece of art.[18]

Given the enormous barbarity of the fratricidal conflict in Europe then in progress, one might expect, in retrospect, perhaps a touch of irony or an acknowledgment of an element of relativism in Holmes's use of such terms as *savagery*, *barbarism*, and *civilization*. In July of 1916, after all, at virtually the same time that Holmes was writing the article on the Great Dragon, the Allies and the Germans would commence the First Battle of the Somme, a bloodbath of staggering proportions that alone claimed over a million casualties. The moral foundation on which Holmes's science rested, however, remained free of any doubt, and, indeed, would survive the Great War unscathed. But in any case, Holmes was not given to such self-reflection or doubt. To be fair, in this he was hardly alone. (But, as we shall see, in his willingness to condemn those who were so inclined to question the powers that be and the underlying assumptions and values of society, he was perhaps exceptional among his peers.) Even in his discussion of the decline of Mayan culture, the belief in the superiority of his own civilization prevented him, or others of his generation for that matter, from seeing that there may be something to learn from what happened to non-Western peoples at other times. Instead, Holmes was focused on what separated cultures and on how they should be ranked from the primitive to the advanced. As yet, there were few other ways to think about such things. The cultural relativism of Franz Boas and his students had yet to revolutionize American anthropology.

Thus, Holmes's graphic conjecture as to what befell the Maya, based on a very close reading of a large embellished rock, bears no trace of irony, analogy, or metaphor, however tempting it may be to read something larger into his discussion of the subject. According to Holmes, to "account for the decay of the Mayan culture and the ruin of its wonderful cities we do not have to call primarily on the more drastic agencies of destruction—war, pestilence, changes in the level of the land, floods, and earthquakes, one or all of which, however, may have aided in precipitating the disaster." Instead, Holmes suggested, "the seeds of decay were inherent in the system, as they are inherent in every organization and structure of whatsoever kind that involves the long-continued, ever-growing, and unrequited waste of the energies and resources of a people." Holmes specifically blamed the powerful Mayan religious establishments for the degeneration that would overtake their culture.

"Under the undisputed control," Holmes wrote, "of an organized body of wide influence and a religio-political system hoary with age, the people doubtless believed themselves working for the common good and in obedience to the bidding of deities whose reality and authority were constantly impressed upon them." "They had," Holmes continued,

> no means of arriving at a correct knowledge of the truth that the gods of the entire pantheon were mere fictions and that the revered priesthood, although the embodiment of the highest wisdom, the promoters of learning, and perhaps the conservators of moral standards, was at the same time a body of organized parasites, their position and authority being sustained by the cunning use of the images in stone and the complex system of festivals connected with their conjuration.

And to drive home his point even further, Holmes speculated

> that under the evergrowing requirements of the shammanistic body in carrying forward their ambitious schemes, the energies and resources of the people were absorbed in larger and larger measure—in quarrying, hewing, transporting, building, carving, providing, and serving, and that as the natural agencies of deterioration and decay made inroads on the splendid establishments which they had builded, they were called on to quarry and carve and build again in an ever-losing struggle against the elements and against the undetected incubus of the ambitious and selfish priestcraft. We can readily conceive that these conditions prevailed until the energies and resources of the people were impaired or exhausted . . . so that disintegration and decay rapidly supervened, so that the end came on apace.[19]

If Holmes failed to find anything of contemporary relevance in the jungles of Guatemala, he did find lessons there for the future. His involvement in the U.S. preservation movement as head of the BAE had sensitized him to the threats posed to antiquities, chief among them perhaps exploration itself. Now he saw that such threats transcended borders, although he believed the problem should be addressed on a nation-by-nation basis. In visiting archaeological sites in Guatemala and Honduras, which until very recently had been protected by thick layers of overgrowth, he saw the damage that had already occurred to the newly exposed ruins. "No wall," he warned, "howsoever strong, will stand exposure in the open in this climate for a single generation." He noted that the restoration work that had been performed in 1910 by Hewett's School of American Archaeology (of Santa Fe) had, by 1916, already fallen into disrepair. The Portland cement was in no better condition than the original materials. Seeing firsthand how rapidly ruins could disintegrate once they were reexposed to the elements led Holmes to the logical conclusion that "as soon as the work of exploration and record is completed the work of preservation, of covering in, should be taken up as a national obligation of the Republic in whose custody these monuments must remain." His thinking had evolved considerably since the Armour expedition to Mexico and the Yucatán over two decades before. There was no question in his mind, however, that despite the risks involved such sites should continue to be explored and excavated. And there was certainly no evidence in his thinking of a later humility that held that some sites or parts of sites should be left undisturbed and set aside for later generations of archaeologists, who presumably would develop less intrusive methods and technology.

The year 1916 was a good one for Holmes. It began with the expedition to Central America; it ended with his seventieth birthday (December 1), when he was presented with a five-hundred-page "Anniversary" volume of anthropological essays at a large dinner and tribute at the Lafayette Hotel. Holmes was honored by his peers for his forty-five years of contributions to science. Morley and Frederick Webb Hodge staged the surprise event. The volume contained no less than forty-four original essays by many of the top people in anthropology, including Franz Boas, Walter Hough, Aleš Hrdlička, Neil Judd, George Grant MacCurdy, Sylvanus Morley, Alfred Tozzer, Berthold Laufer, Gerard Fowke, Alice Fletcher, Edgar Hewett, George Heye, Charles Peabody, Charles Willoughby, Alfred Kidder, S. A. Barrett, Theodoor de Booy, David Bushnell, William Churchhill, Roland B. Dixon, William Farabee, R. E. Goddard, George Gordon, Albert Jenks, Alfred Kroeber, Robert Lowie, Charles Mead, William Mills, Warren Moorehead, Nels Nelson, George Pepper, Marshall Saville, Frank Speck, Herbert Spinden, and Clark Wissler. Needless to say, Holmes was overwhelmed by this gesture of respect. Typical of his response was a note to Boas: "Conspiring with Mr. Hodge and forty-four other good friends, you have given me a great surprise and a token that must rank among the greatest—the most gratifying experiences of my life. The book is a marvel. What you have written and what you have said are treasured and shall not be forgotten."[20] Holmes had reached the pinnacle of his career. Sadly, the war, which brought out the worst in

Holmes—as it did in so many others—would spoil the goodwill represented here and destroy his formidable standing in the anthropology profession.

The Fall of Holmes

On August 5, 1916, Holmes received a letter from President Woodrow Wilson. The president asked if Holmes would agree to serve on the National Research Council. Without hesitation, Holmes accepted the invitation. In April, the same month that Holmes returned to Washington from Guatemala, the National Academy of Sciences "voted unanimously to offer its services to the President of the United States in the interest of national preparedness," and it was suggested that the academy "might advantageously organize the scientific resources of educational and research institutions in the interest of national security and welfare." Wilson accepted the offer and on June 19, 1916, an organizing committee formed the National Research Council,

> whose purpose shall be to bring into cooperation existing governmental, edu-
> cational, industrial, and other research organizations with the object of en-
> couraging the investigation of natural phenomena, the increased use of
> scientific research in the development of American industries, the employment
> of scientific methods in strengthening the national defense, and such other ap-
> plications of science as will promote the national security and welfare.[21]

With the war in Europe showing no signs of ending, military preparedness seemed to many of the nation's scientists reasonable and prudent. Not every-one agreed, however. Franz Boas was outspokenly critical of Wilson's han-dling of foreign policy in general and of preparedness in particular. In fact, he accused the president of not "guarding American rights as neutrals against all attacks," and had instead "chosen to select certain rights which he will pro-tect, others which he will disregard."[22] To Boas, the "foremost duty of every individual and every country is to serve the interests of mankind," and he de-clared, "There are higher duties than patriotism, as at presently generally con-ceived."[23] Given the temper of the times, especially the growing anti-German feeling, Boas, a German American, showed real courage in taking this stand. In 1917, Smithsonian secretary, Charles Walcott fired Leo J. Frachtenberg from the BAE for making "derogatory remarks about the United States and the President."[24] But needless to say, others did not appreciate Boas's opinion, including the organizers of the National Research Council. By definition, these men, including Walcott, saw no conflict between science and patriotism (few did, for that matter—on either side of the Atlantic), and Boas was passed over for membership on the Council's Committee on Anthropology. Holmes and Aleš Hrdlička were chosen instead.[25]

Holmes certainly saw no conflict, either. In fact, his willingness to put patriotism ahead of reason was remarkable, even in the context of those hyperpatriotic times. Evidence of how far he was willing to go in this direction became clear early on. As head of the anthropology section, he, along with Hrdlička, submitted names of proposed committee members for the Research Council's approval. Their suggestions, however, were repeatedly turned down. Finally, the director of the Council, George E. Hale, named two nonanthropologists, Madison Grant and Charles B. Davenport, to the committee.[26] Both of these men were eugenicists. Grant, who held leadership positions in the American Eugenics Society and the Immigration Restriction League, is best known for his racist polemic *The Passing of the Great Race* (1916). Grant argued that the blood of the Nordic race was being diluted by inferior sources, and that, if not checked, the United States would decline as a great power. The irony here is almost too rich to be believed. Holmes, as a former head of the BAE, had dedicated much of his career to the proposition that the American race (Native Americans) was being replaced by the stronger white race—a process that was always viewed as something tragic but nevertheless inevitable. Holmes was now serving on a committee with a man who argued that the Nordic race was being polluted by foreign strains, and that if strong action were not taken this race would, in effect, share the same fate as the American race—that is, disappear. Unfortunately, there is no record of what Holmes thought of all of this. What we do know is that Holmes and Hrdlička, two men who had fought all of their lives for the professionalization of American anthropology, acquiesced in the naming of two nonanthropologists to the committee, rather than resigning in protest. They, in effect, sold out their colleagues and they would pay a price for it.

Given the composition of this committee, it is not surprising that at meetings held in 1917 in Washington, New York, and Boston, the concerns of physical anthropology outweighed everything else. The committee decided on behalf of the profession that the best way anthropology could aid the army and navy in war preparedness was to recommend that these branches adopt methods to ensure that the collection of physical data accurately took into account the nationalities and races of the new recruits.[27] It was, in effect, a way to conduct a limited national anthropological survey. Building on this momentum, Hrdlička founded the *American Journal of Physical Anthropology* early in 1918 and Davenport and Grant organized the Galton Society of New York to support the study of "racial anthropology."[28] And Holmes worked to secure Hrdlička's election to the National Academy of Sciences.

The issue of Hrdlička's election came to the fore in the fall of 1919. By then, things had changed. The war had ended in November 1918, but the postwar fear and reaction that swept the nation was in full swing. The National Research Council survived the war and Boas, with the help of his students, a group the historian George W. Stocking, Jr. called the "cultural anthropologists" or "Boasians," managed to recover some of the ground lost to the other major group in the profession, whom Stocking identified as the "physical anthropologists." To wit, they gained control of the National Research Council's peacetime division of anthropology and psychology and in the process excluded Holmes and Hrdlička because of their earlier role on the Council's Committee on Anthropology. Boas did see to it that Hrdlička was later elected as a divisional representative, but he refused to support Holmes's candidate for the National Academy.[29]

Holmes was furious at these moves, especially at Hrdlička's treatment. Holmes, unlike Boas, had not produced a number of distinguished students who were fanning out across the nation and taking their places in all of the major centers of anthropological study, from museums to universities. But if he did not have any students, he did have Hrdlička. From the time Hrdlička started at the National Museum in 1902, Holmes had taken an almost paternal interest in Hrdlička and had done all that he could for his career. That the two saw eye to eye on the antiquity question was no doubt a crucial factor in their relationship. They were also good friends. They lunched together and confided in one another. Thus, when Boas blocked Hrdlička's election, Holmes's reaction was intensely emotional.

But there is more to Holmes's strong reaction than that. Boas was not just anybody. He was a person with whom Holmes had a relationship dating back to 1894, when he got what Boas thought should have been his job at the Field Columbian Museum. The men were able to work through that situation, but Boas always held a grudge against Holmes and Walcott. Then, in 1902, when Holmes became chief of the BAE, Boas made it clear that McGee was the better man for the job, in part, because McGee was the one Washingtonian who was decent to Boas during the Chicago episode. Still, the men worked through that situation as well. When Holmes went to Stuttgart in 1904, for instance, he met Boas there, who then showed him around. In 1906, Holmes made a contribution to the anniversary volume prepared in Boas's honor and Boas returned the honor in 1916, by contributing an article, "Representative Art of Primitive People," to Holmes's anniversary volume.[30] In the meantime, Holmes, as bureau head, had worked closely with Boas for years on the Handbook of American Indian Languages. Their relationship thus was complicated but constrained. The passions generated by the war and professional rivalries and jealousies would destroy it and help precipitate one of the ugliest incidents in the history of American anthropology.

On May 17, 1919, Holmes went to New York City on business with Charles Walcott (who, incidentally, lost a son in the war). While in New York, he paid Boas a visit at Columbia University to discuss Hrdlička's candidacy to the National Academy, and, as it turned out, Boas's candidate and student Alfred L. Kroeber.[31] At this point, it is not clear whether an understanding was reached. But there were apparently no problems raised at the New York meeting. Holmes left assuming his man had Boas's support.

The main reason Holmes was in New York was to attend a meeting of the American Federation of the Arts, which was probably related to the creation of the Smithsonian's National Portrait Gallery. After the war, prominent art patrons formed a National Art Committee to see to it that the likeness of the American and Allied leaders in the Great War, both civil and military, were captured in portraits for posterity. The members of this committee included J. Pierpont Morgan, Henry C. Frick, Mrs. E. H. Harriman, Abram Garfield, Herbert L. Pratt, and Charles Walcott. This committee was endorsed by the Smithsonian Institution, the American Mission to Negotiate Peace, and the American Federation of Arts. In the end, twenty-one portraits were painted and displayed at the National Gallery of Art in May 1921 (the collection was subsequently exhibited at museum and galleries across the nation).[32] As curator of the National Gallery, Holmes gave his full support to this commemorative and patriotic movement.

By October 1919, however, at the same time that the Boasians were excluding Holmes and Hrdlička from the division of anthropology and psychology, Boas made it clear to Holmes that he could not support Hrdlička's election to the National Academy of Sciences. Apparently Boas claimed that, based on his conversation with Holmes, as far as he was concerned Hrdlička had nominated himself, which he said was inappropriate. What is more, Boas then shared Hrdlička's "self-nomination" with the members of the anthropology section of the National Academy. Defensive, Holmes responded to Boas on October 28:

> I happened to say in a friendly conversation with you, speaking of possible additional members for the National Academy of Sciences, that Dr. Hrdlicka "would be glad" to become a member. This careless remark was only an expression of my own wish in the matter and in which I expected you would concur. I had said to the Doctor on my own initiative, recognizing his great merit, that I hoped he might some day become a member of the Academy. He did nothing more than to indicate his pleasure at the suggestion, as any one else would have done under like circumstances. That you would write to members of the Anthropological Section of the Academy that "Dr. Hrdlicka has nominated himself for the academy," astonishes me. This was uncalled for and unjust and little short of malicious. You cannot expect support for your friends while you are ready to tear down others. I had intended to vote for your protégé, Dr. Kroeber, but cannot do so now. I am compelled to explain this matter fully to all members of the Academy who are directly concerned.[33]

Boas responded to this letter two days later, in copy that went to all members. He reiterated his earlier position, adding that "I do not see what my opinion of this peculiar move has to do with the merits of Dr. Kroeber, but, of course, we all have our own judgement." Holmes was incensed. In a letter to the philosopher and educator John Dewey, he tried to explain what had happened. "Dr. Boas had previously asked me to vote for his candidate. I sought to learn his attitude toward mine. I learned it. I resent his Prussian method of advertising it."[34]

The adjective "Prussian" was close to one of the worst things Holmes could think of to describe Boas's actions. He would think of a few more after Boas's bombshell letter (written on October 16) to the editor (Henry Raymond Mussey) of *The Nation* appeared on December 20, 1919, under the heading "Scientists as Spies."

Boas wrote:

> In his war address to Congress, President Wilson dwelt at great length on the theory that only autocracies maintain spies; that these are not needed in democracies. At the same time that the President made this statement, the Government of the United States had in its employ spies of an unknown number. I am not concerned here with the familiar discrepancies between the President's words and the actual facts, although we may perhaps have to accept his statement as meaning correctly that we live under an autocracy; that our democracy is a fiction. The point against which I wish to enter a vigor-

ous protest is that a number of men who follow science as their profession, men whom I refuse to designate any longer as scientists, have prostituted science by using it as a cover for their activities as spies.

A soldier whose business is murder as a fine art, a diplomat whose calling is based on deception and secretiveness, a politician whose very life consists in compromises with his conscience, a business man whose aim is personal profit within limits allowed by a lenient law—such may be excused if they set patriotic devotion above common everyday decency and perform services as spies. They merely accept the code of morality to which modern society still conforms. Not so the scientist. The very essence of his life is the service of truth. We all know scientists who in private life do not come up to the standard of truthfulness, but who, nevertheless, would not consciously falsify the results of their researches. It is bad enough if we have to put up with these, because they reveal a lack of strength of character that is liable to distort the results of their work. A person, however, who uses science as a cover for political spying, who demeans himself to pose before a foreign government as an investigator and asks for assistance in his alleged researches in order to carry on, under this cloak, his political machinations, prostitutes science in an unpardonable way and forfeits the right to be classed as a scientist.

By accident, incontrovertible proof has come to my hands that at least four men who carry on anthropological work, while employed as government agents, introduced themselves to foreign governments as representatives of scientific institutions in the United States, and as sent out for the purpose of carrying on scientific researches. They have not only shaken the belief in the truthfulness of science, but they have also done the greatest possible disservice to scientific inquiry. In consequence of their acts every nation will look with distrust upon the visiting foreign investigator who wants to do honest work, suspecting sinister designs. Such action has raised a new barrier against the development of international friendly cooperation.[35]

This was by all accounts a remarkable letter. In the super-patriotism and hyper-hysteria of the postwar era, the reaction to it was predictable and swift. At the Smithsonian Institution, a move was launched to sever Boas's connection with the BAE (he was still an honorary philologist there), just as Leo Frachtenberg had been driven out for his un-American views two years before. Not everyone in the Smithsonian agreed with this course of action, however. James Mooney of the BAE, for instance, warned Boas immediately what was afoot. "With surprise indignation," Mooney wrote, "I have just learned within the hour that a petition was yesterday passed around in this office in the Museum for signatures calling for your detachment from official connection or for other discipline, because of your article in *The Nation* of December 20."[36] John R. Swanton was also sympathetic, but wrote:

> Pardon me for saying so but I can't help feeling that you made a mistake in not breaching the subject privately among the anthropologists, explaining all circumstances, when it is possible that some expression of opinion regarding the ethics of the question might have been secured of advantage in future international emergencies. As it is the most erroneous constructions have been placed upon your letter and I regret to say that scientists show the same tendencies toward lynch law that are so distressing in the rest of the world.[37]

And Holmes was holding the rope.

Holmes turned to Frederick Webb Hodge (who had resigned from the bureau in 1918 to take a position at George Heye's Museum of the American Indian in New York), assuming that he shared with him his views on the Boas matter. Hodge, after all, had tried to resign in the fall of 1917 from the American Anthropological Association when Leo J. Frachtenberg had been nominated to become a member of the AAA council. On January 2, 1918, Hodge explained his reasons to Kroeber, the president of the AAA. Hodge wrote that he felt he had no other choice, given that Frachtenberg had been "recently dismissed from this Bureau by the Secretary of the Smithsonian Institution, to whom my loyalty is due." Kroeber explained that no insult was intended to the Smithsonian or anyone else and refused to accept Hodge's resignation.[38]

In late December 1919, Holmes wrote a violent letter to Hodge in which he stated the following:

> You have doubtless seen the traitorous article by Boas in the last Nation, and I want to say to you and to Saville and others who do not favor Prussian control of Anthropology in this country that we are determined to end the Hun regime. The position of Honorary Philologist in the Bureau of Ethnology *has been abolished*, and this, I am sure, is not the final step in the official assault upon the Hun positions.
>
> My attitude is this. In case Boas or any of his henchmen is selected to fill the $6,000.00 position in the National Research Council, I shall resign from the Association and shall advocate the organization of a new Association which shall be American in reality. I am sure that the majority of anthropologists outside of New York will be glad to join any movement that will tend to purge the stables.[39]

Hodge's reply is missing, but Holmes's terse response to it is not. Holmes wrote: "I have your recent favor and am surprised that you should wish the continuance of the Prussian regime, the vicious, scheming minority of the association has ruled long enough, and if it is to continue I shall close my connection with anthropology for good."[40]

As it turned out, Holmes got his way, at least in the short term. At the meeting of the AAA, held in Cambridge on December 30, 1919, Boas was censured (the only time the AAA ever took such action against a member), his membership in the association's governing council was taken away, his membership in the association was threatened, and he was forced to resign from the National Research Council, and then was prevented from explaining his position or from even apologizing.[41] Holmes wrote the resolution of censure, which ended with:

> Boas and his followers have sought to gain control of and direct anthropological researches in this country, especially those undertaken on behalf of the nation. There appears now danger that the Research Council may give this group control of researches and measures affecting the most intimate and vital interests to the nation—interests which should be entrusted to those, and those only, whose standard of citizenship is wholly above criticism.[42]

Despite this massive assault, Boas quickly recovered. He still had his institutional base at Columbia University and his many students who, as Stocking points out, "by 1926 headed every major department of anthropology in American universities."[43] Holmes, on the other hand, resigned his position at the museum in 1920 to serve as director of the National Gallery of Art, when it was established as a new department within the Smithsonian Institution. His influence in anthropology waned, especially after the Folsom discovery in 1926 seemed to discredit much of what he tried to do over the course of his long career.

Hrdlička may have seen which way the wind was going to blow. Holmes may have had the option of going into art; Hrdlička, however, would remain in the anthropology profession for the rest of his career. In a letter to Boas, written on January 13, 1920, he tried to explain his difficult position: his loyalty to Holmes, on the one hand, and his debt to Boas, which he had accumulated over the years, on the other.

> Resolutions in condemnation of your letter were passed by the Council of the Anthropological Society of Washington at a special meeting and have been sent to *The Nation* and *Science* for publication . . . I refused to support it, but I must tell you it was not because I agreed with your position but because I did not think we ought to take action as a scientific body and because I did not agree with the terms of the resolutions either. I promised at that time to draw up an independent statement, but have been waiting for the publication

of the resolutions before doing so. It is extremely unpleasant because I feel indebted to both you and Professor Holmes. All of the raises in salary I received here, except the first and last, were while he was Chief of the Bureau. I hope I deserved them but it makes a difference just the same. As I honestly differ from both of you it may look as if I were trying to carry water on both shoulders, which I'm not. I was absent from the Cambridge meeting solely for financial reasons.[44]

Given everything that had happened over the past few months, this was not a bad first attempt at postwar reconstruction.

The Consolation of Art

From 1920 until his retirement in 1932, Holmes served as director of the Smithsonian's National Gallery of Art. He was very much a part of the old guard and he personally saw little of interest in the post-Moran art world. He continued to enjoy painting and water-coloring and took pleasure in showing it. He worked hard to try to get a building for the ever-growing and increasingly valuable National Gallery, even taking his case to the public by radio in 1923. "The last effort," he wrote, toward this end

> was the publication in 1927 of an illustrated article "A Plea for a National Gallery Building," but this was promptly cast into the discard as wholly unavailing. Early in 1927 an announcement was made by Senator [Reed] Smoot [of Utah] in the public press that he had knowledge of a wealthy patron [Andrew W. Mellon, Secretary of the Treasury] who was planning to contribute ample funds for the erection of the needed building. With this prospect in view all efforts to induce Congress to appropriate public funds for the purpose was necessarily abandoned.[45]

It was not until after Holmes passed away on in 1933, that Mellon offered the funds to build a gallery of art building. And when he did, Mellon wanted to found his own National Gallery of Art, and he wanted to be able to use that name. The government happily agreed to his terms and the Smithsonian's National Gallery of Art was renamed the National Collection of Fine Arts on March 24, 1937 (now the National Museum of American Art), in order to accommodate the new institution, with which it shared the Mall.

On April 9, 1925, Holmes's wife Kate passed away after enduring, in his words, "a most painful illness."[46] Holmes tried to sell his home on Belmont Street, but was unable to find a buyer. During this difficult period, his sister-in-law, Agnes Osgood Clifton, stayed with him and "kept house."[47] After

Holmes's friends from the Hayden Days Enjoying a Reunion in 1927. Posing before Moran's *Grand Canyon of the Yellowstone* at the Smithsonian's National Gallery of Art are William H. Jackson (*standing left*), William H. Holmes (*standing right*), Story B. Ladd (*sitting left*), and George B. Chittenden (*sitting right*). Note Holmes' crutch under his right arm. (Photograph , no. 65,224, courtesy Yellowstone National Park Reference Library, Albright Visitor Center, Mammoth Hot Springs, Wyoming.)

several months, Holmes took up residence at the Cosmos Club, where he was well received and liked, leaving the house to his son, Osgood. The following year, he suffered from blood poisoning in his foot and had to have his left leg amputated above the knee. Although he was seventy-nine years old, this operation barely slowed him down, even though he was forced to depend on crutches and a wheelchair to get around, and he reported that he was "soon at my desk at the Gallery as usual."[48] On December 1, of that same year, his many friends marked his eightieth birthday with a volume of letters as a token of their esteem for him and his distinguished career in science and art. The time clearly seemed right for Holmes to take his leave of government service. But the failure to prepare for retirement kept him on the job for six more years. Holmes spent part of this time organizing his papers for posterity. The result of this labor, which he had finished by June 10, 1929, was the twenty-volume work that he called the "Random Records," which was anything but *random*. It was a remarkably thorough, if selective, compilation of his life's documents. Holmes had them bound at his own expense.[49]

In 1932—sixty years after he had gone West with Hayden—Holmes finally left Washington for good and joined his other son, William Heberling, in Royal Oak, Michigan. There he was well taken care of by those who loved him and where he was affectionately known as "Mitter." According to his granddaughter Mary, his "avowed materialism" held until the end. His position apparently softened, however, after suffering a stroke on January 11, 1932, in which he lost the use of his right arm. In a letter Mary Holmes wrote to Hrdlička (Holmes and Hrdlička remained close until the end), she shared with him a discussion she and Holmes had about philosophy and the meaning of life. She wrote that while she was a believer, Holmes was not. Toward the end of this conversation, Holmes mentioned Hrdlička, saying he "will persist in believing in some divine origin." To which Mary recorded her response as "Hurrah for Hrdlička." After a pause, "Mitter smiled very sweetly and then said [to Mary], 'Oh well . . . I guess it does no harm after all, if people want to believe those things.'"[50]

Holmes passed away a few months later on April 20, 1933, at the age of eighty-six. He was cremated in Detroit and then buried in the same lot with his wife, Kate, at Rock Creek Cemetery in Washington, D.C. Their marker reads: "They gave to art and science." This remembrance was as true as it was understated.

Notes

Introduction

1. William H. Goetzmann, *Exploration and Empire: The Explorer and the Scientist in the Winning of the American West* (New York: W. W. Norton and Company, 1978), 512–13.

2. Ibid., xi.

3. Wallace Stegner, *Beyond the Hundredth Meridian: John Wesley Powell and the Second Opening of the West* (Lincoln: University of Nebraska Press, 1982), 137.

4. Frederick S. Dellenbaugh to William Henry Holmes, Apr. 11, 1922, William Henry Holmes Papers, Smithsonian Institution Archives (hereafter cited as SIA), Record Unit 7084.

1. "What is the Species of the Bird?"

1. Albert C. White, *A History of the Rectangular Survey System* (Washington, D.C.: U.S. Government Printing Office, 1983), 18–24. See also Walter Havighurst, *Ohio: A Bicentennial History* (New York: W. W. Norton and Company, 1976), 33; H. J. Eckley and William T. Perry, *History of Carroll and Harrison Counties, Ohio* (Chicago: Lewis Publishing Company, 1921), 209–10.

2. Henry Howe, *Historical Collections of Ohio in Three Volumes* (Columbus: Henry Howe and Son, 1891), 2:168.

3. "Brief Biography of William Henry Holmes: Artist, Geologist, Archaeologist and Art Gallery Director, 1846–19–," *Ohio Archaeological and Historical Society Publications* 36 (1927): 493–527. Holmes probably wrote this article or at least edited it. Unless otherwise indicated, the account of Holmes's childhood is drawn from this source. Also, John R. Swanton, "Biographical Memoir of William Henry Holmes, 1846–1933," *National Academy of Sciences Biographical Memoirs*, vol. 17 (Washington, D.C.: National Academy of Sciences, 1937), 223.

4. *Commemorative Biographical Record, Harrison, Ohio, Containing Biographical Sketches of Prominent and Representative Citizens, and Many of the Early Settled Families* (Chicago: J. H. Beers and Co., 1891), 217.

5. Charles A. Hanna, *Ohio Valley Genealogies* (1900; repr., Baltimore: Genealogical Publishing Company, 1968), 63–64.

6. Ibid, 64.

7. William Henry Holmes, "Random Records of a Lifetime, 1846–1931: Cullings, Largely Personal, From the Scrap Heap of Three Score Years and Ten, Devoted to Science, Literature and Art," 1:19 (hereafter cited as "Random Records"). These records make up twenty volumes of materials—newspaper clippings, personal documents, correspondence, memoirs, anecdotes, articles, photographs, and notes. The first sixteen original volumes are in the Library of the National Museum of American Art and the National Portrait Gallery, and are on microfilm. The other four volumes are in the possession of Holmes's granddaughter, Mrs. Laughlin A. Campbell, who resides in Washington, D.C. She kindly made available these volumes, which are largely of personal interest.

8. Ibid., 1:18.

9. "Brief Biography," 496.

10. "Random Records," 1:10.

11. Ibid., 1:15.

12. "Brief Biography," 497.

13. H. A. Clark to Holmes, Oct. 9, 1870, William Henry Holmes Papers, SIA, Record Unit 7084.

14. Letter of introduction from Edwin Regal to D. B. Hagar, Apr. 15, 1871, "Random Records," 1:17.

15. Andrew J. Cosentino and Henry H. Glassie, *The Capital Image: Painters in Washington, 1800–1915* (Washington, D.C.: Smithsonian Institution Press, 1983), 102, 105, 215, 264.

16. Theodore Kaufmann to John Simmons, Apr. 11, 1871, "Random Records," 1:22.

17. Henry Adams, *The Education of Henry Adams*, ed. Ernest Samuels (1918; repr., Boston: Houghton Mifflin Company, 1973), 256.

18. "Random Records," 1:46; "Brief Biography," 498.

19. "Random Records," 14:47.

20. "Brief Biography," 498–99.

21. "Random Records," 13:152–55; "Random Records," 14:160.

22. Charles A. White, "Memoir of Fielding Bradford Meek, 1817–1876," *National Academy of Sciences Biographical Memoirs*, vol. 4 (Washington, D.C.: National Academy of Sciences, 1902): 77–81; Ellis L. Yochelson, "Fielding Bradford Meek," *Dictionary of Scientific Biography*, vol. 4 (1974): 255–56.

23. W. P. Woodring, "William Healey Dall, August 21, 1845–March 27, 1927," *National Academy of Sciences Biographical Memoirs*, vol. 31 (New York: Columbia University Press, 1958), 95–98; see also Melody Webb, *The Last Frontier: A History of the Yukon Basin of Canada and Alaska* (Albuquerque: University of New Mexico Press, 1985), 53–55.

24. Clifford M. Nelson, "William Henry Holmes: Beginning a Career in Art and Science," *Records of the Columbia Historical Society of Washington, D.C.* 50 (1980): 256.

25. Clifford M. Nelson and Fritiof M. Fryxell, "The Antebellum Collaboration of Meek and Hayden in Stratigraphy," *Two Hundred Years of Geology in America*, ed. Cecil J. Schneer (Hanover, N.H.: University Press of New England, 1979), 187.

26. Herman J. Viola, in *Exploring the West* (Washington, D.C.: Smithsonian Books, 1987), draws needed attention to the activities of this crucial figure in the history of American scientific discovery.

27. David Starr Jordan, "Spencer Fullerton Baird and the United States Fish Commission," *Scientific Monthly* 27 (August 1923): 101; E. F. Rivinus and E. M. Youssef, *Spencer Baird of the Smithsonian* (Washington, D.C.: Smithsonian Institution, 1992).

28. "Brief Biography," 499; Rivinus and Youssef, *Spencer Baird*, 32.

29. William H. Holmes to Fielding B. Meek, Sept. 9, 1871; Holmes to Meek, Sept. 19, 1871; Meek to Holmes, Sept. 28, 1871, Fielding B. Meek Papers, SIA, Record Unit 7062; Nelson, "William Henry Holmes," 263.

30. Stegner, *Beyond the Hundredth Meridian*, 178–79.

31. Unless indicated otherwise, I have drawn these details about Hayden's career from Mike Foster, *Strange Genius: The Life of Ferdinand Vandeveer Hayden* (Niwot, Colo.: Roberts Rinehart Publishers, 1994); see also, Charles A. White, "Memoir of Ferdinand Vandiveer Hayden, 1838–1887," *National Academy of Sciences Biographical Memoirs*, vol. 3 (1895): 397–413.

32. "Random Records," 1:55.

2. Yellowstone Expedition, 1872

1. For a highly readable account of Schliemann's excavations of ancient Troy and Greece, which coincided with Holmes's own work in the Southwest, see C. W. Ceram, *Gods, Graves, and Scholars: The Story of Archaeology*, trans. E. B. Garside and Sophie Wilkins, 2d rev. ed. (New York: Alfred A. Knopf, 1967), chaps. 4–7.

2. Peter Hassrick, *The Way West: Art of Frontier America* (New York: Abradale Press/Harry N. Abrams, 1983), 17–20; Brian W. Dippie, "The Visual West," in *The Oxford History of the American West*, ed. Clyde A. Milner II, Carol A. O'Conner, and Martha A. Sandweiss (New York: Oxford University Press, 1994), 675–705.

3. On the subject of the relationship between science and western art, I am indebted to the works of William H. Goetzmann, especially to his *Exploration and Empire*, cited above.

4. Unless otherwise indicated, the details of Holmes's trip in 1872 to Yellowstone National Park were drawn from William Henry Holmes, "Extracts from the Diary of W. H. Holmes," 1872, 1878, Typescript, Yellowstone National Park Library.

5. Anne Farrar Hyde, *An American Vision: Far Western Landscape and National Culture, 1820–1920* (New York: New York University Press, 1990), 45.

6. For facts about Jackson's life, I have drawn on William Henry Jackson, *Time Exposure* (1940; Albuquerque: University of New Mexico Press, 1986); Peter B. Hales, *William Henry Jackson and the Transformation of the American Landscape* (Philadelphia: Temple University Press, 1988); and Rowe Findley, "The Life and Times of William Henry Jackson: Photographing the Frontier," *National Geographic* 175 (February 1989): 216–51.

7. F. V. Hayden, *Sixth Annual Report of the United States Geological Survey of the Territories Embracing Portions of Montana, Idaho, Wyoming, and Utah; Being a Report of Progress of the Explorations for the Year 1872* (Washington, D.C.: U.S. Government Printing Office, 1873), 5. For an overview of the Hayden Survey, see Richard A. Bartlett, *Great Surveys of the American West* (Norman: University of Oklahoma Press, 1962), pt. 1; William H. Goetzmann, *Exploration and Empire*, chap. 14.

8. This description holds at least for the year 1875. See General William E. Strong, *A Trip to the Yellowstone National Park in July, August, and September, 1875* (Norman: University of Oklahoma Press, 1968), illustration opposite p. 24.

9. Albert Charles Peale, Transcript of 1872 A. C. Peale Diary (July 21–October 24), Yellowstone National Park Library, 56.

10. See Fritiof M. Fryxell, "Albert Charles Peale: Pioneer Geologist of the Hayden Survey," *Annals of Wyoming* 34 (October 1962): 175–92.

11. Peale, Transcript of 1872 A. C. Peale Diary, 15.

12. Hayden, *Sixth Annual Report*, 144–45.

13. Foster, *Strange Genius*, 237.

14. "Random Records," 2:47.

15. Ibid.

16. See Nancy K. Anderson, "'The Kiss of Enterprise': The Western Landscape as Symbol and Resource," in *The West as America: Reinterpreting Images of the Frontier, 1820–1920*, ed. William H. Truettner (Washington, D.C.: Smithsonian Institution Press, 1991), 237.

17. Thurman Wilkins, *Clarence King: A Biography*, 2d rev. ed. (Albuquerque: University of New Mexico Press, 1988), 409.

18. Hayden, *Sixth Annual Report*, 44.

19. Ibid., 27.

20. Peale, Transcript of 1872 A. C. Peale Diary, 9.

21. Hayden, *Sixth Annual Report*, 43.

22. Peale, Transcript of 1872 A. C. Peale Diary, 8.

23. Hayden, *Sixth Annual Report*, 47.

24. Peale, Transcript of 1872 A. C. Peale Diary, 14.

25. Thomas Moran's *The Grand Cañon of the Yellowstone* was placed on exhibition in the Smithsonian gallery in early May 1872, so Holmes had an opportunity to study the painting before his trip to Yellowstone. Thurman Wilkins, *Thomas Moran: Artist of the Mountains* (Norman: University of Oklahoma Press, 1966), 5.

26. Peale, Transcript of 1872 A. C. Peale Diary, 14.

27. Moran had Hayden inspect the *Grand Cañon of the Yellowstone* for its geological accuracy. Wilkins, *Thomas Moran*, 69–70.

28. The following Moran quotes were taken from Robert Taft, *Artists and Illustrators of the Old West, 1850–1900* (New York: Charles Scribner's Sons, 1953), 250. See Joni Louise Kinsey, *Thomas Moran and the Surveying of the American West* (Washington, D.C.: Smithsonian Institution Press, 1992), 12–19; Wilkins, *Thomas Moran*, 69.

29. Wilkins, *Thomas Moran*, 99.

30. Taft, *Artists and Illustrators*, 250.

31. Not until January 20, 1877, however, did Henry Stanley, an American journalist and explorer, prove incontrovertibly that Lake Victoria was the Nile's source. See James Morris, *Heaven's Command: An Imperial Progress*, vol. 1 (1973; repr., Harmondsworth, Engl.: Penguin Books, 1979), 296.

32. Peale, Transcript of 1872 A. C. Peale Diary, 22.

33. Swanton, "Biographical Memoir of William Henry Holmes," 224.

34. Carl I. Wheat, *Mapping the Transmississippi West, From Lewis and Clark to Fremont 1804–1845* (San Francisco: Institute of Historical Cartography, 1958), 2:1–5.

35. Hayden, *Sixth Annual Report*, 57.

36. Ibid, 167.

37. Peale, Transcript of 1872 A. C. Peale Diary, 66.

38. F. V. Hayden, *[Seventh] Annual Report of the United States Geological and Geographical Survey of the Territories, Embracing Colorado, Being a Report of the Progress of the Exploration for the Year 1873* (Washington, D.C.: Government Printing Office, 1874), 1.

3. Mount of the Ephemeral Cross

1. Hayden, *[Seventh] Annual Report*, 1.

2. Wheat, *Mapping the Transmississippi West, From the Civil War to the Geological Survey* (San Francisco: Institute of Historical Cartography, 1963), 5:347.

3. Wilkins, *Clarence King*, 187.

4. John Noble Wilford, *The Mapmakers: The Story of the Great Pioneers in Cartography from Antiquity to the Space Age* (New York: Vintage Books, 1981), 163–66.

5. James T. Gardner, "Sketch of the Methods of Survey in the Geographical Department," in Hayden, *[Seventh] Annual Report*, 627–28.

6. Archibald R. Marvine, "Report," in Hayden, *[Seventh] Annual Report*, 94.

7. Ibid., 95.

8. William H. Holmes, "Field Book: Colorado, 1873–1876," Denver Federal Center, United States Geological Survey, Field Records Library, Accession no.: NO-7448, sheet page 6/1. (Hereafter cited as Field Book: NO-7448, sheet page.) In the process of turning Holmes's field sketch into an illustration for Marvine's report, Golden City's only suburb—a number of scattered structures south of town—disappeared. See fig. 5 of Marvine, "Report," in Hayden, *[Seventh] Annual Report*, facing 130.

9. See "Ideal Section of Dyke" in Hayden, *[Seventh] Annual Report*, facing 28.

10. George P. Merrill, *The First One Hundred Years of American Geology* (New Haven: Yale University Press, 1924), 520–21; Stephen J. Pyne, *Grove Karl Gilbert: A Great Engine of Research* (Austin: University of Texas Press, 1980), 84–85.

11. The mountains Holmes named were Italia, Grizzly, Gothic, Crested Butte, Castle Peak, Capitol, and Powell. See "Random Records," 4, pt. 1:11.

12. Ibid., 26.

13. The survey calculated the elevation of the Mount of the Holy Cross at 14,176 feet above sea level, which, by today's standards, was 171 feet too high. Owing to the level of sophistication of topography in Holmes's day and to the haste in which some of the work was carried out—such errors were unavoidable.

14. Jackson, *Time Exposure*, 217.

15. See Field Book: NO-7448, 66/2–70/1.

16. On Aug. 29, 1869, William H. Brewer (of the California Geological Survey and Sheffield Scientific School) recorded the first official citing of the Mount of the Holy Cross from Grays Peak, which stands at a distance of forty miles. *Rocky Mountain News*, Aug. 31, 1990, 88.

17. *Rocky Mountain News*, July 29, 1874, 4.

18. Holmes and Jackson both stressed the cross's fleeting nature, but given how rarely the cross appears in the condition in which Jackson first photographed it, the question has been raised whether the snow cross was a hoax that the Hayden Survey deliberately perpetrated. And in 1950, twenty-one years after President Herbert Hoover had set aside the Mount of the Holy Cross as a national monument, President Harry S. Truman decommissioned the famous site. See Robert L. Brown, "A Controversy: William H. Jackson and Mount of the Holy Cross," *Trail and Timberline* 590 (February 1968): 37–41; Mathias S. Fisch, "The Quest for the Mount of the Holy Cross," *The American West: The Magazine of Western History* 16 (March/April 1979): 32–36, 57–58.

19. "Random Records," 4, pt. 1:60–61.

20. Ibid.

21. See plate 59 (opposite p. 168) in Patricia Trenton and Peter H. Hassrick, *The Rocky Mountains: A Vision for Artists in the Nineteenth Century* (Norman: University of Oklahoma Press, 1983).

22. The 1890 version is part of the art collection of the Western History Department, Denver Public Library.

23. One version of the wandering Spanish padre can be found in J. A. D., "The Mount of the Holy Cross: A Legend of Colorado," *Potter's Monthly: Illustrated Magazine of History, Literature, Science and Art* 11 (1878): 326–27; several of the old myths are discussed in Robert L. Brown, *Holy Cross—The Mountain and the City* (Caldwell, Idaho: Caxton Printers, 1970), 52–56. Fritiof M. Fryxell, in the foreword to Clarence S. Jackson and Lawrence W. Marshall's *Quest of the Snowy Cross* (Denver: University of Denver, 1952), makes the point that the "'early legends' about this peak which have been persistently circulated are so palpably made to order as to be wholly unconvincing, even as fiction."

24. Jackson, *Time Exposure*, 216.

25. Ibid.

26. Holmes stated that Jackson's famous photograph of the Holy Cross truthfully represented what they saw that day and that it "had not been subject to the least retouching on the part of the photographer." See "Random Records," 4, pt. 1:60–61. According to Peter B. Hales, however, Jackson did make two changes to the picture:

> As it originally stood, the picture portrayed a stony wall without sign of life, an irregular cross carved into its face. Jackson's initial improvement was minimal; besides opaquing the sky, he regularized the cross by retouching one arm. The second alteration, however, was more drastic; it was the addition of the stream and waterfall to the picture.

Quoted from Hales, *William Henry Jackson*, 132.

27. William H. Holmes, "Mountain of the Holy Cross," *Illustrated Christian Weekly* (May 1, 1875): 210.

28. Jackson, *Time Exposure*, 218.

29. Holmes, "Mountain of the Holy Cross," 209–10; Jackson, *Time Exposure*, 217; Swanton, "Biographical Memoir of William Henry Holmes," 225.

4. Opportunity

1. Erwin Raisz, *General Cartography* (New York: McGraw-Hill Book Company, 1948), 52.

2. Indeed, contemporary foreign observers had taken favorable note of the American innovation of combining the traditionally separate disciplines of topography and geology. In the words of Capitaine Prudent, which were written in 1879, this practice was "tres logique." See Emmanuel de Margerie, *Commentaire de L'Atlas of Colorado (1877)* (Paris: Imprimerie Nationale, 1925), 61–62.

3. Hayden, *[Seventh] Annual Report*, 3.

4. Unless otherwise indicated, the details of Holmes's exploration of the Elk Mountains and quotes are drawn from his "Report on the Geology of the Northwestern Portion of the Elk Range" (hereafter cited as "Report on the Elk Range"), in Hayden's *[Eighth] Annual Report of the United States Geological and Geographical Survey of the Territories, Embracing Colorado and Parts of Adjacent Territories; Being a Report of Progress of the Exploration for the Year 1874* (Washington, D.C.: Government Printing Office, 1876), 59–71.

5. Goetzmann, *Exploration and Empire*, 492–93.

6. Today Holmes's route around the northwestern base of the Elk Mountains can be retraced from the side of Colorado's mountain roads. From the town of Aspen, follow Highway 82 north to Highway 133, and observe to the left of the road the eastern slope of the Elk Range. Then turn south on 133, and drive at least as far as the town of Redstone. From this stretch of highway, note the western slope of the range on the left.

7. See Field Book: NO-7448, 47/2. This sketch shows where the intrusive granite met its metamorphic counterpart at the top of Italian Mountain.

8. See Holmes, "Report on the Elk Range," 68 and fig. 11.

9. Ibid., fig. 10.

10. Grove Karl Gilbert, *Report on the Geology of the Henry Mountains*, 2d ed. (Washington, D. C.: Government Printing Office, 1880), 64.

11. Thomas Moran and Holmes had by now become good friends. One of the illustrations to Holmes's report on the Elk Mountains, in fact, bore Moran's famous colophon. See Holmes, "Report on the Elk Range," fig. 8, which was probably based on a Holmes sketch.

12. Artistic considerations aside, Holmes's work provided a valuable public service as well. In 1879, prospectors appeared along the Roaring Fork River equipped with copies of the Hayden reports, which helped them locate some of the richest silver deposits in the world. Malcolm J. Rohrbough, *Aspen: The History of a Silver-Mining Town, 1879–1893* (New York: Oxford University Press, 1986), 3–6.

13. Holmes to Hayden, June 13, 1875, in *Records of the U.S. Geological and Geographical Survey of the Territories "Hayden Survey" 1867–79*, Roll 8, *"Letters Received, 1871–79"* (Washington, D. C.: The National Archives and Records Service, General Services Administration, 1965), microcopy no. 623, arranged alphabetically and chronologically (hereafter cited as "Letters Received").

14. Hayden, *Ninth Annual Report of the United States Geological and Geographical Sur-*

vey of the Territories, Embracing Colorado and Parts of Adjacent Territories: Being a Report of Progress of the Exploration for the Year 1875 (Washington, D.C.: Government Printing Office, 1877), 4.

15. Holmes to Hayden, June 17, 1875, "Letters Received."

16. Chittenden to Hayden, June 18, 1875, "Letters Received."

17. James Jefferson, Robert W. Delaney, and Gregory C. Thompson, *The Southern Utes: A Tribal History* (Ignacio, Colo.: Southern Ute Tribe, 1972), 30.

18. Duane Vandenbusche and Duane A. Smith, *A Land Alone: Colorado's Western Slope* (Boulder, Colo.: Pruett Publishing Company, 1981), 79; Francis Paul Prucha, *The Great Father: The United States Government and the American Indians*, abridged ed. (Lincoln: University of Nebraska Press, 1986), 172–73.

19. Holmes to Hayden, July 18, 1875, "Letters Received."

20. Jackson, *Time Exposure*, 230–31.

21. Ibid. Evidently in return for services rendered as host and guide, Jackson and the other men in his expedition cast what were decisive votes for Moss in his bid for office in Rio Grande County.

22. Holmes to Hayden, July 18, 1875, "Letters Received."

23. Jackson, *Time Exposure*, 241.

24. Unless otherwise indicated, the story of Holmes's encounter with the Utes and Navajo in the valley of the San Juan River is drawn from "Random Records," 4, pt. 1: "Field Notes of W. H. Holmes in Charge of the San Juan Division of the Geological Survey of the Territories, 1875," 153–97 (hereafter cited as "San Juan Field Notes").

25. Chittenden reported to Hayden that "Tom [Cooper] did a clean bit of recapture on the San Juan & deserves a good deal of credit for it." Chittenden to Hayden, Aug. 25, 1875, "Letters Received."

26. Gardner, *Rocky Mountain News*, Sept. 21, 1875, 2.

27. Holmes, "Geological Report on the San Juan District," in Hayden, *Ninth Annual Report*, 239.

28. Gardner, *Rocky Mountain News*, Sept. 22, 1875, 2.

29. Gardner, *Rocky Mountain News*, Sept. 21, 1875, 2.

30. Unless otherwise indicated, the following account of the Indian attack is drawn from Gardner, *Rocky Mountain News*, Sept. 5, 1875, 4.

31. A. C. Peale, "Description of an Indian Fight," *The Denver Westerners Monthly Round Up* 12 (July 1956): 3–5. This account was taken from Peale's diary.

32. Jackson, *Time Exposure*, 242.

33. Gardner, *Rocky Mountain News*, Sept. 17, 1875, 4. Before Gardner could reach the two men, a score of mounted Utes had arrived at the supply camp and threatened to kill the men, but instead set fire to the tall grass around the tents as a less-than-friendly warning for them to leave.

34. Chittenden opined to Hayden that Gardner's party was "in a pretty tight place" and that Gardner had "enough back bone there. The after-clap has made the trouble and the great general is miserable for it." Chittenden to Hayden, Oct. 2, 1875, "Letters Received."

35. Gardner, *Rocky Mountain News*, Sept. 21, 1875, 2. These strong words notwithstanding, Gardner clearly had enough of the West. That autumn he resigned his position

with the Hayden survey and took over New York State's less hazardous trigonometrical survey.

36. Holmes, "San Juan Field Notes," August 5 entry.

37. Jackson, *Time Exposure*, 242.

5. Ghosts

1. Holmes, "Report on the Ancient Ruins of Southwestern Colorado, Examined During the Summers of 1875 and 1876," in Hayden, *Tenth Annual Report of the United States Geological and Geographical Survey of the Territories, Embracing Colorado and Parts of Adjacent Territories, Being a Report of Progress of the Exploration for the Year 1876* (Washington, D.C.: Government Printing Office, 1878), 383.

2. For a discussion of Holmes's place within the emerging anthropology profession, see Curtis M. Hinsley, Jr., *Savages and Scientists: The Smithsonian Institution and the Development of American Anthropology, 1846–1910* (Washington, D.C.: Smithsonian Institution Press, 1981), passim; Joan Mark, *Four Anthropologists: An American Science in Its Early Years* (New York: Science History Publications, 1980), 131–71.

3. James H. Simpson, *Journal of a Military Reconnaissance from Santa Fe, New Mexico, to the Navajo Country, made with the Troops under the Command of Brevet Lieutenant Colonel John M. Washington, Chief of the 9th Military Department, and Governor of New Mexico, in 1849*, 31st Cong., 1st sess., Sen. Exec. Doc. 64 (Washington, D.C.: Union Office, 1850), 75–85; John S. Newberry, "Geological Report," in John N. Macomb, *Report of the Exploring Expedition from Santa Fe, New Mexico, to the Junction of the Grand and Green Rivers of the Great Colorado of the West, in 1859, Under the Command of Capt. J. N. Macomb; with a Geological Report by Prof. J. S. Newberry* (Washington, D.C.: Government Printing Office, 1876), 80, 88–89. In the latter work, Newberry explained in a prefatory note, written June 1, 1875, that the Civil War had indefinitely postponed publication of his geological report, but the recent interest in the San Juan region has now "rendered [its] publication desirable." No doubt the issue of priority for his scientific discoveries was also a consideration.

4. Richard Kern's brother, Edward, was also a member of Simpson's party. Edward served as topographer. See David J. Weber, *Richard H. Kern: Expeditionary Artist in the Far Southwest, 1848–1853* (Albuquerque: University of New Mexico Press, 1985), 57–113. See also Robert V. Hine, *Edward Kern and American Expansion* (New Haven: Yale University Press, 1962).

5. William H. Goetzmann, *Army Exploration in the American West, 1803–1863* (New Haven: Yale University Press, 1959), 240–41.

6. Ibid., 394–96.

7. Holmes was probably familiar with Edward Palmer's article, "Exploration of a Mound in Utah," which the *American Naturalist* published in 1876. Later, archaeologists would identify three major horticultural traditions in the Southwest: 1) the Mogollon; 2) the Hohokam; and 3) Anasazi or the ancestral Pueblo Indians. The Anasazi, a people whom Holmes called the cliff builders, occupied the Four Corners region where the Rio San Juan stood in the center, with the Virgin River defining the western limit and the Pecos River the eastern.

8. Duane A. Smith, *Mesa Verde National Park: Shadows of the Centuries* (Lawrence: University Press of Kansas, 1988), 7.

9. Holmes, "Report on the Ancient Ruins of Southwestern Colorado," 384.

10. See Alfred Vincent Kidder's "Bibliography of the San Juan," in his 1924 classic, *An Introduction to the Study of Southwestern Archaeology, with a Preliminary Account of the Excavations at Pecos,* rev. ed. (New Haven: Yale University Press, 1962), 252–53.

11. The Mormons, however, were inclined, based on the teachings of the *Book of Mormon,* to view the local Indians, whom they called "Lamanites," as a fallen race that had once built mighty civilizations in the Americas, including the remains found throughout the Southwest. Equally plausible to the Mormons was that the white "Nephites" had built the cities of the Southwest. They believed that "Nephites" (descendants of ancient Jewish immigrants) eventually fell away from the Lord's commandments and were consequently utterly destroyed by the even more wicked Lamanites in a race war. In 1854, Brigham Young sent W. D. Huntington to explore the San Juan area. The remoteness and inaccessibility of the cliff ruins in Mancos Canyon suggested to Huntington that they were once inhabited by the West's first outlaws. "We very readily came to a conclusion," Huntington reported in the *Deseret News,* "drawn from the *Book of Mormon* in the second chapter of Nephi that ancient possessors of these strongholds were robbers of the Gadianton Band." Quoted from C. Gregory Crampton, *Standing Up Country: The Canyon Lands of Utah and Arizona* (1964; repr., Salt Lake City: Gibbs M. Smith, Peregrine Smith Books, 1983), 173.

12. Holmes, "Report on the Ancient Ruins of Southwestern Colorado," 383.

13. Simpson, *Journal of a Military Reconnaissance . . . to the Navajo Country,* 77.

14. Ibid., 83. Simpson consulted with Hosta, the governor of Jemez pueblo; Sandoval, a Navajo chief; and Rafael Carravahal, a Mexican who served as his guide. Regardless of the views of modern archaeologists, it is important to note the acceptance of the Aztec origins of the ruins on the part of at least some of the Indians of the Four Corners region, for the idea served to unite them in a common belief of brotherhood. Sandoval, for example, told Simpson that the ruins had been "built by Montezuma . . . [and] that the Navajos and all the other Indians were once one people, and lived in the vicinity of the Silver Mountain . . . [and] that the Pueblo Indians separated from them (the Navajos), and built towns on the Rio Grande and its tributaries." See p. 83 of Simpson's *Journal.* In the late 1960s, several Chicano writers resuscitated this old idea in the "myth of Aztlan." See David J. Weber, "The Spanish Legacy in North America and the Historical Imagination," *Western Historical Quarterly* 23 (February 1992), 19–21.

15. Quoted from Weber, *Richard H. Kern,* 88–89.

16. Newberry, "Geological Report," 89. Modern archaeologists still make a case for cultural continuity between the ancient and the historic Pueblos, although today they have more evidence to support their generalizations than Newberry was able to collect on his brief tour in 1859. William M. Ferguson and Arthur H. Rohn, *Anasazi Ruins of the Southwest in Color* (Albuquerque: University of New Mexico Press, 1987), 72.

17. Another antebellum government scientist, Lieutenant William H. Emory of the Corps of Topographical Engineers, also took issue with the Aztec hypothesis and argued that the modern Puebloans had built the ancient ruins of the Southwest. Goetzmann, *Exploration and Empire,* 325–26.

18. Holmes, "Report on the Ancient Ruins of Southwestern Colorado," 408.

19. F. W. Putnam to Holmes, April 24, 1876, "Random Records," 4, pt. 2:20. In a letter sent to Holmes before he published his report on the ruins, Putnam wrote:

I am as yet not at all satisfied with [your] theory regarding the ancient ruins of Col[orado] and I hope you will be able to get more information from them and clear up the question . . . The more I find out about the ruins the more I am convinced that we must look to the south for their origin.

20. Hewett, "Excerpt from School of American Research, *Director's Report, 1928,* 'Appendix 1: The Status of Ethnological & Archaeological Research in the Southwest,'" in "Random Records," 4, pt. 2:89. Hewett is worth quoting on this point at length:

[Holmes] prepared the way through his geological studies in the Southwest and then proceeded with his masterly interpretations of the remains left by man. He wiped out the mythical ideas of "Vanished Races," demonstrating that the ancient cliff dwellers were the Pueblo Indians of the centuries preceeding [*sic*] the European occupation. We owe it to him that students of man now concede that the archaeology of the American Southwest is mainly the early history of the Pueblo Indians.

21. Holmes, "Report on the Ancient Ruins of Southwestern Colorado," 408.

22. See Don D. Fowler, *The Western Photographs of John K. Hillers: Myself in the Waters* (Washington, D.C.: Smithsonian Institution Press, 1989), 77–79. Before Hillers became photographer for the Bureau of American Ethnology in 1879, he had produced a number of photographs of modern pueblos for Powell's survey, including photographs of the Hopi Mesas (such as the famous *Dance Rock at Walpi Pueblo, Arizona*) shown at the Philadelphia Centennial Exhibition.

23. Jackson, *Time Exposure,* 243.

24. "Report of Professor Henry, Secretary of the Smithsonian, to the Board of Regents, for the Year 1876," in the *Annual Report of the Board of Regents of the Smithsonian Institution, Showing the Operations, Expenditures, and Condition of the Institution for the Year 1876* (Washington, D.C.: Government Printing Office, 1877), 57.

25. Hayden, *Eleventh Annual Report of the United States Geological and Geographical Survey of the Territories, Embracing Idaho and Wyoming, Being a Report of Progress of the Exploration for the Year 1877* (Washington, D.C.: Government Printing Office, 1879), xxiii. A photograph of the model of the cliff ruin in Mancos Canyon may be found in Holmes, "Random Records," 4, pt. 2:19.

26. Hayden, *Eleventh Annual Report,* xxiv.

27. Jackson noted that as of 1940 several of the models could still be enjoyed at the American Museum of Natural History in New York City. Jackson, *Time Exposure,* 243.

28. "Report of the Secretary," in *Annual Report of the Board of Regents of the Smithsonian Institution, Showing the Operations, Expenditures, and Condition of the Institution to July, 1894* (Washington, D.C.: Government Printing Office, 1896), 18; "Random Records," 6:109.

29. Holmes, "San Juan Field Notes," July 31 entry.

30. Jackson, "Ancient Ruins in Southwestern Colorado," in Hayden, *[Eighth] Annual Report,* 380.

31. Newberry, "Geological Report," 89.

32. Holmes, "Report on the Ancient Ruins of Southwestern Colorado," 383.

33. Ibid.

34. Ferguson and Rohn, *Anasazi Ruins,* 72.

35. See Foster, *Strange Genius,* 181–84; Henry Nash Smith, *Virgin Land: The American West as Symbol and Myth* (1950; repr., Cambridge, Mass.: Harvard University Press, 1978), 179–83. Foster argues that the drubbing Hayden received from historians has been unjust, that Hayden's support of the "Rain follows the Plow" theory was, at the time at least, scientifically defensible.

36. Quoted from Smith, *Virgin Land,* 180.

37. Donald Worster, *Rivers of Empire: Water, Aridity, and the Growth of the American West* (New York: Pantheon Books, 1985), 133.

38. Holmes, "Report on the Ancient Ruins of Southwestern Colorado," 384. This interpretation placed the "nomadic Indians" of the area—the Navajo, Paiute, and Ute—in double jeopardy, in the sense that they were tried for being barbarians twice: first, when they overthrew the civilized Anasazi; and second, when they resisted the embrace of civilized Americans.

39. Ibid.

40. Living in an age when the West was superabundant in resources and optimism, it never occurred to Holmes that a climatic change may have led to fierce competition, if not outright civil war, among the Anasazi for the remaining areas of arable land. This dark interpretation, however, has a morbid appeal among the Jeremiahs in today's West, as the region struggles with the mounting costs of growth and diminishing resources. The archaeologist Christy Turner II has advanced another view, a decidedly politically incorrect one, that it was cannibalism and other terrors that led to the disintegration of Anasazi society. See Douglas Preston, "Cannibals of the Canyon," *The New Yorker* (November 30, 1998), 76–89.

41. Holmes, "Report on the Ancient Ruins of Southwestern Colorado," 397.

42. Ibid., 389.

43. Ibid., 384. Holmes was not sure whether the cave dwellers were of the "same tribe and contemporaneous" with the people who lived in the agricultural settlements.

44. Ibid., 401.

45. Modern archaeologists have largely rejected the theory that the rock art of the Southwest is a form of writing or "hieroglyphics." See Polly Schaafsma, *Indian Rock Art of the Southwest* (Santa Fe, N.M.: School of American Research, 1980), 10–13.

46. Holmes, "Report on the Ancient Ruins of Southwestern Colorado," 401–3.

47. Ibid., 402.

48. Ibid., 403.

49. Ibid.

50. Jackson, *Time Exposure,* 228–30.

51. Holmes, "Report on the Ancient Ruins of Southwestern Colorado," 390.

52. Ibid., 408. According to Ferguson and Rohn, the Great Migration from Mesa Verde, Kayenta, and Chaco Canyon occurred toward the end of the thirteenth century. See their *Anasazi Ruins,* 68–72.

53. Holmes, "Report on the Ancient Ruins of Southwestern Colorado," 408. Within this report, Holmes included sketches of eleven rock panels. Townsend S. Brandegee provided another three sketches. See plates opposite pp. 401, 402.

54. See Holmes, "Random Records," pt. 4. 1: "Jornal of Trip to the Rocky Mountains, Beginning August 6, 1876." Sept. 23 entry (hereafter cited as "Journal of Trip to the Rocky Mountains."

6. Laccoliths and Lithographs

1. "Journal of Trip to the Rocky Mountains," September 19 entry.
2. Ibid.
3. Stegner, *Beyond the Hundredth Meridian*, 140–43. According to Stegner, the Henry Mountains (and the Escalante River to the south) were the last topographical features of the West "to go onto the map." See p. 142.
4. Holmes, "Report on the Geology of the Sierra Abajo and West San Miguel Mountains," in Hayden's *Tenth Annual Report*, 191. For a modern overview of this area, see Donald L. Baars, *The Colorado Plateau: A Geologic History* (Albuquerque: University of New Mexico Press, 1972), 210–17.
5. Gilbert, *Report on the Geology of the Henry Mountains*, 157. In addition to Holmes's work on "intrusive phenomena comparable with those of the Henry Mountains," Gilbert gave due credit to A. C. Peale, G. M. Dawson, Henry Newton, N. H. Winchell, E. S. Dana and G. B. Grinnell, and F. V. Hayden. It should be noted that although Holmes's geological study of 1875 was published in 1877, the same year that the *Report on the Geology of the Henry Mountains* (first edition) appeared in print, Gilbert was nevertheless aware of Holmes's work well before going to press.
6. Holmes was very proud of this christening. He kept a typescript excerpt from Gilbert's report of 1877 pertaining to his two namesakes. See "Random Records," 2:70–81. See also Swanton, "Biographical Memoir of William Henry Holmes," 236. Two weeks before Gilbert passed away on May 1, 1918, Holmes wrote a letter to his old friend in which he recalled Gilbert's gesture through a play on words: "Among the pleasant memories of a more or less intimate association with you for many years, one episode always rises to the surface of my mind, namely your generous thoughtfulness in naming a mountain for me—a favor not at all embarrassed as a compliment by the naming for me also a hypothetical mountain—a mountain as yet unborn." Holmes to Grove K. Gilbert, Apr. 13, 1918, Letters to G. K. Gilbert on the occasion of his 75th birthday, May 6, 1918, NO-7704, Field Records Library, Geological Division, U.S. Geological Survey, Denver Federal Center.
7. Holmes to Walter C. Mendenhall, Nov. 12, 1916, William Henry Holmes Papers, SIA, Record Unit 7084. In the same letter, Holmes appraised Gilbert as a man who was "approachable, unassuming, considerate, patient, helpful, generous, companionable, cheery, appreciative, candid, consistent, well poised, wise, judicial, noble—an ideal man exercising in many ways a helpful influence upon all who came within his circle."
8. Holmes, "San Juan Field Notes," August 13 entry.
9. Ibid.
10. William Morris Davis, *Biographical Memoir of Grove Karl Gilbert, 1843–1918*, National Academy of Sciences Biographical Memoirs 21, no. 5 (Washington, D.C.: Government Printing Office, 1926), 80.

11. Holmes, "Geological Report on the San Juan District," in Hayden's *Ninth Annual Report*, 244.

12. Ibid., 273.

13. Charles B. Hunt, "G. K. Gilbert, on Laccoliths and Intrusive Structures," in *The Scientific Ideas of G. K. Gilbert: An Assessment on the Occasion of the Centennial of the United States Geological Survey (1879–1979)*, ed. Ellis L. Yochelson, Special Paper 183 (Boulder, Colo.: Geological Society of America, 1980), 30, 33.

14. Gilbert, *Report on the Geology of the Henry Mountains*, 157.

15. Holmes, "Journal of Trip to the Rocky Mountains," September 19 entry.

16. Hunt, "G. K. Gilbert, on Laccoliths and Intrusive Structures," 30.

17. Albert C. Peale, "On a Peculiar Type of Eruptive Mountains in Colorado," in *Bulletin of the United States Geological and Geographical Survey of the Territories* (Washington D.C., Government Printing Office, 1877), 3:551–64.

18. See Thomas S. Kuhn's famous study, *The Structure of Scientific Revolutions*, 2d ed., (1962; repr., New York: New American Library, 1970).

19. Pyne, *Grove Karl Gilbert*, 94.

20. Davis, *Biographical Memoir*, 83.

21. Holmes, "Journal of Trip to the Rocky Mountains," September 23 entry.

22. Hayden, *Geological and Geographical Atlas of Colorado and Portions of Adjacent Territory* (New York: Julius Bien, 1877). By preparing a second edition (1881), Hayden's men handed future historians a beautiful source for gauging the amount of change in Colorado's cultural geography during its first five years of statehood.

23. Walter W. Ristow, *American Maps and Mapmakers: Commercial Cartography in the Nineteenth Century* (Detroit: Wayne State University Press, 1985), 300, 499.

24. Holmes to Hayden, Aug. 1, 1877, "Letters Received."

25. Carl I. Wheat's high praise has already been mentioned; more recent historians of cartography, however, were no less enthusiastic. Of Hayden's *Atlas*, Seymour I. Schwartz and Ralph E. Ehrenberg exclaimed: it is "one of the most artistic and beautiful American atlases ever issued." See Schwartz and Ehrenberg, *Mapping America* (New York: Harry N. Abrams, 1980), 304–7.

26. Of the four Great Surveys of the American West, the forward-looking civilians Hayden, Powell, and King adopted the more accurate if less attractive contour system, whereas Lieutenant Wheeler mostly continued to use hachures to express relief. See Henry Gannett, "The Mother Maps of the United States," *National Geographic Magazine* 4 (March 31, 1892): 105–7.

27. According to Schwartz and Ehrenberg, the State Geological Survey of California was the first to use the technique of plastic shading in 1874. See their *Mapping America*, 307.

28. Hayden, *Tenth Annual Report*, xxv.

29. Hayden, *Geological and Geographical Atlas of Colorado*, sheets xix–xx.

30. Hayden, *[Eighth] Annual Report*, opposite p. 49.

31. See the William Henry Jackson Photographs, number 1111, "Triangulation, summit of Sultan Mountain. Wilson and Rhoda. San Juan, Colorado. 1874 (Stereoscopic view)," Denver Federal Center, U.S. Geological Survey Photograph Library.

32. "Random Records," 2:115. In 1870, Gifford joined the Hayden Survey in

Wyoming and painted several of the same scenes that Jackson photographed, such as the painter's *Valley of the Chug Water, Wyoming Territory* and the photographer's *Castellated Rocks on the Chugwater*. A comparison of these two works shows Gifford's strong commitment to rendering nature accurately and his preference for subtlety over the more dramatic effects common in the works of other American landscapists. It is not difficult to understand his appeal to Holmes. *Sanford Robinson Gifford, 1823–1880*, Catalog of an Exhibition Organized by the University of Texas Art Museum (Austin: University of Texas Art Museum, 1970), 11, 67; Hales, *William Henry Jackson*, 90–91.

7. New Wests

1. Historians and biographers—Wallace Stegner, Mary C. Rabbitt, Thurman Wilkins, William H. Goetzmann, Thomas G. Manning, Mike Foster, Henry Nash Smith—have analyzed the complicated behind-the-scenes politics that led to establishment of the United States Geological Survey in 1879. For the best overview, see Goetzmann, *Exploration and Empire*, 578–91.

2. Although Jackson was married, he was separated from his wife during this period. Unless otherwise indicated, the source for these quotes and facts pertaining to Holmes's experiences in Washington during the spring of 1878 is Holmes, "Extracts from the Diary of W. H. Holmes," 1872, 1878, Typescript, Yellowstone National Park Library.

3. For observations of how Holmes appeared to others, I am indebted to Neil M. Judd's vignette that appeared in the *Cosmos Club Bulletin* 5 (March 1952): 2–5. As to the question of character, one source concluded that Holmes "was a very human and very lovable companion and friend to those who had the pleasure of an intimate acquaintance with him." Swanton, "Biographical Memoir of William Henry Holmes," 237. For similar views, see David J. Meltzer and Robert C. Dunnell, eds., *The Archaeology of William Henry Holmes* (Washington, D.C.: Smithsonian Institution Press, 1992), viii; W. Lyle Dockery, "William Henry Holmes," in Harry K. Veal, ed., *Exploration Frontiers of the Central and Southern Rockies* (Denver: Rocky Mountain Association of Geologists, 1977), 481–82.

4. See chromolithographs in Hayden, *Twelfth Annual Report of the United States Geological and Geographical Survey of the Territories: A Report of Progress of the Exploration in Wyoming and Idaho for the Year 1878, Part II* (Washington, D.C.: Government Printing Office, 1883).

5. See Holmes, "Field Book: Topographical Sketches [of Western Wyoming], 1878," Denver Federal Center, United States Geological Survey, Field Records Library, Accession no.: 830-E, 3.

6. Hayden, *Twelfth Annual Report*, xx.

7. Holmes, "Report on the Geology of the Yellowstone National Park," in Hayden, *Twelfth Annual Report, Part II*, 1 (hereafter cited as "Report on Yellowstone National Park").

8. Bernard DeVoto, ed., *The Journals of Lewis and Clark* (Boston: Houghton Mifflin Co., 1953), 481–87.

9. Holmes, "Report on Yellowstone National Park," 1.

10. Ibid., 47.

11. Ibid., 2.

12. Ibid., 11.

13. Ibid., 15.

14. Peale, Transcript of 1872 A. C. Peale Diary, 6.

15. Lee H. Whittlesey, *Yellowstone Place Names* (Helena: Montana Historical Society Press, 1988), 104–5.

16. Holmes, "Report on Yellowstone National Park," 23; Holmes to Horace M. Albright, Nov. 2, 1920 and M. P. Skinner to Holmes, Nov. 10, 1920, William Henry Holmes Papers, SIA, Record Unit 7084. According to M. P. Skinner, who in 1920 wrote to Holmes on behalf of Horace M. Albright, superintendent, Yellowstone National Park, "It is particularly fitting that the structure of Mount Holmes should bear your name, in view of your work in describing the laccolithic character of the Henry Mountains. Mount Holmes is an instance of the structure to which the term 'bysmalith' has been applied; for this mountain is clearly a plug of dacite-porphyry thrust up from below. When first formed this dacite was of laccolithic character, although later somewhat modified by profound faults immediately to the west and to the east of this peak."

17. Hayden, *Sixth Annual Report*, 44.

18. Holmes, "Report on Yellowstone National Park," 29.

19. See Foster, *Strange Genius*, 189–91.

20. Homes, "Report on Yellowstone National Park," 32. Holmes published a short account of the obsidian quarry in the *American Naturalist* (April 1879), entitled "Notes on an Extensive Deposit of Obsidian in the Yellowstone National Park." See "Random Records," 3:160–63.

21. Meltzer and Dunnell reached the same conclusion about the significance of Holmes's work at Obsidian Cliff. See *Archaeology of William Henry Holmes*, xiii.

22. Homes, "Report on Yellowstone National Park," 34.

23. William R. Keefer, *The Geologic Story of Yellowstone National Park*, U.S. Geological Survey Bulletin 1347 (Washington, D.C.: Government Printing Office, 1971), 34–51.

24. Holmes, "Report on Yellowstone National Park," 39–40.

25. Ibid., 42.

26. Ibid., 48.

27. Holmes, "Fossil Forests of the Volcanic Tertiary Formations of the Yellowstone National Park," in *Bulletin of the United States Geological and Geographical Survey of the Territories* (Washington, D.C.: Government Printing Office, 1880), 5:125–32. This article is a revision and enlargement of the account that appears in Hayden's *Twelfth Annual Report*.

28. Holmes also published this section on glacial phenomena almost in toto in the *American Naturalist* (March 1881). See "Random Records," 3:142–45.

29. John Muir, *The Mountains of California* (1894; repr., New York: Century Co., 1913), 28; the *Overland Monthly* articles, which first appeared in 1874 and 1875, are available in one volume—John Muir, *Studies in the Sierra* (San Francisco: Sierra Club, 1950).

30. Holmes's observations on living glaciers in the Rocky Mountains appeared in 1884 as part of Israel C. Russell's article on glaciers in the United States. John Wesley Powell, "Fifth Annual Report of the Geological Survey," in *Report of the Secretary of the Interior*, 48th Cong., 2d sess., House Ex. Doc. 1, pt. 5, 1884, 344–47.

31. Holmes, "Report on Yellowstone National Park," 53; Richard A. Bartlett, *Nature's Yellowstone* (Albuquerque: University of New Mexico Press, 1974), 24–30.

32. Holmes, "Report on Yellowstone National Park," plate XXX.

33. Ibid., 55.

34. Merrill, *The First One Hundred Years*, 615–42.

35. Kenneth L. Pierce, *History and Dynamics of Glaciation in the Northern Yellowstone National Park Area*, U.S. Geological Survey Professional Paper 729-F (Washington, D.C.: Government Printing Office, 1979), 4, 11–12.

36. Hayden, *Sixth Annual Report*, 57; for Hayden's theory on freshwater lakes, see Foster, *Strange Genius*, 190.

37. William Booth, "'Now or Never' Surveys of Earth's Diversity," *Washington Post*, Oct. 1, 1990.

38. William H. Goetzmann, *New Lands, New Men: America and the Second Great Age of Discovery* (New York: Viking, 1986), 1–5.

39. John Wesley Powell to A. Bastian, Aug. 15, 1879, William Henry Holmes Papers, SIA, Record Unit 7084.

40. Holmes to Kate [Clifton Osgood], Aug. 26, 18[79], "Random Records," 5:12. The two married on Oct. 9, 1883.

41. From Holmes's journal, "Random Records," 5:13.

42. Trenton and Hassrick make the convincing argument that Holmes was simply more competent in the use of lighter mediums such as watercolors than in oils. As evidence, they cite Holmes's oil, *Cliff-Houses of the Rio Mancos, Colorado*, which was reproduced in Hayden's annual report for 1876. See their *Rocky Mountains*, 172–74.

43. Unfortunately, "hundreds" of these works have, according to Holmes, "gone into other places." A handful, however, may be seen in "Random Records," 5.

44. Norbert Heermann, *Frank Duveneck* (Boston: Houghton Mifflin Company, 1918), 1.

45. Ibid., 45–50.

46. "Random Records," 5:4–6. See Robert Neuhaus, *Unsuspected Genius: The Art and Life of Frank Duveneck* (San Francisco: Bedford Press, 1987).

47. "Random Records," 2:115.

48. Russell Ash, *The Impressionists and Their Art* (New York: Crescent Books, 1980), 9–12.

8. "The Great Innovation"

1. John Wesley Powell, "Second Annual Report of the United States Geological Survey," in *Report of the Secretary of the Interior*, 47th Cong., 1st sess., House Ex. Doc. 1, pt. 5, 1882, 5–8.

2. Clarence E. Dutton, *Tertiary History of the Grand Cañon District, with Atlas*, United States Geological Survey Monographs, 2 (Washington, D.C.: Government Printing Office, 1882), vii.

3. Unless otherwise stated, this account of Holmes's trip to the Grand Canyon is based on his diary. "Random Records," 5:35–41. Today Pipe Spring is a national monument.

4. Dutton, *Tertiary History*, viii.

5. See the superb collection of pencil drawings contained in Holmes's "Sketches of the

Grand Canyon and Vicinity," (1880), 19 1/2 x 13 inch sheets, 55 sheets, in the "Green Book" located at the Denver Federal Center, United States Geological Survey, Field Records Library.

6. Plate V, "The Pink Cliffs (Eocene) upon the Southern End of the Paunsagunt Plateau" was, according to the credits, a woodcut based on a Holmes photograph. Dutton, *Tertiary History*, xi.

7. A chromolithograph from the *Atlas* accompanying Dutton's *Tertiary History*. See plate VI.

8. W. Kenneth Hamblin and Joseph R. Murphy, *Grand Canyon Perspectives: A Guide to the Canyon Scenery by Means of Interpretive Panoramas*, Brigham Young University Geology Studies, Special Publication No. 1, rev. ed. (1969; repr., Provo, Utah: H and M Distributors, 1980), 46–47.

9. Quoted from C. Gregory Crampton, *Land of Living Rock, The Grand Canyon and the High Plateaus: Arizona, Utah, Nevada* (1972; repr., Layton, Utah: Gibbs M. Smith, 1985), 56.

10. Dutton, *Tertiary History*, 141.

11. Ibid., 142.

12. Edward Abbey, *Desert Solitaire: A Season in the Wilderness* (1968; repr., New York: Ballantine Books, 1971), xii.

13. Dutton, *Tertiary History*, 86.

14. Byrd H. Granger, *Grand Canyon Place Names* (Tucson: University of Arizona Press, 1960), 15. Deer remain plentiful in this area. In the summer of 1986, the author was roused from sleep well before dawn by a large herd not about to let his poor choice of campsites stand in the way of its destination.

15. These chromolithographs appeared in Dutton's atlas accompanying the *Tertiary History*, sheets xv, xvi, xvii. For a brief discussion of Holmes's canyon art, see William H. Goetzmann, *William H. Holmes, Panoramic Art* (Fort Worth: Amon Carter Museum of Western Art, 1977); and Goetzmann's "Limner of Grandeur: William Henry Holmes and the Grand Canyon," *The American West: The Magazine of Western History* 15 (May/June 1978): 20–21, 61–63.

16. Dutton, *Tertiary History*, 144.

17. Stegner, *Beyond the Hundredth Meridian*, following p. 92; Stegner, "The Scientist as Artist: Clarence E. Dutton and the Tertiary History of the Grand Cañon District," *The American West: The Magazine of Western History* 15 (May/June 1978): 18–19, 61; and Stegner, *Where the Bluebird Sings to the Lemonade Springs: Living and Writing in the West* (New York: Random House, 1992), 53–56; Egloffstein's *Black Cañon*, incidentally, was based on a sketch by Lieutenant Joseph Christmas Ives. See Joseph Christmas Ives, *Report upon the Colorado River of the West, Explored in 1857 and 1858 . . .* U.S. 36th Cong., 1st sess., Sen. Ex. Doc. (Washington D.C.: Government Printing Office, 1861), plates v, vi, ix.

18. William H. Goetzmann and William N. Goetzmann, *The West of the Imagination* (New York: W. W. Norton and Co., 1986), 111.

19. Dutton, *Tertiary History*, 143–44.

20. In the summer of 1873, Moran made his first trip to the North Rim of the Grand Canyon as a guest of John Wesley Powell. Sketches he made at that time formed the basis of his famous *The Chasm of the Colorado*. In *Thomas Moran and the Surveying of the American West*, Joni Louise Kinsey argues that Moran's *Chasm* formed one part of a

great triptych that included *The Grand Cañon of the Yellowstone* (1872) and *The Mountain of the Holy Cross* (1875).

21. John Muir, *Steep Trails*, ed. William Frederic Bade (1902; repr., Boston: Houghton Mifflin, 1918), 360–61.

22. M. Emm. De Margerie to Holmes, Nov. 30, 1883, William Henry Holmes Papers, SIA, Record Unit 7084.

23. William Morris Davis to Holmes, July 4, 1901, William Henry Holmes Papers, Smithsonian Institution Archives, Record Unit 7084, Box 1.

24. See Wallace Stegner's introduction to the re-publication of Dutton's *Tertiary History of the Grand Cañon District, with Atlas* (1882; repr., Santa Barbara and Salt Lake City: Peregrine Smith, 1977), viii–ix.

25. In appreciation of Holmes's work, George Wharton James elected to name a rock feature, located northwest of Shiva Temple, the "Holmes Tower." James, *In and Around the Grand Canyon: The Grand Canyon of the Colorado River in Arizona* (Boston: Little, Brown and Company, 1900), 35, 92; Holmes kept a copy of James's references in his "Random Records," 5:74–75.

26. See Holmes's pencil "Field Sketches of the Vermilion Cliffs and the Valley of the Rio Virgin" (1880), 191/2 x 13 inch sheets, 20 sheets, located at the Denver Federal Center, United States Geological Survey, Field Records Library.

27. Pyne, *Grove Karl Gilbert*, 110–13.

28. Grove Karl Gilbert to Holmes, Sept. 13, 1880, Smithsonian Institution Archives, Record Unit 7084, William Henry Holmes Papers, 1870–1931.

29. Holmes to Kate Holmes, May 8, 1909, "Random Records," 5:55. In his later life, Holmes loved these sort of affairs, but in this case he seemed sincere in writing, "As grand as all this is I would rather be with you on the little farm and I shall hurry back as soon as my duties will permit." The little farm, which they endearingly called "Holmescroft," was located north of Washington in Rockville, Maryland.

30. Dutton to United States Geological Survey Director (King), Oct. 30, 1880, National Archives Microfilm Publications, *Letters Received by the United States Geological Survey, 1879–1901*, Roll 5, No. 812, May 28, 1880–October 28, 1880 (Washington, D.C.: The National Archives and Records Service, General Services Administration, 1964), microcopy no. 590.

31. Foster, *Strange Genius*, 323–27. Hayden died in 1887 at the age of fifty-nine.

32. Elliot Coues to Holmes, Dec. 9, 1880, and Coues to Holmes, Dec. 14, 1880, William Henry Holmes Papers, SIA, Record Unit 7084; "Random Records," 5:41–42.

33. See Hayden to Holmes, Mar. 16, 1881; Hayden to Holmes, Mar. 17, 1881, William Henry Holmes Papers, SIA, Record Unit 7084.

34. On June 30, 1883, Holmes was promoted from assistant to full geologist, a position that he held until June 30, 1889, when he transferred to the BAE. His salary, however, remained the same: twenty-four hundred dollars. "Random Records," 1:55–56. See also, Mary C. Rabbit, *Minerals, Lands, and Geology for the Common Defence and General Welfare, Volume 2, 1879–1904* (Washington, D.C.: United States Government Printing Office, 1980), 51, 54.

35. Spencer F. Baird's letter of introduction for Holmes, June 27, 1883, William Henry Holmes Papers, SIA, Record Unit 7084.

36. For recent historiographical essays on western American art, consult Martha A.

Sandweiss, "Views and Reviews: Western Art and Western History," in *Under an Open Sky: Rethinking America's Western Past*, ed. William Cronon, George Miles, and Jay Gitlin (New York: W. W. Norton and Company, 1992), 185–202; Nancy K. Anderson, "'Curious Historical Artistic Data': Art History and Western American Art," in *Discovered Lands, Invented Pasts: Transforming Visions of the American West*, Jules David Prown (New Haven: Yale University Press, 1992), 1–35.

37. The men who worked directly under Holmes were Delancy W. Gill, who would take over the division in 1889; John L. Ridgway; and Frederick W. von Dachenhausen. John K. Hillers headed the photography unit. During the 1880s, it should be noted, women started to play a role in government illustration. Miss Moorhead (first name unknown), who worked under Lester F. Ward at the National Museum, specialized in fossil botany subjects; Mrs. R. D. Irving prepared her husband's microscopic plates. Regarding the quality of the latter's work, Holmes stated that "she is unsurpassed." Her efforts, however, went uncompensated. See Holmes's administrative report in Powell's "Sixth Annual Report of the United States Geological Survey," in *Report of the Secretary of the Interior*, 49th Cong., 1st sess., House Ex. Doc. 1, pt. 5, 1886, 94–97.

38. Ibid., 96.

39. Lorenzo J. Hatch to Holmes, Apr. 2, 1888, William Henry Holmes Papers, SIA, Record Unit 7084.

40. Powell's "Eighth Annual Report of the United States Geological Survey," in *Report of the Secretary of the Interior*, 50th Congress, 1st sess., House Ex. Doc. 1, pt. 5, 1889, 29–30.

41. Charles C. Glover to Holmes, Nov. 10, 1921, William Henry Holmes Papers, SIA, Record Unit 7048.

42. Paul Bartsch, "William Henry Holmes," in Harris E. Starr, ed., *Dictionary of American Biography* 21 (1944): 427–28. Not all of Holmes's hostility was unfounded. For Holmes, who had devoted his life to museums, the sensationalist call of the Futurists to "Burn the museums" must have struck him as either dangerous or insane. Joshua C. Taylor, "The Futurist Goal, The Futurist Achievement," in Patricia Kaplan and Susan Manso, eds., *Major European Art Movements, 1900–1945: A Critical Anthology* (New York: E. P. Dutton, 1977), 165.

43. "Random Records," 2:97–98. This painting of the Grand Canyon was not the famous 1872 version, which was 7 x 12 feet. It was even larger, measuring a gigantic 8 x 14 feet.

44. "Random Records," 2:97–98.

45. William Henry Holmes, "Biographical Memoir of Lewis Henry Morgan, 1818–1881," *National Academy of Sciences Biographical Memoirs*, vol. 6 (1909): 219–39.

46. Ibid., 236. For an excellent discussion of Holmes's contributions to the history of archaeology, see David J. Meltzer and Robert C. Dunnell's introductory remarks to *Archaeology of William Henry Holmes*, xxv–xxxviii. This volume reprints "four of Holmes's most influential works." They are: "Natural History of Flaked Stone Implements" (1894); "Stone Implements of the Potomac-Chesapeake Tidewater Province" (1897); "Origin and Development of Form and Ornament in Ceramic Art" (1886); and "Aboriginal Pottery of the Eastern United States" (1903).

47. Hinsley, *Savages and Scientists*, 133–40. Later, in a paper read before the Congress of Americanists in Stuttgart, Germany, on Aug. 21, 1904, entitled "Contributions of

American Archaeology to Human History," Holmes, who at this time was serving as chief of the Bureau of American Ethnology, added a fifth and earlier stage of development: "the stage of prehuman development through and out of which the race arose." See "Random Records," 2:206–28.

48. Holmes, "Order of Development of the Primal Shaping Arts," in the *Annual Report of the Board of Regents of the Smithsonian Institution, . . . 1901* (Washington, D.C.: Government Printing Office, 1902), 510.

49. Holmes, "Origin and Development of Form and Ornament in Ceramic Art," in John Wesley Powell's *Fourth Annual Report of the Bureau of Ethnology to the Secretary of the Smithsonian Institution, 1882–1883* (Washington, D.C.: Government Printing Office, 1886), 458.

50. Holmes, "Order of Development of the Primal Shaping Arts," 512.

51. Joan Mark's discussion of Holmes's views on race is worth quoting at length: "Holmes was perceptive and careful, and he insisted on two principles in [his] search for the evolution of art. For him, as for Powell, the differences between culture stages were not owing to biological 'race' for neither of them took any such categories seriously.. . . Repeatedly Holmes insisted that human beings seem to be 'almost the same' in natural wants and capacities, and the 'almost' here is a gesture in the direction of scientific caution. Physical anthropologists might come up with some innate differences between groups of people, but he thought whatever they might find would be so slight as to be negligible." See Mark, *Four Anthropologists*, 146.

52. Holmes, "On the Evolution of Ornament—An American Lesson," *The American Anthropologist* 3 (April 1890): 137–46. See also Holmes, "Studies in Aboriginal Decorative Art, Part 1," *The American Anthropologist* 5 (January 1892): 67–72; Holmes, "Studies in Aboriginal Decorative Art, Part 2," *The American Anthropologist* 5 (April 1892): 149–52.

53. Holmes, "Order of Development of the Primal Shaping Arts," 512.

54. "Random Records," 5:86; Hales, *William Henry Jackson*, 144, 172; Jackson, *Time Exposure*, 259.

55. *Annual Report of the Board of Regents of the Smithsonian Institution, . . . 1884* (Washington, D.C.: Government Printing Office, 1885), 72–73.

56. Mark, *Four Anthropologists*, 142–43; Robert C. Dunnell, "Five Decades of American Archaeology," in David J. Meltzer, Don D. Fowler, and Jeremy A. Sabloff, eds., *American Archaeology, Past and Future: A Celebration of the Society for American Archaeology, 1935–1985* (Washington, D.C.: Smithsonian Institution Press, 1986), 26–27; Gordon Randolph Willey, "One Hundred Years of American Archaeology," in J. O. Brew, ed., *One Hundred Years of Anthropology* (Cambridge: Harvard University Press, 1968), 38. Willey credits Alfred V. Kidder as the first to use the stratigraphic method "intensively," while at the Pecos excavations. Gordon R. Willey, *Portraits in American Archaeology: Remembrances of Some Distinguished Americanists* (Albuquerque: University of New Mexico Press, 1988), 307.

57. Holmes, "The Trade in Spurious Mexican Antiquities," *Science: An Illustrated Journal* 7 (Feb. 19, 1886): 170–72. Interestingly enough, on the trip home Jackson made a photograph of the party at ease in their private railway car. Holmes is sitting by the window, his face brightly illuminated by the incoming light of truth. The large fake vase that he acquired is situated below Holmes in a half-lighted, half-darkened corner. This is admittedly, to use Holmes's term, an "over-elaborate" interpretation, but in this par-

ticular historical context, it is not hard to infer the point. See photograph no. 118 in Hales, *William Henry Jackson*, 172. Holmes illustrated his article, "The Trade in Spurious Mexican Antiquities," with a drawing of the eleven-inch-high fake vase.

58. Holmes, "Trade in Spurious Mexican Antiquities": 170–72.

59. Spencer Baird, the second secretary of the Smithsonian Institution, stepped down on doctor's orders in May of 1887, but not before arranging for the astronomer and physicist Samuel Pierpont Langley to succeed him. Baird passed away on August 18, 1887. Rivinus and Youssef, *Spencer Baird of the Smithsonian Institution*, 181.

60. "Random Records," 5:126; William H. Holmes, "In Memoriam: Matilda Coxe Stevenson," *American Anthropologist*, n.s., 18 (1916): 552–59. Swanton, "Biographical Memoir of William Henry Holmes," 227.

61. "Random Records," 14:8–9.

62. William H. Holmes, "Notes on the Antiquities of the Jemez Valley," *American Anthropologist*, n.s., 7 (1905): 198. See Hal Rothman's study, *America's National Monuments: The Politics of Preservation* (Lawrence: University Press of Kansas, 1989).

9. The Death and Rebirth of Pleistocene Man

1. Robert Wiebe, *The Search for Order, 1877–1920* (New York: Hill and Wang, 1967).

2. Holmes, "A Sketch of the Great Serpent Mound," *Science, An Illustrated Monthly* 7 (December 1886): 624, 626–28.

3. Ibid., 627.

4. Samuel P. Langley, *Annual Report of the Board of Regents of the Smithsonian Institution, Showing the Operations, Expenditures, and Condition of the Institution to July, 1893* (Washington, D.C.: Government Printing Office, 1894), 23. In dramatic fashion, Langley announced that "it is the united opinion of the officers of the Bureau that [Cyrus Thomas's work] contains the solution to the mystery of the mounds; very greatly to the surprise of the investigators who began the work." In Holmes's case, this claim of pure induction seems highly unlikely. The investigators "have been led to believe," Langley continued, "that the mounds and the art products contained therein are in no wise distinct from the works of the modern Indians, and that the distribution of tribes can now be studied from the mounds themselves as well as from other aboriginal records."

5. Holmes, "Sketch of the Great Serpent Mound," 627.

6. Ibid., 628.

7. Thomas Wilson, "The Paleolithic Period in the District of Columbia," *The American Anthropologist* 2 (July 1889): 235–41. According to Wilson, "Paleolithic implements have been found in the United States which correspond in every particular with those of Western Europe—correspond in form, appearance, material, mode of manufacture—in short, they are the same implements in every essential." See p. 236.

8. In Holmes, *Handbook of Aboriginal American Antiquities*, (Washington, D.C.: Government Printing Office, 1919), 75, the author states, no doubt incorrectly, that Powell first asked him to work on the antiquity problem when he was still "engaged in the geological survey of Colorado." See Mark, *Four Anthropologists*, 149–54.

9. William H. Holmes, "A Quarry Workshop of the Flaked-Stone Implement Makers in the District of Columbia," *The American Anthropologist* 3 (January 1890): 3.

10. For Holmes's role in the debate over early man, I am indebted to David J. Meltzer's "The Antiquity of Man and the Development of American Archaeology," in *Advances in Archaeological Method and Theory*, ed. Michael B. Schiffer (New York: Academic Press, 1983), 6:1–51; Meltzer's "On 'Paradigms' and 'Paradigm Bias' in Controversies Over Human Antiquity in America," in Tom D. Dillehay and David J. Meltzer, *The First Americans: Search and Research* (Boca Raton, Fla.: CRC Press, 1991), 13–49; Meltzer's "The Discovery of Deep Time: A History of Views on the Peopling of the Americas," in *Method and Theory for Investigating the Peopling of the Americas*, ed. Robson Bonnichsen and D. Gentry Steele (Corvallis, Ore.: Center for the Study of the First Americans, 1994), 7–26. Also, see Curtis M. Hinsley, Jr., "Amateurs and Professionals in Washington Anthropology, 1879–1903," in *American Anthropology: The Early Years*, ed. John V. Murra (St. Paul: West Publishing Co., 1976), 47–51.

11. Holmes, *Handbook of Aboriginal American Antiquities*, 92–94.

12. The above quotes are from a reprint entitled "Traces of Glacial Man in Ohio," which appeared in *Journal of Geology* 1 (1893): 149, 158, in Holmes, Collected Papers, Reprints, etc., on Prehistoric Man, No. 1–5, Library of Congress.

13. Holmes, *Handbook of Aboriginal American Antiquities*, 52–54, 93.

14. F. W. Putnam to Holmes, July 5, 1892, William Henry Holmes Papers, Smithsonian Institution Archives, Record Unit, 7084.

15. G. F. Wright to Holmes, Apr. 12, 1893, William Henry Holmes Papers, SIA, Record Unit 7084.

16. Neil M. Judd, *The Bureau of American Ethnology: A Partial History* (Norman: University of Oklahoma University Press, 1967), 15; Meltzer and Dunnell, *Archaeology of William Henry Holmes*, xvi.

17. Meltzer, "Antiquity of Man," 11–25.

18. For the colorful Kidder quote, see Douglas R. Givens, *Alfred Vincent Kidder and the Development of Americanist Archaeology* (Albuquerque: University of New Mexico Press, 1992), 18.

19. "Random Records," 6:73; Hinsley, *Savages and Scientists*, 104–5.

20. See Holmes, "An Ancient Quarry in Indian Territory," *Bureau of Ethnology Bulletin 21* (Washington, D.C.: Government Printing Office, 1894), 7–19.

21. Ibid.

22. Ibid.

23. See Joseph G. Rosa and Robin May, *Buffalo Bill and His Wild West: A Pictorial Biography* (Lawrence: University Press of Kansas, 1989). A recent example of the tenaciousness of the stereotype of Native Americans as noble warriors and buffalo hunters was the popular film *Dances with Wolves* (1990).

24. Holmes, "The World's Fair Congress of Anthropology," *The American Anthropologist* 6 (October 1893): 433.

25. Holmes, "Modern Quarry Refuse and the Palaeolithic Theory," *Science* 20 (Nov. 25, 1892): 295.

26. "Random Records," 8:88–90.

27. Holmes, " Obsidian Mines of Hidalgo, Mexico," *American Anthropologist*, n.s., 2 (July–September 1900): 408–9. See also "Obsidian Mines" in "Random Records," 8:95–104.

28. Holmes, "Obsidian Mines of Hidalgo, Mexico": 409.

29. Holmes, "Modern Quarry Refuse," 295.

30. Ibid., 297.

31. Dutton to Holmes, Dec. 10, 1892, in "Random Records," 6:51–52.

32. Holmes, "Gravel Man and Palaeolithic Culture; A Preliminary Word," *Science* 21 (Jan. 20, 1893): 29–30.

33. Mark, *Four Anthropologists*, 151.

34. Holmes, "Stone Implements of the Potomac-Chesapeake Tidewater Province," *Fifteenth Annual Report of the Bureau of Ethnology to the Secretary of the Smithsonian Institution, 1893–94* (Washington, D.C.: Government Printing Office, 1897); repr. in Meltzer and Dunnell, *Archaeology of William Henry Holmes*. See "Introduction," xviii, xxxii–xxxv.

35. Fay-Cooper Cole, "Eminent Personalities of the Half Century," *American Anthropologist* 54 (April–June 1952): 160.

36. See Meltzer and Dunnell, *Archaeology of William Henry Holmes*, xxxii.

37. Holmes, "Stone Implements of the Potomac-Chesapeake Tidewater Province," in Meltzer and Dunnell, *Archaeology of William Henry Holmes*, 61.

38. Ibid.

39. Ibid., 13.

40. Holmes, "Vestiges of Early Man in Minnesota," *American Geologist* 9 (1893): 219–40.

41. Holmes, "Gravel Man and Palaeolithic Culture" : 29–30.

42. Holmes, "Preliminary Revision of the Evidence Relating to Auriferous Gravel Man in California," First Paper and Second Paper, *American Anthropologist*, n.s., 1 (1899): 107–121 and 614–645, respectively; "Random Records," 8:60; Wilkins, *Clarence King*, 86–87.

43. Holmes, "A Question of Evidence," *Science* 21 (March 10, 1893): 135–36.

44. Holmes, "On the Antiquity of Man in America," *Science*, n.s., 47 (June 7, 1918): 562.

45. "Appendix to Secretary's Report," in *Annual Report of the Board of Regents of the Smithsonian Institution, Showing the Operations, Expenditures, and Condition of the Institution to July, 1892* (Washington, D.C.: Government Printing Office, 1893), 49.

46. "Random Records," 6:48.

47. "Random Records," 6:47–48.

48. Thomas Wilson to Holmes, Dec. 5, 1894, William Henry Holmes Papers, SIA, Record Unit 7084.

49. Holmes, *Handbook of Aboriginal American Antiquities*, 57–58.

50. Holmes, "The Antiquity Phantom in American Archaeology," *Science* 62 (September 18, 1925): 256–58.

51. Edgar L. Hewett to Holmes, June 6, 1925, William Henry Holmes Papers, SIA, Record Unit 7084.

52. F. W. Sardeson to Holmes, Sept. 25, 1925, William Henry Holmes Papers, SIA, Record Unit 7084.

53. Holmes, "Some Problems of the American Race," *American Anthropologist*, n.s., 12 (April–June 1910): 169.

54. Holmes to Lieut.-Colonel Clarence O. Sherrill, Apr. 29, 1925, "Random Records," 6:59–63.

55. Undated and unidentified newspaper article; it was probably written after May of 1928 when Clarence Sherill tried to condemn the Piney Branch land so that it could be added to Washington, D.C.'s park system. See "Random Records," 6:66.

56. Meltzer and Dunnell, *Archaeology of William Henry Holmes*, xxxiv.

57. Meltzer, "Antiquity of Man," 30–34; E. H. Sellards, "Further Notes on Human Remains from Vero, Florida," *American Anthropologist*, n.s., 19 (1917): 239–51; Oliver P. Hay, "Further Considerations of the Occurrence of Human Remains in the Pleistocene Deposits at Vero, Florida," *American Anthropologist*, n.s., 20 (1918): 1–36.

58. See Frederic B. Loomis's angry "Reply to Dr. Holmes on Florida Man," William Henry Holmes Papers, SIA, Record Unit 7084.

59. Credit for the first sighting of extinct bison bones in close association with points may go to George McJunkin, former slave and foreman of the Crowfoot Ranch, who noticed the items in Wild or (Dead) Horse Gulch after they were exposed by a flood in 1908. McJunkin later informed Carl Schwachheim, an "avocational paleontologist," who in turn contacted J. D. Figgins. E. Steve Cassells, *The Archaeology of Colorado* (Boulder: Johnson Books, 1983), 37–40; Marc Simmons, *New Mexico: An Interpretive History* (1977; repr., Albuquerque: University of New Mexico Press, 1988), 51; Meltzer, "Discovery of Deep Time," 15.

60. J. D. Figgins, "The Antiquity of Man in America," repr. from *Natural History* 27 (1927): 229–39, Western History Department, Denver Public Library. See p. 232.

61. Ibid.

62. Figgins to Oliver P. Hay of the Carnegie Institution of Washington, Feb. 23, 1927, Figgins Papers, Denver Museum of Natural History Archives (hereafter cited as DMNHA); Figgins, "Antiquity of Man in America," 232–34.

63. Hay to Figgins, Nov. 17, 1926; Hay to Figgins, Dec. 6, 1926, Figgins Papers, DMNHA.

64. Figgins to Barnum Brown of the American Museum of Natural History, Feb. 16, 1927, Figgins Papers, DMNHA.

65. Figgins, "Antiquity of Man in America," 229.

66. Figgins to Barnum Brown, Feb. 16, 1927, Figgins Papers, DMNHA.

67. Figgins to Barnum Brown, June 8, 1927, Figgins Papers, DMNHA.

68. Ibid.

69. Figgins to Barnum Brown, June 8, 1927; Figgins to Hay, July 1, 1927, Figgins Papers, DMNHA.

70. Figgins to Hay, Sept. 29, 1927, Figgins Papers, DMNHA.

71. Frank H. H. Roberts, Jr., "A Folsom Complex: Preliminary Report on Investigations at the Lindenmeier Site in Northern Colorado," *Smithsonian Miscellaneous Collections*, 94 (June 1935): 5.

72. Ibid.

73. Ibid.

74. Ibid., 5–6.

75. Cassells, *Archaeology of Colorado*, 39.

76. For a fuller discussion of Webb's *The Great Plains* and its place in the literature of western American history, see Elliott West, "Walter Prescott Webb and the Search for the West," in *Writing Western History: Essays on Major Western Historians*, ed. Richard W. Etulain (Albuquerque: University of New Mexico Press, 1991), 167–75.

77. Consensus on the significance of Figgins's discovery was not reached in the American archaeological community until the results of his third season of work were made available. Cassells, *Archaeology of Colorado*, 39.

78. E. H. Sellards to Holmes, Feb. 24, 1930, William Henry Holmes Papers, SIA, Record Unit 7084. Sellards addressed the letter to the Cosmos Club, which was Holmes's address after his wife, Kate, passed away in 1925.

79. Holmes to Sellards, Mar. 6, 1930, William Henry Holmes Papers, SIA, Record Unit 7084.

80. Holmes, *Handbook of Aboriginal American Antiquities*, 94.

81. See the abstract of Holmes's paper, "The Peopling of America," which he delivered in 1908 at the First Pan-American Scientific Congress in Santiago, Chile, in the *Annual Report of the Board of Regents of the Smithsonian Institution, Showing the Operations, Expenditures, and Condition of the Institution for the Year Ending June 30, 1909* (Washington, D.C.: Government Printing Office, 1910), 42.

82. Swanton's sound judgment on this matter is worth quoting in full:

> [Holmes] regarded his opposition to, and virtual explosion of, the early theory of a paleolithic period in America as one of his great accomplishments, and it did indeed exert a wholesome, restraining influence over archaeologic thought, but men seldom attain permanent fame for their negative accomplishments, and Holmes's contribution here did little more than shorten the pathway of his contemporaries and save them some useless and wasteful meanderings.

Swanton, "Biographical Memoir of William Henry Holmes," 236–37.

10. "On the Ragged Edge of Uncertainty"

1. Meltzer and Dunnell, *Archaeology of William Henry Holmes*, 120–39; Mark, *Four Anthropologists*, 151.

2. Holmes, "The World's Fair Congress of Anthropology." See frontispiece in Holmes, "Stone Implements of the Potomac-Chesapeake Tidewater Province," 4.

3. *Annual Report of the Board of Regents of the Smithsonian Institution . . . 1893* (Washington, D.C.: Government Printing Office, 1894), 39.

4. "Random Records," 2:127.

5. Ibid., 2:129.

6. Ibid., 2:127–29. For two general treatments, see Robert W. Rydell, *All the World's a Fair: Visions of Empire at American International Expositions, 1876–1916* (Chicago: Uni-

versity of Chicago Press, 1984); Burton Benedict, *The Anthropology of World's Fairs* (London and Berkeley: Scolar Press, 1983).

7. "Random Records," 7:11.

8. Unless otherwise indicated, Holmes's account of his troubled Chicago period is based on the documents in "Random Records," 7:150–64.

9. Thomas W. Goodspeed to Holmes, Aug. 31, 1892, "Random Records," 7:19.

10. Holmes to Thomas C. Chamberlain, August 1892, "Random Records," 7:21; in Allen Johnson, ed., "Thomas Chrowder Chamberlain", *Dictionary of American Biography* 3: 600–601.

11. See William Cronon, *Nature's Metropolis: Chicago and the Great West* (New York: W. W. Norton, 1991).

12. "Random Records," 7:22–24.

13. Swanton, "Biographical Memoir of William Henry Holmes," 229.

14. In 1892–1893, the officers of instruction of the Department of Geology at the University of Chicago were: Thomas C. Chamberlain, Rollin D. Salisbury, Joseph P. Iddings, R. A. F. Penrose, Charles R. Van Hise (nonresident), Charles D. Walcott (nonresident), William H. Holmes (nonresident), George Baur, and Edmund Jüssen. See "Random Records," 7.

15. *Annual Report of the Board of Regents of the Smithsonian Institution . . . 1894* (Washington, D.C.: Government Printing Office, 1896), 49.

16. See Marshall Hyatt, *Franz Boas, Social Activist: The Dynamics of Ethnicity* (New York: Greenwood Press, 1990), 30–33; Hinsley, *Savages and Scientists*, 250–51; and George W. Stocking, Jr., *Race, Culture, and Evolution: Essays in the History of Anthropology* (1968; repr., Chicago: University of Chicago Press, 1982), 280–81.

17. Franz Boas to Frederick Ward Putnam, Feb. 18, 1894, *The Professional Correspondence of Franz Boas* (hereafter cited as the Boas Papers). Microfilmed in 1972 by Scholarly Resources. Quoted with the permission of the American Philosophical Society.

18. F. J. V. Skiff to Holmes, Oct. 27, 1894, William Henry Holmes Papers, SIA, Record Unit 7084.

19. Boas to Putnam, Feb. 18, 1894, Boas Papers.

20. Boas to Skiff, Feb. 19, 1894; Boas to Putnam, Feb. 18, 1894, Boas Papers.

21. Chamberlain to Holmes, Jan. 23, 1894, William Henry Holmes Papers, SIA, Record Unit 7084; Chamberlain to Holmes, Jan. 27, 1894, "Random Records," 7:8–9.

22. Chamberlain to Holmes, Jan. 27, 1894, "Random Records," 7:8–9.

23. Boas to Holmes, Oct. 7, 1893, Boas Papers.

24. Skiff to Holmes, Feb. 27, 1894, "Random Records," 7:27–28.

25. Ibid.

26. Holmes to Boas, Feb. 21, 1894; McGee to Boas, Mar. 21, 1894, Boas Papers. George W. Stocking, Jr., "Franz Boas," *Dictionary of American Biography*, Supplement 3 (1941–1945): 81–86.

27. "Random Records," 7:16–17.

28. Holmes believed that Skiff's "attitude toward [him] was doubtless due in part to jealousy, due to his fear that [Holmes] was undermining him with the view of becoming Director." Holmes, "Random Records," 8:4.

29. "Random Records," 7:32–33; Holmes to Charles D. Walcott, Jan. 28, 1897, "Random Records," 7:150–53.

30. Ibid.

31. Ibid.

32. Ibid.

33. Ibid.

34. See Victor Wolfgang Von Hagen, *Maya Explorer: John Lloyd Stephens and the Lost Cities of Central America and Yucatán* (Norman: University of Oklahoma Press, 1948).

35. The title of Charnay's work, *Les Anciennes Villes du Nouveau Monde* (1885), translated from the French in 1887, was clearly the source of inspiration for the title of Holmes's own work on Mexico.

36. Holmes, *Archaeological Studies among the Ancient Cities of Mexico* (Chicago: Field Columbian Museum, 1895–1897), Vol. 1, Anthropological Series, 149–50.

37. Ceram, *Gods, Graves, and Scholars*, 388–400.

38. Holmes to McGee, Jan. 14, 1895, "Random Records," 7:47.

39. Holmes, *Archaeological Studies among the Ancient Cities of Mexico*, 149.

40. Ibid., 15.

41. Holmes to McGee, Jan. 14, 1895, "Random Records," 7:47.

42. See Holmes's field notes, "Random Records," 7: Section 2.

43. See Holmes's correspondence with Kate Holmes, "Random Records," 7: Section 2.

44. Since Stephens's trip to the Yucatán, the peninsula had exploded in the terrible but little-known War of the Castes (1847–1855), in which the Maya Indians nearly reclaimed their ancient lands from the white Mexicans or "Ladinos." They failed, but the Mexican government also was unable to reestablish its authority over every corner of the state—a stalemate that lasted for decades. The standard work on this conflict is Nelson Reed, *The Caste War of Yucatan* (Stanford, Calif.: Stanford University Press, 1964).

45. John Burroughs, John Muir et al., *Alaska: The Harriman Expedition, 1899*, 2 vols. (1901; repr., New York: Dover Publications, 1986), xxi–xxxi.

46. This work, in fact, established Holmes as one of the early authorities of ancient Mexican architecture.

47. Walter Krickeberg, *Las Antiguas Culturas Mexicanas*, trans. Sita Garst y Jasmin Reuter (1956; repr., Mexico City: Fondo de Cultura Economica, 1985), 22.

48. Quoted from a lecture entitled "Development of Architecture in Mexico," which Holmes delivered in Chicago at the Field Columbian Museum on Nov. 30, 1895. William Henry Holmes Papers, SIA, Record Unit 7084, Box 4.

49. Holmes, "Origins and Development of Form and Ornament in Ceramic Art," 458.

50. Ibid., 443.

51. Holmes, *Archaeological Studies among the Ancient Cities of Mexico*, 52.

52. Ibid., 17–18.

53. Ibid.

54. During the 1890s, Holmes devoted himself more and more to water-coloring and in 1900 won the first Corcoran prize (Washington Water Color Club, 1900). Edna Maria Clark, *Ohio Art and Artists* (Richmond [Va?]: Garrett and Massie, 1932), 467.

55. Holmes, *Archaeological Studies among the Ancient Cities of Mexico*, 15–16.

56. Holmes to Walcott, Jan. 28, 1897, "Random Records," 7:150–53.

57. Ibid.

58. See Walcott correspondence, "Random Records," 7: Section 3.

59. Holmes to S. P. Langley, June 22, 1897, "Random Records," 7:165.

11. The Significance of the "Frigid Gateway" in American Anthropology

1. "Random Records," 7:168, 191; see "List of Papers Published by William Henry Holmes, 1874–1896," William Henry Holmes Papers, SIA, Record Unit 7084.

2. Holmes, "Aboriginal Pottery of the Eastern United States," in the *Twentieth Annual Report of the Bureau of American Ethnology to the Secretary of the Smithsonian Institution, 1898–1899* (Washington, D.C.: Government Printing Office, 1903); this piece is reprinted in Meltzer and Dunnell, *Archaeology of William Henry Holmes.*

3. See plate 4 of Holmes's "Aboriginal Pottery."

4. Ibid., 18, 24–25.

5. Ibid., 68.

6. Ibid., 69.

7. Franz Boas, "The Methods of Ethnology," *American Anthropologist,* n.s., 22 (October–December 1920): 317.

8. Quoted from Jesse Green, ed., *Zuñi: Selected Writings of Frank Hamilton Cushing* (Lincoln: University of Nebraska Press, 1979), 17.

9. Ibid.

10. Holmes, "Aboriginal Pottery," 62.

11. Ibid., 21–22.

12. Ibid., 22–23.

13. Ibid.

14. Holmes, "Areas of American Culture Characterization Tentatively Outlined as an Aid in the Study of the Antiquities," *American Anthropologist,* n.s., 16 (1914): 413–46.

15. Holmes, "Anthropological Studies in California," in *Report of the U.S. National Museum, 1900* (Washington, D.C.: Government Printing Office, 1902), 161.

16. Holmes, "Preliminary Revision of the Evidence Relating to Auriferous Gravel Man in California, First Paper," *American Anthropologist,* n.s., 1 (1899): 108; and Holmes, "Preliminary Revision of the Evidence Relating to Auriferous Gravel Man in California, Second Paper," in *American Anthropologist,* n.s., 1(1899): 614–15.

17. Holmes, "Preliminary Revision . . . First Paper," 109.

18. Holmes, "Preliminary Revision . . . Second Paper," 645.

19. Holmes, "Preliminary Revision . . . First Paper," 110.

20. Holmes, "Preliminary Revision . . . Second Paper," 640.

21. Holmes, "Anthropological Studies in California," 167–68.

22. Ibid., 161.

23. Ibid., 162.

24. Ibid., 168.

25. Ibid., 162.

26. Ibid., 164.

27. Ibid., 162.

28. Ibid., 163.

29. Ibid., 164.

30. Hinsley, *Savages and Scientists*, 110.

31. Holmes, "Anthropological Studies in California," 164. See also "Random Records," 8:60–86.

32. "Random Records," 8:88–90.

33. Quoted from Hinsley, *Savages and Scientists*, 246.

34. Ibid.

35. Richard Rathbun (Assistant Secretary) to Holmes, Feb. 19, 1900, "Random Records," 8:18–19.

36. Holmes to Kate Holmes, "Random Records," 8:20–23; Samuel P. Langley to Holmes, Mar. 11, 1900, "Random Records," 8:25.

37. From an extract of a letter from Holmes to Kate Holmes, Mar. 11, 1900, "Random Records," 8:45–48.

38. John Wesley Powell, "Report of the Director of the Bureau of American Ethnology for the Year Ending June 30, 1900," in the *Annual Report of the Board of Regents of the Smithsonian Institution, Showing the Operations, Expenditures, and Condition of the Institution for the Year Ending June 30, 1900* (Washington, D.C.: Government Printing Office, 1901), 59, 61.

39. Ibid., 59.

40. J. B. Bellinger (Major and Quartermaster) to All Quartermasters of Cuba and Puerto Rico, Feb. 6, 1900, "Random Records," 8:17.

41. Powell, "Report of the Director" (1900), 61.

42. Holmes to Kate Holmes, Feb. 11, 1900, "Random Records," 8:10–11.

43. Ibid.

44. Ibid.

45. Holmes to Kate Holmes, Feb. 24, 1900, "Random Records," 8:20–23.

46. Robert B. Meyer, Jr., ed., *Langley's Aero Engine of 1903* (Washington, D.C.: Smithsonian Institution Press, 1971), 3–4.

47. Edmund Morris, *The Rise of Theodore Roosevelt* (New York: Coward, McCann and Geoghegan, 1979), 840, n. 76.

48. Stegner, *Beyond the Hundredth Meridian*, 242; Wilcomb E. Washburn, *The Cosmos Club of Washington: A Centennial History, 1878–1978* (Washington, D.C.: The Cosmos Club, 1978), 15–17.

49. Quoted from Morris, *Rise of Theodore Roosevelt*, 608.

50. Ibid., 840, n. 76; Charles H. Gibbs-Smith, *The Invention of the Aeroplane (1799–1909)* (London: Faber and Faber, 1966), 43–45.

51. Gibbs-Smith, *Invention of the Aeroplane*, 36.

52. Langley to Holmes, Mar. 11, 1900, "Random Records," 8:25–27.

53. In Holmes's words: "With the help of the natives specimens were easily caught by throwing out rats with looped cords, so that when they lit to pick up the rats, their feet were caught up in the loops." See the extract of a letter from Holmes to Kate Holmes, Mar. 11, 1900, "Random Records," 8, Section 1.

54. Gibbs-Smith, *Invention of the Aeroplane*, 43–47.

55. Two Pencil Sketches, "Random Records," 8:41.

56. See reprint of the editorial cartoon, "The Birds Chorus: 'Wonder Which of Us Was the Model!'" *The Evening Star*, Dec. 9, 1903, in Meyer, *Langley's Aero Engine of 1903*, vii.
57. Ibid., vi.

12. The Racial Frontier

1. *Annual Report of the Board of Regents of the Smithsonian Institution showing the Operations, Expenditures, and Condition of the Institution for the Year Ending June 30, 1902* (Washington, D.C.: Government Printing Office, 1903), 35. According to Stephanie Livingston and Claudia Miner, "We still do not know whether people preyed on them, scavenged the carcasses of mammoths that died of other causes, competed with them for vegetative food resources, or simply coexisted with them." See Livingston and Miner, "Mammoths, Prehistoric Archaeology, and Interdisciplinary Research," in Stephen Tchudi, ed., *Science, Values, and the American West* (Reno: The Nevada Humanities Committee, 1997), 81–102.

2. Unless indicated otherwise, Holmes's account of his appointment as chief of the BAE comes from "Random Records," 8: Section 5; 9: Section 1.

3. See Curtis M. Hinsley, Jr.'s discussion of Langley's long-standing opposition to McGee, in Hinsley, *Savages and Scientists*, 248–56; also, see Judd, *Bureau of American Ethnology*, 22–23.

4. Charles Fletcher Lummis, a friend of Holmes, wrote: "I think I am not mistaken in sizing you up when I feel that you personally would sooner have had [McGee] in there." Lummis to Holmes, Nov. 29, 1902, William Henry Holmes Papers, 1870–1931, SIA, Record Unit 7084.

5. Franz Boas reports that he "took the opportunity, during the meeting of the Americanists' Congress in New York in 1902, to point out to Professor Holmes that if he were to decline the office, nobody would take it, to which he replied that when his superior (that is, the Secretary of the Smithsonian Institution) ordered him to take the office, he had to do so." Boas to Dr. Abraham Jacobi, Sept. 2, 1909, Boas Papers. For a more detailed account of Boas's response to McGee's demotion, see Hyatt, *Franz Boas*, 56–59.

6. According to Neil M. Judd, the Adams Building was the home of the BAE from 1893 to 1910. Judd, *Bureau of American Ethnology*, caption of photograph facing p. 5.

7. It is hard not to share the negative assessments of Holmes's leadership of the BAE that have been advanced by Curtis M. Hinsley, Jr. and Virginia Noelke. See Hinsley, *Savages and Scientists*, 277.

8. Ibid., 252.

9. Ibid.

10. McGee to Holmes, July 31, 1903; Holmes to McGee, Aug. 1, 1903, William John McGee Papers, Manuscript Division, Library of Congress.

11. McGee to Boas, Dec. 21, 1902, Boas Papers.

12. McGee to Boas, June 16, 1903, Boas Papers.

13. Judd, *Bureau of American Ethnology*, 22.

14. Boas to McGee, Oct. 29, 1902, McGee Papers.

15. Quoted in Hyatt, *Franz Boas*, 57.

16. *The Popular Science Monthly,* November 1902 issue; *Science,* November 21, 1902, issue.

17. Lummis to Holmes, Dec. 18, 1902, William Henry Holmes Papers, 1870–1931, SIA, Record Unit 7084. In 1924, Lummis recalled the first time the two met: "It is twenty-six years to-day since you and M'Gee peeled off your plug hats and Prince Alberts," and nobly passed up buckets of "mort" to me as I built the wall of my Zaguan. I have never forgotten that day, nor the lovely talk we had after our mutual work as Masons." Lummis to Holmes (or rather the "Old Dean"), Oct. 28, 1924, William Henry Holmes Papers, 1870–1931, SIA, Record Unit 7084.

18. Boas to Dr. Abraham Jacobi, Sept. 2, 1909, Boas Papers.

19. Ibid.

20. Hyatt, *Franz Boas,* 34–35.

21. Ibid.

22. Boas to Carl Schurz, Aug. 12, 1903, Boas Papers.

23. Boas to Alexander Graham Bell, Aug. 7, 1903, Boas Papers.

24. Boas to Carl Schurz, Aug. 12, 1903, Boas Papers.

25. Ibid.

26. Boas to Alexander Graham Bell, Dec. 7, 1903, Boas Papers.

27. *Annual Report of the Board of Regents of the Smithsonian Institution, Showing The Operations, Expenditures, and Condition of the Institution for the Year Ending June 30, 1904* (Washington, D.C.: Government Printing Office, 1905), 31.

28. *Annual Report of the Board of Regents of the Smithsonian Institution, Showing The Operations, Expenditures, and Condition of the Institution for the Year Ending June 30, 1906* (Washington, D.C.: Government Printing Office, 1907), 37.

29. See "Random Records," 9, Section 4, "Election to Membership in the National Academy of Sciences."

30. Holmes, *Handbook of Aboriginal American Antiquities.* (Washington, D.C.: Government Printing Office, 1919).

31. See Holmes's "Plan for Establishment of Physical Anthropology Department under the Smithsonian Institution" and "Researches Relating to the Racial and National Elements Now Entering into the Composition of the American Nation," "Random Records," 8: Section 5, 112–13 and 114–17, respectively.

32. Holmes, "Plan," "Random Records," 8: Section 4, 112–13.

33. Hinsley, *Savages and Scientists,* 276.

34. See Audrey Smedley, *Race in North America: Origin and Evolution of a Worldview* (Boulder, Colo.: Westview Press, 1993), 275–82.

35. See Vernon J. Williams, Jr., *Rethinking Race: Franz Boas and His Contemporaries* (Lexington: The University Press of Kentucky, 1996), 33.

36. Holmes to Langley, Nov. 5, 1902, "Random Records," 8: Section 5, 111.

37. Smedley, *Race in North America,* 274–75.

38. C. Loring Brace and M. F. Ashley Montagu, *Man's Evolution: An Introduction to Physical Anthropology* (New York: Macmillan, 1965), 212; A. Hrdlička, *The Skeletal Remains of Early Man,* Smithsonian Miscellaneous Collections, vol. 83 (Washington, D.C.: Smithsonian Institution, 1930).

39. Richard Rathbun (Assistant Secretary) to Holmes, Nov. 15, 1902, "Random Records," 8: Section 5, 118.

40. "Random Records," 9:39; Holmes, "Sketch of the Origin, Development, and Probable Destiny of the Races of Men," *American Anthropologist*, n.s., 4 (July–September 1902): 369–91.

41. Frank B. Livingston, "On the Non-Existence of Human Races," *Current Anthropology* 3 (3) (1962): 279.

42. C. Loring Brace, "Foreword to the Sixth Edition," in Ashley Montagu, *Man's Most Dangerous Myth: The Fallacy of Race*, 6th ed. (Walnut Creek, Calif.: AltaMira Press, 1997), 15–16. The skin color example is Brace's as well.

43. Mark Nathan Cohen, "Culture, Not Race, Explains Human Diversity," in *The Chronicle of Higher Education* 44, no. 32, April 17, 1998: B4–B5. However, the traditional view that traits can be linked is by no means dead. See Richard J. Herrnstein and Charles Murray's controversial study, *The Bell Curve: Intelligence and Class Structure in American Life* (New York: The Free Press, 1994).

44. Montagu, *Man's Most Dangerous Myth*, 47. Franz Boas, incidentally, served as Montagu's dissertation advisor at Columbia University and, according to C. Loring Brace, was a reader of Montagu's manuscript before it first went to publication in 1942. See Brace, "Foreword to the Sixth Edition," in Montagu's *Man's Most Dangerous Myth*, 14.

45. Holmes, "Sketch," 371.

46. Ibid., 371–73.

47. Ibid., 373.

48. Ibid., 381.

49. Ibid.

50. Holmes, "Researches Relating to the Racial and National Elements Now Entering into the Composition of the American Nation," "Random Records," 8: Section 5, 114–17.

51. Holmes, "Sketch,"389–90.

52. Ibid., 390.

53. In *Man's Most Dangerous Myth*, the authority on race theory, Ashley Montagu, writes a passage that speaks directly to the milieu in which Holmes operated.

Exalted in their citadels of infallibility, scientists by their consensus gave security and comfort to those who believed in a hierarchy of races. . . . But the collective judgement of the specialized community of anthropologists during the nineteenth, and well into the twentieth, century was abysmally wrong concerning the "fact" of race. For this the scientists who subscribed to the concept of race cannot be faulted, for it was a product of a social environment which, through the distorting glass of prejudice, saw people divided by caste and class, and segregated by race. In a society that segregated people by caste and class, "race" was the term that categorized the most visibly distinguishable groups of people. (p.43)

54. Holmes, "Some Problems of the American Race," *American Anthropologist*, n.s., 12 (April–June 1910): 149.

55. Ibid., 159–61.

56. Ibid., 161.

57. Ibid.

58. "Random Records," 9:159. The article, which carried the headline "No 'Happy Hunting Ground' for the Redskin. Fallacies about American Indian Disposed of," appeared in *The Evening Star* on Aug. 17, 1907. Under the headline there were several portraits with captions. On the left was an Indian male with long hair and in traditional native dress, including ceremonial feathers, over the caption "A Grandeur That is Fast Waning." On the right was a photograph of a clean-cut Indian male in suit and tie over the caption "The Twentieth Century Indian." Significantly, in between the two contrasting pictures was a portrait of a well-groomed Prof. W. H. Holmes. And below all three pictures was another portrait of an Indian woman. The caption here read "The Indian is Most Like the Oriental."

59. Ibid. The Native American population did recover in absolute numbers from its late nineteenth-century low of under 300,000. According to the 1990 census, Native Americans now form 0.8 percent of the American population or two million strong.

13. History and Prophecy

1. "Random Records," 9:149. Ten million was the generally accepted figure in Holmes's day. Since then, the debate over pre-Columbian demography has become almost as intense as the ongoing debate over the antiquity of the first Americans.

2. Holmes, "Some Problems of the American Race," 163–64.

3. Holmes, "Bearing of Archeological Evidence on the Place of Origin and on the Question of the Unity or Plurality of the American Race," *American Anthropologist*, n.s., 14 (1912): 36.

4. Holmes, "Some Problems of the American Race," 169–70.

5. Ibid., 166.

6. "Random Records," 9:158. The article, cited above, appeared in the Aug. 17, 1907, issue of *The Evening Star*.

7. Ibid., 9:43–45.

8. *Annual Report of the Board of Regents of the Smithsonian Institution, Showing the Operations, Expenditures, and Condition of the Institution for the Year Ending June 30, 1904* (Washington, D.C.: Government Printing Office, 1905), 47–48.

9. *Annual Report of the Board of Regents of the Smithsonian Institution, Showing the Operations, Expenditures, and Condition of the Institution for the Year Ending June 30, 1907* (Washington, D.C.: Government Printing Office, 1908), 27–28; "Random Records," 9:147.

10. "Random Records," 9:165.

11. *Annual Report of the Board of Regents of the Smithsonian Institution, Showing the Operations, Expenditures, and Condition of the Institution for the Year Ending June 30, 1909* (Washington, D.C.: Government Printing Office, 1910), 21.

12. "Random Records," 9:170; *Annual Report of the Board of Regents of the Smithsonian Institution . . . for the Year Ending June 30, 1909* (Washington, D.C.: Government Printing Office, 1910), 43.

13. See Richard W. Etulain's discussion of Lummis's regional significance, in *Re-Imagining the Modern American West: A Century of Fiction, History, and Art* (Tucson: University of Arizona Press, 1996), 85.

14. *Annual Report of the Board of Regents of the Smithsonian Institution . . . for the Year Ending June 30, 1909* (Washington, D.C.: Government Printing Office, 1910), 44.

15. See Donald E. Worcester, "Herbert Eugene Bolton: The Making of a Western Historian," in Richard W. Etulain, ed., *Writing Western History: Essays on Major Western Historians* (Albuquerque: University of New Mexico Press, 1991), 199.

16. *Annual Report of the Board of Regents of the Smithsonian Institution, Showing the Operations, Expenditures, and Condition of the Institution for the Year Ending June 30, 1905* (Washington, D.C.: Government Printing Office, 1906), 25.

17. "Random Records," 9:46.

18. Ibid., 47–49.

19. See the "Report" in "Random Records," 9:50–59.

20. Ibid., 53.

21. *Annual Report of the Board of Regents of the Smithsonian Institution, Showing the Operations, Expenditures, and Condition of the Institution for the Year Ending June 30, 1911* (Washington, D.C.: Government Printing Office, 1912), 17.

22. In 1904, the situation in Latin America was, of course, much worse. In a letter to Holmes, Adolph Bandelier of the American Museum of Natural History described the effect of international politics on science and exploration. Bandelier wrote: "It is not certain that we may not again undertake explorations in western South America, should a favorable opportunity offer itself. Only, some time must elapse yet . . . we want to wait until the unfavorable impression caused by the Panama affair upon the masses has worn off some. While the government of Peru and Chile are far from being dissatisfied with the turn suddenly taken by affairs on the Isthmus, the PEOPLE, especially the people in remoter mountain districts, look upon the action of the United States with mistrust and their feelings are rather hostile. Explorations of ruins by parties from here might easily be construed as preliminary "surveys," with the view of political ends and aims. ("Random Records," 9:177)

23. "Random Records," 9:120–21.

24. Ibid., 21.

25. Ibid., 95–96.

26. Ibid.

27. Ibid., 69–71.

28. Ibid., 71.

29. *Annual Report of the Board of Regents of the Smithsonian Institution, Showing the Operations, Expenditures, and Condition of the Institution for the Year Ending June 30, 1905* (Washington, D.C.: Government Printing Office, 1906), 42.

30. Richard Rathbun to Holmes, Aug. 10, 1906, "Random Records," 9:143.

31. Biographical Sketch of Richard Rathbun, William Henry Holmes Papers, SIA, Record Unit 7084.

32. *Annual Report of the Board of Regents of the Smithsonian Institution, Showing the Operations, Expenditures, and Condition of the Institution for the Year Ending June 30, 1907* (Washington, D.C.: Government Printing Office, 1908), 32.

33. Rothman, *America's National Monuments*, 39.

34. *Annual Report of the Board of Regents of the Smithsonian Institution, Showing the Operations, Expenditures, and Condition of the Institution for the Year Ending June 30, 1907* (Washington, D.C.: Government Printing Office, 1908), 23–25.

35. Gifford Pinchot to Holmes, Oct. 15, 1905; Holmes to Pinchot, Oct. 23, 1905 "Random Records," 9:213–14; Holmes to Francis E. Leupp (Commissioner of Indian Affairs), Dec. 5, 1905, William Henry Holmes Papers, SIA, Record Unit 7084.

36. *Annual Report of the Board of Regents of the Smithsonian Institution, Showing the Operations, Expenditures, and Condition of the Institution for the Year Ending June 30, 1905* (Washington, D.C.: Government Printing Office, 1906), 49.

37. Quoted in Washburn, *Cosmos Club of Washington*, 24.

38. Ibid., xiv.

39. Neil M. Judd, "William Henry Holmes," in Washburn, *Cosmos Club of Washington*, 308–311; George Crossette, *Founder of the Cosmos Club of Washington, 1878: A Collection of Biographical Sketches and Likenesses of the Sixty Founders* (Washington, D.C.: The Cosmos Club, 1966), 92–94.

40. Washburn, *Cosmos Club of Washington*, 182.

41. "Random Records," 9:134–35.

42. William Dall to Holmes, Apr. 20, 1905, "Random Records," 9:136.

43. Holmes to Hrdlička, Jan. 7, 1933, Papers of Aleš Hrdlička, Box 33, National Anthropological Archives.

44. Judd, "William Henry Holmes," 309.

14. The Great Dragon of Quirigua

1. "Random Records," 10:9.

2. Ibid., 129.

3. Ibid., 7.

4. Ibid., 129.

5. Mark, *Four Anthropologists*, 155.

6. Ibid.

7. Holmes, "Areas of American Culture Characterization", 413–14.

8. Ibid., 414.

9. Ibid., 416.

10. Ibid., 414–15.

11. Ibid.

12. Ibid., 416.

13. "Random Records," 10:7, 129.

14. *Annual Report of the Board of Regents of the Smithsonian Institution Showing the Operations, Expenditures, and Condition of the Institution for the Year Ending June 30, 1910* (Washington, D.C.: Government Printing Office, 1911), 33; "Random Records," 10:133, 134.

15. "Random Records," 10:12–13.

16. Mark, *Four Anthropologists*, 161.

17. Unless otherwise indicated, the account of Holmes's trips is based on his piece

"The Great Dragon of Quirigua, Guatemala," in *Annual Report of the Board of Regents of the Smithsonian Institution Showing the Operations, Expenditures, and Condition of the Institution for the Year Ending June 30, 1916* (Washington, D.C.: Government Printing Office, 1917), 447–60.

18. Ibid., 456–57.

19. Ibid., 459–60.

20. Holmes to Boas, Dec. 9, 1916, Boas Papers.

21. *Annual Report of the Board of Regents of the Smithsonian Institution Showing the Operations, Expenditures, and Condition of the Institution for the Year Ending June 30, 1916* (Washington, D.C.: Government Printing Office, 1917), 16–17.

22. Quoted in Hyatt, *Franz Boas*, 125.

23. Ibid., 126.

24. Quoted in William C. Sturtevant, "Huns, Free-Thinking Americans, and the AAA," in *History of Anthropology Newsletter* 2, No. 1 (Winter 1975): 5.

25. Stocking, "The Scientific Reaction against Cultural Anthropology, 1917–1920," in *Race, Culture, and Evolution*, 287.

26. This version of events is according to Boas. See Stocking, "Scientific Reaction," 288.

27. "Random Records," 10:147–48.

28. Quoted in Stocking, "Scientific Reaction," 289.

29. Ibid., 292. Stocking's analysis of this stormy period is masterful. Essentially, he argues that the Boasians, or the "cultural anthropologists," ultimately prevailed over the rest of the profession, including the "physical anthropologists." The result was that "by the middle of the twentieth century, it was commonplace for educated Americans to refer to human differences in cultural terms, and to say that 'modern science has shown that all human races are equal.' In fact," Stocking stated pointedly, "what science had shown was better put negatively than positively: there was no scientific basis for assuming that one race was inferior or superior to another" (p. 306).

30. Mark, *Four Anthropologists*, 160.

31. "Random Records," 10:155–56.

32. *Annual Report of the Board of Regents of the Smithsonian Institution Showing the Operations, Expenditures, and Condition of the Institution for the Year Ending June 30, 1923* (Washington, D.C.: Government Printing Office, 1925), 48–49.

33. Holmes to Boas, Oct. 28, 1919, Boas Papers.

34. Holmes to John Dewey, Nov. 3, 1919, Hrdlička Papers.

35. Franz Boas, "Scientists as Spies," *The Nation* 109 (Dec. 20, 1919): 797.

36. James Mooney to Boas, Dec. 25, 1919, Boas Papers; see L. G. Moses, *The Indian Man: A Biography of James Mooney* (Urbana: University of Illinois Press, 1984), 212–15.

37. John R. Swanton to Boas, Jan. 16, 1920, Boas Papers.

38. Sturtevant, "Huns, Free-Thinking Americans, and the AAA," 5.

39. Ibid.

40. Ibid., 6.

41. Stocking, "Scientific Reaction," 273.

42. Quoted in Mark, *Four Anthropologists*, 162.

43. Stocking, "Scientific Reaction," 296.

44. Hrdlička to Boas, Jan. 13, 1920, Boas Papers.
45. "Random Records," 11:4.
46. "Random Records," 1: "Personal (1926)," 189.
47. Ibid.
48. Ibid.
49. "Random Records," 1: "The Story of the 'Random Records,'" 5–6.
50. Mary Holmes to Hrdlička, Jan. 22, 1933, Hrdlička Papers.

Bibliography

Archival Sources

American Philosophical Society:

Franz Boas Papers (on microfilm as *The Professional Correspondence of Franz Boas*, Scholarly Resources, 1972).

Denver Federal Center:

A. United States Geological Survey, Field Records Library. William Henry Holmes, Sketchbooks.

B. United States Geological Survey, Photographic Library. William Henry Jackson Photographs.

Denver Museum of Natural History:

Jesse D. Figgins Papers

Denver Public Library, Western History Division:

Newspaper Files.

Library of Congress:

William John McGee Papers

National Archives Microfilm Publications, Washington, D.C.:

"Records of the Geological and Geographical Survey of the Territories 'Hayden Survey', 1867–79, Roll 8, Letters Received, 1871–79," in Record Group 57 (USGS). The National Archives, National Archives and Records Service, General Services Administration. Washington, D.C., 1965. Microcopy No. 623.

Smithsonian Institution:

A. Library of the National Museum of American Art and the National Portrait Gallery, William Henry Holmes, "Random Records of a Lifetime, 1846–1931: Cullings, Largely Personal, From the Scrap Heap of Three Score Years and Ten, Devoted to Science, Literature and Art," in 20 vols. Vols. 17–20, however, are in the possession of Holmes's granddaughter, Mrs. Laughlin A. Campbell, of Washington, D.C.

B. Smithsonian Institution Archives, Record Unit 7084, William Henry Holmes Papers, 1870–1931; Record Unit 7062, Fielding B. Meek Papers, 1843–1877; Record Unit 7208, Albert Charles Peale Papers, ca. 1891; Record Unit 31, Office of the Secretary (Samuel P. Langley), 1891–1906, and Related Records to 1908; Record Unit 45, Office of the Secretary (Charles D. Walcott), 1903–1924.

C. National Anthropological Archives, Papers of Aleš Hrdlička (1869–1943).

Yellowstone National Park Library and Museum Association:

William Henry Holmes, "Extracts from the Diary of W. H. Holmes," 1872, 1878, Typescript.

Albert Charles Peale, Transcript of 1872 A. C. Peale Diary (July 21–October 24).

Government Publications

Annual Reports of the Board of Regents of the Smithsonian Institution, from 1876 to 1920.

Gilbert, Grove Karl. *Report on the Geology of the Henry Mountains.* 2d ed. Washington, D.C.: Government Printing Office, 1880.

Ives, Joseph Christmas. *Report upon the Colorado River of the West, Explored in 1857 and 1858 . . .* U.S. 36th Cong., 1st sess., Sen. Exec. Doc. Washington D.C.: Government Printing Office, 1861.

Macomb, John N. *Report of the Exploring Expedition from Santa Fe, New Mexico, to the Junction of the Grand and Green Rivers of the Great Colorado of the West, in 1859, Under the Command of Capt. J. N. Macomb; with a Geological Report by Prof. J. S. Newberry.* Washington, D.C.: Government Printing Office, 1876.

Schmeckebier, Lawrence F. *Catalogue and Index of the Publications of the Hayden, King, Powell, and Wheeler Surveys.* U.S. Geological Survey Bulletin 222. Washington, D.C.: Government Printing Office, 1904.

Simpson, James H. *Journal of a Military Reconnaissance from Santa Fe, New Mexico, to the Navajo Country, made with the Troops under the Command of Brevet Lieutenant Colonel John M. Washington, Chief of the 9th Military Department, and Governor of New Mexico, in 1849,* U.S. 31st Cong., 1st sess., Sen. Exec. Doc. 64. Washington, D.C.: Union Office, 1850.

Hayden Survey Annual Reports

1872

Hayden, F. V. *Sixth Annual Report of the United States Geological Survey of the Territories Embracing Portions of Montana, Idaho, Wyoming, and Utah; Being a Report of Progress of the Explorations for the Year 1872.* Washington, D.C.: U.S. Government Printing Office, 1873.

1873

Hayden, F. V. *[Seventh] Annual Report of the United States Geological and Geographical Survey of the Territories, Embracing Colorado; Being a Report of the Progress of the Exploration for the Year 1873.* Washington, D.C.: Government Printing Office, 1874.

1874

Holmes, William H. "Report on the Geology of the North-West Portion of the Elk Range." In F. V. Hayden, *[Eighth] Annual Report of the United States Geological and Geographical Survey of the Territories, Embracing Colorado and Parts of Adjacent Territories; Being a Report of Progress of the Exploration for the Year 1874.* Washington, D.C.: Government Printing Office, 1876.

1875

Holmes, William H. "Geological Report on the San Juan District." In F. V. Hayden, *Ninth Annual Report of the United States Geological and Geographical Survey of the Territories Embracing Colorado and Parts of Adjacent Territories; Being a Report of Progress of the Exploration for the Year 1875.* Washington, D.C.: Government Printing Office, 1877.

1876

Holmes, William H. "Report on the Geology of the Sierra Abajo and West San Miguel Mountains." In F. V. Hayden, *Tenth Annual Report of the United States Geological and Geographical Survey of the Territories, Embracing Colorado and Parts of Adjacent Territories; Being a Report of Progress of the Exploration for the Year 1876.* Washington, D.C.: Government Printing Office, 1878.
——— . "Report on the Ancient Ruins of Southwestern Colorado, Examined during the Summers of 1875 and 1876." In ibid.

1877

Hayden, F. V. *Eleventh Annual Report of the United States Geological and Geographical*

Survey of the Territories, Embracing Idaho and Wyoming; Being a Report of Progress of the Exploration for the Year 1877. Washington, D.C.: Government Printing Office, 1879.

Hayden, Ferdinand Vandeveer. *Geological and Geographical Atlas of Colorado and Portions of Adjacent Territory.* New York and Washington, D.C.: Julius Bien, 1877; 2d. ed., 1881.

1878

Holmes, William H. "Report on the Geology of the Yellowstone National Park." In F. V. Hayden, *Twelfth Annual Report of the United States Geological and Geographical Survey of the Territories: A Report of Progress of the Exploration in Wyoming and Idaho for the Year 1878. Part 2.* Washington, D.C.: Government Printing Office, 1883.

Hayden Survey Bulletins

Holmes, William Henry. "Fossil Forests of the Volcanic Tertiary Formations of the Yellowstone National Park." In *Bulletin of the United States Geological and Geographical Survey of the Territories.* Washington, D.C.: Government Printing Office, 1880.

Peale, Albert C. "On a Peculiar Type of Eruptive Mountains in Colorado." In *Bulletin of the United States Geological and Geographical Survey of the Territories.* Washington, D.C.: Government Printing Office, 1877.

United States Geological Survey Reports

Dutton, Clarence E. *Tertiary History of the Grand Cañon District, with Atlas.* United States Geological Survey Monographs, 2. Washington, D.C.: Government Printing Office, 1882.

Powell, John Wesley. "Second Annual Report of the United States Geological Survey." In *Report of the Secretary of the Interior,* U.S. 47th Cong., 1st sess., House Ex. Doc. 1, pt. 5, 1882.

——. "Fifth Annual Report of the Geological Survey." In *Report of the Secretary of the Interior,* U.S 48th Cong., 2d sess., House Ex. Doc. 1, pt. 5, 1884.

——. "Sixth Annual Report of the United States Geological Survey." *Report of the Secretary of the Interior,* U.S 49th Cong., 1st sess., House Ex. Doc. 1, pt. 5, 1886.

——. "Eighth Annual Report of the United States Geological Survey." In *Report of the Secretary of the Interior,* U.S 50th Cong., 1st sess., House Ex. Doc. 1, pt. 5, 1889.

Books and Articles

Abbey, Edward. *Desert Solitaire: A Season in the Wilderness.* 1968. Reprint, New York: Ballantine Books, 1971.

Adams, Henry. *The Education of Henry Adams*. Edited by Ernest Samuels. 1918. Reprint, Boston: Houghton Mifflin Company, 1973.

Ambrose, Stephen E. *Undaunted Courage: Meriwether Lewis, Thomas Jefferson, and the Opening of the American West*. New York: Simon and Schuster, 1996.

Anderson, Nancy K. "'Curious Historical Artistic Data': Art History and Western American Art." In *Discovered Lands, Invented Pasts: Transforming Visions of the American West*, Jules David Prown. New Haven: Yale University Press, 1992.

———. "'The Kiss of Enterprise': The Western Landscape as Symbol and Resource." In *The West as America: Reinterpreting Images of the Frontier, 1820–1920*, edited by William H. Truettner, 237–83. Washington, D.C.: Smithsonian Institution Press, 1991.

Ash, Russell. *The Impressionists and Their Art*. New York: Crescent Books, 1980.

Baars, Donald L. *The Colorado Plateau: A Geologic History*. Albuquerque: University of New Mexico Press, 1972.

Babcock, Barbara A., and Nancy J. Parezo. *Daughters of the Desert: Anthropologists and the Native American Southwest, 1880–1980*. Albuquerque: University of New Mexico Press, 1988.

Bartlett, Richard A. *Great Surveys of the American West*. Norman: University of Oklahoma Press, 1962.

———. *Nature's Yellowstone*. Albuquerque: University of New Mexico Press, 1974.

Bartsch, Paul. "William Henry Holmes." In *Dictionary of American Biography* 21, Supplement One, edited by Harris E. Starr. New York: Charles Scribner's Sons, 1944: 427–28.

Benedict, Burton. *The Anthropology of World's Fairs*. London and Berkeley: Scolar Press, 1983.

Blum, Ann Shelby. *Picturing Nature: American Nineteenth-Century Zoological Illustration*. Princeton, N.J.: Princeton University Press, 1993.

Boas, Franz. "The Methods of Ethnology." *American Anthropologist*, n.s., 22 (October–December 1920): 311–21.

Brew, J. O., ed. *One Hundred Years of Anthropology*. Cambridge: Harvard University Press, 1968.

"Brief Biography of William Henry Holmes: Artist, Geologist, Archaeologist And Art Gallery Director, 1846–19–." *Ohio Archaeological and Historical Society Publications* 36 (1927): 493–527.

Brown, Robert L. "A Controversy: William H. Jackson and Mount of the Holy Cross." *Trail and Timberline* 590 (February 1968): 37–41.

———. *Holy Cross—The Mountain and the City*. Caldwell, Idaho: Caxton Printers, 1970.

Burroughs, John, John Muir et al. *Alaska: The Harriman Expedition, 1899*. 2 vols. 1901. Reprint (2 vols. in 1), New York: Dover Publications, 1986.

Bryson, Michael A. "Controlling the Land: John Wesley Powell and the Scientific
     Management of the American West." In *Science, Values, and the American West,*
     edited by Stephen Tchudi. Reno: The Nevada Humanities Committee, 1997.
Cassells, E. Steve. *The Archaeology of Colorado.* Boulder, Colo: Johnson Books, 1983.
Ceram, C. W. *Gods, Graves, and Scholars: The Story of Archaeology.* Translated by E. B.
     Garside and Sophie Wilkins. 2d rev. ed. New York: Alfred A. Knopf, 1967.
Clark, Edna Maria. *Ohio Art and Artists.* Richmond [Va?]: Garrett and Massie, 1932.
Cole, Fay-Cooper. "Eminent Personalities of the Half Century." *American Anthropolo-
     gist* 54 (April-June 1952): 157–67.
*Commemorative Biographical Record, Harrison, Ohio, Containing Biographical Sketches
     of Prominent and Representative Citizens, and Many of the Early Settled Families.*
     Chicago: J. H. Beers and Co., 1891.
Conzen, Michael P., ed. *The Making of the American Landscape.* Boston: Unwin
     Hyman, 1990.
Cook, Harold J. "Definite Evidence of Human Artifacts in the American Pleistocene."
     Science 62 (Nov. 20, 1925): 459–60.
———. "New Geological and Palaeontological Evidence Bearing on the Antiquity of
     Mankind in America." Reprinted from *Natural History* 27 (1927): 240–47. West-
     ern History Department, Denver Public Library.
Cosentino, Andrew J., and Henry H. Glassie. *The Capital Image: Painters in Washing-
     ton, 1800–1915.* Washington, D.C.: Smithsonian Institution Press, 1983.
Crampton, C. Gregory. *Land of Living Rock, The Grand Canyon and the High Plateaus:
     Arizona, Utah, Nevada.* 1972. Reprint, Layton, Utah: Gibbs M. Smith, 1985.
———. *Standing Up Country: The Canyon Lands of Utah and Arizona.* 1964. Salt Lake
     City: Gibbs M. Smith, Peregrine Smith Books, 1983.
D., J. A. "The Mount of the Holy Cross: A Legend of Colorado." *Potter's Monthly:
     Illustrated Magazine of History, Literature, Science and Art* 11 (1878): 326–27.
Davis, William Morris. *Biographical Memoir of Grove Karl Gilbert, 1843–1918.* National
     Academy of Sciences Biographical Memoirs 21, no. 5. Washington, D.C.: Govern-
     ment Printing Office, 1926.
de Margerie, M. Emm. *Commentaire de L'Atlas of Colorado (1877).* Paris: Imprimerie
     Nationale, 1925.
DeVoto, Bernard, ed. *The Journals of Lewis and Clark.* Boston: Houghton Mifflin Co.,
     1953.
Dillehay, Tom D., and David J. Meltzer. *The First Americans: Search and Research.*
     Boca Raton, Fla.: CRC Press, 1991.
Dippie, Brian W. "The Visual West." In *The Oxford History of the American West,* ed-
     ited by Clyde A. Milner, II, Carol A. O'Conner, and Martha A. Sandweiss,
     675–705. New York: Oxford University Press, 1994.
Dockery, W. Lyle. "William Henry Holmes." In *Exploration Frontiers of the Central*

and Southern Rockies, edited by Harry K. Veal. Denver: Rocky Mountain Association of Geologists, 1977.

Dunnell, Robert C. "Five Decades of American Archaeology." In *American Archaeology, Past and Future: A Celebration of the Society for American Archaeology, 1935–1985*, edited by David J. Meltzer, Don D. Fowler, and Jeremy A. Sabloff. Washington, D.C.: Smithsonian Institution Press, 1986.

Eckley, H. J., and William T. Perry. *History of Carroll and Harrison Counties, Ohio.* Chicago: Lewis Publishing Company, 1921.

Etulain, Richard W. *Re-Imagining the Modern American West: A Century of Fiction, History, and Art.* Tucson: University of Arizona Press, 1996.

Fagan, Brian M. *The Great Journey: The Peopling of Ancient America.* New York: Thames and Hudson, 1987.

Ferguson, William M. and Arthur H. Rohn. *Anasazi Ruins of the Southwest in Color.* Albuquerque: University of New Mexico Press, 1987.

Figgins, J. D. "The Antiquity of Man in America." Reprinted from *Natural History* 27 (1927): 229–39. Western History Department, Denver Public Library.

Findley, Rowe. "The Life and Times of William Henry Jackson: Photographing the Frontier." *National Geographic* 175 (February 1989): 216–51.

Fisch, Mathias S. "The Quest for the Mount of the Holy Cross." *The American West: The Magazine of Western History* 16 (March/April 1979): 32–36, 57–58.

Folsom, Franklin. *Black Cowboy: The Life and Legend of George McJunkin.* Niwot, Colo.: Roberts Rinehart Publishers, 1992.

Foster, Mike. *Strange Genius: The Life of Ferdinand Vandeveer Hayden.* Niwot, Colo: Roberts Rinehart Publishers, 1994.

Fowler, Don D. *The Western Photographs of John K. Hillers: Myself in the Waters.* Washington, D.C.: Smithsonian Institution Press, 1989.

Fryxell, Fritiof M.. "Albert Charles Peale: Pioneer Geologist of the Hayden Survey." *Annals of Wyoming* 34 (October 1962): 175–92.

Gallenkamp, Charles. *Maya: The Riddle and Rediscovery of a Lost Civilization.* 3d rev. ed. New York: Viking Penguin, 1985.

Gannett, Henry "The Mother Maps of the United States." *National Geographic Magazine* 4 (March 31, 1892): 101–16.

Gidley, Mick, and Robert Lawson-Peebles, eds. *Views of the American Landscape.* New York: Cambridge University Press, 1989.

Givens, Douglas R. *Alfred Vincent Kidder and the Development of Americanist Archaeology.* Albuquerque: University of New Mexico Press, 1992.

Goddard, Piny Earle. "Fact and Theories Concerning Pleistocene Man in America." *American Anthropologist*, n.s., 29 (1927): 262–66.

Goetzmann, William H. *Army Exploration in the American West, 1803–1863.* New Haven: Yale University Press, 1959.

———. *Exploration and Empire: The Explorer and the Scientist in the Winning of the West.* 1966. Reprint, New York: W. W. Norton and Company, 1978.

———. "Limner of Grandeur: William Henry Holmes and the Grand Canyon." *The American West: The Magazine of Western History* 15 (May/June 1978): 20–21, 61–63.

———. *New Lands, New Men: America and the Second Great Age of Discovery.* New York: Viking, 1986.

———. *William H. Holmes, Panoramic Art.* Fort Worth: Amon Carter Museum of Western Art, 1977.

Goetzmann, William H., and William N. Goetzmann. *The West of the Imagination.* New York: W. W. Norton and Co., 1986.

Granger, Byrd H. *Grand Canyon Place Names.* Tucson: University of Arizona Press, 1960.

Green, Jesse, ed. *Zuñi: Selected Writings of Frank Hamilton Cushing.* Lincoln: University of Nebraska Press, 1979.

Hagen, Wolfgang von. *Maya Explorer: John Lloyd Stevens and the Lost Cities of Central America and Yucatán.* Norman: University of Oklahoma Press, 1948.

Haines, Aubrey L. *The Yellowstone Story: A History of Our First National Park.* 2 vols. Yellowstone National Park, Wyo.: Yellowstone Library Museum Association, 1977.

Hales, Peter B. *William Henry Jackson and the Transformation of the American Landscape.* Philadelphia: Temple University Press, 1988.

Hamblin, W. Kenneth, and Joseph R. Murphy. *Grand Canyon Perspectives: A Guide to the Canyon Scenery by Means of Interpretive Panoramas.* Brigham Young University Geology Studies, Special Publication No. 1. Rev. ed. Provo, Utah: H and M Distributors, 1980.

Hanna, Charles A. *Ohio Valley Genealogies.* 1900. Reprint, Baltimore: Genealogical Publishing Company, 1968.

Hassrick, Peter. *The Way West: Art of Frontier America.* New York: Abradale Press/Harry N. Abrams, 1983.

Havighurst, Walter. *Ohio: A Bicentennial History.* New York: W. W. Norton and Company, 1976.

Hay, Oliver P. "Further Considerations of the Occurrence of Human Remains in the Pleistocene Deposits at Vero, Florida," *American Anthropologist,* n.s., 20 (1918): 1–36.

Hinsley, Curtis M., Jr. "Amateurs and Professionals in Washington Anthropology, 1879 to 1903." In *American Anthropology: The Early Years,* edited by John V. Murra. St. Paul: West Publishing Co., 1976.

———. *Savages and Scientists: The Smithsonian Institution and the Development of American Anthropology, 1846–1910.* Washington, D.C.: Smithsonian Institution Press, 1981.

———. *The Smithsonian and the American Indian: Making a Moral Anthropology in Victorian America.* Washington, D.C.: Smithsonian Institution Press, 1994.

Holmes, William H. "Aboriginal Copper Mines of Isle Royale, Lake Superior." *American Anthropologist*, n.s., 3 (1901): 684–96.

———. "Aboriginal Pottery of the Eastern United States." In *Twentieth Annual Report of the Bureau of American Ethnology to the Secretary of the Smithsonian Institution, 1898–1899*. Washington, D.C.: Government Printing Office, 1903. Reprinted in Meltzer and Dunnell, eds., *The Anthropology of William Henry Holmes*.

———. "Aboriginal Shell-Heaps of the Middle Atlantic Tidewater Region." *American Anthropologist*, n.s. 9 (1907): 113–28.

———. "An Ancient Quarry in Indian Territory." *Bureau of Ethnology Bulletin 21*. Washington, D.C.: Government Printing Office, 1894.

———. "Anthropological Studies in California." *Report of the U.S. National Museum, 1900*. Washington, D.C.: Government Printing Office, 1902.

———. "The Antiquity Phantom in American Archaeology." *Science* 62 (September 18, 1925): 256–58.

———. *Archaeological Studies among the Ancient Cities of Mexico, Part I: Monuments of Yucatan; Part II: Monuments of Chiapas, Oaxaca and the Valley of Mexico*, Vol. 1, No. 1. Chicago: Field Columbian Museum, 1895–1897.

———. "Areas of American Culture Characterization Tentatively Outlined as an Aid in the Study of Antiquities." *American Anthropologist*, n.s., 16 (1914): 413–46.

———. "Bearing of Archaeological Evidence on the Place of Origin and on the Question of the Unity or Plurality of the American Race." *American Anthropologist*, n.s., 14 (1912): 30–36.

———. "Biographical Memoir of Lewis Henry Morgan, 1818–1881." *National Academy of Sciences Biographical Memoirs*, vol. 6, 221–39. City of Washington: National Academy of Sciences, 1909.

———. "Burial-Masks of the Ancient Peruvians." *Science: An Illustrated Journal* 4 (July 4, 1884): 10–11.

———. "Caribbean Influence in the Prehistoric Art of Southern States." *The American Anthropologist* 7 (January 1894): 71–79.

———. "Certain Notched or Scalloped Stone Tablets of the Mound-Builders." *American Anthropologist*, n.s., 8 (1906): 101–8.

———. "Classification and Arrangement of the Exhibits of an Anthropological Museum." *Science*, n.s., 16 (September 26, 1902): 487–504.

———. "Discussion and Correspondence on the Antiquity of Man in America." *Science*, n.s., 47 (June 7, 1918): 561–62.

———. "Distribution of Stone Implements in the Tidewater Country." *The American Anthropologist* 6 (January 1893): 1–14.

———. "Excavations in an Ancient Soapstone Quarry in the District of Columbia." *The American Anthropologist* 3 (October 1890): 321–30.

———. "Flint Implements and Fossil Remains from a Sulphur Spring at Afton, Indian Territory." *American Anthropologist*, n.s., 4 (July–September 1902): 108–29.

———. "Fossil Human Remains Found Near Lansing, Kansas." *American Anthropologist*, n.s., 4 (July–September 1902): 743–52.

———. "Gravel Man and Palaeolithic Culture; A Preliminary Word." *Science* 21 (January 20, 1893): 29–30.

———. "The Great Dragon of Quirigua, Guatemala." In *Annual Report of the Board of Regents of the Smithsonian Institution Showing the Operations, Expenditures, and Condition of the Institution for the Year Ending June 30, 1916*, 447–60. Washington, D.C.: Government Printing Office, 1917.

———. *Handbook of Aboriginal American Antiquities*, Washington, D.C.: Government Printing Office, 1919.

———. "Modern Quarry Refuse and the Palaeolithic Theory." *Science* 20 (Nov. 25, 1892): 295–97.

———. "Natural History of Flaked Stone Implements." *Memoirs of the International Congress of Anthropology*. Chicago: Schulte Publishing Co., 1894. Reprinted in Meltzer and Dunnell, eds., *The Archaeology of William Henry Holmes*.

———. "The Obsidian Mines of Hidalgo, Mexico." *American Anthropologist*, n.s., 2 (1900): 405–16.

———. "On the Antiquity of Man in America." *Science*, n.s., 47 (June 7, 1918): 561–62.

———. "On the Evolution of Ornament—An American Lesson." *The American Anthropologist* 3 (April 1890): 137–46.

———. "On the Race History and Facial Characteristics of the Aboriginal Americans." In *Annual Report of the Board of Regents of the Smithsonian Institution Showing the Operations, Expenditures, and Condition of the Institution for the Year Ending June 30, 1919*, 427–32. Washington, D.C.: Government Printing Office, 1921.

———. "Order of Development of the Primal Shaping Arts." In *Annual Report of the Board of Regents of the Smithsonian Institution, Showing the Operations, Expenditures, and Condition of the Institution for the Year Ending June 30, 1901*. Washington, D. C.: Government Printing Office, 1902.

———. "Origin and Development of Form and Ornament in Ceramic Art." In *Fourth Annual Report of the Bureau of Ethnology to the Secretary of the Smithsonian Institution, 1882–1883*. Washington, D.C.: Government Printing Office, 1886. Reprinted in Meltzer and Dunnell, eds., *The Archaeology of William Henry Holmes*.

———. "Pottery of the Potomac Tide-water Region." *The American Anthropologist* 2 (July 1889): 246–52.

———. "Preliminary Revision of the Evidence Relating to Auriferous Gravel Man in California, First Paper." *American Anthropologist*, n.s., 1 (1899): 107–21.

———. "Preliminary Revision of the Evidence Relating to Auriferous Gravel Man in California, Second Paper." *American Anthropologist*, n.s., 1 (1899): 614–45.

———. "A Quarry Workshop of the Flaked-stone Implement Makers in the District of Columbia." *The American Anthropologist* 3 (January 1890): 1–26.

———. "A Question of Evidence." *Science* (March 10, 1893): 135–36.

———. "A Sketch of the Great Serpent Mound." *Science, An Illustrated Journal* 7 (December 1886): 624, 626–28.

———. "Sketch of the Origin, Development, and Probable Destiny of the Races of Men." *American Anthropologist*, n.s., 4 (July–September 1902): 369–91.

———. "Some Problems of the American Race." *American Anthropologist*, n.s., 12 (April–June 1910): 149–82.

———. "Some Spurious Mexican Antiquities and Their Relation to Ancient Art." In *Annual Report of the Board of Regents of the Smithsonian Institution, Showing the Operations, Expenditures, and Condition of the Institution for the Year Ending June 30, 1886*, 319–34. Washington, D.C.: Government Printing Office, 1889.

———. "Stone Implements of the Potomac-Chesapeake Tidewater Province." In *Fifteenth Annual Report of the Bureau of Ethnology to the Secretary of the Smithsonian Institution, 1893–94*. Washington, D.C.: Government Printing Office, 1897. Reprinted in Meltzer and Dunnell, eds., *The Archaeology of William Henry Holmes*.

———. "Studies in Aboriginal Decorative Art, Part 1." *The American Anthropologist* 5 (January 1892): 67–72.

———. "Studies in Aboriginal Decorative Art, Part 2." *The American Anthropologist* 5 (April 1892): 149–52.

———. "Textile Fabrics of Ancient Peru." *Bureau of Ethnology Bulletin* 7. Washington, D.C.: Government Printing Office, 1889.

———. "Traces of Aboriginal Operations in an Iron Mine Near Leslie, Missouri." *American Anthropologist*, n.s., 5 (1903): 503–7.

———. "The Trade in Spurious Mexican Antiquities." *Science: An Illustrated Journal* 7 (February 19, 1886): 170.

———. "Use of Textiles in Pottery Making and Embellishment." *American Anthropologist*, n.s., 3 (1901): 397–403.

———. "A West Virginia Rock-Shelter." *The American Anthropologist* 3 (July 1890): 217–25.

———. "The World's Fair Congress of Anthropology." *The American Anthropologist* 6 (October 1893): 423–34.

Howe, Henry. *Historical Collections of Ohio in Three Volumes*. Columbus: Henry Howe and Son, 1891.

Howell, J. V. "Geology Plus Adventure: The Story of the Hayden Survey." *Journal of the Washington Academy of Sciences* 49 (July 1959): 220–24.

Hrdlička, Aleš (in collaboration with W. H. Holmes, Bailey Willis, Fred. Eugene Wright, and Clarence N. Fenner). "Early Man in South America." *Bureau of American Ethnology Bulletin 52.* Washington, D.C.: Government Printing Office, 1912.

Hunt, Charles B. "G. K. Gilbert, on Laccoliths and Intrusive Structures." In *The Scientific Ideas of G. K. Gilbert: An Assessment on the Occasion of the Centennial of the United States Geological Survey (1879–1979),* edited by Ellis L. Yochelson. Special Paper 183. Boulder, Colo.: Geological Society of America, 1980.

Hyatt, Marshall. *Franz Boas, Social Activist: The Dynamics of Ethnicity.* New York: Greenwood Press, 1990.

Hyde, Anne Farrar. *An American Vision: Far Western Landscape and National Culture, 1820–1920.* New York: New York University Press, 1990.

Jackson, Clarence S., and Lawrence W. Marshall. *Quest of the Snowy Cross.* Denver: University of Denver Press, 1952.

Jackson, William Henry. *Time Exposure.* 1940. Reprint, Albuquerque: University of New Mexico Press, 1986.

James, George Wharton. *In and Around the Grand Canyon: The Grand Canyon of the Colorado River in Arizona.* Boston: Little, Brown and Company, 1900.

Jefferson, James, Robert W. Delaney, and Gregory C. Thompson. *The Southern Utes: A Tribal History.* Ignacio, Colo.: Southern Ute Tribe, 1972.

Jennings, Jesse D. "Origins." In *Ancient North Americans,* edited by Jesse D. Jennings. New York: W. H. Freeman and Company, 1978.

Jordan, David Starr. "Spencer Fullerton Baird and the United States Fish Commission." *Scientific Monthly* 27 (August 1923): 96–107.

Judd, Neil M. *The Bureau of American Ethnology; A Partial History.* Norman: University of Oklahoma Press, 1967.

———. *Cosmos Club Bulletin* 5 (March 1952): 2–5.

Keefer, William R. *The Geologic Story of Yellowstone National Park.* U.S. Geological Survey Bulletin 1347. Washington, D.C.: Government Printing Office, 1971.

Kidder, Alfred Vincent. *An Introduction to the Study of Southwestern Archaeology, with a Preliminary Account of the Excavations at Pecos.* Rev. ed. New Haven: Yale University Press, 1962.

Kinsey, Joni Louise. *Thomas Moran and the Surveying of the American West.* Washington, D. C.: Smithsonian Institution Press, 1992.

Krickeberg, Walter. *Las Antiguas Culturas Mexicanas,* translated by Sita Garst y Jasmin Reuter. 1956. Reprint, Mexico City: Fondo de Cultura Economica, 1985.

Kuhn, Thomas S. *The Structure of Scientific Revolutions.* 1962. 2d ed., New York: New American Library, 1970.

Lawrence, Bill. *The Early American Wilderness as the Explorers Saw It.* New York: Paragon, 1991.

Lee, Ronald F. *The Antiquities Act of 1906*. Washington, D.C.: Office of History and Historic Architecture, Eastern Service Center, 1970.

Lindstrom, Gaell. *Thomas Moran in Utah*. 68th Faculty Honor Lecture. Logan: Utah State University Scholarly Publications Committee, n.d.

Livingston, Stephanie, and Claudia Miner. "Mammoths, Prehistoric Archaeology, and Interdisciplinary Research." In *Science, Values, and the American West*, edited by Stephen Tchudi. Reno: The Nevada Humanities Committee, 1997.

Lorenzo, Jose Luis. "Los Origenes Mexicanos." In *Historia General de Mexico*, vol. 1, 85–123. México, D.F.: El Colegio de México, 1976.

Manning, Thomas G. *Government in Science: The U.S. Geological Survey, 1867–1894*. Lexington: University of Kentucky Press, 1967.

Mark, Joan. *Four Anthropologists: An American Science in Its Early Years*. New York: Science History Publications, 1980.

Martin, Calvin. "Ethnohistory: A Better Way to Write Indian History." *Western Historical Quarterly* 9 (January 1978): 41–56.

Mead, Margaret, and Ruth L. Bunzel, eds. *The Golden Age of American Anthropology*. New York: George Braziller, 1960.

Meltzer, David J. "The Antiquity of Man and the Development of American Archaeology." In *Advances in Archaeological Method and Theory*, edited by M. B. Schiffer, 6:1–51. New York: Academic Press, 1983.

———. "The Discovery of Deep Time: A History of Views of the Peopling of the Americas." In *Method and Theory for Investigating the Peopling of the Americas*, edited by Robson Bonnichsen and D. Gentry Steele. Corvallis, Ore.: Center for the Study of the First Americans, Oregon State University, 1994.

Meltzer, David J., and Robert C. Dunnell, eds. *The Archaeology of William Henry Holmes*. Washington, D.C.: Smithsonian Institution Press, 1992.

Merrill, George P. *The First One Hundred Years of American Geology*. New Haven: Yale University Press, 1924.

Miller, Helen Markley. *Lens on the West: The Story of William Henry Jackson*. Garden City, N.Y.: Doubleday, 1966.

Morris, Edmund. *The Rise of Theodore Roosevelt*. New York: Coward, McCann and Geoghegan, 1979.

Morris, James. *Heaven's Command: An Imperial Progress*. Vol. 1. 1973. Reprint, Harmondsworth, Engl.: Penguin Books, 1979.

Moses, L. G. *The Indian Man: A Biography of James Mooney*. Urbana: University of Illinois Press, 1984.

Muir, John. *The Mountains of California*. 1894. Reprint, New York: Century Co., 1913.

———. *Steep Trails*. Edited by William Frederic Bade. 1902. Reprint, Boston: Houghton Mifflin, 1918.

———. *Studies in the Sierra*. San Francisco: Sierra Club, 1950.

Naef, Weston, and James N. Wood. *Era of Exploration: The Rise of Landscape Photography in the American West, 1860–1885.* Buffalo: Albright-Knox Art Gallery; Boston: distributed by New York Graphic Society, 1975.

Nash, Gerald D. "The Conflict Between Pure and Applied Science in Nineteenth-Century Public Policy: The California State Geological Survey, 1860–1874." *Isis* 54 (1963): 217–28.

Nelson, Clifford M. "William Henry Holmes: Beginning a Career in Art and Science." *Records of the Columbia Historical Society of Washington, D.C.* 50 (1980): 252–78.

Nelson, Clifford M., and Fritiof M. Fryxell. "The Antebellum Collaboration of Meek and Hayden in Stratigraphy." *Two Hundred Years of Geology in America,* edited by Cecil J. Schneer. Hanover, N.H.: University Press of New England, 1979.

Nelson, Clifford M., Mary C. Rabbitt, and Fritiof M. Fryxell. "Ferdinand Vandeveer Hayden: The U.S. Geological Survey Years, 1879–1886." *Proceedings of the American Philosophical Society* 125 (1981): 283–43.

Neuhaus, Robert. *Unsuspected Genius: The Art and Life of Frank Duveneck.* San Francisco: Bedford Press, 1987.

Nichols, Roger L., and Patrick L. Halley. *Stephen Long and American Frontier Exploration.* 1980. Reprint, Norman: University of Oklahoma Press, 1995.

Orosz, Joel J. *Curators and Culture: The Museum Movement in America, 1740–1870.* Tuscaloosa: University of Alabama Press, 1990.

Peale, A. C. "Description of an Indian Fight." *The Denver Westerners Monthly Round Up* 12 (July 1956): 3–5.

Pierce, Kenneth L. *History and Dynamics of Glaciation in the Northern Yellowstone National Park Area.* U.S. Geological Survey Professional Paper 729-F. Washington, D.C.: Government Printing Office, 1979.

Proudfit, S. V. "Ancient Village Sites and Aboriginal Workshops in the District of Columbia." *The American Anthropologist* 2 (July 1889): 241–46.

Prown, Jules David, et al. *Discovered Lands, Invented Pasts: Transforming Visions of the American West.* New Haven: Yale University Press, 1992.

Prucha, Francis Paul. *The Great Father: The United States Government and the American Indians.* Abridged ed. Lincoln: University of Nebraska Press, 1986.

Pyne, Stephen J. *Dutton's Point: An Intellectual History of the Grand Canyon.* Published by the Grand Canyon Natural History Association, Monograph Number 5, 1982.

———. *Grove Karl Gilbert: A Great Engine of Research.* Austin: University of Texas Press, 1980.

———. *The Ice: A Journey to Antarctica.* Iowa City: University of Iowa Press, 1986.

Rabbitt, Mary C. *Minerals, Lands, and Geology for the Common Defence and General Welfare,* 3 vols [to 1939]. Washington D.C.: U.S. Geological Survey, Government Printing Office, 1979–1986.

Rainger, Ronald. *An Agenda for Antiquity: Henry Fairfield Osborn and Vertebrate Pale-ontology at the American Museum of Natural History, 1890–1935.* Tuscaloosa: University of Alabama Press, 1991.

Raisz, Erwin. *General Cartography.* New York: McGraw-Hill Book Company, 1948.

Reed, Nelson. *The Caste War of Yucatan.* Stanford, Calif.: Stanford University Press, 1964.

Reingold, Nathan. *Science, American Style.* New Brunswick, N.J.: Rutgers University Press, 1991.

Reingold, Nathan, ed. *Science in Nineteenth-Century America: A Documentary History.* 1964. Reprint, New York: Octagon Books, 1979.

Ristow, Walter W. *American Maps and Mapmakers: Commercial Cartography in the Nineteenth Century.* Detroit: Wayne State University Press, 1985.

Rivinus, E. F., and E. M. Youssef. *Spencer Baird of the Smithsonian.* Washington, D.C.: Smithsonian Institution Press. 1992.

Roberts, Frank H. H., Jr. "A Folsom Complex: Preliminary Report on Investigations at the Lindenmeier Site in Northern Colorado." *Smithsonian Miscellaneous Collections* 94 (June 1935): 1–11.

Robertson, Janet. *The Magnificent Mountain Women: Adventures in the Colorado Rock-ies.* Lincoln: University of Nebraska Press, 1990.

Rohrbough, Malcolm J. *Aspen: The History of a Silver-Mining Town, 1879–1893.* New York: Oxford University Press, 1986.

Rothman, Hal K. *America's National Monuments: The Politics of Preservation.* Lawrence: University Press of Kansas, 1989.

Rydell, Robert W. *All the World's a Fair: Visions of Empire at American International Expositions, 1876–1916.* Chicago: University of Chicago Press, 1984.

Sandweiss, Martha. "Views and Reviews: Western Art and Western History." In *Under an Open Sky: Rethinking America's Western Past,* edited by William Cronon, George Miles, and Jay Gitlin. New York: W. W. Norton and Company, 1992.

Sanford Robinson Gifford, 1823–1880. Catalog of an Exhibition Organized by the University of Texas Art Museum. Austin: University of Texas Art Museum, 1970.

Schaafsma, Polly. *Indian Rock Art of the Southwest.* Santa Fe, N.M.: School of American Research, 1980.

Schwartz, Seymour I., and Ralph E. Ehrenberg. *Mapping America.* New York: Harry N. Abrams, 1980.

Simmons, Marc. *New Mexico: An Interpretive History.* 1977. Reprint, Albuquerque: University of New Mexico Press, 1988.

Smedley, Audrey. *Race in North America: Origin and Evolution of a Worldview.* Boulder, Colo: Westview Press, 1993.

Smith, Duane A. *Mesa Verde National Park: Shadows of the Centuries.* Lawrence: University Press of Kansas, 1988.

Smith, Henry Nash. *Virgin Land: The American West as Symbol and Myth.* 1950. Reprint, Cambridge, Mass.: Harvard University Press, 1978.

Smith, Michael L. *Pacific Visions: California Scientists and the Environment, 1850–1915.* New Haven: Yale University Press, 1987.

Stegner, Wallace. *Beyond the Hundredth Meridian: John Wesley Powell and the Second Opening of the West.* 1953. Reprint, Lincoln: University of Nebraska Press, 1982.

———. "Introduction." In Clarence E. Dutton, *Tertiary History of the Grand Cañon District, with Atlas.* 1882. Reprint, Santa Barbara: Peregrine Smith, 1977.

———. *Mormon Country.* 1942. Reprint, Lincoln: University of Nebraska Press, 1970.

———. "The Scientist as Artist: Clarence E. Dutton and the Tertiary History of the Grand Cañon District." *The American West: The Magazine of Western History* 15 (May/June 1978): 18–19, 61.

———. *Where the Bluebird Sings to the Lemonade Springs: Living and Writing in the West.* New York: Random House, 1992.

Stinger, Christopher, and Clive Gamble. *In Search of the Neanderthals: Solving the Puzzle of Human Origins.* New York: Thames and Hudson, 1993.

Stocking, George W., Jr. *Race, Culture, and Evolution: Essays in the History of Anthropology.* 1968. Reprint, Chicago: University of Chicago Press, 1982.

Strong, William E. *A Trip to the Yellowstone National Park in July, August, and September, 1875.* Norman: University of Oklahoma Press, 1968,

Stuart, David E., and Rory P. Gathier. *Prehistoric New Mexico: Background for Survey.* 1981. Reprint, Albuquerque: University of New Mexico, 1988.

Swanton, John R. "Biographical Memoir of William Henry Holmes, 1846–1933." *National Academy of Sciences Biographical Memoirs,* vol.17, 223–52. Washington, D.C.: National Academy of Sciences, 1937.

Taft, Robert. *Artists and Illustrators of the Old West, 1850–1900.* New York: Charles Scribner's Sons, 1953.

Taylor, Joshua C. "The Futurist Goal, The Futurist Achievement." In *Major European Art Movements, 1900–1945: A Critical Anthology,* edited by Patricia Kaplan and Susan Manso. New York: E. P. Dutton, 1977.

Trenton, Patricia, and Peter H. Hassrick. *The Rocky Mountains: A Vision for Artists in the Nineteenth Century.* Norman: University of Oklahoma Press, 1983.

Truettner, William H. "What You See is Not Necessarily What You Get: New Meaning in Images of the Old West." In *Montana: The Magazine of Western History,* 42 (Summer 1992): 70–76.

Truettner, William H., ed. *The West as America: Reinterpreting Images of the Frontier, 1820–1920.* Washington, D.C.: Smithsonian Institution Press, 1991.

Van Riper, A. B. *Men among the Mammoths: Victorian Science and the Discovery of Human Prehistory.* Chicago: University of Chicago Press, 1993.

Vandenbusche, Duane, and Duane A. Smith. *A Land Alone: Colorado's Western Slope.* Boulder, Colo.: Pruett Publishing Company, 1981.

Viola, Herman J., *Exploring the West.* Washington, D.C.: Smithsonian Books, 1987.

Washburn, Wilcomb E. *The Cosmos Club of Washington: A Centennial History, 1878–1978.* Washington, D.C.: The Cosmos Club, 1978.

Webb, Melody. *The Last Frontier: A History of the Yukon Basin of Canada and Alaska.* Albuquerque: University of New Mexico Press, 1985.

Weber, David J. *Richard H. Kern: Expeditionary Artist in the Far Southwest, 1848–1853.* Albuquerque: University of New Mexico Press, 1985.

———. "The Spanish Legacy in North America and the Historical Imagination." *Western Historical Quarterly* 23 (February 1992), 5–24.

West, Elliott. "Walter Prescott Webb and the Search for the West." In *Writing Western History: Essays on Major Historians,* edited by Richard W. Etulain. Albuquerque: University of New Mexico Press, 1991.

Wheat, Carl I. *Mapping the Transmississippi West.* 6 vols. San Francisco: Institute of Historical Cartography, 1958–63.

White, Albert C. *A History of the Rectangular Survey System.* Washington, D.C.: U.S. Government Printing Office, 1983.

White, Charles A. "Memoir of Ferdinand Vandiveer Hayden, 1839–1887." *National Academy of Sciences Biographical Memoirs,* vol. 3, 397–413. Washington City: National Academy of Sciences, 1895.

———. "Memoir of Fielding Bradford Meek, 1817–1876." *National Academy of Sciences Biographical Memoirs,* vol. 4, 77–81. Washington, D.C.: National Academy of Sciences, 1902.

White, Richard. *"It's Your Misfortune and None of My Own": A History of the American West.* Norman: University of Oklahoma Press, 1991.

Wiebe, Robert H. *The Search for Order, 1877–1920.* New York: Hill and Wang, 1967.

Wilford, John Noble. *The Mapmakers: The Story of the Great Pioneers in Cartography from Antiquity to the Space Age.* New York: Vintage Books, 1981.

Wilkins, Thurman. *Clarence King: A Biography.* 2d rev. ed. Albuquerque: University of New Mexico Press, 1988.

———. *Thomas Moran: Artist of the Mountains.* Norman: University of Oklahoma Press, 1966.

Willey, Gordon R. *Portraits in American Archaeology: Remembrances of Some Distinguished Americanists.* Albuquerque: University of New Mexico Press, 1988.

Williams, Vernon J., Jr. *Rethinking Race: Franz Boas and His Contemporaries.* Lexington: University of Kentucky Press, 1996.

Wilmsen, Edwin N. *Lindenmeier: A Pleistocene Hunting Society.* New York: Harper and Row, 1974.

Wilson, Thomas. "The Paleolithic Period in the District of Columbia." *The American Anthropologist* 2 (July 1889): 235–41.

Woodring, W. P. "William Healey Dall, August 21, 1845–March 27, 1927." *National Academy of Sciences Biographical Memoirs*, vol. 31. New York: Columbia University Press, 1958.

Worster, Donald. *Rivers of Empire: Water, Aridity, and the Growth of the American West.* New York: Pantheon Books, 1985.

Yochelson, Ellis L. "Fielding Bradford Meek." *Dictionary of Scientific Biography* 4 (1974): 255–56.

———. *The National Museum of Natural History: 75 Years in the Natural History Building.* Edited by Mary Jarrett. City of Washington: Smithsonian Institution Press, 1985.

Index

Page numbers in italic type indicate photos.

Abajo Peak, 75; view from, 70–71
Abbey, Edward, xiii, 106
Abbott, Charles C., 128
Aboriginal American Basketry (Mason), 209
aboriginal architecture, 157–58, 161
aboriginal art, 214
aboriginal mining, 172
aboriginal pottery, 164–68
"Aboriginal Pottery of the Eastern United States" (Holmes), 164; and WHH's understanding of collecting and classifying, 165
aboriginal technology, 197
Academy of Sciences (Philadelphia), 164
Act for the Preservation of American Antiquities, 204
Adams, Herbert, 212
Adler, Cyrus, 197
Aerodrome, 175
aerodynamics, 175
Alaska and Its Resources (Dall), 8
Alaska-Yukon-Pacific Exposition, 149, 196, 197
Allegheny Observatory, 174
American Anthropological Association (AAA), 145, 190
The American Anthropologist, 120, 169, 187, 190, 194
American Association for the Advancement of Science, 121
American Federation of Arts, 221

The American Journal of Physical Anthropology, 187
American Mission to Negotiate Peace, 221
American Museum of Natural History, 152, 164, 180, 196; Boas takes job at, 182
American West: and change from general reconnaissance to special investigation, 88–90; and environmental problems, 90; as field in which to test manhood, 45; fragmentation into subregions, 89
Amethyst Mountain, 95–96
"An Ancient Quarry in Indian Territory," (Holmes), 130
Anasazi Indians, 58; dating of, 64–66; rock art and pottery of, 64; theories for disappearance of, 61–64
Anatomical Museum (Paris), 199
Ancient Monuments of the Mississippi Valley (Squire and Davis), 56
Ancient Society (Morgan), 119
Andrews, Eliphalet Frazer, 4–5
Anselmo, Father, 34
Anthropological Society of Washington, 187
"Anthropological Studies in California" (Holmes), 170
anthropometry, 186
antiquities, 116; fraud in, 123–24, 126; relationship between exploration and preservation of, 206; threats posed to, 216; WHH on preservation of, 206
Antiquities Bill, 124
antiquity question, 148, 158–59, 163, 184, 195, 220; and Folsom Man, 141–47

285